The ASIAN FILM INDUSTRY

John A. Lent

TEXAS FILM STUDIES SERIES
Thomas Schatz, Editor

The ASIAN FILM INDUSTRY

John A. Lent

UNIVERSITY OF TEXAS PRESS, AUSTIN

International Standard Book Number 0–292–70421–6 (cloth)
0–292–70422–4 (paperback)

Library of Congress Catalog Card Number 89–51958

Copyright © 1990 by John A. Lent, George S. Semsel,
   Keiko McDonald, Manjunath Pendakur
Printed in England

First University of Texas Edition, 1990

Requests for permission to reproduce material from this work should
be sent to Permissions, University of Texas Press, Box 7819, Austin, Texas
78713–7819

iv

CONTENTS

List of Illustrations   vii

Preface   viii

Introduction
   Diversity of Cultures and Films;
   Commonalities of Asian Films   1

EAST ASIA

1 **China**   *(George S. Semsel)*
   Introduction; The Studios; Film as Literature;
   Beijing Film Academy; The Fifth Generation;
   Independent Film; Notes   11

2 **Japan**   *(Keiko McDonald)*
   Introduction; Historical Background;
   Contemporary Scene; Notes   34

3 **Taiwan**
   Introduction; Historical Background;
   Contemporary Scene; Afterword; Notes   61

4 **Hong Kong**
   Introduction; Historical Background;
   Contemporary Scene; Notes   92

5 **South Korea**
   Introduction; Historical Background;
   Contemporary Scene; Brief View of North
   Korean Film; Afterword; Notes   122

SOUTHEAST ASIA

6 The Philippines
Introduction; Historical Background;
Contemporary Scene; Notes 149

7 Malaysia and Singapore
Introduction; Historical Background;
Malaysianising the Industry; Singapore; Notes 185

8 Indonesia, Thailand and Burma
Introduction 201
INDONESIA
Historical Background; Contemporary Scene 202
THAILAND
Historical Background; Contemporary Scene 212
BURMA
Historical Background; Contemporary Scene;
Afterword; Notes 221

SOUTH ASIA

9 India *(Manjunath Pendakur)*
Introduction; Industry; Notes 229

10 Pakistan, Bangladesh and Sri Lanka
Introduction 253
PAKISTAN
Historical Background; Contemporary Scene 254
BANGLADESH
Historical Background; Post-Liberation Period 262
SRI LANKA
Historical Background; Contemporary Scene;
Afterword; Notes 267

References 279
Interviews 293
Correspondence 296
About the Authors 297
Index 299

ILLUSTRATIONS

A scene from Chen Kaige's *Yellow Earth*
Chen Kaige's *The Big Parade*
Nabuko Miyamoto in Juzo Itami's *A Taxing Woman*
The 'clad in white' gangster (Koji Kakusho) tells the
   audience how to appreciate fine cinema and fine
   cuisine, in Juzo Itami's *Tampopo*
Japanese director, Juzo Itami
Scenes from two early Korean films: Lee Pil-u's
   Mongtongguri (1926) and Lee Gyu-sol's
   Nongjungjo (1926)
Hong Kong director, Allen Fong
Filipino director, Peque Gallaya
Filipino director, Lino Brocka
Jins Shamsuddin, the Malaysian founder of the film
   distribution organisation, Perfima
A scene from the 1983 Korean film *Adada*, directed
   by Im Kwon-t'aek
Mira Nair's *Salaam Bombay!*
A scene from *Damul*, directed by Prakash Jha with
   Manohar Singh and Annu Kapoor, first broadcast
   on Indian television in 1985
An Indian street lined with cinemas and gigantic
   hoardings

PREFACE

T he making of this book has eaten up quite a few outlines since its conception about 20 years ago.

Originally, the idea was to solicit a number of Asian and non-Asian film researchers to write country case studies, but it was abandoned for various reasons. Among these were people who knew cinema in some countries but were too busy to write about it or feared being candid because of government controls or personal affinities to the film profession.

For a brief time, the outline featured topics into which national film industries could be plugged. It too was scrapped, my beliefs being that comparative analysis often dangerously forces national film characteristics into pigeonholes, tosses out traits that do not fit and, generally, purées everything into a homogenised portrayal not striking of reality.

Momentarily, the outline took on some dimensions of an aesthetical analysis. For various reasons, this version was ripped out of the typewriter rather quickly and with some force. One reason was that I was not interested in, nor was I adept at, doing such a study. A second, more important, reason emanated from the days when I taught literature, trying to plough through the symbolism applied by 'those damn English professors', to quote Robert Frost, to creative work. My view has been that if such analyses are to be attempted, they should *begin* with interviews with the makers of films to determine what they wished something to mean or the effect they tried to achieve. However, to have interviewed the major Asian films' scriptwriters, producers and directors would have limited the study to a contemporary perspective, and would have been a never-ending project.

Finally, the outline that was settled on combined historical and contemporary perspectives, primarily of the Asian film industries, carried out in a case-study, problem-oriented approach. The historical perspective was included because an understanding of the present and a prediction of the future rest on knowing the cinematic past;

the industry approach, because it so often has been ignored in film studies, and case study, because it allowed for more emphasis on individual nuances of film in various countries.

I decided to write most of the chapters to keep a uniformity of style, topics and format. Three prolific researchers of Asian film were asked to write on China (George S. Semsel), India (Manjunath Pendakur) and Japan (Keiko McDonald).

The book is organised by regions of East, Southeast and South Asia, as commonly defined by Asian scholars, and by topics. West Asia, some parts of which are called 'Middle East', and Australasia (Australia, New Zealand and Oceania) were not included because of space limitations. Besides these exceptions, and Vietnam, for which the author lacked reliable data, all other major film-producing countries of Asia were studied. Some film industries were emphasised more than others, based on their representativeness of a region, their stages of development or decay or their unique or universal characteristics. In some instances, more attention was given to a country's film industry, because of the amount of interviewing the author did among its personnel, e.g. Hong Kong, the Philippines and Taiwan.

Because of colonial combinings of cultures and their evolutions into nations, as well as other political situations, the roots of film industries sometimes had more than one source. Take the case of Bangladesh, whose film branched from that of Pakistan, which itself stemmed from that of India. Also, Singapore broke away from what is now Malaysia, and the Hong Kong and Taiwan film industries were spawned in China.

In almost all chapters, a uniform set of topics was used, incorporating historical and contemporary overviews. Analysed under the latter were production; distribution and exhibition; directing, acting and scriptwriting; genres; regulation and professionalism. The author of the China chapter used different categories, elaborating upon the studio system and latest generation of filmmakers. Some chapters have an 'Afterword' to make the information as current as possible. All chapters cover film into the latter 1980s; some have information through mid-1989.

Feature films are the central focus, although a few mentions of documentaries and experimental cinema exist. The volume does not pretend to deal in any depth with the latter types of film, or those of a commercial (advertising), animated and educational nature.

Much of the information is based on interviews conducted with 68 leading media, film and government personnel in China, Hong Kong, India, Japan, Korea, Malaysia, Pakistan, the Philippines, Sri Lanka and Taiwan. (See complete list of interviewees in References.) Impressions and concrete data were also gathered through viewing films, visiting sets and examining many secondary sources. (See References.)

All chapters are new to this volume, although very brief parts of the chapters on Korea, Malaysia and the Philippines were extracted from my previous writings (Lent 1976; 1983a, b, c; 1984b).

To the many people who made contacts, provided interviews and secondary data, or otherwise encouraged the preparation of this book, I offer my sincerest gratitude.

John A. Lent
1 June 1989

INTRODUCTION

D
evika Rani turns a number of heads, whether in the Imperial Hotel where she stays when she is in New Delhi, or in the shops of Bangalore, the city the Bengali has adopted as home. Indians still remember her as the grand lady of cinema, even though her career began in the silent film era and ended in 1945, about the time the big studios were closing.

Though reluctant to talk about her stardom, which she abandoned when she married the painter, Svetoslav Roerich, Devika Rani was one of the important pioneers of Indian film.

Her success was anticipated by the great German director, G.W. Pabst, while she was studying theatre in Germany during the 1920s. He made his prediction after putting the young actress 'in front of the camera while he did things to elicit laughter, sadness [and other emotions] and studied my facial expressions,' she said (Interview, Rani, 15 August 1980).

Her break was provided by Indian director Himansu Rai, who asked her to join his Indian Films, which she did, thus breaking the class barrier in acting. Later, he also asked her to marry him. The couple worked together on a number of films, most produced by Bombay Talkies. She described their objective as wishing

> 'to establish Bombay Talkies as a real institution on the basis of a fine business. Everyone who worked with us came from good families and were academically qualified.' (Correspondence, Rani, 27 February 1981)

Claiming there had not been 'any films greater than the ones these studios produced,' Rani said that the big studios collapsed after World War II, when some pioneers died and independents, some supported by 'black [illegally-gained] money', took over (Correspondence, Rani, 25 September 1981).

In mid-1980, I had occasions to chat with Devika Rani over a couple of chicken curry dinners at the Imperial Hotel, in her 1947 chauffeur-driven Chevrolet which took us around Bangalore, at her office and at the Roerich's 500-acre, linaloe berry plantation. We discussed many topics, including the state of Indian films.

'These movies are awful,' she said, explaining they have talent, but not 'know-how or moral structure'. She offered other observations, some of which were:

> 'They are too dedicated to money, instant success' (Interview, Rani, 21 July 1980). 'Movies today copy too much of the West. The arts (and film too) draw inspiration from the society. India is restless now and that is reflected in the films. In the last ten years, too much sex has come into them—women wearing nylons and putting buttons in their bras.' (Interview, Rani, 22 July 1980)

In later correspondence, she elaborated:

> 'Predominance was given to sex and, believe it or not, our own Indian audience in Bangalore broke up the theatre and box office when they found no sex in films so the poor theatre management had to put a card outside the ticket counter saying "no sex" . . . This sort of thing is the trend.' (Correspondence, Rani, 25 September 1981)

Acknowledging that Satyajit Ray is a contemporary director with ideals, Rani said that 'even he is trying to cater to the public'. She did not believe quality movies had an audience in India, pointing out,

> 'There are a few producers and directors who do excellently and whose films win awards abroad for their excellence, but these films are not released in India or taken up by the distributors because they are not a box office draw . . . the distributors do not take them up because they are considered "Art Films" and the themes are not what the public wants to see. For instance, if you are poor and you have to live in the slums and you have to struggle, you don't want to pay money to see all this . . . I personally do not agree with the themes etc. which tend to be unreal or garish and the costumes which are worse, but then, people like all this as it takes their mind off poverty, rising prices, lack of food and accommodation.' (Correspondence, Rani, 25 September 1981)

Devika Rani's opinions are useful to introduce the topic of Asian cinema, for many of the complaints she has of her country's movies are germane to the rest of the continent—the high degree of commercialisation, the heavy influences from the West, the liberalisation of topics (such as sex), the dominating power of the distributor, the plight of the film artist in regard to audience acceptance, and the nostalgia for movies of another time.

DIVERSITY OF CULTURES AND FILMS

That Devika Rani's country is India provides an appropriate starting point in discussing the social, economic and political aspects of Asia. India's use of hundreds of languages, all major religions and extremely varied political and economic systems, in a huge, multi-ethnic context, exemplifies a continent known for its mind-boggling variations.

The diversity is reflected in, and causal to, many characteristics of Asian cinema. In India, movies are produced in all 15 major languages, plus a few sublanguages. Similarly, other countries have multilingual film industries, such as Pakistan, Sri Lanka and Hong Kong. India has religious taboos which dictate against some film content, as have had Malaysia, Indonesia and Pakistan, among others. Indian politics has found its way into cinema, and some movie stars launched important political careers from their box-office appeal. Elsewhere, notably the Philippines, other politicians used movies to promote their campaigns or stepped off the stage into the political arena.

'The mixture of brilliance and mindlessness' (O'Leary 1976:3) of Asian films has been noted rather often, *Time* (1976, p. 40) writing that,

> No other region of the world produces such a concoction of Kung Fu, sci-fi, porn, soapers, chasers and period pieces with such uneven degrees of tackiness and brilliance.'

India again serves as the prototype. Not only can most of these film types be found among the approximately 700 Indian productions a year, but many are meshed within individual pictures called *masala* or *kedgeree* (a spicy, mixed dish). I recall seeing one such three-hour feature in New Delhi a few years ago that included much singing and background music, lots of love and James Bond-type violence, spectacular explosions, breathtaking scenery, miraculous recoveries, trite patriotic displays and much symbolism. My Indian host said many films had these traits.

Before delving further into commonalities of Asian film as introductory chapters are inclined to do, it is necessary to dispel the utter nonsense of referring to Asian cinema as a whole. Though familiar strands may run through the cinema of, let us say, Malaysia and Indonesia, or India and Sri Lanka, the differences between films of Japan and India, or Korea and Pakistan, are as far apart as everything else in those cultures.

Another commonly held perception that should be laid aside is that Asian cinema is unique for being virtually unknown in the West

3

(see Armes 1987: 135). A quick reaction is that most of the film of South America, Africa or even other parts of the West is equally unknown. However, to use unfamiliarity, as Armes (1987, p. 135) does, as a justification for presenting the 'barest sketch' of a region's films is not sound. Much information is available on film of Asian countries through retrospectives and festivals held in the West, and through the burgeoning number of periodicals (e.g. *China Screen*, *Cinema India-International* or *East-West Film Journal*); books, a few recent ones being Quirino (1983), Dissanayake (1988), Desser (1988), Clark (1987), Lee (1988) or Downing (1987); and conferences and symposia (such as those of Asian Cinema Studies Society) (see Lent 1984a, 1985, 1986, for bibliographies).

Granted, except for the works of Kurosawa, Ray, Brocka and a few other directors, Asian cinema has not been well known in the West. But some factors have tended to change this situation, among which are the trend to internationalism, with Asian companies seeking co-production arrangements and directors having their works honoured at festivals such as Cannes or Berlin; the push to export Asian cinema, especially through videocassettes; and the expansion of economic relations with non-Asian areas, with corresponding exchanges of films. For example, as economic relations increased between the European Community and ASEAN (Association of Southeast Asian Nations), Southeast Asian film panoramas and retrospectives were featured in Germanic Europe and France.

COMMONALITIES OF ASIAN FILM

With the above-mentioned cautionary notes in mind, some generalisations are ventured about Asian cinema.

First, Asia has been a prolific producer and voracious viewer of movies. For years, India has led the world in filmmaking, with other countries such as Hong Kong and the Philippines not far behind among the top ten producers. Equally profound has been the enthusiasm of Asian cinema audiences. The continent has had the highest number of movie theatres in the world and, even with the inroads made by home video, leading to theatres being torn down or converted into supermarkets, the figure is formidable. The ready explanation given for Asia's huge film attendance is escapism from a hard lifestyle.

The themes and types of films popular with the audiences have reflected their desire to escape—sex, slapstick comedy, kung fu, melodramatic love, cute animal and youth-oriented topics.

Throughout the 1970s and 1980s, low-budget 'quickie' films with explicit sex scenes set box-office records in some Asian countries. Hong Kong and the Philippines far out-distanced their neighbours in this regard, but almost all other countries enthusiastically accepted erotica as a theme—e.g. Sri Lanka, Indonesia, Japan, Pakistan, India and Thailand. As with other film types, the tendency has been to imitate Western prototypes. Thus, the box-office of the French movie, *Emmanuelle*, gave birth to at least four Asian varieties —*Tokyo Emmanuelle*, *Hong Kong Emmanuelle*, *Black Emmanuelle* and *Yellow Emmanuelle*. Some film companies changed their emphasis entirely to take advantage of the popularity of erotica; for example, Japan's Nikkatsu, realising it had lost the general audience to television, switched to soft porn in 1972 (see *Asiaweek* 1980b).

Much of the comedy in Asian film has been the slapstick variety, which diverts audiences' attentions and arouses a raucous belly laugh. In some cases, comedy has been combined with other mass appeal genres, a recent example being kung fu comedy. Comedy's importance to the industry has been attested to by the huge salaries (some of the highest in the industry) paid to comedians such as Dolphy of the Philippines or Michael and Samuel Hui of Hong Kong. More subtle types of comedy have been popular in some countries at various times. In Japan, parody films boomed in the 1980s, mainly through the works of Juzo Itami (Bornoff 1989: 60). China was short on satire films until the 1980s when that type of comedy became somewhat popular.

Kung fu's appearance in the early 1970s (and resurgence in 1979) marked the first time that an Asian film type spawned a world-famous vogue. In Asia a number of countries joined Hong Kong in producing kung fu movies, including Japan, Korea, Thailand, Indonesia, Taiwan and the Philippines (see *Asiaweek* 1979b).

A much older escapist formula common to Asian cinema has combined melodrama with a love theme of rich boy meets poor girl. Especially popular in the Philippines and South Asia with lower class audiences, this type of film has been relied upon by top directors, e.g. Satyajit Ray of India and Lino Brocka of the Philippines, to keep them financially afloat while they pursue more sophisticated themes in other films.

Besides the formulaic, commercially designed fare, Asia has been home to much high quality cinematic work. Directors such as Lino Brocka, Akira Kurosawa, Nagisa Oshima, Yasujiro Ozu, Lester Peries, Ishmael Bernal, Allen Fong, Satyajit Ray, Teguh Karya, Cherd Songsri, Chen Kaige, Zhang Yimou and others have been associated with technically and thematically sound work. Because of the national self-confidence of the past generation, many Asian countries have generated their equivalent of a 'new wave', featuring young directors who capture realistic aspects of their societies on film, using sophisticated techniques (see Eichenberger 1986: 16).

In most instances, it has been difficult to market domestically the works of such directors trying to make personal films for less sophisticated audiences; the price they pay to keep their dignity is often quite high. Even great directors such as Kurosawa and Ray have not been very popular among their own people; in the late 1980s, Kurosawa had to seek United States funding for his film, *Dreams*.

Also common to most Asian film industries has been the domineering threat of Western movies. In many areas, local films consistently had difficulties finding exhibition sites, as foreign movies took up large proportions of the screening time. Over the past generation, national governments and film associations have countered with a number of protectionist moves, epitomised in the South Korean demonstrations and boycotts of US films in 1988. Among tactics used by various governments have been heavy taxation of foreign films, state co-ordination of foreign distribution of local films (see Schnitman 1981), established quotas of screening days for domestic movies and import quotas on foreign ones, granting of loans and subsidies to local producers, and awarding of prizes for artistically and socially relevant national films.

Governments have reacted in other ways, in some cases strengthening censorship regulations, and generally re-examining copyright legislation in the light of rampant videocassette piracy. The degree of censorship fluctuates throughout the region, with Malaysian and Singaporean authorities remaining tough in the implementation of laws, those in the Philippines quashing 'pene' (sexual penetration) films and those in other countries loosening up a bit. By 1988, governments of at least Taiwan, China, Korea, India and Pakistan eased their controls on the screening of sex.

A common complaint Asian film producers have had relates to the arbitrary application of censorship laws. In most countries, a different standard existed for foreign movies; in other instances, e.g. Indonesia, authorities were tougher on sex than on violence themes. Some restriction policies were hard to fathom: in parts of India, film kissing was taboo, yet *frottage* (rubbing of one clothed body against another) was allowed; in Hong Kong, censors stopped a wide shot of love-making, but permitted a close-up of the upper body of a woman during love-making.

As is the trend world-wide concerning all mass media, concentration of ownership has plagued Asian film. A few large production houses, interlocking with large business and political concerns, have monopolised many industries. For example, Japanese film is lorded over by Toho, Shochiku, Toei and Nikkatsu; Hong Kong by Shaw, Cinema City, Golden Harvest and D and B, and the Philippines by Regal, Seiko and Viva. Invariably, companies of this magnitude are also knotted to distribution and exhibition, as well as non-film industries and businesses, e.g. development, financial interest, transportation or rubber (Interview, Raman Kutty, 1986).

An encouraging aspect of Asian film has been the development of a number of professional agencies involved in film training, protectionism, promotion and preservation. Asia has hosted international film festivals, such as those of Manila, Hong Kong (see *Asiaweek* 1983c) and Tokyo, as well as its own Asian Film Festival, an annual event since 1954. A regional ASEAN Film Festival, started in 1971, has presented annual awards to deserving movie talent and proposed film enhancement projects such as an ASEAN film school library. Additionally, many countries have their own national film festivals, e.g. Taiwan (whose festival now includes Hong Kong), Korea, Indonesia, Pakistan, the Philippines, Thailand, India and Japan.

All Asian film industries are organised into professional groups. On the regional level, Southeast Asia has had the ASEAN Motion Picture Producers Association since 1974. Among some of its activities have been the encouragement of co-productions and the fostering of an appreciation of films of member states (see Anwar 1988: 137).

Finally, it seems to be a common feeling among Asian film personnel that some of the national film industries may be tottering near death as they explore alternatives and implore government agencies to lend a helping hand.

EAST ASIA

EAST ASIA

1

CHINA

George S. Semsel*

INTRODUCTION

'I d like us to talk very informally about film in China,' said Chen Mei, editor of *World Cinema*, a magazine published by the China Film Association. We were talking over tea in my apartment at the Friendship Hotel in Beijing, where I was spending a year working as a 'foreign expert' at the China Film Export and Import Corporation, the state-run organisation which manages the international business of the film industry. With us was my wife, Rosemary, and Wang Rui, head of the translation section, the man responsible for my appointment.

'Let's just make this a dialogue between friends. It's very important that we note the date of this interview, 2 February 1985, because even after a year, many things change here. There have been a lot of changes since 1983, when I went to the States, and there will be a lot more before long. You will have to come back in two or three years, just to take a close look at whatever's happened.' (Interview, Chen Mei, 1985)

In 1989, as I prepared to return to China, this time as a Fulbright Scholar, we met again, in Iowa City, at the annual meeting of the Society for Cinema Studies. 'You know you can't believe everything you read,' Chen Mai admonished, 'especially in the Chinese press. Everyone is interested in building themselves up these days. They all have a story to tell. Everyone has his version of the truth.' (Interview, Chen Mei, 1989) I had just finished delivering a paper in which I had gone on about the fitful rise of independent filmmaking in the People's Republic. The industry had been changing rapidly since the end of the Cultural Revolution. In 1985, I had found a few people talking about the commercial potentials for independent

* This chapter © 1990 George S. Semsel.

11

productions, but there hadn't been any official position publicised. Since leaving China, I had learned that official sanction had been granted at last, and there had already been some efforts by film-makers to make use of the new freedom, though they had not apparently succeeded. Chen Mei was concerned that the recent reports in the overseas edition of *People's Daily* were not telling the whole picture. Her warning in itself is a good indication of how the Chinese film world operates.

Much of Chinese film has remained somewhat mysterious to the rest of the world. Few films had been released to the international markets until early in 1985, when *Yellow Earth* (1984) proved a sleeper at the Hong Kong Film Festival. In fact, although China traces its film industry back to the turn of the century, its progress had nearly come to a standstill during the Cultural Revolution period (1966–76), often spoken of in China as the 'ten chaotic years'. Officially, during that decade of turmoil, when China's doors remained tightly closed to the outside world, only eight films were released, and these were primarily operas adapted to political ends. Contemporary Chinese film, as a result, can be conventionally traced back to the renewal of the industry after the fall of the 'Gang of Four' in 1976.

Since the mid-1970s, film production gradually but steadily increased until the annual production of feature films settled into a range from 125 to 150, most of them made in the 16 studios officially permitted to produce commercial works. The majority of features are produced at the larger, well-established studios in Beijing, Changchun and Shanghai, yet some of the most interesting work is being done at smaller studios as far away as Inner Mongolia and Xinjiang. Other studios are given to the production of agri-cultural films, scientific and educational films, documentaries and newsreels and animations. Additional filmmaking is done in smaller studios owned and operated within individual provinces.

THE STUDIOS

The film industry in China operates very much as did the studio system of the United States in the 1930s and 1940s. Although one cannot always define the kind of production one will see on the basis of the studio which produced it, none the less, each studio has a sufficient reputation that my colleagues at China Film would groan or applaud, depending on where a film we were about to see was made. *On the Hunting Ground* (1984) held only a small audience. Most people left the theatre as soon as they learned it had been made at the Inner Mongolia Film Studio. I learned quickly enough that films made by the PLA's studio usually demonstrate the merits of the army; that films from Changchun, the first studio to operate under communist control, tend to be more conservative in structure and politics than those of Shanghai, whose roots go far back into Chinese film history; that films from Shanghai, because of its background, tend to have a 'Hollywood look' to them; that films from the Pearl River Studio reflect the proximity of Guangzhou to Hong Kong; that films from Xi'an, under the dedicated leadership of Wu Tianming, tend to be fresh and innovative.

Most of the studios are designed to serve their local population. Although not necessarily required to do so, their products are frequently structured around a regional content. Filmmakers from the Emei Film Studio in Chengdu talked to me about their filmmaking in Sichuan Province. 'Emei is, to some degree, committed to regional materials,' Director Liu explained. 'I was born and raised in Sichuan, so naturally I choose subjects with which I am most familiar. In that sense, they're autobiographical' (Semsel 1987: 159–64). Zhang Liang's *Yamaha Fish Stall* (Pearl River Film Studio, 1984) is set on the streets of Guangzhou; screenwriter Xie Fengsong's *On the Elevator* (Beijing Film Studio, 1985) takes place in Beijing.

Other studios have specialised functions. The Youth Film Studio, operated by the Beijing Film Institute, not only provides its faculty members with a facility at which they can remain active in their profession, but also has the potential to earn profits to support the school. 'If our films cannot make money,' Xie Fei, deputy head of the Beijing Film Academy, explained,

'then we do not have the funds to do other things: repair equipment, build new facilities. It is important that we make films that sell well. In the early 1980s, we made a few films that gave us an income. They were art films, too. They won prizes, but they did well at the box office, too. Recent films have not been able to do that. It's a problem for us.' (Interview, Xie, 1985)

The Children's Film Studio makes films for young people. The August First Film Studio, operated by the PLA, makes films primarily for those in military service.

Each studio maintains a full staff of writers, directors, cinematographers, designers and technicians. The Beijing Film Studio, among the largest in China, maintains some 70 directors, yet produces little more than 20 films a year. Each director, therefore, must await the opportunity to direct. The Children's Film Studio, located on the grounds of the Beijing Film Studio, has a staff of 90 professionals, supplementing them as necessary with other personnel. The smaller studios have attracted some of the most interesting young directors, because they offer more opportunities to be active. Chen Kaige, for example, was suggested for the Youth Team of the Guangxi Film Studio by his classmate, cinematographer

13

Zhang Yimou. There he made one of the first films of the 'Fifth Generation' to attract international attention, *Yellow Earth*.

Most studios maintain a professional acting troupe, especially for casting in supporting roles. Major roles, in contrast, are not necessarily cast from the available ensemble. Teng Wenji discovered Yin Tingru working as an announcer for the Shanghai Philharmonic Society and after placing her in a minor role in *Awakening*, gave her major roles in several subsequent films. Zhang Liang, at the Pearl River Film Studio in Guangzhou, cast an untrained amateur in the role of Haizai in *Yamaha Fish Stall*, because the man actually was a self-employed youth, the subject of the film. Extras are cast on location. The August Eight Film Studio, in need of an American to play Agnes Smedley, cast Elizabeth (Lee) Grumman from a group of students at Beijing Normal University.

The studios are generally well-equipped with 35mm equipment. At a number of shoots, I found Arriflex cameras in common use, accompanied by the lighting and sound equipment found in most Western studios. The major difference in filmmaking was that most films are shot without sound, which is dubbed in later. Since there is a multiplicity of dialects and languages in the country, it is useful to work this way. *In the Wild Mountains* (1985), generally celebrated as the first film in the People's Republic to be shot using location sound, won the Golden Rooster Award. Studios' buildings are often spacious, and the larger studios maintain exterior, 'back lot', generic streets, which are the Chinese equivalent of the frontier towns long used in American westerns.

The studio system may be coming to an end in the People's Republic. The box office has steadily declined over the past few years although personal income has improved. The China Film Corporation reported that the annual audience had slipped from a high of more than 27 thousand million in 1984–85 to only 22 thousand million in 1987. The industry has looked for ways to respond to this decline. Part of the blame is placed upon the films themselves, which audiences, beginning to access works from other countries, are finding less interesting. They no longer want to see what they consider little more than time-worn propaganda. At the same time, filmmakers have been looking for more freedom. Even after the studios gained control of their own productions, in 1986, no burst of creative energies ensued. If anything, the financial crisis has led the studios to conservative entertainment films, and these have yet to sell well.

The gradual influx of television has affected the Chinese film market as it has markets elsewhere. The number of television sets sold increases annually. According to Li Xiaohong, doctoral candidate in mass communications at Ohio University, new sets are sold out as quickly as they become availabale. Videocassette recorders (VCRs) too, are spreading across the land at a faster rate than initially anticipated. Chris Berry, who recently spent several years in the People's Republic, told me at the October 1988 meeting of the Asian Cinema Studies Society, that contraband videocassettes are major business on the black markets of China, and that these are often of coarse materials or of low quality. That the government recently burned several thousand videocassettes it confiscated in Beijing verifies his observation.

'Our most serious competition is television,' Chen Xiaolin said to me one day as we talked about the problems of China's film business in her Beijing office.

'When TV broadcasts a new film, we may lose several million RMB in distribution, but it only pays 180 RMB (US $45) for a single transmission. In addition, there are also special clubs in factories and other units, and operations like the Cultural Palace and the PLA, which have their own theatres and thus no overheads. Professional theatres have to pay 50 per cent of their profits in taxes. It's a real constriction. We need to renovate our theatres with new equipment and other facilities to provide better viewing conditions and to attract our audience back. The special clubs splinter the audience. They have better conditions and don't have to pay taxes. The film corporation doesn't have a lot of money and yet it must serve the rural area. The average price of a ticket in 35mm theatres is only 15 fen (US 3 cents). Our main purpose is to make it possible for all the people to see movies so that they gain a better understanding of the world.' (Interview, Chen Xiaolin, 1985)

The mammoth China Film Distribution and Exhibition Corporation, with its sister enterprise, the China Film Export and Import Corporation, until recently, controlled all the film business of the country. The domestic corporation maintains a staff of half a million and operates almost 200,000 projection units in more than 3,000 cinemas. Its foreign counterpart maintains relationships with more than 100 countries. It operates an office in Paris and a subsidiary in Los Angeles, currently headed by Chen Xiaolin. Out of economic necessity, it has started to market videocassettes as well as film.

By the mid-1980s, the system for marketing films had clearly become an anachronism and the studios began to demand a larger share of the profits. After considerable debate on the issue, and numerous backstage manoeuvres, a compromise was reached and China Film and studio representatives met at the Great Hall of the People on Tiananmen Square in Beijing and signed an agreement. One source in 1988 reported four methods of profit allocation:

'1. China film grants a minimum guarantee to a finished film and a distribution fee (50% of the box office) is divided between China Film (71.5%) and the studio (28.5%); 2. China Film and studios share box office at a negotiated percentage in which no minimum guarantee is granted from China Film; 3. China Film acquires a film for a flat fee; 4. China Film acts as an agent for a studio on a commission basis in which China Film is no longer obliged to take a poor film.' (*Variety* 19 October 1988)

Variety also reported that, 'So far, only four studios, Beijing, Xi'an, Pearl River and Emei, have opted for the first method with the rest sticking to the third.' The issue of profits has not been fully resolved.

One alternative solution has been the development of a system for independent producing which places the responsibility for the success of the film into the hands of its producer. While the initial results of this system have been negative, it is much too soon to draw conclusions.

FILM AS LITERATURE

Film in China is understood and taught not as a fine art, but as a form of literature. In fact, in the early 1980s, a relatively heated debate took place among educators and scholars over the 'literature-isation of film', as Chen Mei called it. 'They really do put it that way. I'm quite amazed when they talk about that. I find myself asking: "Why? It's *cinema*. It's *cinematic*. It's *film*. Why should we keep talking about it as a literary form?"' (Interview, Chen Mei, 1985)

The question of film is rooted in the Chinese notion that the story comes first in any work, be it novel, drama or film. Film as an individual art has not been fully recognised by its own practitioners. As a result, the few cinema studies courses found in the universities are usually offered in literature departments, and they usually begin with scriptwriting, the starting place for every film. 'A film depends on its screenplay. That's why reading them has become a specific pleasure of the Chinese, something you Americans seem to find astonishing,' Chen Mei (Interview, 1985) said. She is right. I was tempted to argue that screenplays are only the recipes for film. Films are to be watched, not read. But I resisted the urge. The truth is the Chinese do enjoy reading screenplays, even Chinese screenplays, and devote magazines to them, a workable solution to the fact that film screenings are still a city matter, and that foreign films are seldom seen outside the urban environment. If you can't see a film, at least you might read it.

Chen Mei cites another reason for the reading of scripts:

I love to read them myself. You know, after the ten chaotic years, some very moving ones have been written about them. By reading a screenplay, we get to feel close to the truth, you know, of what happened. People were so very eager to find a way to express their emotions in a concrete form; it didn't matter whether it was fiction, poetry, scriptwriting, whatever, because it was all *literature*.' (Interview, Chen Mei, 1985)

To the Chinese, writing is basic to first impressions. For that reason, the universities, but not the film college, start with screenwriting.

BEIJING FILM ACADEMY

The Beijing Film Academy is the primary institution at which filmmaking is taught, although some young people manage to find other ways into the film industry. It is a relatively small institute located in the northwest section of Beijing. During the Cultural Revolution, it was forced to leave Beijing for the nearby countryside, but it is now completing a new campus near the Beijing Film Studio and the other film units, which make the district the centre of China's film circles.

Only a very small number of students are accepted into the Film Academy, and competition is keen. Xie Fei, deputy head of the Academy, said that overall, there are about 150 students taking eight or nine courses a year. They attend classes for 28 hours spread over a six-day week. On Sundays, new students work on video projects which simulate filmmaking practices. On Mondays, the senior students work on their projects, which are usually shot in 35mm. Everyone works in teams. There is little opportunity to pursue individual projects, although Xie Fei made it clear he would like to see the change. (Interview, Xie, 1985)

The curriculum is divided into various areas of specialisation: directing, photography, design, sound, acting, literature. Literature includes screenwriting as well as theoretical and historical studies. In 1985, the administration decided to enrol no more than 16 students in any given area, in part for lack of funding, but also because with the new campus under construction, facilities were being pushed to the limit. The situation has eased slightly, Xie Fei told me in a visit to Ohio University, but basic problems must still be resolved. 'Before the Cultural Revolution, the school was patterned on the Soviet system,' he explained, adding, 'Now that the years of chaos have ended, the school is giving more attention to Western models. As you know from your own experience, that takes a lot of money. So for the moment, we will have to keep the number of students low.' (Interview, Xie, 1987)

The academy is operated by the government, and all students receive government support, including the money for making movies. My own students are envious when I tell them this. The problem, I make clear to them, is that the government cannot put much money into student filmmaking, and the funding system affects the nature of the training they receive. As it now stands, filmmaking must be done in teams. Students majoring in photography do the shooting on a project, while those in directing never handle a camera. 'We are trying to change this situation,' Xie Fei said, 'We want to allow people to try their hand with everything.' He had visited a number of universities in the United States and was hoping to adapt some Western concepts to his school. Xie said:

> 'We would like to institute a programme where students study many aspects of filmmaking together. We are trying to design a way to relate each major with the other majors to make filmmaking a total process instead of a group of separate discrete areas.' (Interview, Xie, 1987)

One solution already in practice is the separation of new students into two distinct programmes: a two-year programme for those in need of technical training and a more comprehensive four-year programme. This should lead to a more efficient use of available resources.

Financial considerations may prevent Xie Fei from restructuring the film academy totally along Western lines. The main reforms taking place in the People's Republic have not yet brought significant changes to such matters as the way jobs are classified. Until that structure is changed, students will have no choice but to undertake a specific major and later, upon graduation, to be assigned to that field. Xie Fei talked about this:

> 'We made a comparison between students who have trained in a specialty and those who took in a broader range of interests. Those who had the more comprehensive curriculum had a better grasp of their specific field.' (Interview, Xie, 1987)

The changes will come eventually.

Already in operation, the new campus, when completed, will accommodate 600 students and will provide a badly needed space for conferences and film studies. Aside from new buildings, the most important problem the leadership must address is the modernisation of equipment. This means, of course, Xie Fie must gain a major financial commitment from the government, something not easy to achieve under the current economic situation, and will probably need help from private sources as well. 'We might even seek the help of foreign countries,' he laughed—but I sensed he was not joking (Interview, Xie, 1985).

I toured the Beijing Film Academy in 1985, before it moved back into the city. I envied the large studio spaces, but found much of the equipment outdated (compared with tools currently in use elsewhere) but none the less workable. Lighting equipment was made in the 1940s. There were no flat-bed editors, and the upright machines were unquestionably ancient. I assured Xie Fei, that the age of such machines was not necessarily of great significance, that students at my university also cut films on antiques, with good results. He understood this, but pointed to a problem few American universities face:

> 'A lot of money is wasted on useless personnel. Although we have only 150 students, we have a staff of 509. There are 200 on the faculty alone. Whenever I mention this to foreigners, they are shocked. But right now, I can't do anything about it.' (Interview, Xie, 1985)

THE FIFTH GENERATION

Early in 1984, when *One and Eight*, Zhang Junzhao's first film, appeared, it caused a sensation among those who saw it. It was withheld from release to the public, however, for more than a year, while changes mandated by those in power were made. When later that same year, Chen Kaige's first film, *Yellow Earth*, reached the screen, people in the film world began to talk about a new generation of filmmakers, a 'Fifth Generation'. China's youngest directors— Zhang Junzhao (*One and Eight*, 1984), Chen Kaige (*Yellow Earth*, 1984), Tian Zhuangzhuang (*On the Hunting Ground*, 1985), Wu Ziniu (*Secret Decree*, 1985) and, later Huang Jianxin (*Black Cannon Incident*, 1986) and Zhang Yimou (*Red Sorghum*, 1987) — brought Chinese filmmaking to the attention of international film circles. The term stuck.

However, when it comes to defining what precisely is meant by the 'Fifth Generation', there has been continual debate both in and out of China. Cheng Jihua, the major historian of Chinese film, flatly declared:

> 'The term is inaccurate and inappropriate for these filmmakers. There are a number of filmmakers not included in the generally accepted definition who make films of equally high aesthetic value. Besides, we expect the works of the best directors to span more than a single generation.'

Despite his position, Cheng admitted that the division of film-making into generations was a useful strategy for the historian (Interview, Cheng Jihua, 1989).

By the time *One and Eight* appeared in 1984, a number of filmmakers, primarily those considered middle-aged, had already succeeded in re-establishing Chinese film from the ruins of the Cultural Revolution. Yang Yianjin (*Troubled Laughter*, 1979;

Narrow Lane, 1980), Teng Wenji (*Reverberations of Life*, 1979; *A Corner of the City*, 1983), Wu Yigong (*Evening Rain*, 1981; *My Memories of Old Beijing*, 1983), Zheng Dongtian (*Neighbours*, 1982), Zhang Nuanxin (*Sha'ou*, 1982) and Hu Bingliu (*Native Call*, 1984) all contributed significantly to the development of Chinese film. Their achievement in aesthetics, especially clear when their works are compared with films made during the 17 years following Liberation in 1949, laid the groundwork for the new filmmakers.

The appearance of *One and Eight*, followed in a relatively short time by *Yellow Earth*, *On the Hunting Ground*, *The Decree* and *Dove Tree* (Wu Ziniu, 1985), all made by young directors, generated considerable excitement. Here were films not only markedly different from traditional Chinese films, but from those made by contemporaries in terms of the selection and representation of topics, the application of cinematic styles and narrative devices and the reflection of ideology. These young filmmakers, however, are not all alike. Each has distinct differences in the individual characteristics and styles. Facing this new phenomenon, people in Chinese film circles crowned it with a variety of names: 'New Chinese Cinema'; 'Chinese Experimental Film'; 'Exploration Films'. In 1986, in enthusiastic response to the new direction Chinese film had taken, a special theatre was opened in Shanghai as a showcase for what were termed 'art' films, but it later closed for lack of attendance.

The new filmmakers did not go unnoticed by the foreign population in China. They were also acknowledged as the 'Chinese avant-garde', or the 'Chinese New Wave' by those few Westerners who saw them. However, it seemed that no single generalisation accurately described this new phenomenon. Gradually, more and more people opted for the general term, 'Fifth Generation'. At first, the term referred only to filmmakers who graduated from the Beijing Film Institute in the class of 1982, but eventually it was extended to include other young people such as Chen Lizhou (*Road*, 1984) and Huang Jianxin (*Black Cannon Incident*, 1985), who had studied at the Institute, but who were not graduates.

Dividing the filmmakers of a country into generations clearly has its problems, although it provides a convenient way of looking at the history of the medium. The first generation of Chinese filmmakers consists of those who introduced film into the country and subsequently made films themselves (Zheng Zhenqui, Yang Shichuan); the second generation consists of those directors who joined the industry before Liberation and remained active for some time afterwards (Cai Cusheng, Zheng Junli); the third generation refers to those educated during the 17-year period following Liberation, who formed the backbone of the industry during that period (Xie Jin); the fourth generation is the middle-aged directors who received a college-level education in film or theatre before the Cultural Revolution and who became the major force of filmmaking immediately after it ended (Zheng Dongtian, Wu Yigong); the fifth generation, the youngest, is for the most part recent graduates from the Beijing Film Institute. Despite the inaccuracy of such divisions (Chen Mei insists there are six, not five generations), and the seemingly endless disputes among scholars over the issue, the label, 'Fifth Generation', has been so widely accepted that the arguments now seem academic.

The class of 1982 entered the Beijing Film Institute in 1978, the year in which the nation-wide college entrance examination was reintroduced after the Cultural Revolution had ended. What made them different from students today, who enter college directly after high school, is that they had gone through a long period of working experiences in factories or in the countryside. They were, therefore, older upon entering, ranging in age from 25 to 35, and more mature.

Among the most prominent of the young directors, Tian Zhuangzhuang is the most fortunate since, after spending only a year in the countryside, he joined the army. Later, after working as a cameraman in the Beijing Agricultural Film Studio, he was able to study directing at the Beijing Film Institute and was subsequently assigned to the Beijing Film Studio. The others were not so fortunate. Chen Kaige was sent to work in the countryside as an 'educated youth' before spending six years as a PLA soldier. Then, after three years in the Beijing Film Processing Lab, in 1978, he passed the entrance examination for the film institute, where he also studied directing. Zhang Yimou, after three years on a farm in the Shaanxi countryside, spent seven years at the Number Eight Textile Factory in Xianyan. Also a member of the Class of '82, he studied cinematography and was assigned to the Guangxi Film Studio. Wu Ziniu likewise worked in the countryside for several years.

In addition to the experiences these men had in common, the dramatic changes forced upon their families during the Cultural Revolution played a crucial role in shaping their personalities and characteristics. Zhang Yimou, for example, is the son of a Kuomintang army official; Wu Ziniu, the son of a landlord; Chen Kaige and Tian Zhuangzhuang, the sons of intellectuals. These young people became the abandoned children of the time and the 'ruins' of society. The spiritual torment they endured because of their families far exceeded the physical hardships they experienced in the countryside and factories. They came to share the common characteristics of perseverance, deep seriousness and sophistication. Because of this, they are often referred to as a 'generation of thinkers'. These characteristics were later embodied in their films.

As Chen Kaige allegedly put it:

'Everyone agrees that the Cultural Revolution brought us many problems. Aside from the damage caused to our economic

21

system, I believe that the ruin of our national and cultural spirit was the worst. The doomed psychology which resulted from fear, doubt and a laissez-faire attitude made it very difficult to do anything about the situation. Those with the most passionate feelings for a nation are the ones most likely to dissent and that includes its intellectuals. Since we cannot choose the time into which we are born, can we not be more open-minded toward most of what happened?' (Quoted in Hou and Xia 1989)

Chen's words accurately reflect the attitude of the 'Fifth Generation' filmmakers towards their life experiences and towards art. This quality is far more precious than any use they have made of the technology of the medium. This is the heart of the deep solemnity and the imposing emotional power one finds in their films.

If their experience in the Cultural Revolution shaped the thinking of this generation, their education, together with the movement toward ideological liberation and the open-door policy which ensued, provided them with opportunities denied those who came before them. These filmmakers were not only able to view many Chinese films of the 1930s and 1940s, but a variety of contemporary foreign films. The foreign directors most admired and addressed were Antonioni, Fellini and Bergman; the theorists most widely discussed were Bazin and Kracauer.

Compared with the older generations, the 'Fifth Generation' demonstrates two unique characteristics: one is the desire to assimilate all of Western culture. From classicism to modernism, they have tried to take in everything. In contrast, the older generations remain cautiously conservative in such matters. Curiously enough, few traces of Westernisation can be detected in the 'Fifth Generation's' films, easing the fears of many people who worried about this direction. The other is the bold, thoroughly rebellious and thoughtful spirit which saw the virtuous trait of 'listening to the Party' weaken and disappear in them. At the time when the middle-aged directors were torn over whether it was more appropriate to learn from the West or to develop their own tradition, and spent much time in discussions of montage, long takes, theatricality and the redemption of physical reality, the 'Fifth Generation' began its quest for new means of expression. *One and Eight* shocked the depressed and slow-moving film circles, and *Yellow Earth* brought an innovative freshness and vitality to China's screen.

The 'Fifth Generation' has consciously sought a breakthrough in filmic expression. While middle-aged directors such as Zheng Dongtian, Teng Wenji and Wu Tianming targeted their creative efforts against the artificial reality which had become a characteristic of Chinese film and worked for the truths to be found in the portrayal of ordinary people, the 'Fifth Generation' looked for alternatives to the norms of production. They paid little attention to material gain from their films, though they would pay a price for this later, nor did they trouble themselves over remedies for the ailments of Chinese film. Further, they displayed little interest in the depiction of present-day reality in their films, a reality older generations relished and younger generations found boring. On the contrary, as a group, they turned their attentions to the past, to Chinese history. *One and Eight*, *Yellow Earth* and *Secret Decree* are all set in the period before Liberation, during the war with Japan, and *On the Hunting Ground*, because of its setting, seems even more ancient.

Traditional Chinese film is derived from the Hollywood model of the 1930s and 1940s. What the Chinese call 'literary film' means a dramatic and touching story rendered through cinematic techniques. Although clearly the themes and content of Chinese films differ from those of the West, their carefully constructed dramatic structures — beginning, middle and (usually happy) ending — told through a generally accepted cinematic language, were imported from Hollywood and taken as infallible law for Chinese filmmaking.

Thus, the Hollywood model standardised the way the Chinese audiences perceived films, a process of training Chinese viewers which, until the emergence of the 'Fifth Generation', was never seriously challenged. Because of this, the appearance of the films made by Chen Kaige, Zhang Junzhao and other young directors was received with confusion, indifference and, at times, resistance. The narrative styles and the representative devices used in their films, counter to the accepted viewing experience, were strongly resisted by most viewers. Thus, as critics delight in pointing out, these films did badly at the box office. The critics missed the point. *One and Eight*, *Yellow Earth* and the subsequent films of the 'Fifth Generation' represented a revolt against tradition and, consequently, the Hollywood model on which it is based.

Chinese film critics, no matter whether they are for or against the 'Fifth Generation', tend to focus attention on the forms and techniques of the new filmmakers. Their rebellious spirit, however, derives from their concept of film. To them, film is no longer a 'dream-making' machine, nor merely a tool which, by combining sound and image, simply repeats or reconstructs a written tale. Nor is the medium, as had long been held by those in power, merely a means to illustrate or transmit political ideologies. Influenced by the major European film artists, they were led to use film to express their individual thoughts and ideas, their deepest feelings. Films became for them a bridge between their subjectivity and the objective world.

The majority of the young filmmakers express their views of contemporary China through its natural environment and cultural traditions. *Yellow Earth*, for example, offers little significance when examined from the perspective of traditional Chinese film. This has led some to argue that Chen Kaige was wrong to centre on the simple story of a countryside girl. However, by placing his characters diminutively against overwhelming expanses of arid yellow earth, he moves us to observe his passionate and yet depressed feelngs. Chen Kaige has a great deal to say in this film, while, paradoxically, saying nothing. The depth of emotions expressed in his film none the less stimulates us to rich thought. It is ironic that the complex analyses written by the film's critics have more substance than the film itself. Chen's strategy is characteristic of 'Fifth Generation' films, and a major difference between them and traditional Chinese film. Yet, despite similarities in their filmmaking strategies, each 'Fifth Generation' director projects his own personality.

Xia Hong and Hou Jianping argue that the major reason critics cannot accept films made by the 'Fifth Generation' is not their cinematic forms but the ideology they reflect. Mainstream Chinese films, of course, no matter how different in theme or content, are all constructed under the guidance of Marxism, Leninism, Mao Zedong Thought and the policies of the Party. In order to meet the demands of the dominant ideology, characters and events in films have frequently been falsely rendered. This can be seen most clearly in films made after 1957 and during the Cultural Revolution.

In addition, philosophies of life and ethics, that are controversial in contemporary China (feudalism especially), are also found in mainstream films and affect the ideas and behaviour of the characters. In other words, traditional Chinese culture restricts and heavily influences Chinese filmmaking. After 1979, a few middle-aged directors broke with the norms of the tradition. The individualism of Zhang Nuanxin's heroine in *Sha'ou* (1981) and the psychological development of Teng Wenji's youngsters in *Awakening* (1979) foreshadowed subsequent developments. Yet the most significant rebellion did not begin until the works of the 'Fifth Generation' began to emerge (Hou and Xia 1989).

The significance of the appearance of *One and Eight* and *Yellow Earth* in 1984 lies not only in the awakening of cinematic consciousness which critics celebrated but, more importantly, in the awakening of a humanistic consciousness. Daring to be different from public opinion and to resist the accusations of the government, the 'Fifth Generation', for the first time in history, thoroughly represented individualism on the screen. In *One and Eight*, the eight prisoners, from the falsely accused Communist Party member to the bandits, gangsters or deserters with whom he is held captive, are all presented with the dignity of people in a desperate struggle against aggression. Especially moving is a crucial scene near the end of the film. A prisoner under attack uses his last bullet to kill a young nurse about to be raped by the enemy, then dies heroically in a hail of bullets. This shocking scene, which provoked a heated debate, proved too much for the censors to handle and it was altered.

In *Secret Decree*, the Chinese audience was once again severely shocked, this time by the representation of the Communist Party and its political opponent, the Kuomintang. After decades of being taught that the former is inherently good and the latter characteristically evil, the audience had to confront a situation not quite so clear-cut: at a time when the existence of the nation was threatened by invaders from Japan, rather than unite against the enemy, the Communist Party and the Kuomintang fight each other in a quest to secure a document proving that Chiang Kaishek ordered his army to co-operate with the Japanese. The calm objectivity of the film demanded that the audience weigh tremendously painful contradictions. Amazingly enough, the film was considered a detective film and was allowed to pass through the strict censorship of the China Film Bureau. Eventually, *Secret Decree* became the only film of the 'Fifth Generation' to be a box-office hit.

With similar perception, Chen Kaige, in *Yellow Earth*, put much of his love into the hard-working and kind peasant father yet, at the same time, calmly exposed the stubborn ignorance of the man as the heavy burden laid on the shoulders of the entire nation. It is these characteristics that turned the peasant, albeit indirectly and unconsciously, into the killer of his own daughter. Through such strategies, these young directors have stimulated the Chinese audience to think deeply about the issues of national identity, a significant matter as China's open-door policies continue to encourage the importation of technologies and ideas from abroad.

The 'Fifth Generation' directors have brought to the Chinese screen unique and personal observations drawn from their life experiences, which agree neither with the accepted norms nor the thinking of their ancestors or the ideas of foreigners. With the appearance of their films, traditional concepts of right and wrong, of values and ethical standards, have wavered and changed. Underlying such changes are recent developments in economics and politics. At the least, these films have led people to realise the limitations of traditional aesthetics and the potentials of this most popular medium.

The narrative structure and cinematic language inherited from the Hollywood model and long accepted in Chinese films have been challenged and weakened by China's newest directors. Their subjective representations are intense as they break with normal objective structures. Plot and narrative in their films are removed from the dominant position, allowing the audience to concentrate on other values. Thus, the director of *Secret Decree* describes it as a monologue of the filmmaker's mind uninterrupted by editing. In *Yellow Earth*, the drum scene and the rain dance act as a catharsis, a release from the tension of deep meditation. Tian Zhuangzhuang has received the most criticism. In both *On the Hunting Ground* and *Horse Thief* (1986), Tian uses long sequences to depict religious rituals and local customs which have nothing to do with the narration. The resultant power of pictorial expression in these films exceeds that of traditional visual representation.

Two major trends dominate the filmmakers of the 'Fifth Generation'. One is the expansion and development of this group. Aside from those already mentioned, new filmmakers continue to join this force. Among the most recent directors, Huang Jianxin, (*Black Cannon Incident*, 1986), Jiang Haiyang, (*The Last Sun*, 1986) and Hu Mei (*Army Nurse*, 1986) have already received critical acclaim. Though these newcomers do not go as far as the pioneers in construction and visual representation, and their emergence did not shock film circles as did the first group, they have broadened the scope of the movement and added new vitality. Among them, Zhang Yimou, a graduate in cinematography of the class of 1982, is the most outstanding. Prize-winning cinematographer on *One and Eight*, *Yellow Earth* and *Big Parade*, he only recently turned to directing. *Red Sorghum* (1987), his first film, won the Golden Bear Award at the Berlin Film Festival and the Golden Rooster and Hundred Flowers Awards in China. Many consider this film the highest achievement of the 'Fifth Generation'.

The second trend is the gradual diversification and increasing personalisation of 'Fifth Generation' directors. The 'Fifth Generation' did not form as a collective group with common goals and identical characteristics. There was no common agreement among them. In fact, these young people did not communicate much with one another.

The strong shock that their films brought to the Chinese screen is the result of the coming together of a generation of similar age and life experiences. Their films revealed different styles and characteristics from the very beginning. In the few years that have followed, each has made a series of his own films and developed his individual style. Chen Kaige made *Yellow Earth*, *Big Parade*, *King of the Children* (1987); Tian Zhuangzhuang, *September* (1983), *On the Hunting Ground*, *Horse Thief*, *Story-Teller* (1987) and *Rock n' Roll Youth* (1988); Wu Ziniu, *Secret Decree*, *Dove Tree*, *The Last Day of Winter* (1986), *Pleasant Heroes* (1987) and *Borderline Between Male and Female* (1988); Zhang Junzhao, *One and Eight*, *Come On, Chinese Team*, (1985), *The Lonely Murderer* (1986) and *The Arc Light* (1988).

Most recently, the demands and strains of economic reform have led all of China's filmmakers, including the 'Fifth Generation', towards films designed to succeed in the market-place. However, this does not mean the 'Fifth Generation' has ended, but broadened its scope.

The appearance of the 'Fifth Generation' violently stirred the traditional Chinese film. Through their rebellion, they intend to improve and reconstruct. They have been striving to open a creative route for Chinese film, which is neither a duplication of the ancestors, nor an imitation of foreigners. But, they have taken only the first step. Despite critical success with their experimental alternatives to the norms, it is far too early to make a conclusive assessment of the 'Fifth Generation'. Their films do not fit the general notion of experimental or independent filmmaking in the West. All have made feature-length narratives within the state-owned studio system for commercial release. No 'Fifth Generation' director has claimed alliance with the experimental or avant-garde by intent. Experimentation, as the West conceives of it, is probably coming, but is still years away. Independent filmmaking may be another matter.

INDEPENDENT FILM

In early 1988, officials from China's film circles held a seminar to discuss strategies for the development of film. From that seminar came approval for the studios to control distribution, and an acceptance of independent producing. The groundwork for this decision had already been established, primarily through the work of Teng Wenji, a middle-aged director who has been working both out of the Xi'an Film Studio, headed by Wu Tianming, and on his own (Semsel 1987: 115–24).

As an independent filmmaker, I went into China expecting to find elements of filmmaking similar to my own. I knew, of course, that the nature of the Chinese government in all likelihood prevented this, and that the cultural tradition of China, from what I understood about it, might also preclude independent filmmaking, as most film artists think of it. Like Fred Marx and Amy Rothschild, among other American independents I met in Beijing, I eventually concluded that personal filmmaking in China was far in the future, if it was going to happen at all.

In that year (1984–85) spent working within China's film industry, I was able to discuss the medium with virtually all major figures in China's film circles. A majority of those with whom I spoke, such as Xie Fei, felt that Chinese film was reaching maturity in the 'new era', the period which began when the Cultural Revolution ended, and that the medium stood on the threshold of a significant breakthrough in aesthetic quality. 'Within the next few years,' Xie said in 1985, 'you will see many changes in the industry compared to now. You will start to see films made outside of the studios, with independent productions made by individual directors.' (Interview, Xie, 1985) Later, Teng Wenji, a director with whom I had several long conversations, said that he had worked out a system for independent filmmaking which would allow him far greater freedom than he had at the moment. In these conversations, he gave much of the credit for this to Wu Tianming, who headed the Xi'an Film Studio, and to which Teng Wenji was officially assigned at the time (Interview, Teng, 1987).

My job at China Film required that I view new films almost daily. Consequently, I was able to see the majority of film productions for the year, before their release. In addition, I was able to view a number of films still in production. After viewing, within a very short span of time, *Yellow Earth*, *One and Eight* and *On the Hunting Ground*—all seminal works by the 'Fifth Generation'—I began to think that an independent Chinese film was not too far off, for these films were clearly a move in directions I had not seen before. They were innovative and interesting, a compelling departure from the norms of Chinese production, as they have proved subsequently by their success in international film circles.

Yet, what my American colleagues in Beijing and I failed to acknowledge was that the films we celebrated as signs of a Chinese 'new wave', had been produced within the dominant studio system of China, that those who made them did not apparently represent an alternative, independent cinema but, on the contrary, spoke primarily of making a contribution to the growth and development of Chinese film. In fact, it was not from Chen Kaige, Zhang Yimou and Tian Zhuangzhuang, the major figures of the 'Fifth Generation', that I eventually heard talk of independence; it was primarily from middle-aged directors working within the mainstream of Chinese filmmaking. The movement towards independent filmmaking is not a matter of aesthetics, but a matter of market-place. None the less, it has been the work of the 'Fifth Generation' filmmakers which has been the centre of critical attention in China. And it is through examination of the writings of Chinese critics that we can clearly understand the current positions taken towards independent filmmaking, as we generally think of it in the West.

Shao Mujun, editor of *World Cinema*, a leader of the China Film Association and one of China's foremost film critics, responded to the growing tendency, especially among the younger directors, towards the 'art film' rather than the inherent nature of film:

> 'The making of art films is an effort to turn filmmaking into an individualized activity as is the case with the other arts. Art films do not go through commercial distribution and appear to be remote from commerciality. What a pity that art theatres also have ticket-selling windows and people cannot go inside without paying money.' (Shao 1984)

He went on to criticise the Western independent, experimental or 'art' film, which he found a poor model for those seeking innovation in Chinese film:

> 'individualized filmmaking is not only counter to filmmaking as a collective activity, but also to film as an entertainment. Because of this, the art film will always hold an inferior position in every

28

respect with regards to commercial film. Commercially speaking, the art film will never be a dominant force in western film; nonetheless, it often enhances the attraction of commercial film because it continually loses its artists to that realm. This process can be seen in every art movement in the West—the leading artists end up making commercial films.' (Shao 1984)

Later, he concluded:

'On the other hand, in the West, the profits of the producers come from the box office, thus whatever films the audience may enjoy can be made without any limitations. No doubt many vulgar and low films result from this; nevertheless, some new and original works may also come of it. In other words, while economic shackles certainly kill many good ideas, for those who are obsessed with personal expression, or mystical concepts, or who simply toy with forms, such constraints may be reasonable. Therefore I never give my whole-hearted support to new film movements in the West and criticize those who protest against economic limitations. It is not wrong to put limitations on some people. Even if the money is in the hands of capitalists, it comes from the sweat and blood of the people. No one should be permitted to waste it.' (Shao 1984)

A month later, in December, Xie Fei, an active director as well as educator, echoed the dangers Shao Mujun expressed about the failure among China's filmmakers to address the market-place:

'One of the important tasks we face today is the need to adjust our attitude toward the commerciality of film. Most of our filmmakers think art superior and the pursuit of art, most elegant, while they find the making of commercial and entertainment films vulgar and without value. The case is also true of our teaching. In our classes, the films we show to our students are art films. We try by all means to show our students films by different artists and schools of thought, but we seldom touch upon the topic of entertainment films such as musicals, westerns, melodramas and science fiction which are very popular. No wonder some elder artists fear that our students will all think alike, both artistically and philosophically, and lack the ability to meet the various requirements of the audience. Thus we say it is paramount that our filmmakers step out of their ivory towers, in their thinking and in their practice.

'Currently, our whole nation is in the midst of reform, seeking to bring about change according to objective principles, especially those of economics. To apply this to film means we must treat film both as an art and a commodity.' (Xie 1984)

Most recently, Luo Yijun, another current leader of the China Film Association and a major figure in contemporary Chinese film criticism, summarised the current directions of Chinese film:

'Two major trends made their appearance in the New Era. One is the awakening of a self-consciousness in all people, a restoration of the humanism, the esteem and values that had been alienated by blind worship and barbarity [during the Cultural Revolution]. The other is the awakening of a self-consciousness in film, film freed from the direct control and restraints of politics so as to recognise and establish itself on its own. . . . Currently Chinese society is changing from an agricultural economy to a commercial economy. This trend has pushed Chinese film toward commercialization; consequently, entertainment and genre films have become the 'hot topics' in the study of Chinese film theory.' (Luo 1989)

The most pressing need in contemporary Chinese filmmaking is not a matter of aesthetics alone, but of economics, the problem of a serious decline in box-office receipts. The gravity of this problem can be read in the number of reports published both in China and abroad. *Variety* (19 October 1988) reported that of 141 features planned for 1988, only 40 or so had been completed, half of which, the magazine quoted an unnamed official as stating, 'are purely light entertainment. They are thrillers and martial arts films, but most of them are shallow, poorly made and repetitious.' The report stated that after enthusiastic exploration of drama and art in film during the last decade, 'a financial crisis in China's film industry is pushing filmmakers to introduce tough new measures to improve profits.'

The current crisis in the Chinese film industry is strikingly reminiscent of the situation in Hollywood during the 1950s and 1960s, when the box office became increasingly threatened as television proliferated. During that period, as we all know well, the industry gravitated toward a system of independent filmmaking, borrowing this somewhat loose term from the 'underground' and 'experimental' film, which, at the same time, was increasing popularity in the subculture of the 'beat generation' and which would later flower during the 'hip movement'. Since Hollywood has been a major influence on Chinese film far back in its history, we should not be surprised that filmmakers in the People's Republic have been looking westward for potential solutions to their financial problems. One does not know what will come of the music video Chen Kaige is reportedly planning to make with the rock group, 'Duran Duran', but he is only one of a number of prominent Chinese filmmakers to work in the US or in Europe. Xie Jin, Zhang Nuanxin, Xie Fei and Zhang Yimou are among the growing list. That, in 1985, the China Film Corporation established an office in Los Angeles confirms the close relationship between the two industries.

If the Chinese industry has looked westward, film industries in the US and Europe have long sought ways to tap the Chinese film market. The recent international successes of films such as *Yellow Earth*, *Red Sorghum* and *Evening Bell* (1988) have led to increased interest in the People's Republic. Hardly a week passes when one cannot read new articles about co-productions between China and western nations, and other exchanges. This intercourse is not taking place on a one-way street.

Clearly with a dwindling box office, there is a great deal of pressure upon the Chinese film industry to find viable solutions as quickly as possible. Having already achieved well-publicised success with 'free markets' and other endeavours of the private sector under the responsibility system, the government quite logically has instituted a system for independent producing. Unlike the general concept in the West, which considers independent filmmaking a way to artistic freedom, independent filmmaking in China is considered a matter of economics. An individual may, via contracts, gain access to production moneys. A contract system through which an individual filmmaker could access private funding was already in place as early as 1985, though only recently has it received much attention. Certainly, by 1984, the structure through which the industry achieved renewal at the end of the Cultural Revolution was in need of revision, and there was considerable discussion at the time of the road to follow.

At the time I was working at China Film Corporation, studios made a bid to distribute their own products, rather than give them over to the state agency established for that purpose. In response, China Film argued that if the studios could control their own films, then China Film had the right to produce films without going through a studio, i.e. to contract directly with a filmmaker. The studios, for the moment, were at a disadvantage, for they lacked direct access to the exhibition houses. The China Film Corporation controlled the professional movie houses in the country, and owned most of the exhibition equipment as well. Consequently, when the government agreed to allow the studios the right to distribute their own films, the corporation maintained it had no obligation to exhibit them, and would show only those films given to it by the studios. The studios did not press the issue at the time, but they have since returned and apparently have strengthened their position. China Film, incidentally, established a production office that year, which it maintained even after the studios backed down.

Independent filmmaking in the People's Republic has been addressed most clearly in a series of articles published early in 1989 in the international edition of *People's Daily*. Summarising the movement, the author of the series, Li Li wrote:

'The so-called "independent filmmaker" is the result of economic motivation in the same way that entertainment films shifted their direction. . . . There were three noticeable "independent filmmakers" in 1988: Huangpu Keren of the Beijing Film Studio, Mi Jiashen of the Emei Film Studio, and Chen Yuewu of the Chongqing Hardware Store. Producer/director Huangpu Keren's funding comes from outside the film studio. Mi Jiashan, likewise producer/director, has been funded through a normal investment in film by the government. Chen Yuewu, not from a studio, is a financial sponsor and producer whose funding comes from outside of the industry.' (Li, 1989)

Li Li went on to say that though these three people do not make films with their own moneys nor control distribution of their work, and hence, other than Chen Yuewu, do not quite fit the normal concept, they none the less are best described as independent filmmakers. He elaborated:

'Independent film contract is unquestionably a feasible method of resolving problems of capital. The Inner Mongolia Film Studio has already made seven films using this approach. The advantage is that while a producer is responsible for not covering production costs, he/she may earn a profit as well, something Chinese filmmakers normally have little cause to consider. Obviously the motivation for the independent contract originates from economic considerations, with the success of a filmmaker determined by the number of prints sold.' (Li 1989)

According to the report, independent filmmaking has lowered production costs considerably. *Fengkuangenu* (*The Frenzied Singing Girl*), directed by Liu Gouquan and shot in 40 days, cost only about 600,000 Yuan (US $150,000), but sold more than 200 prints.

With the potential for profit a motivating force, the role of producer shifts to a central position under the contract system. Li Li reported that when Chen Yuewu, producer of *Kongbuyie* (*Night of Terror*), who got his capital from a hardware store, realised his director was costing him money, he fired him, the first such instance in PRC film history, and Huangpu Keren, to save money, made a film in 13 days, a Chinese record.

The primary advantage of the independent contract system is that it expands the financial resources of Chinese filmmaking. However, the long-range effects of this remain to be seen. It places a heavy responsibility for box-office success on both producers and directors, and may well elevate the control a producer has over a film. Yet, it should also provide opportunities for gifted filmmakers who could not, under the established system, hope to direct, and in the process, it should increase competition among all participants.

The system is not without problems. Independent filmmakers do not anticipate financial failure, yet they cannot promise financial success. According to Li Li, there is currently nothing in Chinese law to address this reality and 'even if there were, it would not solve anything'. Further, the system places economics above aesthetics and does not make allowances for films which appeal to a limited audience. The 'Fifth Generation' filmmakers, who have brought Chinese film to international attention, would probably not have been able to make films like *Yellow Earth*, *On the Hunting Ground*, *Black Cannon Incident* or *Red Sorghum* under the independent system. The exploration of film aesthetics might well decrease and the medium could stagnate.

In the final article of the series, Li Li wrote:

> 'Independent filmmaking may be an appropriate term for what has been taking place. Better might be "Collective Funding Contract". Independent filmmakers in China at present do not have legal rights, nor is the capital investment privately owned by the producer.'

Yet, those already involved are optimistic: Huangpu Keren said that if possible he would set up an independent film company (Li 1989).

Ni Zhen head of theoretical studies at the Beijing Film Institute, wrote in a letter to me in 1989:

> 'I fully understand your interests in the reform of Chinese filmmaking. But this reformation faces many problems. We are staggering rather than marching. I must tell you that what is said outside of China is not necessarily what is happening. For example, although we are allowed to make film independently, a truly private system of film production has yet to be founded. While it is true that one or two producers have attempted to work this way, in the end their attempts were aborted because of the incompleteness of the system and the rough quality of the films.' (Correspondence, Zhen, 1989)

In the 1989 meeting of the CCP Congress, the government announced that it must reconsider and, perhaps, substantially revise some of its policies in order to deal with the current economic crisis. How this will affect reforms within China's film world remains to be seen. Yet the films of the 'Fifth Generation' and the potentials for independent filmmaking suggest that Chinese film will continue to expand and solidify its position in the international film world.

NOTE

I am grateful to Hou Jianping and Xia Hong for their kind help with this material; to the former for her translations, and to the latter for his research and information about the Fifth Generation.

2

JAPAN

*Keiko McDonald**

INTRODUCTION

'The more adverse the conditions for filmmaking are, the more challenging the task of creation becomes. Using this as an incentive, I try to make a better film. And now I do have such an opportunity' (Interview, Ogawa, 1988). Ogawa's manner was enthusiastic as we spoke at the Hawaii International Film Festival in December 1988. He was talking after a screening there of his most recent documentary, *Ichimannen Kizami no Hidokei: Magino-mura Monogatari* (*Magino Village: A Tale*, 1987).

At 55, Ogawa is considered one of Japan's top documentary artists. Moreover, his films are independent productions, often backed in unconventional ways. One example is the *Sanrizuka* series (1968–72); another masterpiece of dedicated pursuit of his subject is *Nippon-koku Furuyashiki-mura* (*A Japanese Village: Furuyashiki-mura*, 1984). In this case, director and staff got close to their subject by taking up life in the village, tilling the soil and using the profits from the sale of their produce to pay film production costs. Eight years of communal farming yielded a 210-minute documentary (Desser 1988: 158–63, 167–70).

Ogawa has chosen to beat adversity at its own game. And while he can scarcely be considered a director in the mainstream of commercial filmmaking, his 'outsider' diagnosis of difficult working conditions reminds us that the Japanese film industry has a long tradition of boom and bust. Today's statistical graphs, for example, exhibit an alarming decline in the number of movie-goers. At the same time, television's challenge of 25 years ago has been matched now by amazing gains in the home video market. The net result is severe cut-backs in films produced each year, denying directors, old and new, access to the medium.

* This chapter © 1990 Keiko McDonald

Yet, paradoxically, the Japanese film industry on the whole is very much alive. Some major studios have shown again that Japanese ingenuity can work profit wonders by experimenting with net patterns of market control. And, as so often elsewhere in the business sector, collaboration is the key as studios have learned to link up with other enterprises reacting sensitively to audience demand.

As one commentator put it, 'Film production can be viewed as one facet of modern society's overriding industrial complex.' (Thomas 1982: 5) Even though Japanese filmmaking has long been an industry in Japan, the *business* end of the art has been more acutely felt in the past two years, both at home and abroad. In fact, one critic saw 1987 as marking a significant turning point in the motion picture industry:

> 'The cinema industry constantly changes. However, these changes are hardly noticeable to those who are steeped in this industry for a long time . . . The rapid growth of videocassettes, the emergence of many new filmmakers, deaths of veteran stars who made their epoch, the successive construction of new types of theater, and participation of other industries in production . . . half of the ten major events [of 1987] indicate the structural transformation of the film industry.' (*Kinema Jumpo* 1988: 217)

The word 'producer' has taken on new meanings recently as publishers and other media entrepreneurs work ever more closely with the major film studios. This spirit of collaboration also extends to a wide range of large corporations engaged in trade and advertising. The stronger purchasing power of the yen has also worked to establish this trend abroad.

The possibility of a Japanese take-over of Hollywood, one critic noted, 'surfaced with sensational effect in 1988 and is likely to be debated throughout 1989' (Segers 1989a: 78). Certainly alarms are sounding from that quarter as a group of investors from Japan has pooled US $50 million to form a new film production company: Apricot Entertainment, Inc. Businessman Toshihiro Nagayama is already the world's top investor in the Hollywood film industry.

As we shall see, a discussion of the Japanese industry, emphasising production, distribution and subject matter (genres/themes), must show how these interacting phrases today are controlled and, indeed, shaped by the 'business interest'.

HISTORICAL BACKGROUND

The history of the Japanese film industry from its beginning to 1981 is well documented in Joseph Anderson and Donald Richie's 1982 expanded edition of *The Japanese Film: Art and Industry*. Yet the radical transformation in production policy which took place in the early 1980s must be taken into account now if we are to complete the post-war historical record.

Compared with other parts of Asia, Japan's filmmaking tradition is a long one, dating back to 1899. A golden age of business prosperity and international recognition of artistic excellence came in the 1950s. In that decade, film studios took their place among industries working the Japanese economic miracle of recovery and innovation.

New construction soon restored the number of theatres to the pre-war figure of 2,641. By 1959, that number had nearly tripled, to 7,401. The return to national independence with the San Francisco Peace Treaty of 1951 had a direct effect on both commercial and artistic aspects of cinema. The *jidaigeki* (period film), especially its swashbuckling *chambara* variety, returned to captivate an audience hungry for a source of cultural continuity cut off by the Occupation ban on feudal tales.

At this point, the Japanese film industry was dominated by four major companies: Toho, Shin-Toho, Daiei and Shochiku. They were joined by the Tokyo Eiga Company, commonly called Toei (est. 1951). An old-timer, Nikkatsu, also resumed filmmaking in 1953. It was Toei that led the way with some notable innovations. First, this newcomer adapted the jidaigeki genre to the vast new market of children and teenagers. It also groomed stars to fit the parts. Then in 1954, Toei tried another market strategy, double-featuring.

These profitable inputs set off a chain reaction in the rival studios, resulting in a division of the market. Shochiku continued to emphasise melodrama, especially the *shomingeki* drama of lower middle-class life aimed at the female audience; Toho Company captured the white-collar market with a comedy series, and Daiei was notably successful with art films, producing international prize-winners such as Kurosawa's *Rashomon* (1950) and Mizoguchi's *Ugetsu* (1953). Nevertheless, Daiei captured a share of the cinema boom with a subgenre of *seiten* (sex series) intended for teenagers. Nikkatsu's prosperity depended on the so-called *taiyozoku* (sun-tribe) films appealing to the younger generation, quick-return productions dealing with disaffected youth in these difficult, hard-driven years. The Shin-Toho Company worked the opposite end of the spectrum with military subjects laden with ultra-conservative overtones.

Toei's energy and ingenuity imposed the unremitting pressure of the double-bill marketing strategy, not just on itself, but on all the other studios. By 1958, a subdivision, Daini-Toei (Second Toei; later, New Toei Company), was formed and put in charge of the mass production of films, especially chambara films. Its Kyoto Uzumasa Studio, specialising in the jidaigeki genre, ran full tilt far into the night to keep up with demand. Some scriptwriters on contract were forced to work on three and four projects at a time. Supporting casts, too, were shifted like items of inventory, serving now in this film, now in that on a given day.

By 1960, the annual production nation-wide peaked at 547 films. But soon, the decade began to generate dismal statistics. For example, by 1963, television had reached 65 per cent of the nation's viewing audience. That same year, the film audience shrank to half of its 1958 peak of 1,127 million. Challenged by this new 'motion picture' medium, and also plagued by poor management and strikes, Shin-Toho went bankrupt in 1961, and New Toei was also dissolved that year. Faced with some hard facts, the remaining four studios had to retrench and re-form their products and marketing strategy in line with audience tastes.

By the 1960s, the jidaigeki was coming to the end of its eight-year reign of prosperity. It began to seem outmoded in plot and theme, and its elaborate sets, costumes and artefacts/props put a strain on tightening studio budgets. Even filming on location became increasingly difficult, given the rapid transformation of the rural landscape. Under these circumstances, in 1968, Shochiku closed its Kyoto studio devoted to jidaigeki.

Significantly, Toei replaced this genre's lost lead with a more timely contemporary *yakuza* (gangster/gambler film) genre. Next to Toei, the most active company in the 1960s was Nikkatsu. Its stiff competition was provided by skilful management of established idols and by grooming new talent. This resulted in a solid claim to pre-eminence in the action drama film.

Despite a general cut-back in the number of films produced, Daiei kept profits high, thanks to revenues from action drama series with popular stars. Toho continued to populate the screen with comedy and science fiction, which proved to be marketable as special interest films throughout the decade.

Shochiku was not so fortunate. Audience interest in its strengths declined as domestic drama and melodrama fell further out of favour in the 1960s. But then, at the eleventh hour, Shochiku made a comedy come-back in 1969, with a series that continues to be a popular favourite today: Yoji Yamada's *Otako wa Tsurai yo* (*It's Tough to Be a Man*), commonly called *Tora-san*.

How then did filmmakers with an artistic bent manage to create under such adverse circumstances? As Joseph Anderson and Donald Richie (1982, p. 468) pointed out, many young directors worked as independents. With the help of production companies formed on their own, often with assistance from the Art Theatre Guild (ATG, est. 1961), many were able to make worthwhile films in the doggedly commercial decades of the 1960s and 1970s. The first ATG financial commitment went to Shohei Imamura's experimental docudrama *Ningen Johatsu* (*A Man Vanishes*, 1964). The usual arrangement was a 10 million yen ATG matching grant; an equal amount raised by the director's production company.

Susumu Hani, Hiroshi Teshigawara, Kihachi Okamoto and Kaneto Shindo worked this way. So did Masahiro Shinoda, Yoshishige Yoshida and Nagisa Oshima after their break with Shochiku. In fact, the first 10 million yen budget film produced with ATG assistance was Oshima's *Koshikei* (*Death by Hanging*, 1968). That film joined two other Art Theatre Guild collaborations in ranking among the top ten films of 1968, as selected by the prestigious film journal, *Kinema Jumpo*. *Death by Hanging* was voted Best Picture. Okamoto's *Nikudan* (*Human Bullets*) ranked second, and Hani's *Hatsukoi Jigokuhen* (*Inferno of Love*), sixth (Shinoda 1986: 65).

Yoji Yamada would seem to be a director who balanced studio demand and professional integrity successfully. His *Tora-san* series fitted in beautifully with the Shochiku emphasis on the shomingeki genre, celebrating family solidarity and values. Interest in making this kind of film, coupled with *Tora-san*'s enormous box-office success, has given Yamada an enviable amount of creative freedom. He writes his own scenarios and, by virtue of succeeding, has earned important privileges in the area of production decisions. He is, in fact, an executive of the Shochiku Company.

Other companies had much less to offer by way of compensating successful directors. As the state of decline continued into the 1970s, the film industry was forced to make more adjustments that considerably altered the character of some studios. A few failed to survive, even so. Daiei went bankrupt in 1971, and was revived four years later on a much smaller level. Nikkatsu scaled down its productions and eventually discontinued regular feature-length films. Its change of production policy began with the introduction of a new genre requiring a lower budget, fewer staff and reduced production time. This was the so-called *roman poruno* ('soft porn' in the American designation), which reached about 500 films during this decade.

Toei continued its production of yakuza films in new formulas emphasising violence. After 18 years away from jidaigeki, the company gambled on a revival of the chambara action film with *Yagyu Ichizoku no Inbo* (released in English as *Shogun's Samurai*, 1978). It was a smash, sweeping the market that year with a profit of US $8.5 million, the largest profit Toei had ever made. Significantly, this film, directed by Kinji Fukasaku, reflected a new economic policy in the Japanese film industry: *taisaku-shugi*, which may be translated and paraphrased as betting on blockbusters. The consequence, of course, was a radical reduction in the number of productions each year.

Yoji Yamada's *Tora-san* series, meanwhile, continued to be the breadwinner for Shochiku, adding another 20 instalments in the 1970s.

Toho began the decade in a slump. Its comedies became hackneyed, and its jidaigeki offerings failed to please, with one notable exception: *Kozure Okami* (*Shogun's Assassin*, 1972), a series with comic-book origins. Toho's precarious finances were also propped by a disaster film, an adaptation of Sakyo Komatsu's best-selling book, *Nihon Chinbotsu* (*Japan Sinks*, 1973), directed by Shiro Moritani.

By the mid-1970s, Toho reversed the downward trend by reviving its use of singing talent last used in the 1950s. Its young star this time was Momoe Yamaguchi, cast opposite another youthful talent, Tomokazu Miura. Together, they made 19 box-office hits. This popular 'golden combination' continued until 1980, when their marriage led to Yamaguchi's retirement from the screen.

Also crucial to recovery in the Japanese film industry in the mid-1970s was a newcomer, the Kadokawa Publishing Company, which was to have a profound influence on events in the 1980s. Kadokawa began by applying the policy of taisaku-shugi with a vengeance, pouring immense amounts of capital into single, large-scale popular features. Its first such success was a screen adaptation of the popular detective novel by Seishi Yokomizo, *Inugami-ke no Ichizoku* (*The Inugami Family*, 1976), directed by Kon Ichikawa. Kadokawa's publishing connections were the silver lining in its enterprises. Massive advertising campaigns were used to promote best sellers and film versions in tandem. These efforts later extended to sound-track recordings of major singing talents. This multiple-entry market-targeting paid off in 1978, when *Yasei no Shomei* (*Proof of Savagery*) surpassed Toei's biggest box-office hit of the season, *Shogun's Samurai*.

As the number of serious films continued to decline in the early 1980s, the film industry tended to reconsider its future in terms of popular cinema. Again, Kadokawa provided the leading case in point. Having identified teenagers as the majority of the audience, it took the lead in production and marketing by grooming young talent. Its cultivation of the teen idol market owed something to Toei's power as distributor to theatres under contract. Meanwhile, Nikkatsu continued to concentrate on soft porn for the male audience. By 1985, Shochiku's *Tora-san* had reached its sixteenth year with more than twice that number of instalments. Even more remarkable was the fact that the studio's longest-lived product was still its largest source of revenue. Toho set itself a new direction in science fiction with the large scale *Sayonara Jupita* (*Goodbye, Jupiter*, 1984). The studio also staged a *Godzilla* revival for the 1985 New Year's holiday season—31 years after the original appeared.

CONTEMPORARY SCENE

Production

'How does one account for the low quality of the films produced these days? How many times do I have to sigh over boring films? Who can one blame but the top brass in the industry? Their hidebound attitudes are effectively squeezing out many talented filmmakers.' (Tayama 1988: 110)

Thus, the noted film critic Rikiya Tayama summarised the present materialistic orientation of the Japanese film industry. Given this kind of fanatical profit motivation, is it any wonder that so few films of genuine artistic merit (often enough compromised by producers) make it to the screen each year?

Though the number of feature films produced in Japan dwindled in the early 1980s, the figure has stabilised in the late 1980s. In 1986, 297 were made, 298 in 1987 and 296 anticipated for 1988.

The noteworthy aspect of these statistics is that more than 60 per cent of annual productions are made by independent production companies. The other approximately 40 per cent are shared by the four major studios of Shochiku, Nikkatsu, Toho and Toei.

'Independent producer' used to be synonymous with small capital; now it means something more like 'huge enterprise'. The Kadokawa Publishing Company has provided a prime example. Others are large corporations such as Mitsui Trading Company and Tokyu Group (associated with department stores, hotels and private railways). Even television stations and advertising agencies are becoming major players.

Of course, newcomers frequently collaborate with existing film studios. A notable exception was Fuji Television's go-it-alone production of *Koneko Monogatari* (*The Story of Chatran*, 1986) by the animal storywriter, Masanori Hata. The timing owed something to the biggest hit of the previous season, Koretsugu Kurahara's *Nankyoku Monogatari* (*Antarctica*, 1983) which grossed close to 70 billion yen (US $50 million at $1 = 125 yen). Fuji Television's kitten protagonist worked a similar miracle in several senses, bringing its producer a profit of 53 billion yen (US $35 million), the second record figure in the Japanese film industry until then.

Other big investors supported this trend. The Tokyu Group and Mitsui Trading company joined Shochiku to produce another animal genre film, *Hachiko Monogatari* (*The Story of the Loyal Dog Hachiko*, 1987). It yielded 19.5 billion yen (US $15 million). The Mitsubishi Trading Company and Toho also shared a hefty

11 billion yen (US $9 million) from their joint venture, *Maririn ni Aitai* (*I Want to See Marilyn*, 1988), a male dog's romance adventure.

The Seibu Saison Group is a diversified investment group affiliated with the Seibu Seiyu conglomerate of department stores and railways. Formed in 1983, it entered the film industry by building Cine Vivant, a small theatre near Roppoingi, Tokyo. Cine Saison followed in 1984, adding foreign film distribution to the company's interests. Actual movie production came in 1985 with the formation of several independent production companies. These have been particularly sensitive to the market created by a further lowering of age in target audiences. Since 'young adults' have deserted the movie theatres, Seibu Saison Group interests have focused on high school and middle school students, with block-buster productions scheduled for release in the two most profitable seasons of summer and New Year's holidays. The success of these strategies speaks for itself. One such project, the science fiction *Story of the Imperial Capital* (*The Teito Monogatari*, 1988), by Akio Jissoji, captured the third-largest box-office of that year with a profit of 10.5 billion yen (US $8.4 million).

On the international scene, Japanese interest in Hollywood is apt to seem most ambitious. One large entry was made recently by an investment group consisting of C. Itoh & Co., a trading company, Suntory Ltd, known for its whisky, and Tokyo Broad-casting System. Their combined US $15 million investment in MGM/UA resulted in *Bright Lights*, *Big City*, *Fatal Beauty* and *Betrayed*, none of them being real 'barnburners' (Segers 1989a: 78).

Statistics more on a Hollywood scale come from Japanese investment in China, where a picture shot on location cost the Marubeni Trading Corporation 45 billion yen (US $36 million). This was *Tonko* (*Dun-Huang*, 1988), directed by Junya Sato.

The Marubeni investment might be put into perspective by considering that the typical programme picture from a major studio is budgeted at 1.5 billion yen (US $1.2 million). A Nikkatsu soft porn film costs on average only 20 million yen (US $160,000). Even a programme picture on a grand scale costs in the neighbourhood of 10 billion yen (US $8 million). One of the lowest budget films of recent years received international recognition. This was Kaizo Hayashi's black and white *Yume Miru Yo ni Nemuritai* (*To Sleep So As To Dream*, 1986), which the 27-year-old director made for just 5 million yen (US $40,000).

The critic who wishes to focus on statistics is hampered by the fact that production budgets are never made public except for promotional purposes. Even so, rumour and surmise indicate that in Japan, as elsewhere, stars are given more than just top billing. Big stars are said to receive somewhere between 15 and 20 million yen per film (US $120,000 to $160,000). As might be expected, much larger sums are earned from appearances in TV commercials, whose contract value far exceeds film earnings.

As early as 1985, Toho gambled 26 billion yen (US $10.4 million at $1 = 250 yen) on Kurosawa's *Ran*, a record amount that could never break even domestically. The difference had to be made up elsewhere, and was. The Marubeni Trading Corporation's shocking cost of 45 billion yen actually paid off in a gross take of 100 billion yen (US $80 million) by the end of 1988. This success against the odds is largely attributed to Yasuyoshi Tokuma from Daiei. Tokuma was instrumental in forming a production committee, setting budget and managing logistics for the large-scale shoot on location. Before the film's release, he also launched a massive campaign for advance sale tickets.

No wonder optimism seems to have soared among major investors. For the first time in the Japanese cinema industry, a consortium of investors was formed in the late 1980s, calling itself 'Feature Film'. Collaboration with studios is no doubt mutually beneficial, since it reduces each party's finanical risk. Not least among studio attractions for such investors is the excellent distribution network already in place. Since there are no anti-cartel laws in Japan, the major film companies control most of the theatres where they can show their own pictures exclusively.

Studios are increasingly aware of themselves as partners in business. Shochiku is a notable example of this, being a studio whose programme offerings, except for the *Tora-san* series, have in general fallen out of favour in the 1980s. A summer venture *Dauntaun Hirozu* (*Downtown Heroes*, 1988) failed completely in a market sector locked up by Toho and Toei. Shochiku's hopes now revolve around collaboration with major corporations, which should help it enrich the 1989 production schedules, in the process breaking with shomingeki-style films.

Studios themselves have ventured forth in a new kind of diversification, sinking capital into related markets. As early as 1975, Toei did exceedingly well in the sightseeing trade by opening its Uzumasa Studio in Kyoto to tourists. A natural extension of that has developed in the past several years with the company actively engaged in real estate and tourism, using workers no longer needed in studio locations shifted elsewhere. Shochiku is opening its own theatres to other kinds of entertainment, such as live stage revues. It has also built a shopping mall on the site of its Ofuna Studio.

Nikkatsu, in the meantime, seems left out of the upward trend in the industry. The soft porn market has been declining on its own, so in May 1988, Nikkatsu abandoned it in favour of a return to regular feature-length films on a variety of subjects. A series of ten such films was produced under the name Nikkatsu Ropponica, but with little success financially. The company is overhauling its entire production policy, which doubtless will entail a further reduction in project numbers.

Directing, Acting and Scriptwriting

The most radical change in contemporary cinema has to do with the age of directors; a number have made their mark while still in their twenties and thirties. No doubt the change in film-going audiences has something to do with it. Theoretically, the younger directors know more about what Japanese teenagers will respond to. This shows, too, in the literary sources favoured by these directors—light novels and even cartoons, very often scripted with the help of the director himself.

Yoshimitsu Morita is a good example. At 18, he made an 8mm film. By the age of 30, he was making his first feature-length work, his twenty-second film. Not wanting to bother with a producer, he borrowed 40 million yen (US $320,000) from parents and friends willing to gamble on his talent. He also mounted his own promotional campaign and managed to get his picture distributed by Herald Enterprise, Inc., a major force in the industry.

The film in question is *No Yo na Mono* (*Something like Yoshiwara*, 1980). This first commercial work says much about Morita's businesslike approach to filmmaking. Later, he had this to say about his progress:

'Aiming for a box-office hit, I came up with the title *No Yo na Mono*, which echoes the language popular at the time. I dressed youths in Ivy League clothes, even though they were pursuing the traditional profession of *rakugo* reciter. All this had audience appeal' (Nukumizu 1981: 109).

Elsewhere, Morita added:

'I have learned to distinguish between "good", "commercially successful", and "commercially unsuccessful" films. In order to make a successful one, a director needs to consider what makes the audience happy. He does not succeed if he continues cranking out the kind of film he wants to make. A director also has to think ahead about audience taste and ways of thinking as they will be in two or three months.' (Kakeo 1985: 50)

Morita has remained faithful to this strategy. Since his 1980 debut, he has made ten films, including *Kazoku Gemu* (*The Family Game*, 1983). His 1985 adaptation of the Meiji novelist Soseki's *Sorekara* (*And Then*) won him both the Best Picture and Best Director awards from *Kinema Jumpo*. This work is a rare combination of artistic accomplishment and commercial savvy.

Interestingly enough, Morita has also been instrumental in helping young directors make a start. His 1988 film *Bakayaro:*

Watakushi Okotte Imasu (You're Stupid: I'm Angry), scripted by Morita himself, consists of four parts, each directed by a new comer under his supervision.

Besides Morita, the active young generation includes Shunichi Nagasaki, Seiji Izumi, Shunsuke Kaneko, Naota Yamakawa and Hiroshi Sugawara. Nagasaki's 1988 film, *Rokku yo, Shizuka ni Nagareyo (Rock, Flow Smoothly)*, artistically portrays friendship among youths tested by a friend's death. It ranked fourth in the *Kinema Jumpo* poll. Sugawara, a US film graduate, also presents an interesting case. His 1988 work, *Bokura no Shichinichi-kan Senso (Our Seven-Day War)*, offers a sort of escape for high school students suffering from 'examination hell', as the eleven heroes and heroines challenge Spartan education in a childish manner.

In contrast to such newcomers, veteran directors, most close to 60 years old, are still active, sometimes following their own styles and themes, but often forced into compromise. Yoji Yamada is still engaged in the *Tora-san* series, which recently celebrated its fortieth instalment, setting a world record recognised by The Guiness Book of Records. Masahiro Shinoda is turning more towards aestheticism, as found in his 1985 film, *Yari no Gonza (Gonza the Spearman)*, another adaptation of Chikamatsu's classical play. His thematic constant being the individual torn between societal duties and personal feelings, he is currently working on *Maihime (The Dancing Girl)*, based on the Meiji novel by Ogai Mori.

Kon Ichikawa, 78 years old in 1989, has survived by virtue of versatile craftsmanship, his works running the gamut from adaptations of serious novels to animation. His work, *Taketori Monogatari (Princess From the Moon, 1987)*, dealt with the world of fantasy. This film, starring the veteran Toshiro Mifune, undoubtedly counted on audience familiarity with the tenth-century classical fairy tale.

Kurosawa and Oshima are unique in that they rely heavily on their popularity overseas. Kurosawa, over 80 years old, is expected to launch a new film in collaboration with Steven Spielberg. This will be *Konna Yuma Mita (I Dreamed a Dream Like This)*. Oshima's recent works included the 1987, *Max, Mon Amour* produced by Serge Silberman and shot in France and, in 1989, he was busy with *Sesshu to Barentino (Sesshu Hayakawa and Rudolph Valentino)*, produced by Jeremy Thomas.

Juzo Itami, in his early fifties, is another notable figure on the contemporary scene. The multi-talented Itami made a debut in *Ososhiki (Funeral, 1984)*, which swept the major film awards domestically. The film, whose production cost was less than 1.2 billion yen (US $960,000), has grossed ten times that amount. Itami has proved that in order to attract the audience, the film must be interesting and amusing (Matsushima, 1986: 163). After a series of box-office hits, he turned producer in the late 1980s. *Suito Homu (Sweet Home)*, released in January 1989, featured the young director

Kiyoshi Kurosawa (unrelated to Akira Kurosawa) who also wrote the script.

Serious filmmaking having lost so much ground to commercial opportunism, it is refreshing to note that Mitsuo Yanagimachi, in his mid-forties, is one independent director who tries to defend the stronghold of 'serious, responsible, and adult pictures' (Richie 1983: 7). His second film *Saraba Itoshiki Daichi* (*A Farewell to the Land*, 1982) and third, *Himatsuri* (1985), are about social changes, such as the complete bankruptcy of the Japanese family. Though dedicated, Yanagimachi also faces the difficulty of maintaining artistic integrity at home. His 1989 project was being undertaken in Hong Kong, its main theme a triangular relationship between a Chinese woman, her Chinese boyfriend and her Japanese journalist lover.

The Japanese film industry does not have a casting system, mainly because actors are not unionised. Thus, the way casting is done is not that consistent. However, in most cases, the producer decides on the cast for main roles, while the director chooses supporting actors and actresses. Independent filmmakers do depart from this practice in some cases. The scriptwriter may ask for changes in main roles even after casting is done, and the director may have the final say about the cast.

Since the star system no longer exists in the Japanese film industry, all major stars are 'free agents'. Notable exceptions are some singer talents who belong to 'productions'. Many 'less famous' actors and actresses opt for joining productions willing to act as their agents. A number of theatrical groups train casts, among them being Haiyu-za, Bungei-za, and groups such as Himawari, specifically devoted to talented children. A unique phenomenon is Mumei-juku (literally translated, Institute for Unknown Talent), established by the veteran actor Tatsuya Nakadai, instrumental in launching the careers of protégés, one of the best known being Taisuke Ryu who appeared in Kurosawa's *Ran*.

Scriptwriters are hired in various ways. Usually, the director's choice counts most. It does not happen that the producer holds out for a scriptwriter of his own choice against the director's decision. Many directors, both old and new, such as Kurosawa, Kinoshita, Morita and Itami, have scripted their own films.

Distribution and Exhibition

The distribution profit for 1988 in the Japanese cinema industry was 325.32 billion yen (US $260.26 million). Though the figure shows a 6.2 per cent increase compared with 1982, it is a dismal statistic when compared with videocassette sales of more than 3 trillion yen (US $2.4 billion).

Numbers of movie theatres have shrunk accordingly. Some 40 to 50 a'year have closed, leaving the cinema industry with something like 2,000. This represents a two-thirds reduction since the peak year of 1958, when the average Japanese saw at least one movie a month. Now, it is fewer—less than one a year. Small cities are losing ground fastest, and few with a population of under 300,000 now have a movie theatre. This means that 70 to 80 per cent of revenue for a film must come from distribution in big cities.

There was a small construction boom in metropolitan areas in the late 1980s. The year 1987 saw the appearance of a five-storey cinema complex in Kawasaki. The same year, Toho, Shochiku and Toei built their own theatres in first-rate downtown areas of Tokyo. Sasaki Entertainment Enterprise opened a series of theatres while Herald, a major independent distributor, joined Fuji Television and the Hata Entertainment Enterprise to open a theatre in the Ginza district, where the Seibu Group also invested in a new theatre. This boom has helped to create a district in the Yurakucho Station section, where more than 20 theatres crowd among department stores, shopping arcades and restaurants. Significantly enough, this construction signals a new co-operation between department stores and theatres courting the purchasing power of the cinema audience.

With the downward trend in attendance, why do more than 47 companies participate in the distribution of so many films (485 foreign and 265 domestic for 1988)? The answer has to do with a simple, long-range business tactic, i.e. to promote videocassette sales in the future.

The absence of anti-cartel laws in the cinema industry makes it easier for major film companies to control distribution. Toei, Nikkatsu, Toho and Shochiku all have theatres under their direct control, in addition to others under special contract. They are mostly devoted to the distribution of films their own companies have produced. Among the four, Toho boasts the largest number of outlets with 531.

Subsidiaries do most of the foreign film distribution. Toho-Towa, Shochiku-Fuji, Toei Yoga (Toei Foreign Film) and Toei Classics are typical examples. Other top-ranking distributors are Japan Herald Film, Inc., Nyuu Serekuto (New Select) and Furansu Eigasha (French Film Company). US film representatives, such as Fox, UIP, WB and COL/TRI, are entering these competitive markets now. UIP is the largest foreign distributor, controlling 16 per cent of the market.

The ratio of distribution for foreign films is higher than that of Japanese films. For example, in 1988, 485 films (351 the previous year) were released while Japanese films reached only 268 (a decrease of 18). The quota system, which still exists in other Asian countries, was abolished as early as the mid-1960s. Thus, this open policy offers the Japanese audience easier access to foreign films. As might be expected, Japan is the largest foreign market for US features, which fare well in the box office, as evidenced by *Top Gun* which grossed US $24 million in 1987. Though 1988 saw *The Last Emperor*, distributed by Shochiku-Fuji, lead the top 30 box-office hits, the next three places were held by American films: *Rambo 3*, distributed by Toho-Towa, and *Fatal Attraction* and *Willow*, both by UIP. Imports from Asia are not widely circulating in Japan. Most often, they are shown for international film festivals. However, notable exceptions are Jackie Chan's films, which always rank in the top 20. *Cannonball 2* and *Project A* ran second and third in 1984, next to *Indiana Jones*.

Despite the higher ratio of distribution enjoyed by foreign films, the revenues they bring in do not compare very favourably with those from Japanese sources. The year 1988 saw 329.9 billion yen (US $263.92 million) from foreign imports in contrast to 325.32 billion yen (US $260.26 million) drawn from domestic films.

The distributors' sensitivity to the market is reflected in their long-run use of the newly-built theatres in the metropolis. The prime example is the French Film Company's relocation to the Hibiya Chante Cine 2 in October 1987. The average film has a two-week run in Japan. But in 1988, the French Film Company chose only five films (four American and one German) for release at the theatre owned by Toho. This was a very successful ploy. The German import *Der Himmel Uber Berlin* (*Sky Over Berlin*) had a full house almost every single day during its 30-week run, sweeping in more than 166,000 patrons. Its success reveals something about consumer taste—the luxurious atmosphere of the theatre suited the content of the film. The Japanese audience, enjoying the purchasing power of the rising yen, is no longer satisfied with film viewing *per se*. It wants to enjoy the decor and all the conveniences that a first-rate theatre can offer.

One of the hottest items in recent years is Toho's achievement for 1988. Thanks to the block-booking of a number of big projects which turned out to be box-office hits, such as *Dun-Huang*, *Iko ka Modoro ka* (*Shall I Go or Return?*) and *Marusa no Onna Ni* (*The Return of the Taxing Woman*), the company grossed more than 100 billion yen (US $80 million).

Admission to a movie theatre is fairly expensive in Japan, starting at 900 yen (US $7.20). In big theatres, a regular seat costs 1,500 yen (US $12), and a reserved one 2,000 yen (US $16). The reason for the maintenance of the average 1,500 yen charge is that there is no admission tax under this amount. A patron also has the advantage of advance purchase at a 10–15 per cent discount. Admission prices continued to rise in the late 1980s. Ten film theatres in Tokyo and Osaka (including three owned by Toho and two by Toei) decided to raise prices from 1,500 to 1,700 yen (US $13.60), beginning in January 1989.

In contrast, other theatres try to draw a larger audience by making admissions more attractive. One example is the creation of a special day, such as the discount day for women. In smaller cities, even local governments participate in boosting attendance; they subsidise theatres with blocks of tickets given to senior citizens on request.

Very few people know that half of the feature-length films made in Japan each year are for overseas distribution. This export trade dates back to the early 1950s. It has shown a steady increase in revenue, especially in the last several years of the 1980s. In 1981, exports reached US $6.8 million; by the late 1980s, it jumped to more than US $9 million.

Among many artistic films of international renown, Kaneto Shindo's low-budget, black and white *Hadaka no Shima* (*The Naked Island*) has fared best. Distributed in 65 countries, this winner of the 1954 Moscow Festival grand prize has grossed about 1 billion yen (US $800,000). Kurosawa's *Kegemusha* (1980) and *Ran* (1985), along with Oshima's *Ai no Korida* (*The Realm of the Senses*, 1975), were successful in the overseas market, but their revenues outside Japan are not fed back into the Japanese film industry.

Detailed data regarding the distribution of Japanese films for export to Asian countries are not available because companies are reluctant to release the information. However, the target market includes Hong Kong, Indonesia and Thailand. Neither North nor South Korea has lifted a ban on the import of Japanese films, which Taiwan did in 1984. Taiwan's move helped expand the Asian market.

Regulation

The Eirin (Motion Picture Code of Ethics Regulation and Control Committee) is the governing body of film censorship in Japan. Originally formed as 'a self-regulatory group in the industry in 1949 under the direction of SCAP [Supreme Commander Allied Powers]', the committee later took over the SCAP's official censorship (Anderson and Richie 1982: 424). Various structural changes ensued. In 1956, for example, the president of five major motion picture companies recommended that Eirin become an autonomous body 'for the fair and impartial administration of motion picture ethics'. As stated in *The Motion Picture Code of Ethics* (1960, p. 1):

'The social responsibility of motion pictures as an artistic entertainment media bearing an important influence on the spiritual and moral life of the nation is duly recognized. It is because of this civic responsibility that the Motion Picture Code of Ethics has been instituted with a view to preventing presentation of such motion pictures that might lower the moral standards of the audience.'

This foreword to *The Motion Picture Code of Ethics*, enacted by the Eirin Sustaining Committee on 10 August 1959, summarises well what the committee considers to be its mission. According to this law, no film can be released before it passes the Eirin Committee review. This process begins with the commissioner's appointment of a reviewer who passes judgement on the film, using *The Motion Picture Code of Ethics* guidelines. If the reviewer recommends changes or deletions, the producer is informed immediately, and an attempt is made to negotiate a settlement. If agreement cannot be reached, the Reviewers' Committee takes over the matter. If the producer still disagrees, the reviewer-in-charge follows the commissioner's instructions.

When the review procedure is completed, the producer affixes the Code Seal to the film. Feature films were originally divided by the committee into three kinds: 'general', which are recommended for juveniles; 'adult'; and 'reissue' for an old film. Into these categories the Eirin in 1976 introduced 'R', which is placed between 'general' and 'adult' and stands for restricted audience 'over the age of 15'.

'The moral standards' mentioned in the foreword need to be explained in the light of articles entitled 'Educations', and 'Sex and Customs'. The former is geared to the respect for and maintenance of democratic educational systems. Therefore, educators should not be ridiculed or insulted in a film. Depiction of scenes considered to have an undesirable influence upon the immature—acts of brutality, for example—must be 'cautiously handled'. More influential are regulations regarding sex and customs which some filmmakers consider very restrictive. The filmmaker, for example, is required to treat the institutions of marriage and home cautiously, so as not to defy their 'sanctity'. He also is required not to present 'promiscuous sex relations and abnormal sexual activities'. More rigorous is the treatment of 'sexual activities' and nudity. Bedroom scenes and 'outrageous activities' must be handled with special care 'so as not to rouse indecent passion in the audience'. 'Indecent language, activities, costume and songs of excessively sexual nature' have to be avoided.

Matters or depictions which are generally considered inappropriate, such as frontal nudity and mixed bathing, must be excluded. An audience frustrated by a number of blurred bedroom scenes in imported foreign films readily understands the restrictions of the Eirin laws. The extreme example was *In The Realm of the Senses*; when released in Japan, it consisted of a succession of blurred shots. Japanese film-goers anxious to see the uncut version had to go to France on special tours designed for this purpose.

As might be expected, Eirin is geared to protect both the film industry and audience. In their execution of duties, Eirin members try to minimise government interference and, often, Eirin and the filmmakers join forces against the authorities. A few incidents involving confiscation and trials shed light on the occasionally troubled though, on the whole, relatively congenial, relationship between Eirin and the film industry.

Any fan of Japanese cinema will recall the 'pink' film, Tetsuya Takechi's *Kuroi Yuki* (*Black Snow*, 1965), which concerns his anti-Americanism, given sexual expression. The film resulted in charges being brought against him for violation of public decency. The matter, taken out of the hands of Eirin and the film industry, involved the police, marking the first trial pertaining to film. Takechi had this to say in court:

> 'The censors are getting tough about *Black Snow*. I admit there are many nude scenes in the film, but they are psychological nude scenes symbolising the defencelessness of the Japanese people in the face of the American invasion. Prompted by the CIA and the US Army, they say my film is immoral. This is of course an old story that has been going on for centuries . . . In fact, it [is] a matter of rank political suppression.' (Quoted in Desser 1988: 99)

Aided by 'intellectuals and filmmakers', such as Nagisa Oshima and Yukio Mishima, Takechi won his first and second cases.

Nikkatsu soft porn had its confrontation with police a year after the studio's conversion to this genre. In January 1972, three Nikkatsu works — *Koi no Kariudo* (*Hunter of Love*), *Mesuneko no Nioi* (*Feline's Smell*) and *Jogakusei Geisha* (*Student Geisha*) — were confiscated by the police on charges of indecency. By September, both the director and the Eirin reviewers were on trial. Not until eight years later (July 1980), were all defendants judged innocent, the prosecutor having decided not to appeal.

There was a six-year litigation involving the book version of *In The Realm of the Senses*. As early as July 1976, the Tokyo Metropolitan Police brought charges against Oshima and Hajime Takemura, president of the publishing firm, for selling an 'indecent' publication, the photobook version of the film. In 1979, the Tokyo local court declared the defendants innocent, but the decision was challenged by the prosecutor, and the case went all the way to the Supreme Court. Only in August 1982, was the original decision upheld.

After the completion of the film version of *In The Realm of the Senses*, Oshima could not risk having the print made in Japan, which would have violated the indecency law. He shipped the negative to France for processing and release, accounting for the blurred scenes in the re-imported version shown in Japan.

More recently, the distributor's self-imposed censorship of Bertolucci's *The Last Emperor*, created a sensation. Shochiku-Fuji edited out 'newsreel footage of the Nanking Massacre in China that showed Japanese military atrocities' (Segers 1989b: 22). The snipping created complaints of censorship from the director and many film critics. Shochiku-Fuji finally conceded, releasing a slightly edited version.

During the heady days of the cinema industry in the 1950s and 1960s, there were a number of regulations, such as *The Five Major Studios' Treaty* (est. 1953), which prevented a studio from poaching talent from its rivals. A number of big stars were victimised by this law and denied appearance on the screen for a long time. However, such a law no longer exists, since the star system itself is a thing of the past.

Impact of Videocassettes

Kinema Jumpo put the impact of videocassettes on film distribution at the top of its list of ten biggest news items in 1987. This is not surprising. The new medium produced 2 trillion yen (US $1.6 billion) in sales, in contrast with 1.611 trillion yen (US $1.28 billion) from distribution of films.

The year 1988 marked an even cleaner sweep of the market. It is estimated that sales of videocassettes broke 3 trillion yen (US $2.4 billion) while films drew only 1.62 trillion yen (US $1.295 billion). At the beginning of 1988, there were 5,000 shops belonging to the Japan Video Association Rental System. A year later, the number soared to above 10,000. The International Film Image Software Council estimated US $3.19 billion revenue from rental videos in Japan for 1988.

Fierce competition among distributors is *de rigueur* in the Japanese cinema/video industry. All stick to the basic business principle that one must sell hard through advertising on a massive scale. As mentioned earlier, in 1988 major distributors showed more feature films than in the previous year. Fully aware that some films would not fare well, they took some long-term risks in order to increase the sale of videocassettes. They also came up with special series, such as the *Best Action* series launched by Herald and the *Platform* series by Shochiku-Fuji. Their rivals, Joy Pack Film, Inc. and Toei Classic Film, challenged them with the *Best Selection Film* and the *Cinema Land* series, respectively.

These distributors' exhibition, totalling more than 100 films, showed a vast array of genres, ranging from action to horror. Significantly, these films were shown at special theatres blocked for sales campaigns. In fact, the number of mini video theatres under construction said something about the potential of market expansion.

Japanese filmmakers' threat from foreign concerns was reflected in a business transaction involving a major US video company, CBS/FOX. At the beginning of 1988, CBS/FOX refused to renew

Shochiku's sales contract. Instead, it let its own Japanese corporation, CBS/Fox Video Far East, take charge of production/advertisement and transfer the sales right to Nippon AVC. The CBS/FOX move suddenly collapsed a market share that Shochiku had taken several years to establish. Rescue came from an import, *The Last Emperor*, which grossed more than 24.5 billion yen (US $19.6 million) in Japan. Thus, the transfer of sales rights has become a threat to native companies who must face their fiercely competitive foreign rivals in the Japanese market.

In Japan, as in many Asian countries, the spread of pirate videocassettes has become a major worry. As a counter measure, in March 1988, the Japan Video Association Rental System formed a special committee represented by six major distributors—Toho, Toei, Shochiku, Nippon AVC, Pony Canyon and Warner. The committee's proposal for 'dealing with the confusion in the video-soft market', identified three major targets. First, in order to prevent illegal production and distribution, the distributor has to monitor the flow of merchandise by adjusting or changing contract stipulations. Second, while monitoring, the distributor also encourages the rental shop to become a member of the Japan Video Association Rental System (Morii 1989: 277). The third item on the proposal has to do with the control of the rental fee, establishing 5 per cent of the wholesale purchase price of a video as a minimum charge. Needless to say, this was triggered by a drastic fall of the rental fee from 505 yen (US $4.04) in 1987 to 479 yen (US $3.83) in early 1988.

The proposal thus implemented in June 1988 brought a favourable gain for the Japanese video industry, resulting in the decrease of illegal rental shops. According to a survey by the Japanese branch of the American Film Association, rental shops stocked with pirate videos had fallen from 51 to 38 per cent in 1988. Pirated videos confiscated by the police dropped to a little over 30,000, from 114,367 the previous year. As the 'Crime of Possessing Pirate Editions' became a fact in December 1988, the figure was expected to drop more.

Two companies took advantage of the price adjustment proposed by the special committee. In June 1988, Toei negotiated new contracts with rental stores nation-wide, adding a stipulated minimum 500 yen (US $4) for Toei films only. A month later, Toho followed suit. However, in September of the same year, their practices met a fierce challenge from the Government, when its Fair Trade Committee warned that the minimum rental fee might be in violation of the anti-monopoly law. The warning at first appeared to generate controversy over the discrepancy between copyright law and anti-monopoly law. None the less, rather than challenge the Government's warning, the two companies discontinued their price control.

This outcome led to a price war among rental shops with smaller ones quickly losing out. Now, some major rental stores charge only 300 yen (US $2.4) per day. In more competitive areas, the price is 200 yen (US $1.60) and quite often only 100 yen (US 80 cents).

The potential of video rental has attracted other industries. Since September 1988, the CCC (Cultural Convenience Club), a franchise of more than 300 rental stores nation-wide, has been consolidating its position in conjunction with the Nissan Automobile Company. Elsewhere, noted trading companies, such as Marubeni and C. Itoh & Co., have been pouring their efforts into automatic lending machines, while another company is developing a home delivery system and mobile video rental shops known as 'video liners'.

Another interesting development comes in soft video sales. In general, soft videos are fairly expensive in Japan, the average price being about 15,000 yen (US $125). However, increasing Japanese interest is boosting sales and lowering prices. One noteworthy example at the end of 1988 was the *Video Library* series sold through CIC/Victor. A feature film such as *Roman Holiday* was priced at only 3,500 yen (US $28).

In order to cope with video copyrights, makers have come up with alternatives such as television feature films on video, or the production of an animation film specifically designed for video use. The forerunner of the latter was *Kuraimu Hantaa* (*Crime Hunter*), which Toei released in March 1989.

The difficulty the movie-theatre management must face as a result of the encroachment of videos was summarised by one critic:

'The video industry benefits from the advertisement of a distributor at the time of the film's release, [and] the sensation and the popularity that the released film creates. But the expenses for advertisement also mean a big financial burden for the distributor, dipping into revenues from the film's release. This one-sided gain must be adjusted somewhere, and this is the biggest problem that lies ahead in the cinema industry.' (Morii 1989: 281)

As long as distributors enjoy a lead in profits through supply to rental stores and soft video makers, they can afford to risk the expense of advertising, and their investment cannot be a one-sided gain. But one ought to consider this question: why is the video industry in Japan putting movie theatres in jeopardy, while in the United States, videos have brought a favourable impact—an increase in the theatre-going population?

Genres and Themes

Filmmaking is a business, just as a film is a form of mass entertainment. Directors nowadays are more sensitive to this commercial connection. Conflict between creative drive and the profit motive must be as old as art itself, yet the fierce competition for survival does not really force any director to undergo the conflict. Most directors either choose between creativity or profit or they compromise. A few giants, such as Akira Kurosawa, would appear to have risen above it all, yet even he has to count on foreign producers, since no one in his home country is rushing to help him follow his artistic integrity.

Juzo Itami was Japan's most sought-after director in the late 1980s. Though he seemed to reconcile the artistic and commercial values of film, he summarised this awareness when he claimed that *Marusa no Onna* (*A Taxing Woman*, 1986) was made as an entertainment film. On one occasion, he said: 'a film is a means of communication, and I am most thrilled when my film attracts a big audience'. (Hachimori 1988: 215)

As mentioned earlier, the nature of the market—the lowering of the movie-theatre population—appears to be affecting film content, aesthetics and genres. A glance at a vast array of contemporary films suggests that directors either adhere to a familiar subject matter/theme/genre or create a new one. The former choice presents an interesting case in that many directors approach the familiar from a uniquely refreshing perspective or mode of representation.

Itami has said that the most important thing for him in filmmaking is the ordinary things a film deals with. His debut film, *Ososhiki* (*The Funeral*, 1984), which won the *Kinema Jumpo* Best Picture of the Year Award, took its cue from familiar funeral scenes explored by master filmmakers, such as the one from Kurosawa's *Ikiru* (1952) and Ozu's *Tokyo Monogatari* (*Tokyo Story*, 1953). Yet, Itami transformed the sad, solemn event into a kind of satirical farce, thus investing the film with a uniquely fascinating touch. His *Tampopo* (1985), which won critical acclaim overseas, again concerned an everyday need, that of food. Yet, by using a parody of *Shane* throughout as a structural principle and adopting a Buñuel style, he made the film, dealing with such ordinary raw material, a pointed satire of the Japanese society's obsession with rituals and status.

A Taxing Woman and *The Return of the Taxing Woman* again drew critical inspiration from an everyday concern of the Japanese people, taxes. As Itami claimed, he created a new type of woman consonant with contemporary society: a tough tax investigator who must compete in the male-dominated world of bureaucracy.

The theme of the Japanese family has been an age-old topic for many directors. However, new kinds of Japanese experiences with contemporary society offer directors different avenues to explore. As might be expected, their works in the late 1980s have run the gamut from simplistic to complicated approaches; from conventional treatments to some that are boldly experimental. A director such as Kohei Oguri has given his somewhat idealised view of family life the benefit of a stepback of a generation. *Doro no Kawa* (*Muddy River*, 1981) was set in the years of the Korean War, which he considered most relevant to his own experience. His nostalgic look celebrated values of tightly knit family life, poor in material goods but rich in spirit and human affection.

Yoji Yamada's *Tora-san* series exhibited the same values in a comic setting. In these features starring the good-natured protagonist, Tora, Yamada managed to affirm values of familial solidarity still intact in contemporary Japan. Tora is a peddler, an anti-hero, who falls in love with a beautiful new heroine in each episode, only to find himself perpetually rejected. Here, family represented security, which even the scapegrace vagabond could count on when the chips were down.

It was not so for the heroes of Mitsuo Yanagimachi's *Saraba Itoshiki Daichi* (*Farewell to the Land*, 1982) and *Himatsuri* (1985). This young director has presented a Japanese family in a state of moral bankruptcy, without all the relationships and values fostered by traditional Confucian virtues.

The more traditional dilemma of old age was the theme related to a Japanese family and revived in *Hana Ichimonme* (*Song About Flowers*, 1985), by Shunya Ito, one of Toei's veteran directors. The same subject matter was treated by Shiro Toyoda in *Kokotsu no Hito* (*Twilight Years*, 1973) in a familiar vein—the taking in of an aged grandparent and the problems this presents to the nuclear family. Ito, however, was less resigned in his approach, presenting a tragic ending, more in tune with present-day doubts about the power of family as a shield against the horrors of final helplessness.

After a 12-year absence, Yoshishige Yoshida returned to directing with a similar theme in *Ningen no Yakusoku* (*Promise*, 1986). A powerful study of senility, the film showed the anguish engendered in two younger generations who faced the terrifying dilemma of euthanasia.

Significantly, two directors offered the rich vein of comic satire—a uniquely new method—to this familiar theme. One was Morita Yoshimitsu with *Kazoku Gemu* (*The Family Game*, 1983). The 1983 work, which *Kinema Jumpo* voted the Best of the Year (a film shot in just 18 days by a 33-year-old director), aimed at two targets in post-war Japan: affluent, middle-class, nuclear family life in the city; and the nose-to-the-grindstone education system. The other, Yojiro Takita, director of *Kommiku Zasshi Nanka Iranai* (*Comic Magazine*, 1986), created a slapstick satire on materialistic aggression in contemporary Japanese society. Another family-type film was *Kimura-ke no Hitobito* (*Yen Family*, 1988), which concerned a Japanese suburban family obsessed with making money.

The sudden growth of the 'animal genre' in the late 1980s illustrated the complex interplay between the Japanese audience's cultural specificity and the studio's shrewdness in capitalising on it. On the surface, a sizeable number of these pictures reflected a present-day mania for keeping pets, as most of them deal with 'cute' kittens and dogs.

The upsurge of this genre was triggered by the box-office hit, *Nankyoku Monogatari* (*Antarctica*, 1985), a film about the sacrifice which accompanied Japan's first successful post-war expedition to Antarctica, a source of great national pride at the time. The sacrifice in question entailed the fate of dogs left in the Antarctic by the expedition. The familiar themes of survival and bonding yielded a predictable reunion, a narrative pattern well calculated to meet audience expectations of joyous relief. The film functioned as an entertainment and escape, because many Japanese viewers are more favourably disposed to a happy ending and entertaining 'content', than to serious realism. Other notable examples of 'animal genre' included *Koneko Monogatari* (*The Story of Chatran*, 1986), the second ranking box-office hit in 1986, and *Maririn ni Aitai* (*I Want to See Marilyn*, 1988), seventh ranking in 1988.

Some other films in this genre were variations on such familiar themes as values of loyalty and bond. *Hachiko Monogatari* (*The Story of the Loyal Dog Hachiko*), which turned out to be the second biggest box-office sweep in 1988, counted on the Japanese audience knowing an actual event—a faithful dog which waited for its owner's return at the station, many days after he died. The film was a celebration of loyalty in a contemporary society in which every familial and corporate bond is constantly put to test. Another such film, *Yushun* (*Oracion*, 1988), dealt with various phases of human lives as they are interwoven into the fate of a pony trained for the derby. Again, the theme of a deep bond immensely appealed to the contemporary audience, echoing a theme similarly explored nearly a half century earlier in Kajiro Yamamoto's *Uma* (*Horse*, 1941).

War has been a favourite thematic constant for many directors, even four decades after Japan's defeat in World War II. Kei Kumai's 1986 film, *Umi to Dokuyaku* (*The Sea and Poison*), voted the Best Film of the Year by *Kinema Jumpo*, explored the Japanese perception of social crime and punishment. Based on Susaku Endo's controversial novel about the Japanese army's use of American prisoners of war for medical experiments, the film concerned the capture and clinical murder of eight US flyers in the last months of the war. This type of film, which involves the Japanese medical profession as a guilty party, would have met much more resistance from conservative domestic audiences if made earlier.

The Sea and Poison was intended to analyse, rather than attack, as the director himself explained:

'The film was never intended as a means of denouncing the
medical profession. Man has long been noted for loss of
conscience when placed in extreme situations. I wanted to define,
examine and describe this horror through the medium of film.'
(*The Sea and Poison* 1986: 1)

The year 1988 was characterised by a number of films with such
thematic orientation. Kazuo Kuroki's *Tomorrow: Asu* (*Tomorrow*)
recaptured the horror of the atomic bomb through a portrayal of the
ordinary lives of people in Nagasaki the day before the atomic
bombing. In *Sakuratai Chiru* (*The Last Moment of Sakura Troupe*),
Kaneto Shindo dealt with an entertainment troupe's encounter with
fate, reviving a theme he explored more than three decades before in
Genbaku no Ko (*The Children of Atom Bomb*, 1952). Isao Takabata's
Hi Taruru no Haka (*Tomb Afire*, 1988) took advantage of the
expressive power of animation to depict the sufferings of a four-year-
old child left alone with her elder brother. The trauma of hunger and
solitude might not have been rendered realistically if the director had
used an actual child star (Takahashi 1989: 102). This thematic
interest in war manifested itself in documentary films, too, as Kazuo
Hara's *Yukiyukite Shingun* (*Emperor's Naked Army Marches On*), the
best of 1987 in this category, touched upon the controversial subject
of cannibalism.

Shinoda's *Setouchi Shonen Yakyudan* (*MacArthur's Children*,
1984), though set during the post-war period, also projected the
director's life-long question: 'why did I think that I would not regret
dying for the emperor? It's still a mystery'. (Yajima 1986: 52) Shinoda
approached this question by examining the world of children—
children who are introduced to baseball and begin to enjoy the game
during the aftermath of the war.

Another emergent genre in recent years has been animation.
This is an expected phenomenon, given the popularity of the comic
magazine among Japanese intellectuals—students and white-collar
workers alike. The animation boom dates back to 1977, when *Uchu
Senkan Yamato* (*Spaceship Yamato*) was released. None the less, 1988
marked a high point in the achievement of animation, when *Kinema
Jumpo* ranked *Tonari no Totoro* (*Totoro: Our Neighbour*), Best Picture
of the Year, and *Tomb Afire*, sixth best. *Totoro: Our Neighbour* was
drawn by Shun Miyazaki, noted for adventure romance films, such as
Kaze no Nakano Naushika (*Warriors of the Wind*, 1984) and *Tenka no
Shiro Ruputa* (*Laputa*, 1987). However, in this award-winning
picture, he returned to a world of fantasy reminiscent of Disney. The
film, set in the mid-1960s, concerned the animal Totoro embodying
the dream of children living in the countryside. Miyazaki's style
differed from that of Tabata, who tried to explore the realistic
dimension of non-animation film through animation.

Though it has lost ground to the contemporary film genre, the jidaigeki has continued to hold on in the competitive market. The few films of this genre which studios manage to crank out each year are far removed from those serious films charged with social criticism produced two or three decades ago. Notable examples include the *Hissatsu* (*Kill*, 1985–88) series, taking its cue from a popular novel, and *Shogun Iemitsu no Ranshin: Gekitotsu* (*Shogun's Madness*, 1989), with cartoon-like characters. The *Zatoichi* series, which drew large audiences in the 1960s, has recently returned to the screen, the current instalment directed by its star, Shintaro Katsu.

It is common practice that a big box-office hit often leads to a series. This is even more conspicuous in the Japanese cinema industry, resulting in an overflow of quick return 'series'. Thus, Toei has been catering to teenagers with the *Bii Bappu Haisukuru* (*Bebop Highschool*) series. Taking its cue from a serialised comic magazine story, *Bii Bappu Haisukuru* celebrated its sixth and final instalment in the late 1980s. Shochiku has recently landed the *Hei no Naka* (*Inside Prison*) series (1987), based on autobiographical works by the former *yakuza* (ex-con) turned-writer Joji Abe. However, the commercial failure of the second instalment, *Hei no Naka no Pureiboru* (*Freedom Inside Prison*, 1987), has jeopardised any further Shochiku commitment.

Professionalism

> 'Since, in the final analysis, the Japanese audience creates the Japanese film, one can only wait and see whether the recent growing intellectual and aesthetic poverty of the Japanese film product is a reflection of a more and more materialistic audience or whether, as in America, this materialism reflects only the industry itself.' (Anderson and Richie 1982: 427)

As early as the 1970s, Joseph Anderson and Donald Richie described the moral dilemma that the Japanese film industry faced in terms of professionalism. This pressing need to improve the quality of films lingers in the contemporary period when, indeed, the need seems even greater. Yet, the problem is not seriously dealt with by most film organisations and foundations in Japan. Given the fiercely competitive world of media (in which the film is, after all, a marketable commodity), the film organisations' efforts and energies are spent on the much wider issue on which the survival of the Japanese cinema industry depends—the promotion of the motion picture itself.

The League of Japanese Filmmakers, whose history dates back to 1946, is composed of motion picture companies and distributors. The League was instrumental in inaugurating, in May 1985, the Tokyo International Film Festival, a ten-day event (31 May–9 June), which enjoyed an audience of 105,000. As a biennial event, now held in October, the festival attracts participants from around the world, who come to see many films, new and old, shown at various local theatres reserved for this purpose. A number of symposia and lectures are conducted with film critics, directors and actors/actresses as participants. As with other international festivals, the event also serves as an avenue for overseas markets.

Among the many foundations engaged in cultural exchange through films are the Japan Film Library Council (renamed Kawakita Memorial Film Institute in 1982) and the National Film Center. The most significant activity of the first is the *Japan Film Worldwide* series, which began in 1974. Annually, the foundation chooses a group of films arranged thematically or topically. Equipped with English, or sometimes French, subtitles, these films are sent worldwide to various film libraries and public cultural organisations. The foundation's 1988 series—its fourteenth—was devoted to the director Hiroshi Shimizu. The Kawakita Memorial Film Institute is also consulted by other international festivals regarding selection of Japanese films for exhibition.

On a smaller scale, the National Film Center, affiliated with the Tokyo Museum of Modern Art, is engaged in cultural exchange through films. Some of its rare holdings are shown at major cultural organisations world-wide. However, one of its main activities is the year-round exhibition of both domestic and foreign films, some of which are retrospectives and others special, 'topical' series. The Film Center also publishes special issues devoted to each series.

Unlike Western academic institutions, Japanese universities do not boast the popularity of film studies. Only a few, such as Nippon University, Waseda University and Tokyo University of Plastic Arts offer a degree in film studies as an academic discipline. Some private institutes are actively engaged in training personnel for the film industry. Best known is the Japan Academy of Visual Arts, located in Yokohama. Originally started as a broadcasting/film institute in 1974, it now has acting, photography, directing and other divisions. Since its inception, the academy has sent many graduates to the cinema industry. Students in the late 1980s realised a long-cherished dream—directing and scripting their own film. With ATG assistance, they made *Kimi wa Hadaka no Kami o Mitaka* (*Have You Seen Naked God?* 1986), with Shohei Imamura, president of the academy, as producer.

Finally, as a conscientious stronghold of the values of artistic integrity in the motion picture industry, ATG's activities, however limited they may be, should be studied. Since its establishment in 1961, this guild has introduced unmarketable high-quality films as a counterbalance to the prevailing commercial orientation. By the end of 1985, it had exhibited 76 foreign and 102 national films, and helped fund 73 others, working with independent directors. Equipe de Cinema, another organisation established by two women—Kashiko

Kawakita and Etusko Takano has made a valuable contribution to bringing foreign creative works to the Japanese audience. The Iwanami Hall, managed by Equipe de Cinema, serves as the centre for such cultural exposure.

NOTE

I am deeply indebted to two persons for offering me valuable information on contemporary Japanese cinema: Ms Kanako Hayashi of the Kawakita Memorial Film Institute and Dr Kyoko Hirano of the Japan Society.

3

TAIWAN

INTRODUCTION

Veteran director and cinematographer Chen Kun-Hou poked at his noodles as he thought about my questions over dinner in a Taipei restaurant. Punctuated by occasional periods of contemplative silence, his diagnosis of the Taiwanese film industry in 1986 was that it was submerged in problems, some so close to home he did not wish to discuss them.

Forty-five years old, he had already directed eight films and was cinematographer of about 40 others in a 24-year career. He is unique in the industry because he has worked with nearly every director in Taiwan. All of the films he worked on made money, and one of them, *Growing Up*, was the first big hit of the 'new cinema', capturing the nation's top movie awards in 1983.

But 1986 was a low point in his career. The industry was beset with too many problems, he said, ticking them off—wrong selection of topics, limited market, difficult relationships between producer and director and director and audience, the out-of-proportion power of distributors and exhibitors and inadequate equipment. The latter problem particularly affected Chen, who had to buy his own camera and an editing table with borrowed money.

With these purchases, he may own some of the best equipment among his colleagues, but, he argued, what he has is only basic compared with other film industries. He explained:

'Film people here think in terms only of adequate equipment—in fact, they may think the basics are more than enough. The audiences have been conditioned by distributors and exhibitors who use the thinking that if you give the people only white rice, they think that is enough. If you change the styles the people will know there are different types of rice, and would want the added variety. The same in film.' (Interview, Chen Kun-Hou, 1986)

Chen's pessimism about the situation in 1986 was offset by optimism for the future. Personally, his own low point was temporary, he said, a time for thinking about the future of Taiwan. 'It is characteristic of the Chinese that they start slowly,' he said. 'We are only beginning to realise what film can be; now, we have to think about what to do.'

Some filmmakers agreed with Chen's latter point, emphasising that cinema already had a rejuvenation in the 1980s, partly because of the encouragement of a film buff high up in government, Dr James Soong.

While he was director of the Government Information Office, Soong helped rebuild the financially beleaguered industry with a number of innovations. Among these were:

(1) Reorganisation of the national film award (Golden Horse) to honour artistic innovation rather than thematic content, and to be judged by film professionals, not government representatives.
(2) Creation of the Golden Horse Awards International Film Festival to bring in award-winning films that might raise local standards.
(3) Encouragement of Taiwan films' entry in international competitions.
(4) Updating of the infrastructure of film law, lifting the medium to the cultural level.
(5) Engineering tax reductions on ticket sales and providing tax shelters for producers (*Free China Journal* 1984: 3).

HISTORICAL BACKGROUND

Those who have followed the history of Taiwan film realise that by the late 1970s, something was amiss. Government regulations remained stifling, production plummeted, overseas markets caved in and thematic and stylistic aspects of film were monotonously imitative. It seemed that much of what had been accomplished in the short history of Taiwan's film industry was endangered.

Compared with other parts of Asia, filmmaking is relatively new in Taiwan. During World War II, the occupying Japanese set up Taiwan Motion Picture Association and Taipei News Picture Association, merged in 1945 to form Taiwan Film Studio. The latter was under the Taiwan Provincial Department of Information. During the next five years, and especially after 1949, a number of movie organisations and filmmakers migrated from China. Included among these was China Movie Studio[1], which co-operated with Agricultural Educational Film Corporation to bring out *Re Men Chu China*, an anti-communist film considered one of the first local pictures[2].

Throughout the 1950s, four government-owned studios dominated most filmmaking, which concentrated on the crimes of communism and the development of Taiwan as the Republic of China. Besides Taiwan Film Studio and China Movie Studio, the others were China Educational Film Studio, which moved from Nanking in 1956 and, after financial problems, was given to the National Taiwan Arts University two years later, and the Central Motion Picture Corporation (CMPC), established in 1954 with the merger of Agricultural Educational Film Corporation and Taiwan Motion Picture.

Managed by the Kuomintang, CMPC continued to make films which boasted of Taiwan's prosperity and propagated that communism was evil. Most of its early work consisted of documentaries for the party or armed forces, although the studio produced five feature-length movies in 1958–9.

Gradually other production houses opened, but mainly to release imported films. In the mid-1950s, some breakthroughs occurred in the industry, such as the first Mandarin film, released by a private company (*Wind and Cloud on Ali Mountain*); government encouragement of producers to work with Hong Hong in co-productions and the release of the first Taiwanese dialect picture (*Six Talents in West Chamber*). In fact, Tang (1975, p. 56) called 1956 the beginning of six golden years in Taiwan's film industry. For example, the 21 features produced in 1956 equalled the total of all studios in the previous seven years. Most were in Taiwanese as 70 per cent of the population used that dialect; Mandarin was not known by many people.

Film companies used the studios of CMPC, China Movie Studio and Taiwan Film Studio to help produce the 110 Taiwanese-dialect pictures of 1957. That year, a newspaper, in conjunction with film associations, gave the first film awards of Taiwan. Themes of these movies were traditional local stories, biographies of famous Taiwanese, stories from popular Taiwanese songs and contemporary stories based on fact.

However, the heyday of Taiwanese-dialect films was short-lived, partly because,

(1) With the lack of high quality scripts, the Taiwanese began adapting from Mandarin, Japanese, French, United States and German films that were unfamiliar to the people,
(2) The low quality of many of these films sapped audience interest,
(3) Some producers changed from Taiwanese to Japanese films after 1959 as the people, after years of Japanese occupation, understood that culture,
(4) Television took away some of the audience with the advent of Taiwan Television Enterprises in 1961 (Tang 1975: 57).

In the 1960s, the Republic of China government took another active role in the film industry, stating that movies should be cultural and educational in a 'positive way', as well as entertaining, and signing, through CMPC, a contract with Japan's Daiei Film Co. to produce *Emperor Chin Shih*, with the aim of exploring markets abroad. The film was not a success, nor was a second co-production with Nikkatsu, *Rainbow over the Kinmen Bay*. The result was that CMPC reorganised in 1963, with a new goal of producing realistic pictures. The first of these, *Oyster Girl*, won best picture at the Tenth Asian Film Festival.

China Movie Studio also changed its direction in 1966, from making military education documentaries and newsreels, to high quality features. However, Taiwan Film Studio's attempt at making big budget features was not a box-office success and the company reverted to making documentaries and newsreels.

In the 1960s, the Government Information Office (GIO) tried to encourage private filmmakers to upgrade quality by allowing Chinese film producers to share in imported film distribution, the guideline being, the more Chinese films a company made, the more chance it had of importing foreign pictures; by loaning up to NT $200,000 (NT $1 = 2.5 US cents at the time) for black-and-white production (doubled for colour) to civilian Taiwan and Hong Kong companies; by setting up annual meetings of Chinese motion picture personnel to help solve industry problems and by awarding the annual Golden Horse for meritorious quality (Tang 1975: 72).

Whether these motivators took effect is a matter of conjecture. However, more certainty can be expressed about the impact the changing of thematic content had upon the industry. In 1963, a Hong Kong-produced Chinese ancient costume musical, *Liang Shan-po and Chu Ying-tai*, broke the Taiwan box-office record by eightfold, a much-needed boost of confidence to an ailing industry. Also that year, a Hong Kong director Lee Han-Hsiang of Shaw Brothers, moved to Taipei to establish the Grand Movie Company. With Taiwan Film Studio and Union Film Company, Grand made the first local ancient costume musical, *Seven Fairies*, setting the trend for the next few years. In 1964, eight of the top ten grossing films in Taiwan were ancient costume musicals; the following year, all ten best sellers fell into this category. Although bankrupt by 1967, Grand had injected much adrenalin into the business in its short life.

About the time Grand was going bankrupt, another Shaw Brothers Studio director, Hu Chin-Chuan, migrated from Hong Kong, bringing with him another genre of film that has endured since 1967—swordsman. Hu's first Taiwan-produced swordsman picture, *Dragon Inn*, came out of Union Film Company Studios, which, with its associated companies International Film Company and China Arts Motion Picture Company, then went on to build the largest civilian studio in Taipei—International Motion Picture Studio.

Swordsman movies poured out of these and other studios at a blistering rate between 1967 and the mid-1970s. In 1967, Taiwan made 190 films, 38 of which were in colour, and the figure pushed up to 198 in 1968 and 230 in 1969. Although some used contemporary themes, the majority were swordsman. Of 609 colour films made in Taiwan between 1972 and 1974 (an average of 17½ per month), more than half (327) were built around fist or sword fighting. Other themes dealt with singing, dancing, historical legends and educational matters (Tang 1975: 77).

Popular throughout this period were the star system and use of studios, the latter required by most swordsman films. Director Chen Yao-Chi (Richard Y. Chen) described the film scene he found upon coming to Taiwan in the mid-1960s:

'Dominated by big studios[3] — Shaw Brothers, CMPC, Cathay — the industry was at its high point. CMPC did nice pictures of the transition in Taiwan life from agrarian to industrial. They were top value productions, old classic filmmaking. All of a sudden, custom kung fu movies — first using weapons, and then fists — came in. Simultaneously, in the late 1960s and early 1970s, so-called melodrama (*wenyi*) based on popular love-story novels, proliferated. When I first arrived here, it was difficult to break in because studios hired veteran directors. Film was the dominant entertainment form here and we had markets for our products in Hong Kong and Southeast Asia as well. In fact, the thinking was to recuperate investments in the overseas markets.' (Interview, Chen Yao-Chi, 1986)

But not all aspects of filmmaking were so rosy. Censorship policies were still strict, forcing directors to find alternative ways to express social concerns. Veteran director Liao Hsiang-Hsiong said he and others made historical pictures to express ideas and themes that might also apply to the contemporary situation. In 1973, a 'sarcastic' picture by Liao, entitled *Money, Money, Money*, was banned by the authorities because it was 'too real'. The story described the change of heart people had over a poor soul after he won the lottery and became wealthy (Interview, Liao, 1986).

CONTEMPORARY SCENE

Production

'All companies claim they are the largest producers, but that is not important. What is important is how long a production company lasts,' Wade Yao of Tom Son Motion Picture Company stated with conviction. But that is not an accurate gauge either, because, in Taiwan, some companies can last a long time by not producing anything. In 1986, of Taiwan's 188 film producers, only 76 were active. An effort was made to prod all companies into activity, when the Government Information Office required that a company, to stay registered as a filmmaker, had to make at least one movie a year. After a couple of years, not much progress had been made in implementing that policy (Interviews, Chiang and Liu, 1986). The situation was compounded by the fact that some companies were solely producers, while others were producers, distributors and exhibitors.

Overall, the number of feature films produced in Taiwan steadily dwindles. From the highs of well over 200 a year in the 1960s and 1970s, the figure has shrunk to considerably fewer than the 99 recorded in 1985. Even a huge producer such as the Kuomintang-controlled Central Motion Picture Corporation, which averaged 16 films a year through 1986, finished only three short and two feature-length films by the end of the summer of 1988. One filmmaker thought the reasons for these cut-backs were changes in the government leadership after Chiang Ching-Kuo's death led to a wait-and-see policy at CMPC, independent producers being short of money and film attendance being down because of added recreational diversions (Interview, Lee Daw-Ming, 1988).

Independent film companies have had less-consistent production patterns than that of CMPC. In 1985, Fee Tang Motion Picture Company did seven features, its total for a previous five-year period. Some years, Fee Tang did not produce films, but helped other companies make theirs (Interview, Chou Ling-Kong, 1986).

Production slices have been blamed on still other factors. Some producers claim the big stars chew up too much of the budgets. 'The problem here is that the actors are too greedy,' H.S. Chou, president of the Motion Picture Association of Taiwan, said. 'The big stars take a large part of the budget, and not much is left for production. If a company will not give 20 per cent of its picture budget to a star, he goes elsewhere.' Chou said up to 40 per cent of production budgets ended up in the pockets of leading actors and actresses (Interview, H.S. Chou, 1986). A 'new cinema' director, Wan Jen, agreed, saying that in an NT $8 million production, one star might take NT $3 million (in the 1980s, the NT dollar was worth about 3.3 US cents). New directors, such as Wan Jen, changed this by not depending on big stars, putting the money saved into film stock. The result for him has been that, whereas previously the ratio of film shot to that used was three to one, now it is eight to one. In an NT $8 million movie, as much as NT $2.5 million might be spent on film stock (Interview, Wan Jen, 1986).

Another producer said the stars did not now take such sizeable chunks of budgets as they did in the late 1960s, when half of the budget would go to them. He broke down the costs of a typical Mandarin picture:

'If today, we invest NT $20 million on a movie, one famous star would get NT $1.5 million maximum. Winners of the Golden Horse award would get NT $1.2 to 1.5 million. In an NT $20 million production we're doing right now, a comedy about a tiger breaking into a hospital, we have to spend NT $3.5 million on the hospital setting alone as no hospital will let us shoot on location. It is a 10,000 foot setting. Another NT $4 million is spent on actors, and the rest on lighting, film, music, and equipment.' (Interview, Chou Ling-Kong, 1986)

Still other filmmakers believe that the major financial difficulty is the inability to get outside investors in films. A long-time producer who quit making films in 1984 said filmmakers tried to get investment capital from well-endowed corporations, most of which did not have the 'guts' for that type of investment. 'Banks do not want to invest as they are not familiar with businesses such as film,' he said (Interview, Liao, 1986).

A variety of approaches is used to seek funding. Golden Harvest, which produced three movies in 1986 on an average of NT $10 million each, receives financial boosts from its parent company in Hong Kong (Interview, Lee Pai-Kwi, 1986), while all money invested in Tom Son pictures comes from within the company (Interview, Wade Yao, 1986). Scholars Motion Picture Company, which is in production, distribution and exhibition, has some investment money from Taiwanese businessmen, but most financing is out of the coffers of the owner, Tsai Sung-Lin. Scholars produced one or two films a year in the mid-1980s, and invested in ten to twelve productions of its satellite companies. A typical film coming out of this studio budgets at NT $6 to $12 million, not counting distribution (Interview, Wang, 1986).

The national film company, CMPC, survives on its own resources, a producer claiming the government provides no help except in the few films dealing with government policy. In one such film showing in 1986, *Battle of Artillery—August 23*, CMPC put up NT $20 million, the government another NT $10 million. CMPC earns large profits from auxiliary activities; as a result, in a generation, it has moved from huge deficits to surplus profits (US $800,000 in 1979). CMPC maintains a film printing branch, which brings in NT $600,000 in attendance revenues, as well as the largest studios rented at NT $15,000 per day. Like a number of production houses, CMPC also owns a string of twelve theatres. Another profitable satellite is its video production house, Thirty-One Audio Visual Company, which produces and distributes video-cassettes under contract to 1,600 video rental shops. Each shop gives CMPC an annual guarantee of NT $10,000. Sources of material for the videocassettes are old CMPC movies which are copied (20 a year), new stories produced especially for video by CMPC (eight a year) and copies of United States or European tapes (six a year) (Interview, Benny Chao, 1986).

Wade Yao (Interview, 1986) summarised the main ways Taiwan films are financed as, personal investment of the company owner, pooling of money from a group of investors, supplementing of the producer's investment with money from a distributor line and advanced money from Hong Kong or Singapore entrepreneurs.

As indicated earlier, Central Motion Picture Corporation is the largest producer of motion pictures in Taiwan. Owned by the government and controlled by the Cultural Department of the Kuomintang, CMPC's structure includes a board of chairmen with a general manager in charge. Six departments make up the corporation: production, distribution, accounting, personnel, research and development and administration. More than 700 people are employed. CMPC owns one of the six studios in the country, the others belonging to the Ministry of National Defence, which produces mainly military-oriented film; Taiwan Provisional Motion Picture Company; and the three independents, Hua Guo Movie Productions, developed in 1978; Lien Pun and Guo Lien. Elaborating upon what was mentioned earlier, CMPC has other facilities, such as the Film Laboratory, launched as a CMPC adjunct in 1977, after being purchased from International Film Laboratory; the Chinese Cultural Movietown, founded in 1975; Folk Custom Museum; Wax Figures Museum; swimming pool with underwater cameras; and the Advertisement Short Film Department. CMPC also publishes *Movie Pictorial Monthly* and *Movie and Drama Weekly* (Interview, Benny Chao, 1986; Government Information Office 1978: 152).

Perhaps because it is financially healthy, CMPC has not always put profits above all else; at times, the company has opted for quality films (more than 100 prize-winning pictures attesting to this fact) and for new directions. In the early 1980s, CMPC gave a group of young directors a chance to bring out their sensitive and realistic pictures, made on budgets as low as US $170,000. This 'new cinema' moved beyond the stereotypical fare that had dominated Taiwan screens for many years. But, according to two of these new directors, CMPC policy veered somewhat by 1986. Li Yuan (Hsian Yeh) and Lee Daw-Ming said that CMPC now expects young directors intending to make a company-funded film to prove its marketability, including overseas. In fact, for a short time, CMPC hired someone specifically to market its movies abroad. Lee said CMPC's head proclaimed the main tasks of directors must be to 'keep each film well controlled within the budget' and assure it will not lose money (Interviews, Li Yuan and Lee Daw-Ming, 1986).

An example of a smaller-scale company is Tom Son Motion Picture Company. Started in 1983 by actress Tom Shu-Fen and David Tom, this company produced six to eight features a year by 1986. Tom Son does not own a studio or any theatres. 'Everything at Tom Son is on contract; we go out and find actors, actresses, scriptwriters for individual pictures,' sales director Wade Yao explained. 'With whomever we contract, they are expected to bring in the equipment. If I hire a cameraman, he must provide the cameras, an editor the editing machine,' he said. The company used to contract CMPC and other studios but, to save costs, abandoned this practice in favour of location shooting. Twenty people work at Tom Son (Interview, Wade Yao, 1986).

Directing, Acting, Scriptwriting

The big changes in film style came with the above-mentioned new directors of the early 1980s. Besides dealing with social awareness and consciousness issues of an economic and political bent, the new directors differed from most predecessors in other ways. They told their stories without melodramatic techniques; shunned the famous stars, occasionally using non-actors to depict the common people in their stories and composed for the regular-sized screen, disdaining cinemascope (Interview, Li Yuan, 1986).

The new directors numbered only about ten. They were usually personal friends who collaborated; it has not been unusual to find one director acting, writing or doing the cinematography for another director's film. As an article in *Asiaweek* (1984, p. 48) pointed out, the new directors have a number of common stylistic and thematic traits, focusing on 'detail more than drama, and they are intensely concerned with the process of personal and social growth' and sharing 'an unabashed affection for the strengths and foibles of the ordinary people of Taiwan'.

The wave of 'new cinema' certainly split directors into 'old' and 'new' categories, and film people point out the differences between them. Director Chen Kun-Hou said the 'new' ones have a 'more assured, personal style' whereas the 'old' directors take an 'average, common stand' (Interview, Chen Kun-Hou, 1986).

Still other traits of 'new' directors are, they often studied filmmaking abroad, usually in the United States; they work as freelancers, not connected to an individual film company (except, in a few cases, the CMPC); make fewer pictures a year (usually one) and abandon studios for more natural settings.

Middle-aged directors (those 40 to 45 years old) were classified by Wan Jen (Interview, 1986) as using a mix of old and new styles and themes. It is very possible such a blending will become the familiar manner of directing.

Hu Ying Mon's story tells much about acting in Taiwan. The very popular actress broke into the profession at age 19 after dropping out of her second year of college. 'I was observing paintings at a gallery here when a director spotted me and asked me to be the leading actress in his film, *Somewhere in the Midst of Clouds*,' she said, adding:

> 'I knew nothing about acting or the film industry. After that film, I realised I was not interested in acting and went to New York where I drifted around. This was good for me as it was the first time I had my freedom. I came back to Taiwan, restarted my film career, and in 14 years, did about 50 films. Sometimes, I do three films at a time, getting them mixed up in my mind.' (Interview, Hu, 1986)

Believing she has grown with the industry, Hu remembered the popular melodramas in which she starred during the 1970s, as 'quite shallow', often made in 15 to 20 days. 'Sometimes an actor just went to the location completely unprepared because some pictures did not even have a script,' she said. Actors were not trained, and there was no theory of acting; some of this changed with the 'new cinema' of the early 1980s. Hu said she was not proud of most of her previous work, which was done with directors who asked actors to imitate their actions. The new directors, she said, 'communicate much beforehand and allow actors to grow more freely as the film is progressing'. Also, new directors are easier to work with because they are of the same generation and background and have had international filmmaking experience (Interview, Hu, 1986).

The image of actors and actresses in Taiwan's society is beginning to change for the better, according to Hu, but, some negative feelings still persist, e.g. that all actors and actresses are basically immoral. 'We have to respect ourselves, our craft,' she said, 'and we are not doing that. Maybe the government can help in this regard because producers, who are concerned only about money, certainly will not.'

The Taiwan film industry does not have a casting or agent system. Hu said directors 'just hire people with the best records, a "most wanted" list', because there is no tradition of reading for a part. An actor's guild exists, but because unions in Taiwan do not have the right to protest, it is ineffective. 'Those in charge are old, too nice, and too conservative,' Hu said. A result is that complaints are not filed against producers, such as CMPC, which pay a Hong Kong actress a quarter of a film's budget, while the rest of the cast, all from Taiwan, split 1 per cent (Interview, Hu, 1986).

To be fair to her colleagues, Hu said the film environment often does not allow actors to be more serious, because they usually have to make quick decisions. She gave the following example:

> 'On one occasion, I was asked the previous evening to do a film that started shooting in the morning. When I arrived on the set, I did not have the right jogging outfit called for in the film. We had

to wait until a shop opened to get the jogging suit. Even Meryl Streep would not be able to act in this lousy environment.'
(Interview, Hu, 1986)

A film reporter for Taipei's *United Daily News* had similar misgivings about the acting profession. Lan Tsu-Wei said some new stars 'only own a beautiful face' and usually are not trained. Furthermore, he said Taiwan has not developed a school of acting of its own; instead, directors tell actors to be natural and real, but not too dramatic. The star system has declined in Taiwan, partly because some directors do not want to see the same faces in films, and because they cannot pay the demanded salaries. To make a living, actors and actresses perform in more than one picture simultaneously, not giving any one their best efforts. Lan said the movie-going public wanted to see the stars even if they were in stories with poor plots; when they did not appear, attendances were down. His complaint about the stars is that 'all their performances are the same. They don't try to capture new ideas or new ways of performing.' (Interview, Lan, 1986)

Poor scriptwriting also makes up part of the problem, according to Lan. 'Directors and scriptwriters don't know how to bring interesting elements to a story; these are still experimental years for them,' he added. On a positive note, Lan thought this aspect would improve (Interview, Lan, 1986).

Distribution and Exhibition

If there is consensus on anything among Taiwan's film people, it is that distributors have far too much clout. Even distributors admit to that accusation. The managing director of Golden Harvest, a branch of the Hong Kong company whose purpose in Taiwan is to distribute Hong Kong films, explained the distributors' strength emanated from their control of the only outlets for Taiwanese films. Hong Kong films could be sold to other countries, but those made in Taiwan normally did not have overseas markets (Interview, Lee Pai-Kwi, 1986).

The lack of foreign markets is a familiar lament. A decade or more ago, Taiwan shipped movies on a regular basis to Singapore, Malaysia, Thailand, Vietnam and the many Chinatowns outside Asia. However, a number of factors dried up these outlets—the plentiful supply of videocassettes, protectionist policies of countries with their own film industries, the inability to compete with Hong Kong as a distributor of Chinese films because of higher-budget, better-quality products and the inability of Taiwan films to communicate internationally[4]. As one filmmaker said, 'traditional Chinese drama and China-style love stories are not accepted in many places' (Interview, Tu, 1986). Kung fu movies, successful internationally in the past, are seen as the only way to open up the Southeast Asia market to Taiwan producers (Interviews, Tu, Wade, 1986). The largest potential market, that of China, remains closed because of a policy that does not allow export to communist countries.

Another reason given for minimal overseas exposure is insufficient promotion. Chen Yao-Chi felt Taiwan pictures were as good as those of Japan, but the Japanese have

> 'promoters who push the films elsewhere, translating where necessary, and explaining them to international audiences. In the 1960s and 1970s, we made 200 films yearly; there must be a lot that are good—as good as those of Kurosawa, in fact. As the People's Republic of China was opened up, there were rave reviews of their films. Ours are politely ignored. We need someone to market our film productions. We don't want to continue being known as the makers of Adidas jogging shoes only.' (Interview, Chen Yao-Chi, 1986)

Because of the resultant strength of the distributors, producers have been known to relinquish their prerogatives in choice of directors, actors, actresses and scripts in order to gain the support of distributors, whom they depend upon for a line of theatres for their films. Benny Chao, head of productions at CMPC, explained:

> 'The power of distributors is great. When we produce a movie, we put a lot of money into it. Since we usually do not have theatres, distributors put a lot of pressure on us to do certain types of movies. They dominate sometimes. Usually distributors are very profit-motivated.' (Interview, Benny Chao, 1986)

A successful distributor believed distributors should be more powerful than producers as they are 'in the first line with the audience and know audience wants and needs, which producers do not know' (Interview, Tchii, 1986).

The power of the distributor was challenged, although not very successfully, by the crop of new directors in the early 1980s, who sought distribution through alternative pipelines. This resulted because most new directors had radically different perceptions of film from tradition-bound distributors. Chen Kun-Hou said:

> 'The major problem rests on one thing—the distributor and exhibitor have control of the audience. They have a say about the type of film producers will make. Producers have to listen to the distributors or their films will not be shown. And, the eyesight of the distributor is too narrow, narrower than that of producers. Anyone who wants to produce new things will not be supported as enthusiastically as those who produce the old-type film; thus, the adventurous filmmaker in both creative and commercial films does not have a chance.' (Interview, Chen Kun-Hou, 1986)

Perhaps confusing the scene in Taiwan is the large number of distribution companies and theatres, and the fact that many distributors also own theatres and some produce films. In 1986, 936 companies claimed to be distributing films, although, according to the Government Information Office, only 212 distributed the one required film each year. The other 724 were considered inactive. At the same time, the country had 792 theatres, 110 of which were in Taipei, another 90 in Kaohsiung (Interviews, Chiang and Liu, 1986).

Although, on paper, the large number of distribution houses should point to decentralisation, this is not the case. Some sources point to fewer than a half dozen companies that control distribution. The largest domestically invested distributor is Scholars Motion Picture Company, created in the early 1980s by Tsai Sung-Lin. By 1986, Scholars dealt strictly with Taiwan-made movies, distributing at least 15 a year—one or two produced by its production arm, another ten or twelve by satellite companies. According to Scholars' production manager, Wang Ming-Tsann, the owner, Tsai, invests in the productions of satellite companies, but no other relationship exists. However, Tsai's friends own the satellites (Interview, Wang, 1986).

In 1986, Tsai strengthened his hold on the film industry by reorganising a number of theatres into a link owned by him. When he had finished, he owned 15 to 20 theatres in Taipei (about a sixth of the total). Not even the two largest Hong Kong-invested distributors, Golden Harvest[5] and Cinema City, rivalled that ownership chain. Tsai derives capital to invest in the productions of satellite companies by milking his theatre chain. Wang explained:

Tsai has abandoned using partners. Instead, he gets money from the theatres. A proposal for a movie title, with cast and themes, is provided the theatres, which then put up the money for production. The theatres, which only invest a little money, deal only with those production companies that have a reputation. The pay-off to the theatres is a box-office guarantee. They invest so they can realise good productions that guarantee box-office success.' (Interview, Wang, 1986)

The potential of theatre managers exercising control over what gets produced exists in this scheme, as it does in the cases of other distributors/exhibitors who are also into production. Besides Scholars and Golden Harvest, Central Motion Picture Corporation, as indicated elsewhere, is in all three aspects. In the mid-1980s, CMPC produced 16 films a year, distributed twelve to 14 others (usually from the US), and owned twelve theatres. Other distributors also own theatres.

A trend in Taiwan is towards more smaller theatres for high rise apartments[6]. This, the multitude of daily showings (seven from 10.30 a.m. to midnight), and short film runs, tend to exhaust film stocks, requiring a number of imports. Some sources claimed the increasing number of theatres meant a lowering of quality in Taiwan movies (Interview, Chen Yao-Chi, Lee Pai-Kwi, Chou Ling-Kong, 1986). Chou Ling-Kong of Fee Tang Motion Pictures Company said, 'We have to produce so many films to fill theatres, the result is quality is not very good.' He added that when a good film does come along, the pressure to fill theatres often does not permit it to be advertised and promoted properly[7] (Interview, Chou Ling-Kong, 1986).

Films have very short runs in Taiwan. In two weeks or less, a film will be show in 40 to 60 theatres, and then it is shelved. One filmmaker said 80 per cent of all films are shown in two-week runs, another 10 per cent for ten or fewer days, and 10 per cent for 18 days (Interview, Wan Jen, 1986). With the absence of other types of theatres (e.g. art), the movie does not stand much chance of being seen again. This phenomenon had the impact of driving at least one director from the business. Chen Yao-Chi explained:

'A film is out and the whole island is blanketed. After ten days, it is gone and lost. If it stays a month here, that is a miracle. Some films need time to build up. I quit directing three years ago because I'd spend months on a film and in a week, it was gone. If you don't get paid well, and there is not enough time to have people appreciate the work, then it's not worth doing.' (Interview, Chen Yao-Chi, 1986)

Depended upon to fill many theatres are foreign movies, most popular of which are those from the US, attributable, in part, to the advantageous position US films have had under Taiwan's import quota system. In the 1980s, parts of this system were changed to the chagrin of US exporters and their pressure group, Motion Picture Export Association of America (MPEAA).

The changes came gradually. In 1977, of 275 foreign pictures allowed to be imported, 110 came from the US; in 1980, although the total imports stayed firm, the number of US films that could be distributed by US companies was sliced by 15. Ten of those options were reserved for new Taiwan companies which produced outstanding Chinese films, five others were added to the 35 to which the Chinese industry was entitled. The number of US films allowed decreased even more, to 50 in 1984, causing the MPEAA to rail against Taiwan regulations in 1985. These laws required importers to contribute US $5,000 to a government film fund for each title brought in, imposed high duties and limited the number of prints of each title to four. Adding to the dilemma of US exporters was Taiwan's 1984 decision to lift a 14-year embargo on Japanese films.

The US movie industry is represented in Taiwan by at least seven major companies, four of which (Paramount of China, Universal of China, United Artists of China and MGM of China) have operated together since 1982. General manager of that organisation (formerly called Cinema International Corporation) Frank Fan said he, along with MPEAA officials, had worked hard through diplomatic channels to 'improve the US industry position', seeking the abandonment of the quota system, among other changes. He explained that in 1985–6, Taiwan independent distributors were given 160 licences to import a film, while the seven US companies were allocated 70. 'We used all 70 of ours, but the independents used fewer than 20 of theirs,' he said. The reason, according to Fan, had to do with another government regulation that US $5,000 an import should be donated to the film fund. 'Independents could not use their quota, because it was too expensive,' he said.

The quota system, in effect since 1949, was reviewed by the government in 1986. One government official discussed what might happen if quotas were lifted:

'If we abolish the quota, it will mean that the foreign films in this country will not be good ones. Already a lot of the quotas (150 of 230) are not used, partly because the foreign film market here is not lucrative now. If we lift the quota, it will be to balance the trade deficit between the Republic of China and the US. The US through MPEAA gets US $8 to 9 million every year from our market. The US is in a super position with regard to our film market.' (Interview, Liu, 1986)

The Government Information Office decided in 1986 to drop the quota system, although it still had to be considered by the legislative *yuan*. Local film people feared the possibility of an open policy on foreign film, because of the impact it would have upon viewership of Mandarin pictures (Interview, Chang King-Yuh, 1986). CMPC's production head said it was very hard to compete with the US majors, claiming his company plays both sides — giving its theatres over to US major distributors but, at other times, distributing mainly films of US independents (Interview, Benny Chao, 1986).

A Taiwan independent distributor, Richard C. Tu of China Educational Recreation, felt the US distributors had benefited immensely over the years, partly through manipulation of Taiwan regulations. According to Tu:

'Government regulations originally gave US film branch offices here rights only to US films that were 100 per cent invested by US films. In other words, if a film is 50 per cent made by a US independent and 50 per cent by European company, it could not be distributed by the branch office. Now, US majors have other deals, such as a European company sells 100 per cent rights to its film to a US major film firm, and the US firm's Taiwan branch gets it. We Taiwan independents cannot distribute these films, nor do we have a chance to buy "A" or "B" class US pictures, again because they are distributed by the US branches here.' (Interview, Tu, 1986)

Tu's concern was not whether the quota system should be abolished, but whether Taiwan independents would be able to buy quality imports. He also believed taxes on the distribution of foreign films had to be dropped from 35 per cent to at least 25 per cent (Interview, Tu, 1986). One government regulation change that affected China Educational Recreation favourably was the abolishment of the Japanese embargo; it received all four Japanese film releases allowed in 1985. (The number was increased to six in 1986). Japanese films are more popular than other imports, according to Tu, because Taiwan was under Japanese occupation for more than 50 years, and the people in the southeast part of the island understand Japanese as well as they do Mandarin (Interview, Tu, 1986).

A successful Taiwan independent distributor dealing almost exclusively with US pictures is ESC Incorporated, owned by Danny Tchii. Started in 1979, ESC distributes 15 US or British films a year. He discussed his methods of operating:

'Fifteen pictures distributed yearly is the right size. To have more means running two or three films at the same time, and they won't do well. Sometimes, we have trouble with US producers who cannot provide pictures promised to us. As a back-up, we import 30 pictures yearly, but distribute 15. Eventually, we show all 30. And we don't have too much inventory (only one or two in back-up) as they come out at different times. We seek action pictures and avoid US drama and comedy because they do not fit here.' (Interview, Tchii, 1986)

ESC spends more money on imports than other distributors (US $2 million a year) but the pay-offs are compensatory. In 1985, the company outgrossed US major distributors such as Fox, Columbia and Warner. ESC distributes in its own two theatres in Kaohsiung[8] and its Taipei circuit of four theatres. Tchii does not release his films in more than ten cities, because the smaller towns do not have much of an audience (Interview, Tchii, 1986).

Regulation

Film laws in Taiwan have been some of the most forbidding in Asia. They seem to encompass every aspect of the movie picture process:

76

'Regulations for the Guidance and Management of the Motion Picture Industry and Film Actors and Actresses'. 'Movie Censorship Law', 'Motion Picture Law', 'By-laws Governing the Execution of the Motion Picture Law', 'Criteria of Movie Censorship', 'Procedures of Foreign Film Import Control', 'Essential Points of Allocation of Import Quotas for Foreign Movies', 'A Method of Soliciting and Selecting Superior Film Scripts', or 'Qualifications of China Film Industry Development Foundation Grant for Experimental Films'. Most of these have been amended regularly over the years (Government Information Office 1978: 31–51 and 1980: 59).

'The Motion Picture Law', most recently changed in 1983, stipulates that no film can be screened before it is censored and licensed, with heavy censorship fees paid by the producer. The censorship licence is for four years, after which, each film must be resubmitted for review if it is to continue to be shown. There are restrictions on films that impair the interest and dignity of the country (meaning that praise of China or the Soviet Union is not allowed, nor is bad-mouthing of the head of state), on films that disrupt the public order, that violate good taste or customs or advocate hearsay or superstition. Changes in this law in 1983 required movie companies to produce at least one full-length feature beginning in their second year of incorporation, distributors to distribute at least one film a year and exhibitors to refrain from uniting with other entities to monopolise the market. By-laws of 1984 spell out more specifically aspects of the movie law. For example, the by-laws state that no more than 20 minutes should be allocated between film showings to clean the theatre, that the projection room cannot be locked during a screening and that the film exhibition place cannot be located higher than the eighth floor in a multi-purpose building.

The guidance and management law requires a potential producer to be a high school graduate, licensed and with NT $8 million paid-up capital; would-be distributors need the same qualifications, but only NT $1 million paid-up capital. To be an actor or actress, the law requires that the candidate possess a registration card, junior high school education and at least three months' acting training (*Yearbook*, 1980: 59).

Enacting and enforcing most film laws is the Government Information Office and, more specifically, its Motion Picture Department. The department screens all films publicly shown in Taiwan and is permitted to censor. The directors of the department said about 30 per cent of all pictures are censored, but the number actually banned goes down every year because of the liberalisation of ideas. In 1985, of 456 foreign and Mandarin pictures reviewed, 37 were banned. Part of the reason outright banning occurs less frequently pertains to a film rating system implemented in 1985. 'After that, many films can be shown that would have been banned before,' deputy director of the Motion Picture Department Liu Shou-Chi (Interview, 1986) explained, adding, 'producers know the rating system so when they shoot a film, they should think about the possibility of losing 30 per cent at the box office by doing something that will get an "R" [restricted] rating'. Ratings enforcement is by theatre owners, who can be fined NT $60,000 for permitting those under 18 years old to see an 'R' rated movie.

Reviewing of a film is done by a committee of three people, one of whom hails from the department and two others from a pool of 45 individuals made up of invited psychologists, historians, drama scholars, critics or audience representatives. Claiming the reviewing process is much more flexible now, department directors said that if they decide to ban a movie, its producer and/or distributor can apply for another review later—after cuts are made. 'We do change decisions on appeal if we think we made a mistake,' Liu said (Interview, Chiang and Liu, 1986).

Besides its regulatory code, the department facilitates movie-making by loaning seed money to producers, funding film personnel's attendance at international film festivals, getting up film and drama scholarships at some universities, awarding the Golden Horses each year and giving five-year business tax-free status to new production houses and monetary awards to winners at international film festivals to make additional prints (Interview, Liu, 1986).

Contrary to government claims, filmmakers do not see much flexibility in either censorship or ratings. As the director-general of Government Information Office, Chang King-Yuh, sensed, producers and critics stress complete freedom from the government in censorship matters. Invariably when industry problems are cited, strict government censorship or lack of a clear policy rank high on the list. One distributor of foreign films, claiming censorship was too rigorous, said that 99 per cent of the times, nudity was cut from pictures; the policy on violence, horror or cruelty was more uncertain. According to him, the US movie, *Cobra*, was rated 'general' and not cut, while less violent films were given an 'R' (Interview, Fan, 1986). Inconsistency in applying regulations bothered other film personnel. One showed that more regulatory attention was paid to sex and political matters than to violence (Interview, Lan, 1986), while others (Interviews, Hu and Chou Ling-Kong, 1986) believed a double standard operated over foreign films exhibited in Taiwan. Chou Ling-Kong explained:

'The board always cuts Taiwan's films, but sometimes not those of Hong Kong. Policies of the preview committee are not clear. Also, our Taiwan standards are reflected in movies we export. We should keep the country we export to in mind. We filmmakers always question the qualifications of the 45 member preview board. We consider movies entertainment and wish the board would think of them as such, and not as political or cultural media.' (Interview, Chou Ling-Kong, 1986)

Some producers and directors do not see government restrictions as severe (especially compared with those of the past) or insurmountable. Chen Yao-Chi, a director prominent in the 1960s and 1970s, said in his day he could 'not touch violence, nudity, sex or social criticism'. Today, he said, directors could say 'almost anything politically and socially'; love scenes were 'much more frank, open and graphic' and subject matter censorship since 1984 was 'virtually non-existent' (Interview, Chen Yao-Chi, 1986). The owner of a picture distribution company said his products were not banned because he was 'very careful with such large investments'. He explained:

'We don't want our pictures banned. Therefore, when we make a film, one of our concerns is how to avoid the censor. If a picture of ours has to be cut, we obtain the necessary certificate, the government cuts the film, and we release it. About 5 per cent of my company's pictures must be censored. We can appeal to the authorities not to tamper with our films but, as a result, we can't release our picture. In effect, we ban it ourselves. I respect the government's decision on what to cut.' (Interview, Tchii, 1986)

Other complaints about the government regulatory process have been discussed elsewhere. The rating system, made up of general and restricted categories only, has been the cause of arbitration between the Government Information Office and the Motion Picture Association of Taiwan, the latter representing the industry (Interview, H.S. Chou, 1986), while the quota on foreign pictures and excessive taxation of the industry have also sparked much controversy.

Impact of Videocassettes
Much government and industry energy has been expended in attempts to curb the spread of illegally produced and distributed videocassettes, yet video remains largely out of the bounds of the law.

With increasing economic affluence, the number of homes with videocassette recorders has sky-rocketed to about 800,000, or 15 per cent of the total (Interview, Hu Joe-Yang, 1986), one of the highest penetration levels in Asia (Interview, Kuang, 1986). In August 1986, 5,173 registered, and from 1,500 to 3,000 illegal, video shops provided cassettes to this market. A total of 5,566 titles (4,387 foreign and local feature films, 788 local video productions and 391 television shows) were registered with authorities; undetermined thousands of others circulated illegally (Interview, Kuang, 1986). The general manager of a US majors distribution company said all legal shops also handled unregistered cassettes in an effort to make up for losses incurred from paying royalties on the legal ones (Interview, Fan, 1986).

Pirated videocassettes are hard to control in any country, but more so in Taiwan because it is not a member of the international copyright community and because smuggling is made easier by its island configuration (Interview, Kuang and Chang, 1986). Shops have regularly made available by noon, versions of Japanese television shows copied onto a master the night before when shown in Tokyo, flown to Taipei and duplicated during the night. Distributors play cat and mouse with illegal cassette operators, trying to find ways to beat them in exhibiting foreign films. Often they lose, as one distributor explained:

'A picture opens in the United States and, by the time we obtain it, a pirated version has already circulated here. My policy is to speed release to reduce the damage from pirated video. Most of the Spielberg films are speed released and get an audience. But usually, pirated versions of other films are released a month before the legal prints.' (Interview, Fan, 1986)

Even local producers cannot get their films into theatres much sooner than a pirated duplicate is circulated. Claiming video threatened to destroy Taiwan's film industry, director Wan Jen said:

'We release our film today and two days from now, it will be all over the country on illegal videocassettes. The legal video version of such a film, for whose use we get only NT $200,000, is released two weeks to a month later.' (Interview, Wan Jen, 1986)

Often the video version has been copied from US or Japanese television, especially cable systems which show more recent films, or directly from theatre screens in the US (and in Taiwan at Saturday midnight previews) or from master prints. One distributor believed video pirates received copies of master prints directly from US producers and distributors. He said:

'When a picture is released in the US, the master gets here within a week and the following day, 2,000 copies will come out. The copy that comes here is very clear so it must be a master. In "B" type movies, we lose big if there is video piracy. The big budget "A" movies from the US are not so anxious to sell video rights as "B". Thus, we go more to "A" movies.' (Interview, Tchii, 1986)

A number of effects were laid at video's door. Of course, film personnel and government officials believed the proliferating video piracy would wipe out the Mandarin movie business (Interview, Chang and Liao, 1986), one producer claiming that by the mid-1980s, overall box-office receipts already suffered a 20 per cent loss (Interview, Benny Chao, 1986). Distributors of foreign pictures also felt the pinch as mentioned before. Golden Harvest's one-third profit loss between 1984 and 1985 was blamed on illegal video, as well as audience preferences for other entertainment fare (Interview, Lee Pai-Kwi, 1986). Others blamed video for impairing Chinese culture, morality and television viewing. Perhaps the director of GIO's Department of Radio and Television, Sunshine Kuang, best represented these concerns when she said:

> 'Culturally, my office is concerned with the impact of videocassettess. Some people say we should treat video like books and let the public make up its own mind on what to see. But cassettes are different—more severe—as they have audio and visual aspects. Although video viewing might be a good stimulus for the imagination, our point of view is that it is kind of dangerous because the viewer watches too much fantasy and does not touch with reality enough. Also, fast-paced video makes young people more anxious and impatient. They always expect the exciting, the unexpectable. But life is expectable. If young people see hours of videocassettes that favour homosexuality or living together unmarried, they believe it is normal activity, which it is not in our culture.' (Interview, Kuang, 1986)

Kuang said illegal videocassettes affected television show ratings, top programmes dropping by 20 to 27 per cent in share of audience (Interview, Kuang, 1986).

Even the then director-general of Government Information Office admitted attempts at regulation had not worked (Interview, Chang, 1986). He and Sunshine Kuang said the pace of regulation promulgation did not keep up with the technology. Videocassette control was dealt with in the 1976 broadcasting act, revised in the 1980s partly to include video. One aspect of the law—that video-cassettes can be shown only in theatres—was 'ridiculous', according to Kuang, because the normal viewing place is the home. Some restaurants illegally set up rooms for video viewing and, in 1988, MTV (movie television) clubs, believed to be piracy dens, were the rage in Taiwan. The government, at that time, revised the 1982 broadcasting act to account for these clubs. The new law specified that MTV operators must obtain business licences from local governments, with failure to do this resulting in fines of US $100 to $1,000.

Video shops and individual tapes must be registered with the authorities but, as we have seen, many pirates survive, often selling illegal tapes in backrooms of electronic appliance stores, or in 'small shops in dark corners' (Interview, Kuang, 1986). The GIO Department of Radio and Television, in conjunction with the Motion Picture Association of Taiwan and Union of Videogram Distributors, tried to implement the law by visiting shops and, in some cases, arranging for raids. 'The anti-piracy law is all right,' according to Kuang, 'but its enforcement needs work.' She said her department's nine-person video section was not large enough to enforce the law, and did not have the power to arrest. 'When we visit a shop, we check its tapes and, if they are illegal, we confiscate them,' she added. Each cassette, to be legal, must be screened by the Department of Radio and Television, which assigns a person drawn from its pool of 50 to 60 scholars, former government officials, movie personnel and lay people. Believing her department had become more liberal in the 1980s, Kuang said that 5 to 10 per cent of all videocassettes reviewed were banned, most of them being foreign films with overt sex and violence (Interview, Kuang, 1986).

The president of the Motion Picture Association of Taiwan, H.S. Chou, believed the cassette registration procedure was effective with Mandarin movies, because as soon as they were produced in Taiwan, the prints were assigned a registration number. But the system was 'not ideal as some applications are handled under the table and, in some cases, film unions help distributors obtain registration numbers in an easy manner,' Chou said (Interview, 1986). The president of a video production company said the registration law had done some good in its first three years, getting 40 per cent of the cassettes copyrighted. The 60 per cent not registered, according to him, were pirated Japanese and Western films and TV shows (Interview, Hu Joe-Yang, 1986).

Other plans to control illegal videocassettes were in the pipeline in the 1980s. One concerned educating the public about the poorer quality of other-than-original videocassettes and bringing the prices of 'A' prints to those of second or third generation copies. This, according to Kuang, was more difficult than it seemed on the surface, because,

> 'The people have developed the bad habit of using less money to get illegal cheap video. They blame GIO for having to pay NT $50 for legal tapes when, before, they obtained pirated copies for NT $10. They also cannot understand why they have to wait six weeks after a movie is in the theater to get a videocassette of it. The agreement here is that film people do not sell video rights to their movies until they are shown in all theatres.' (Interview, Kuang, 1986)

Other proposed remedies involved increasing the penalties for copyright violation, putting more Mandarin films on videocassette and generally producing a supply of legal videocassettes. At least

CMPC, Empire and Century were active in videocassette production in the 1980s. The largest was Empire Audio Visual Company, started in 1984 as a producer of slides and films, with cassette production commencing two years later. The company began making cassettes to supply its television station, CTS, with educational programmes, and the military with training tapes. Empire produces more than 500 videocassettes a year, at least 300 of which are exported to Southeast Asian markets. Many are reproductions of CTS shows. Empire has also imported 2,500 shows from Hong Kong's ATV, from which 4,000 to 10,000 copies are made for sale in video shops. Cantonese shows are translated into Mandarin by Empire and, because Hong Kong television uses PAL (Taiwan, NTSC), standard conversions must be made (Interview, Hu Joe-Yang, 1986). Century also has relationships with Hong Kong, reproducing shows from TVB telvision.

Genres and Themes of Films

Although most filmmakers agree that the 'new cinema' has provided an alternative to the traditional movie fare, they also point out that other types still dominate. But they do not always agree on which types are most popular. For example, Scholars Motion Pictures, in 1986, distributed five comedies (one of which was made by a new director), two mystery and two popular tragedies and one based on a contemporary novel and a political theme (Interview, Wang, 1986). The government CMPC had three categories of films, divided into commercial (six made in 1985), 'new cinema' (four) and governmental policy (two). Benny Chao of CMPC said the company, which regularly mixes the three types, realised that love stories replaced kung fu as the favourite commercial film theme. According to him, movie audiences are much younger now (15–25 years old) — older people choosing to watch television at home — and younger people, and the growing number of married women attending films alone, prefer love stories (Interview, Benny Chao, 1986).

A veteran director said the most popular genres are action and comedy, often combined. The day of the love story is over, according to him, and if made, they involve complicated plots, 'not ordinary love stories' (Interview, Liao, 1986).

Golden Harvest concentrates on producing 'contemporary drama', mostly based on novels (Interview, Lee Pai-Kwi, 1986), while Tom Son Motion Picture Company varies the types. For example, in 1986, Tom Son produced one film of the traditional type (*Woman of Wrath*), which included much violence as a woman plots to kill her husband; another based on a modern novel (called *Key of the Heart*), which bordered on soft pornography with the theme of incest; and a third, *Kung Fu Kids*, about the martial arts exploits of three children, aged five, nine and ten. The latter was a huge success as it was sold to hundreds of theatres in Japan, Hong Kong, Thailand and the Philippines (Interview, Wade, 1986). Actually, these Tom Son productions fit closely what were described as the two and-a-half themes of a decade before: martial arts, 90 per cent of whose contents were violence; romance, stories of 'disjointed love, with no content, and phantom characters', and made up of 'love, some singing, and the view of beautiful scenery and luxurious mansions'; and horror, which constituted the one-half theme. When comedies became popular in the late 1970s, this categorisation of popular film types was revised to 'fists, pillows, and now talk' (*Yearbook* 1978: 13).

Popular themes of the crop of new directors of the late 1980s included prostitution, suicide, infidelity, burdens of material success, student life, mainland China, 'real life of small people', transition from 'agrarian to urban life, family and social issues' (Interview, Wan Jen, 1986; also, Specter 1983: 82; Malcolm 1983: 81). Most productions of 'new cinema' directors are based not on original screenplays, but rather on published literary works, usually of the 'nativist' school.

Various filmmakers have described what 'new cinema' directors are attempting. Chen Yao-Chi said they wanted to capture the 'melancholy of the past and the uncertainty of the future', partly because of their own personal stages. He said they were young directors in their late twenties and early thirties who had seen Taiwan go through some quick development, from a 'sleepy island' to a highly industrialised nation. The problems such rapid development creates (environmental, urban life pressure) and the nerve-wracking adaptation process make up the themes of a number of films (Interview, Chen Yao-Chi, 1986).

'New cinema' director Wan Jen said he and his colleagues chose themes of the recent past reflecting common people's thoughts and feelings and the transition from agrarian to urban life. He said the 'shadows of the directors' could be seen in the films—their growing up in the 1960s.

The works of Hou Hsiao-Hsien and Yang De-Chang (Edward Yang) epitomise many of these characteristics. Hou's works have been described as 'bittersweet searches into times past, relying heavily on his own experiences of growing up in a small town' (Buruma 1987: 40). His interest for film having developed while with a film unit in the military, Hou directed his first work, *Cute Girl*, in 1980. Two years later, he and Chen Kun-Hou made *Green, Green Grass of Home*, a story about a teacher who comes to a country elementary school and becomes deeply involved in his pupils' lives.

Hou's *The Sandwich Man* carried a strong political message, questioning capitalism and foreign involvements in Taiwan. The film showed the poverty and humiliation of Taiwan's poorer classes in a manner that brought government censors to their feet (Chang,

1988: 6). *All the Youthful Days* is about a group of restless youths on a one-day trip from their village to the big city of Kaohsiung. The film, like many of this type, weaves together an almost plotless series of events: 'The listlessness and violence of village life, the aimless bravado of boys on an adventure, and the uncertain quality of human relations' (*Asiaweek* 1984: 49).

Growing up in a small town is the theme of *A Time to Live, a Time to Die* (1985), which depicts three generations of Chinese and how they survived when they migrated to Taiwan (see Tobias 1987a). Other films of Hou include *Summer at Grandpa's*, a 1984 story about Tung Tung and his sister, which captures the innocence of youth as they try to understand the complexities of adult life; *Daughter of the Nile*, a 1987 portrayal of a young girl 'trapped in the materialistic world that had smothered the innocence he knew as a youth' (Chang 1986: 6), and *Dust in the Wind* (1987), a controversial film that showed divisions in Taiwan's society, as it told about a boy who lost his girlfriend when he was drafted into the military.

Yang De-Chang's directorial début was the second segment of *In Our Time*, the trend-setting quartet of 'new cinema' works released together in 1982 by CMPC. His first full-length feature, *That Day on the Beach* (1983), deals with the expectations of the upper-middle-class. Told in flashbacks by two friends reunited after 13 years, the story mirrors life—and not orthodox film—in that solutions are not provided for problems encountered. Yang showed the alienation in the modern city, the split of family ties and the great costs that come with growth and material wealth (see Specter 1983: 82).

In 1985, Yang made *Taipei Story*, the portrayal of a baseball player whose marriage and career are failing as he reaches mid-life. It was a financial flop. The next year, he came back with *The Terrorisers*, a box-office success (as was *That Day on the Beach*, which also showed the harshness of urban life). The story concerns an office worker married to a successful novelist, who, when his marriage fails, shoots his wife and her lover (see *Variety* 1987b: 521; Li 1987: 97).

Among other 'new cinema' filmmakers, the works of Chen Kun-Hou, Hsiao Yeh and Wan Jen stand out. Chen's work, as previously indicated, spans a generation; his hit in 'new cinema' was *Growing Up*, the trouble-plagued story of 'Little Bi', an illegitimate child treated severely by his mother, who has big dreams for him, and kindly by his father. Hsiao Yeh, mainly a scriptwriter, was the planner of CMPC's pioneer work with 'new cinema', of which he said, 'no one could believe CMPC supported "new cinema" because all of these films are against certain social conditions or government policy.' Initially, it was not an easy manoeuvre to get the CMPC interested in 'new cinema', but Hsaio believed the time for the movement had come:

'Our generation was reaching the age of 30 or more at a time when the society was becoming more open, mature and affluent. The market for film was very poor so we had to change. The tendency was for all things to change in directing. New directors, trained abroad in the US, came back with more open minds. Before the 1970s, it was difficult for them to go abroad.' (Interview, Hsiao, 1986)

Wan Jen's first job as director was on the four-segment *In Our Time*, after returning from more than three years of film study in the US. He also collaborated on *The Sandwich Man* and directed *Ah Fei* and *Super Citizen*. Released in 1984, *Ah Fei* tells the story of a little girl who watches her mother move from a subservient position in a male-dominated family to one that represented a 'modernised American style'. During the span of years, the family also progressed from a rural village to an urban shanty town to a middle-class flat (Interview, Wan, 1986).

By 1987, 'new cinema' directors and their type of film were on the wane. Edward Yang had gone to Hong Kong to direct a picture for a company there, while others made advertising films, television or dropped out of the industry (Li 1987: 97).

No doubt by the late 1980s, some film people believed that 'new cinema' was, or should be, changing. Director Wan Jen already made the changes by the mid-1980s, concentrating on present problems which are more realistic, more audience-oriented (audiences were tiring of films about the past) and less expensive (pictures of the past require automobiles and settings of those periods) (Interview, Wan, 1986).

Film critic Lan Tsu-Wei said originally these directors, given a choice to concentrate on creating their distinctive styles or satisfy an audience, would choose the former. But now, he continued, 'they care about both, knowing they have to make good at the box office. Two or three young directors have had no pictures to make in two years because earlier they failed at the box office.' Lan believed new directors had to modify their philosophies to survive with audiences. 'People here view movies as entertainment, not as a lesson,' he said, adding, 'the young directors think their mission is to impart their philosophies to audiences, and the audiences do not like this.' (Interview, Lan, 1986) Another 'new cinema' director, Lee Daw-Ming, was rather sharp in his analysis:

'We generally agree that "new cinema" only represents an alternative way of making films. It did not change audience behaviour or the market. It did not change anything. Most new films were flops at the box office. New directors are not making films audiences want to see. Films usually do not influence society, and Taiwan is no exception.' (Interview, Lee Daw-Ming, 1986)

A veteran director, who claimed to have been swept aside by the 'new cinema' directors, criticised them for their sameness. He thought there needed to be a balance of old and new directors and styles; 'before, the films were too commercial, now they are too arty for a country without an art theatre.'[9] (Interview, Chen Yao-Chi, 1986)

Thematic sameness is a characteristic of all of Taiwan's film industry, not isolated to 'new cinema' directors. Whereas in the past, audiences flocked to theatres to see their favourite stars perform the same roles in the same type of movie with different titles, this is less apt to happen now because of the changing tastes of a more affluent audience and the choice of many other types of entertainment. Besides home video, game parlours, more restaurants and parks and more mobility with the growth of the automobile industry, improved television fare is hurting the movie industry. Shows are more polished in format and content (in fact, as already mentioned, many new directors worked first with television and some have returned to the medium). This and the screening of old Mandarin films keep some potential film-goers at home.

Recognising that thematic sameness is not unique to Taiwan, one director claimed the problem was compounded on a small island where the frequency of a theme is more noticeable. Stating that four out of five films showing at any given time were the same, Chen Yao-Chi said the tendency was to 'kill' audience tastes for an overworked theme (Interview, Chen Yao-Chi, 1986). A Government Information Office head added that what usually happened was that a quality production on a particular theme came out, followed by a number of poor-quality imitators (Interview, Liu, 1986).

Professionalism
The lack of training addressed by actress Hu Ying Mon, or the need for better equipment which director Chen Kun-Hou lamented, are on the agendas of the various organisations dealing with Taiwan films. So are problems of creating higher-quality movies, finding overseas markets, preserving and exhibiting old Mandarin films and combating piracy.

Taiwan does not have a shortage of film organisations to deal with such problems. A futile attempt to form the Motion Picture Production Association of the Republic of China in 1962 led to the establishment the following year of the Taiwan Provincial Motion Picture Association (TPMPA) which, along with the Motion Picture Association of Taiwan (1974), Movie and Drama Association

(1974) and its Actors Branch (1976) and Taipei Actors Association (*Yearbook* 1987: 69, 80, 82), enhanced professionalism in the industry.

In the 1980s, a newly created foundation for the Development of the Motion Picture Industry (1978) and the Motion Picture Association of Taiwan (MPAT) spearheaded numerous efforts to improve filmmaking.

The foundation, which functions similarly to a co-operative, is composed of MPAT personnel, owners of motion picture companies and distributors. Financing is provided from money collected in the awarding of foreign film quotas. In its early days, the foundation was supported by the Government Information Office, but, except for the director-general serving as head of the foundation, other connections have ceased (Interview, Hsu, 1986). Among its many activities, the foundation sponsors the Film Library, provides scholarships and encourages experimental films through its Golden Cluster Awards, and gives monetary grants to young directors.

Affiliated with the foundation, the Film Library attempts to provide those interested in film with a gathering place where seminars are held, featuring directors who explain their work. Additionally, the library publishes the bimonthly *Film Review*, a cinema yearbook and eight or nine other books a year. Three weeks out of every month, the library provides the public with foreign films, complete with printed introductory notes (Interview, Hsu, 1986).

Probably the Film Library's most visible activity is sponsorship of the Golden Horse International Film Festival since its inception in 1980. Meant to educate the public and local filmmakers about quality movies, the festival exhibits in two Taipeil theatres about 120 entries from around the world (see Benedicto 1987).

The Motion Picture Association of Taiwan, in existence for nearly 40 years, is not just the forerunner of most film associations, but the largest with 800 members. Functioning similarly to a union, alongside the production, exhibition and acting unions, MPAT has lobbied on behalf of distributors regarding foreign film quotas and, more recently, has worked strenuously to combat piracy and to liberalise censorship laws. Among other activities, MPAT holds training sessions for directors and symposia on Mandarin and Western movies, and arbitrates in disputes between distributors and exhibitors concerning splits of box-office revenues. MPAT's head said the organisation has more power in arbitration than any other union, including that of the exhibitors (Interview, H.S. Chou, 1986).

Insufficient training of movie personnel at all levels continued to be a problem in the late 1980s. Some universities[10] and film organisations offered courses, but filmmakers saw these as only beginnings. CMPC, for example, trains screenwriters and actors, the latter in six-month courses but, according to one producer, more training is needed:

> 'The government has to set up a better training school for movie people. In Taiwan, we have people deeply dedicated to trades such as textiles, because they received the correct training. It is a pity the government has not done this for film. You can't expect immediate results. It's like you plant a tree and wait ten to 20 years to get shade. The government has to nurture such a school.'
> (Interview, Chou Ling-Kong, 1986)

Because film personnel usually work free-lance, film companies hesitate to invest much in training. The demise of the studio system, where actors and directors were under contract with a company, and obliged to make three or four pictures a year, had much to do with this. As one director said,

> 'Now a company makes a new face famous and, after a year, it is hard to control him or her. The CMPC trains people but they are not required to have a contract with that studio afterwards.'
> (Interview, Liao, 1986)

AFTERWORD

Concerns about the quality of film production plagued the industry in 1988–9. At its annual awards show in 1988, Taiwan was able to capture only one of the 14 feature film 'Golden Horse' statues. Hong Kong movies carried away the rest (Liu 1988: 6). In the same year, most film companies failed to make a profit.

The executive producer of CMPC, Liu Yi, said Taiwan's industry was affected by financial difficulties, cut-throat competition with Hong Kong and a lack of technical expertise. To counter the problems, the CMPC continued its attempts to tap the European market by exhibiting at international film festivals (Benedicto 1988a), by expanding its own festival (Benedicto 1988b: 6), and by bringing in new talent, such as Lee Daw-Ming, Peter Wang, Richard Chen and Hou Ping. Of course, more veteran directors, such as Yang De-Chang, remained active (Benedicto 1988c).

Video was as strong as ever. MTV video centres were especially popular. More than 1,000 in number, they offered a wide variety of films, state-of-the-art video equipment and privacy. In Taiwan, MTV stands for 'Movies on TV', not 'Music Television'. Controversy surrounded the centres because many did not obtain licences to compete with movie theatres, some used pirated films and all allowed teenagers privacy, which represented a threat to traditional values. US movie-makers voiced complaints that the clubs showed copyrighted films that violated laws on 'public viewing' (Liu and Chow 1988: 6).

The Taiwan government cracked down on unlicensed MTV operators as a government task force enforced May 1988 regulations throughout late 1988 and early 1989.

Worried about US pressure on the Taiwan government for tougher copyright laws, 600 videocassette shop operators demonstrated in front of the American Institute (the US liaison in Taiwan) on 18 January 1989. The operators thought the US might demand that copyright protection of American movies be extended from the current 1975 to 1955.

NOTES

1   China Movie Studio grew out of the Propaganda Battalion of Nanking in 1933. It was moved to the National Military Council in 1937, and then to Taiwan in 1949, where it found a home in the Ministry of National Defense (*Yearbook* 1978: 141).

2   This was not the first film produced in Taiwan. Tang (1975, p. 50) said that, earlier, Taiwan Film Studio made *Taiwan of Today*. Of course, there were the Japanese-made films of World War II.

3   Described by Chen Kun-Hou (Interview, 1986) as a studio system where 'you start with an idea, go into committee, hire writers, build and design sets, etc. The studio does everything. Economics forced the style of direction to change. With faster and smaller cameras, one can shoot on location more easily and it is more natural.

4   These problems were already manifested in the late 1970s. A Mandarin picture exported to Thailand in 1978, cost US $5,000 import tax a copy and three to five copies were necessary. Indonesia's sole importer of Mandarin films was Sudan Company; because Sudan had a monopoly, whatever it offered, Taiwan producers were obliged to accept. The Indonesian quota on imported films also dwindled from 100 in 1976 to 40 two years later. Singapore had an import tax of 40 per cent and, in Malaysia, the policy was that for every foreign film brought in, importers had to buy two Malaysian ones. Other countries had limits on the number of Mandarin films allowed in each year; South Korea permitted three; the Philippines, two.

With the overthrow of the 'Gang of Four', China began producing quality pictures which cut into Taiwan's market. Political feuds exacerbated the situation. Taiwan films' propagandistic treatments of China often meant they could not be seen in Hong Kong.

5   For example, Golden Harvest owns ten theatres in Taiwan, distributes 30 Hong Kong films and produces three Taiwanese films a year.

6   To attract audiences back to movies, there have been proposals to improve the theatres. One move has been to build more smaller theatres as part of high-rise apartment complexes. The then director-general of Government Information Office said interior designs of theatres must be improved to make going to a movie a 'social event'. He proposed that theatres should be divided for multiple viewings — e.g. 'one picture for

parents, another for children, still another for grandparents, etc.' (Interview, Chang, 1986).

7   Advertising costs normally take US $50,000 of a picture distributor's budget. One distributor said half of the advertising money goes to television commercials, a quarter to newspaper advertisements and the rest to huge marquees (Interview, Tchii, 1986). A director said 'new cinema' films spent a quarter of their entire budgets (as much as NT $2 million) on television commercials because of that medium's nation-wide appeal (Interview, Wan, 1986). In addition to more formal advertising techniques, film people use personal touches, such as giving shopkeepers a couple of free theatre tickets for displaying a movie poster.

8   Taiwanese laws allow a distributor to own only two theatres in cities such as Kaohsiung and Taichung, and one in other cities outside Taipei.

9   An art theatre, Art House Film Theatre, opened in the late 1980s. CMPC turned over part of its hall to the theatre; the film library of the Film Development Foundation brought in high quality films for screening.

10   Among some of these at the advent of the 1980s were the Cinema and Drama Department, created in 1957 at the Political College; the Movie and Drama Section (1972) of the College of Chinese Culture; the Movie Production Department (1966) of the World College of Journalism and the Movie and Drama Section (late 1950s) of the National Junior College of Arts.

4

HONG KONG

INTRODUCTION

I f non-Asians give a fleeting thought to Hong Kong as a film centre, kung fu and Bruce Lee might come to mind. Nothing more.

But, Hong Kong is much more, representing a rich cinematic tradition that has blended all genres, including a few particularly attached to this part of the world, the languages of Cantonese and Mandarin and communist and capitalist ideologies. At various times, the Crown Colony has boasted more than 300 features a year, making it one of the world's top producers, and sported Asia's largest studio complex, Movie Town. Very few places on the globe have such frequent theatre attendance, or a film event as prestigious as the Hong Kong International Film Festival.

The small enclave also represents in a microcosm some of the dilemmas of film everywhere—controlling outside investment by conglomerates, the fight for survival by 'new directors', top-heavy wage scales favouring superstars and some competition from other leisure-time activities. Surprisingly, in an entertainment capital such as Hong Kong, film still retains the position of being most popular. Also, videocassettes have not had the immediate impact in Hong Kong that they have had elsewhere where film attendances have been seriously raided.

HISTORICAL BACKGROUND

American theatre owner Benjamin Polaski is generally credited with producing the first film in Hong Kong. *To Steal a Roasted Duck*, directed by Liang Shaobo and produced by Polaski's Asia Film Company, was made in 1909, as was another Polaski movie, *Redressment of Justice by a Porcelain Pot*[1].

By 1913, an acquaintance of Polaski, Li Min Wei[2], had sought his help in making *Chuang Tsu Tests His Wife*; Tilden (1975, p. 15) claimed they established the Sino-American Film Company together. Short of money, Li apparently did not produce feature movies until a decade later, when he, his brother and cousin established Min-Xin (New People) Film Company.

For about ten years, Li helped the Kuomintang political party, producing documentaries which he called 'film to save the nation'. This service cost him, for when he sought permission to build a Hong Kong studio, the British refused on the grounds it might upset the war lord who ruled Hong Kong. Instead, Li built a studio in Canton and commuted to Hong Kong to do outside scenes. Li's *Rouge* in 1923 was considered the first totally produced, funded and acted theatrical film made by a Hong Kong citizen (Tilden 1975: 21).

Film historians are not sure of developments between 1925 and 1931, although they know some Shanghai studios had offices and production facilities in Hong Kong. In 1930, Lian-Hau Film Company set up its main office in Hong Kong and, two years later, made movies through its Number Three Studio. Others followed, especially after the commencement of Japanese militarist activities. Between 1932 and 1936, approximately 100 films were produced in Hong Kong by about 50 companies, establishing the territory as the centre for Cantonese movies (Jarvie 1977: 9). The introduction of sound in the pre-war era and the many political manifestations in China (e.g. Communist–Kuomintang rivalry and Japanese occupation) helped to encourage Hong Kong's role as a film producer.

At the outbreak of war with Japan in 1937, the second wave of film refugees flooded into Hong Kong from Shanghai. This wave, more political and more Mandarin-oriented, saw film as a way to fight the Japanese. Another reason filmmakers left China in 1937 was the Kuomintang decree that movies were to be in Mandarin. Thus, Cantonese producers moved to Hong Kong, in the process benefiting from financial and trading advantages. Among these were: raw film being freely importable, studio land being cheap and taxes, regulations and licences being minimal (Armes 1987: 158).

The number of Cantonese films made in Hong Kong increased dramatically to 80 in 1940; overall, to 400 between 1933 and 1941, or 44 a year. Many of these carried patriotic, anti-Japanese-invasion messages, especially after a film association showed its displeasure with Hong Kong film quality, saying it weakened the spirit of resistance by not promoting national identity.

Some production occurred during the Japanese occupation, which Jarvie (1977, p. 14) found amazing since electrical power, raw stock and equipment were scarce. The Japanese set up an organisation to regulate film, and did so by controlling stock and banning anti-Japanese movies. The South China Co-operative

Society controlled, amalgamated and reorganised film personnel and facilities; 40 companies (including one Japanese) registered with the society. In June 1942, the Japanese instituted seven censorship regulations; by 1943, 27 theatres reopened and showed 137 new pictures, mostly Japanese and Chinese, the latter made by Kinkuan Picture Corporation in Shanghai (Tilden 1975: 60).

By the end of 1945, at least a dozen companies re-entered the film business. The Shaws, who had exhibited and produced films since the mid-1920s, dug up jewels they had hidden from the Japanese and re-established their Tien Yat (Tan Yee) Studio. One of the brothers, Run Run, described the treasure:

'The pearls were a little brown, the watches rusty, the bank notes mildewed, but the gold was nice and yellow. The diamonds, sapphires and emeralds were in excellent form. We were still rich.' (Block 1974: 161)

A group of Szechuan capitalists joined Hong Kong's Chiang Pai Yin and Yien Yue Hsiang in 1946 to form another well-financed company, Great China Motion Picture Company (Dazhonghua). Even though it produced highly commercialised films, Great China was not very successful with its 34 features and, before the end of the decade, was no longer operating in Hong Kong. Other post-war companies were Sze Tak Kwok Ka, Grandview, Kwon Ming, Rainbow, Yiu Kui and Nan Luen, among others.

The environment they appeared in was hostile as production costs were five to seven times higher than before the war; competition was keen as still another wave of film refugees came to Hong Kong, seeking to escape Kuomintang censorship in China, and confusion and uncertainty marked the industry. For one thing, potential markets had not yet crystallised, as the new governments of Southeast Asia had not settled their censorship policies and in China, the battle between the Communists and Kuomintang kept everything uncertain.

The themes and quality of their films were criticised as 'crude', based on superstitions and nonsensical folk-tales; 'vulgar and coarsely made', and sentimental in thought and content[3]. Some pictures were made in three to seven days and, according to Jarvie (1977, p. 20–1):

'Legend has it that the "directors" of such pictures simply saw to it that the camera was pointing in the right direction, called for action, then wandered off for a bowl of noodles. Ten minutes later, as the film in the camera was running out he [sic] would return, and call "Cut. Print."'

Financing for many post-war films came from abroad. Money would be raised in Singapore by proposing a cast and sometimes a story, and filming would start while the remaining funds were found elsewhere. Distribution and exhibition faced peculiar circumstances. Because of a shortage of prints, the distributor divided a film into four of five reels and had a film messenger take them from theatre to theatre where screening times were staggered. The standard at the box office was two admissions for the price of one until 1961, when the Government's Entertainment Licensing Authority outlawed the practice. The theatre-goer was never treated so well, receiving for 10 cents a programme with synopsis, stills, lyrics, movie gossip, gifts of soft drinks, sweets and cosmetics.

One writer characterised the period 1948–52 as being made up of four movements which stimulated production, increased the intellectual calibre of film workers and advanced concepts of labour relations in filmmaking. Initially, in a unification period, refugee filmmakers entered Hong Kong, bringing with them democratic ideas. They helped to start the Film Director's Guild, which aimed at improving scripts and the roles of scriptwriters and directors and stimulating a healthier atmosphere for the arts.

A clean-up campaign of 1949 attacked reactionary elements in film; film workers declared they would not participate in films that were not in Hong Kong's best interests. By instilling a non-conformist spirit in film personnel, the campaign became the precursor of a film collectivisation movement in the 1950s. A film co-operative (Fifties Film Company) and a partnership company (Tai Kwong Ming Film Company) were established; companies set up art committees to offset the strong pressure of management and workers established their own guidelines.

The fourth movement, 'new democratic enlightenment', was meant to reform the personal and professional lives of filmmakers. It prescribed abstinence from the vices of giving banquets, sending gifts, excessive drinking and gambling, and promoted the virtues of leading a simple, honest life and being punctual (Lin 1979: 18–20).

Perhaps because of these movements, the film industry witnessed its most prosperous period in the 1950s and 1960s. Production techniques changed; for example, between 1948 and 1957, different visual representations, such as deep focus, asymmetrical framing, medium-long shots and full-stage shots, were used (Lin 1979: 15).

The prosperity of the 1950s–60s meant many new production companies joined an already long list, and average production shot up to 200 a year, peaking at 311 in 1956–7 and 303 in 1961–2. About 4,500 films were made in this period, during most of which, until 1966, there was no great division between Mandarin and Cantonese movies, to the benefit of the latter. However, with the introduction of a new style of swordplay to appeal to a modern society, the more traditional Cantonese film did not adapt quickly enough and disappeared (Lin 1979: 15). Cantonese films are peculiar to Hong Kong by nature of their dialect and limited marketability, and are not even exportable to all of Kwantung Province.

Melodramas remained popular during this golden age, many revolving around plots that glamorised sacrifices made for the preservation of familial order (including women becoming prostitutes to keep families together). Every Mandarin film needed many songs, even placed at inappropriate times and replacing dialogue, partly because many Mandarin actresses could sing and producers wished to exploit this talent. Using music in film emanated from the first Chinese sound movie, *Sing Song Girl, Red Peony* (1931); the tradition has been explained as a way of dealing with China's chaotic social and political situations. Describing the insertion of songs into movies in the 1950s, one critic wrote:

'The plot would develop, dialogue would be exchanged in colloquial manner. Suddenly, the mood would change dramatically, emotions would flare, music would swell in the background, and the characters would break out in song!' (Wong 1979: 30)

Politics definitely played a role in film in the early 1950s, with companies oriented to rightist or leftist ideologies. The influx of film refugees after World War II was predominantly rightist, but a number of left-wing companies also sprang up, among them Tai Kwong Ming, Nan Kuen, Tai Kuang, Wen San and Nan Kwok (Southern). A major achievement of the leftists was the infiltration and take-over of Great Wall Films, a co-operative formed by Chang Shin-Kuan and Joseph Sunn.

In May 1950, the Hong Kong government, concerned about politicisation in film, called producers together and asked them not to make movies that caused disturbances. About the same time, 82 stars, believing the communist presence was all-pervasive, issued a manifesto pledging to live a 'Spartan way of life' and to refrain from making movies which contained 'poison'. Despite these concerns, what was baffling, as Jarvie (1977, p. 32) found, was the 'co-existence of capitalist backers, communist film people, neutral film people, propaganda films and commercial films all within the same company'.

To be sure, there were some dedicated Communists abroad in Hong Kong under party instructions, but most film people's concern was staying solvent, not promoting an ideology, and they were willing to take up whichever banner was necessary to stay in business. Eventually, the left's own propaganda and infiltration tactics and the United States' polarisation efforts in Asia had detrimental effects upon producing leftist films. The anti-communist companies Shaw and Cathay flourished with their extensive distribution-exhibition circuit, forcing leftist films to develop their own group of theatres. Although leftist films of Fiftieth Year Film Company and Feng Huang (Phoenix) Motion Picture Company continued to appear, by the 1960s, they were overtaken at the box office by Shaw and Cathay comedies, musicals and romances.

Hong Kong cinema since World War II owes much to pioneers such as Joseph Sunn, Lee Tsu Yung, Chang Shin-Kuan, Loke Wan Tho, Run Run Shaw and Raymond Chow.

Sunn established Grand View Film Company in 1933 and produced the first locally made Cantonese movie, *Song of Yesterday*. After the war, he joined Chang in creating Great Wall Films.

Chang Shin-Kuan, active in Shanghai cinema since 1924, had a huge role in post-war Hong Kong films. During the war, he managed a film company for the Japanese and in 1946, established Far East Film Company in Hong Kong and then Great Wall Films (Tilden 1975: 72). After the latter was infiltrated by leftists, Chang was forced out. He then formed New Hsin Hwa Company (Jarvie 1977: 27).

Chang apparently persuaded wealthy Shanghai businessman, Lee Tsu Yung, to enter films, after which the two started Yung Hwa Company, known for its sophisticated techniques and good equipment. Chang and Lee did not work together for long. Yung Hwa, dogged by back luck, including a fire and many financial woes, survived because the hard-working Lee was not easily dissuaded. With an eye on Western markets, he continued to produce films that were skilfully edited at a time when this was not the norm. Most filmmakers tried to save film by doing minimal editing. By 1953–4, Yung Hwa was increasingly dominated by International Film Distribution Company, a branch of the Cathay Organisation, which provided loans and other financial support (Tilden 1975: 96).

International Film Distribution was established in 1951 to supply films to the growing number of Cathay theatres in Southeast Asia and Hong Kong. Behind its creation, and that of production houses Cathay Film Production Company (1953) and Keris (1951), was Loke Wan Tho. A man of many interests, Loke set up theatres in Kuala Lumpur and Singapore as early as 1935. After the war, these theatres formed the nucleus of the Cathay Organisation. As the group expanded, Loke realised his need for a source of films and went into production in Hong Kong (Jarvie 1977: 35, 37). The first Cathay film was in 1956; although the company eventually made 20 a year, it found competing with Shaw Brothers difficult in the 1960s.

No name has loomed larger in the Hong Kong and Southeast Asia film industry than that of Run Run Shaw. The company he eventually controlled was dominant in all aspects of film until 1986, when it moved out of production[4]. Run Run and his three brothers, part of a wealthy Shanghainese textile manufacturing family, became involved in cinema in the mid-1920s. The eldest brother, Chien Yung, a lawyer, wrote a play for a theatre the family owned, after which, he decided to make a movie, *A Man Came to the World and He Made Good* (1925). From there, the Shaws set up their own company, Tan Yee, which, in the late 1920s, went its own way when six large Shanghai production companies amalgamated. Tan Yee hoped to tap the overseas market.

The family name had been Shiao, but the brothers changed it when their father showed his disapproval of their new venture. They also changed their first names; Chien Yung became Run Ji; Yee Foo, Run Run; Jen Mei, Runme; and Chuen Yan, Runde. Before World War II, two of the brothers, Run Run and Runme, worked from Singapore, where they bought theatres to exhibit films produced by Runde. The latter was dispatched to Hong Kong in 1934 to start a branch of Tan Yee.

Their success was phenomenal. By 1939, the Shaws' empire included at least 110 theatres, nine amusement parks and legitimate theatres in Malaya, Singapore, Thailand, Borneo, Java and Thailand (Sun 1982: 41). During the Japanese control of Southeast Asia, Shaw theatres were confiscated and Run Run was imprisoned on charges of subversion. But after the war they were back in business at full strength, thanks to the hoard of jewels Run Run had hidden. They reopened with *Objective, Burma!*, went to Hollywood where they bought out entire film libraries and generally rebuilt the business (Weber 1986: 39).

Run Run's relocation to Hong Kong in 1958 has been explained variously. One source said the film magnate left Singapore because of high taxes and a desire to produce more movies, believing he could do this better in Hong Kong where capital is sacred (Weber 1986: 39). Jarvie (1977, p. 45) gave another version, claiming Run Run was asked to take over as managing director of Shaw and Sons from Runde, who was to retire. According to Jarvie, a split occurred in the family operations when Runde did not retire but, instead, established Shaw Brothers in December 1958, including his son and brothers, Run Run and Runme, in the operation.[5]

The ambitious Run Run did not waste his time in Hong Kong. He drew up plans for new studios, established an acting school, imported technicians from Japan, the US and Europe to instruct his crew, bought modern equipment and built new theatres. He promised 35 movies a year as he copied Hollywood's big studio system. Everyone at the Shaw studio was contracted for eight years, starting at US $200 a month plus room and board, to produce more films for the ever-growing number of Shaw theatres (about 400 at one time) (Weber 1986: 39).

By 1961, the new studios were completed in what became known as Movie Town, a 46-acre spread that enclosed ten studios,

16 permanent outdoor sets, three dubbing studios, many film-processing labs and dormitory and apartment space for staff. The self-contained unit kept 1,500 actors/actresses under contract, as well as 2,000 other staff; maintained its own drama school of 120 students; published periodicals (e.g. *Hong Kong Movie News*) that boosted Shaw stars; and used a wardrobe of 80,000 costumes of all dynasties (Dadameah 1972: 13).

In its heyday, Shaw studios worked around the clock in three eight-hour shifts, producing an average 40 films a year on a budget of HK $2.5 million each (at US $1 equal to HK $4 or 5). Most of the more than 1,000 films Shaw produced were low budget, formulaic musicals and melodramas, although martial arts films became the staple diet later (Sun 1982: 42), especially in the late 1960s with *One Armed Swordsman*.

Even in the mid-1970s, Shaw Brothers was the largest of 24 Hong Kong companies, its net earnings in the Crown Colony alone being US $6.5 million. A sprawling company, Shaw had an elaborate distribution network of 143 theatres in Hong Kong, Taiwan, Southeast Asia, Canada and the US, owned hotels, banks, real estate and insurance firms and HK-TVB, one of the television channels (see O'Leary 1976: 8, Kulkarni 1976: 9). Its main competitor until the 1970s was Loke Wan Tho's Motion Picture and General Investment Company Ltd (a 1957 reorganisation of International Film Distribution); after that, its main rival was Golden Harvest.

But the situation changed in the 1980s. By 1984, production at Shaw was down to 30 films a year. It dwindled to six in 1986, before Shaw left film production claiming, at various times, that he had lost interest, that suitable scripts and available talent were in short supply or that more money could be made in television. Run Run Shaw was quoted in *Variety* (1986b, p. 443) as saying that if he continued feature film production, he would make HK $60 million annual profits; if he stopped production, his take from TV would be HK $120 million. In 1988, Shaw Brothers posted a 39.7 per cent increase in net profits to US $20.77 million, mostly from television (up 25 per cent in profits) and film distribution and exhibition.

A former employee provided Run Run with competition during his last 16 years of film production. Raymond Chow, a former newspaperman, joined Shaw Brothers in 1958 and quickly became publicity manager and then head of production for a decade. In 1970, believing other companies would cut production with the proliferation of television, Chow started his own company, Golden Harvest, to stockpile movies. In its first year, the company made eight films; it also acquired theatres in Hong Kong and Taiwan and negotiated with Cathay to use its Malaysia/Singapore network.

Chow had a highly profitable association with a Hollywood bit actor named Bruce Lee, which yielded three and-a-half films, international acclaim through the kung fu genre and some of the colony's first co-productions. The Lee film, *Enter the Dragon*, was made with Warner; it grossed US $100 million in the United States alone (Sun 1982: 40). Lee died in 1973, but Chow continued to court the international and kung fu markets. In 1980, he made *Battle Creek Brawl*, his first film with another kung fu star, Jackie Chan. The following year, *Cannonball Run* was released for the international market, starring Chan and a group of US actors, including Burt Reynolds. Chow did not think of the home market first, but overseas distribution. For example, in 1982, when Golden Harvest made 20 pictures, only 10 per cent of its budget went to Hong Kong-produced Chinese movies (Sun 1982: 40).

Throughout the 1970s, Golden Harvest, along with Shaw Brothers, produced about a third of all Hong Kong films. Golden Harvest's growth was mind-boggling. After only five years, the company had the largest circuit of Hong Kong theatres (24), exhibited in 500 other theatres of Japan and Southeast Asia and was part of a 24-company conglomerate (Marchant 1976: viii). In 1978, Golden Harvest acquired Cathay Films Ltd of London, a world-wide distributor.

The company was equally successful at the box office, having 70 per cent of the top films in the mid-1980s and the all-time, highest-grossing movie, *My Lucky Stars* (Pomery 1985: 27). Chow, learning from Shaw and Cathay, keeps studio overhead costs low, centralises his operation, prefers well-known, freelance artists over contracted ones and concentrates on action films which cut across boundaries.

Golden Harvest's entry into Hong Kong film was but one of the significant changes of the 1970s. Some of the familiar companies, such as Hua Da, Zhong Lian, Guang Yi, Cathay, Great Wall, Feng Huang and Xin Lian, either ceased or reduced operations, and the number of theatres and productions dropped. Especially hard-hit were Cantonese films which, by 1970, had already lost their popularity as only 35 were made. The next year, the number plunged to one, after which they ceased. One source said their demise resulted from their poor quality and competition from Cantonese-language television and Mandarin swordsman[6] movies (see Urban Council 1982). Cantonese films had a revival later on.

The 1970s brought more explicit portrayals of sex and violence to the Hong Kong screen; however, strict censorship kept these films from being as daring as US or European counterparts. Most followed the formula of a girl raped or sold into prostitution who avenges herself in the end.

Getting their starts during 1975–79 were 60 new directors (known as 'new wave') who fired new blood into film with their creative and individualistic efforts. Usually trained abroad, these young directors got their starts on the then three Hong Kong television stations, all of which were involved in doing network features. TVB's Film Unit attracted many talents, including Ann Hui and Patrick Tam, and RTHK's *Below the Lion Rock* series was the training ground for Allen Fong, Wong Chi and Lo Chi-Keung. The short-lived RTV made a number of productions between 1976 and 1978 which helped launch directors (Urban Council 1984: 115).

CONTEMPORARY SCENE

Production

Something right happened in the Hong Kong film industry in the 1980s, as a number of big-time investors challenged the production stranglehold held for years by Shaw and Golden Harvest. The new producers were characterised as having large amounts of capital and being backed by important financial institutions.

With the success of movies at home and internationally, they knew there was money to be made in production—lots of money. For example, in 1985, the turnover of the industry was about HK $1 billion (at HK $7 to US $1), when the average film cost HK $4 to 6 million to make (Garcia 1985: 7). Gross income from film continued to rise, to US $76 million in 1986 and US $96 million in 1987 (Chadha 1988: 31). Hong Kong's 5.6 million people each purchased an average of twelve tickets a year (*Asiaweek* 1988c: 48).

The complexion of the industry definitely changed. Between 1972 and 1981, 50 per cent of all film companies went out of business; often, they were replaced by upstart independents connected to conglomerates, with minimum or no film experience.

Typifying this trend was Dickson Poon, a multimillionaire who owns a chain of up-market jewellery stores and boutiques. With no previous experience, the 28-year-old Poon formed D and B Films in 1984 with a personal investment of HK $100 million. He acquired management rights to some Shaw theatres for his exhibition arena and had his sights on the home video market and overseas film distribution in Taiwan, Malaysia and Japan. In 1986, D and B made 15 movies and the following year, 33, from which it had an income of US $25 million. Within a couple years, D and B became one of the top three Hong Kong producers.

Other tycoons jumped into the lucrative business. In 1986, Deacon Chiu—owner of banks, a US hotel chain, Hong Kong theatre circuit and television network, among other interests—started Far East Motion Picture Development Ltd. Far East, which owned 17 theatres, replaced Bang Bang Motion Pictures and Verdull Ltd, both part of the Chiu chain. Before becoming a Chiu property, Bang Bang was already part of a conglomerate, Bang Bang Fashion, a retail fashion clothing and accessories company which owned other stores, manufactured and distributed electronic games, distributed records and owned advertising interests (Pomery 1985: 29).

Fotocine Film Production Ltd is part of Fotocine Holding Group, with interests in colour printing and processing labs, an advertising agency, a screen advertising division and an institute of photography, while Century Films is a division of a diversified financing services group, Tetra Finance. Century's executives are predominantly bankers and managers. In 1986, Sil-Metropole, controller of many outfits trading with China, absorbed Southern Film Corporation which, for years, represented China's films internationally.

The two most profitable companies of the 1980s, Golden Harvest and Cinema City, are big-business based. The largest, Golden Harvest, which in 1987 alone had six of the ten most profitable movies and realised a US $41 million income, is a patchwork of no fewer than 35 companies around the world. Founder Raymond Chow and his partner Leonard Ho own a large part of the companies in the umbrella organisation, including Golden Harvest, Sin Kon International Ltd, Gala Film Distribution, Golden Princess Gala Film Company and Gala Theatres. Golden Harvest is also connected with Kowloon Developments, which has ties with Cinema City and owns Golden Princess Amusements, Lap Yan Films and Always Good Film Company (*Asiaweek* 1983b: 33). Over the years, many banks, including Bank of America, have underwritten Golden Harvest films.

A Golden Harvest vice-president, vowing the company was still owned by its originator, explained that all of its subsidiaries were in the movie industry and were formed to meet specific needs. 'It's easier to form a new company than to have departments as other producers do. For bookkeeping purposes, it's easier to operate this way,' he said (Interview, Chan, 1986). Among the subsidiaries are Golden Communications (world-wide distributor), Bo Ho Films (producer of specific types of films), Pan Asia Films (distributor of US films in Hong Kong), Golden Harvest Hong Kong and Golden Harvest International and Paragon Films and Golden Wave Productions (both in production).

Cinema City was founded in September 1950 by three filmmakers, Carl Mak, Dean Shek and Raymond Wong, who a year earlier had started Warriors Film Company. Mak, an actor, director and producer, had also formed Garbo Films in 1978. Wong began his career as a television scriptwriter, and Shek worked for Shaw and then became a free-lance director[7]. Lam (Interview, 1986) said these men's involvement was what made Cinema City different from Golden Harvest and Shaw, which, he said, was run by business men: 'The major forces behind this company were the three filmmakers who have a preference for creativity rather than making money.' He did grant that there was 'big money' backing Cinema City:

'Mak got to know Lawrence Louey of Kowloon Developments, a bus transport company. Mak had not been very successful in his filmmaking. When he got Louey's support, everything was okay.' (Interview, Lam, 1986)

Cinema City had backing for its first film from Golden Princess Amusements, itself a subsidiary of the investment consortium, Kowloon Developments, which owns Kowloon Motor Bus Company. After a year, Golden Princess formally acquired 51 per cent of Cinema City and, in 1981, became half owner of Golden Princess Gala Film Company, thus creating a relationship between the rival Cinema City and Golden Harvest (*Asiaweek* 1983b: 33).

Cinema City, like others mentioned above, has ready access to huge sums of capital, some of which it used in 1988 to launch a fourth cinema circuit. Its rise in the industry has been phenomenal; in 1987, Cinema City grossed US $30 million. Each year, its films, along with those of Golden Harvest, are the biggest money-makers. During 1981–83, the company released a total of 22 features, including the first of the *Aces Go Places* series, the initial three of which broke all-time box-office records in 1982, 1983 and 1984.

Reasons given for the instant success of companies such as Cinema City or D and B were as different as the individuals who provided them. Law (Interview, 1986) said it had to do with a shift of audience tastes, Shaw losing touch with the scene, and a studio such as Cinema City having a 'beautiful package within their films (setting, design, costumes, special effects) and beyond in publicity'. Chan (Interview, 1986) explained it as part of a recurring production trend syndrome—in the 1970s, the industry was dominated by major studios, then independents working on smaller budgets came in 1977–79, followed again by big studios with blockbusters and then small independents, some of which themselves became 'mini majors'. Tobias (Interview, 1986) felt a lot of companies similar to Shaw attained a certain height, after which they did not take chances. He explained: 'They provide the same pictures without knowing what the public wants.' On the other hand, Tobias said, new companies used production people aware of the public's desires.

In the late 1980s, about 30 companies were into production but only six were active, making most of the 100 or more films; the others made occasional features. The largest were Golden Harvest Cinema City and D and B, followed by Always Good, Seasonal and Sil-Metropole (Interview, Tobias, 1986). Golden Harvest produced about 20 local movies also designed for China and Southeast Asia, and two or three Hollywood pictures a year (Interview, Chan, 1986). Cinema City made ten to twelve, a fifth for the Taiwan market (Interview, Lam, 1986). On the other hand, Sil-Metropole, an amalgamation of Great Wall, Feng Huang and Xin Lian and owned from China, made six movies a year (Interview, Fong, 1986).

Budgets varied according to studio. Sil-Metropole, for example, allocated US $250,000 for Allen Fong's *Just Like Weather* in 1986. Fong said 10 per cent went to the cast, a low figure because he shoots with new talent, not being able to afford stars. Filming and processing made up a huge part of his expenses (Interview, Fong, 1986). At Cinema City, the budget for an average movie was US $500,000, about 30 per cent of which went to hiring a cast. Of course, movies with special effects and foreign actors, such as the *Aces Go Places* series, demanded larger budgets (Interview, Lam, 1986). *Aces Go Places III* cost more than US $3 million to make (Interview, Shi, 1986).

Cinema City owed some of its success to being willing to invest in big-budget movies such as *Aces Go Places*, a mixed genre (James Bond type with comedy) production. When *Aces Go Places* broke box-office records, the company's confidence shot up and it made a sequel. Soon, it was characteristic of the Hong Kong industry to produce big budget films, using a group of superstars. As Li Cheuk-To said:

> 'The industry is very imitative here. For a few years now, those who are successful use superstars and big budgets. This makes it harder for the small independents to compete; they can't afford the price. A recent big budget film lost money here and will have to depend on the foreign market. Maybe the audience is losing interest in these films.' (Interview, Li, 1986)

Because it thinks of itself as an industry trend-setter, Cinema City shells out large sums for overseas locations, stunts and foreign expertise. With much pride, a company official said, 'We send crews to New Zealand and elsewhere; we are the first to bring in foreign expertise to do stunts or makeup.' (Interview, Lam, 1986)

A disproportionate part of budgets has gone to a few superstars, especially those developed by Golden Harvest for its international market. Since the beginning of the 1970s, Golden Harvest has promoted local talent internationally, first Bruce Lee and later Jackie Chan. Initially, the studio was co-producer with US, Italian and Dutch companies but, by 1976, decided it had learned enough to make its own international movies. For the next decade, Golden Harvest produced 21 such films, joining US stars such as Burt Reynolds or Robert Mitchum with Chan to enhance the latter's marketability abroad.

Difficulties in doing these films are the competition with Hollywood majors and costs. A Golden Harvest vice-president said that because his company is not a Hollywood major, it has trouble getting the best scripts and talents. Golden Harvest's budget for stars in its US pictures is astronomical; of the US $16 million spent on

Cannonball Run, US $10 million went to stars (Interview, Chan, 1986).

Cinema City, which earlier hired one star at US $300,000 a picture, discontinued signing up superstars after its first three years in existence. 'When their contracts ended, they wanted higher fees as they had offers elsewhere,' Lam said 'We let them go, deciding to groom other stars.' (Interview, Lam, 1986) Chan (Interview, 1986) said stars now signed per picture deals, not long-term contracts:

> 'They now say "I have this picture. Who wants it?" You have to bid for their talent. I think in the future, the stars will group together and we'll have to bid more money because we're a major studio.'

Most new production companies do not have their own studios. This does not create problems as almost all filming is done outside, on location. The old studios are used to shoot commercials (Interview, Fong, 1986).

As gleaned from the above, big production companies (especially Golden Harveset) have made strenuous efforts to break into the international market. David Chan of Golden Harvest gave a pragmatic reason for this trend:

> 'Breaking into the international market with Chinese films that can be released everywhere, gives producers the potential to move their companies to more politically stable places like Canada and the US [especially after 1997]. I am not sure they can succeed as Hong Kong pictures are so different from those of Western countries.' (Interview, Chan, 1986)

Chan (Interview, 1986) predicted that commercial pictures would use more foreign talent—'a Japanese singer, an American actor'—to obtain foreign video and cable distribution of their works. Tobias (Interview, 1986) acknowledged that Hong Kong filmmakers were increasingly shooting scenes abroad but not just to give their films international appeal. He said local audiences were tired of Hong Kong locations and 'loved to see their stars in other places; the "yuppie" influence here makes them love those things Continental.'

Distribution and Exhibition
Distribution of Hong Kong films abroad is taken seriously for the above reasons and the limited market of the Crown Colony itself.

Producers bank on films making as much in Taiwan, Singapore, Malaysia and Western Chinatowns as they do in Hong Kong. But, parts of these markets have been lost as people turn to videocassettes. Hong Kong movies have become more difficult to distribute abroad because of changing genres. When kung fu was the rage, distributors merely had the films dubbed into other languages. But comedies and films about Hong Kong contemporary life are in now, and they do not export well[8]. Also, Hong Kong distributors find it difficult to satisfy the ideologically split Chinese markets of Taiwan and China. For example, the Taiwan government routinely bars any film made by a director who also makes pictures for China. (Some directors get around that by using pseudonyms.) (Schlender 1985: 7)

Filmmakers certainly recognise the importance of distributing Hong Kong features abroad, and they are aware of the afore-mentioned shifts in the distribution patterns and the needs for new strategies. Chan of Golden Harvest said:

'The problem we face is producing for Southeast Asia and Taiwan markets. The box-office guarantee is not safe; it's a gamble. Tastes of Southeast Asia countries have all gone different ways. Twenty years ago, we'd do a picture and it would be all right everywhere. It's not the case now. We either do a small budget picture now aimed specifically for Taiwan or Singapore or elsewhere in Southeast Asia, or a big budget film that will hit all countries. Nothing in-between.' (Interview, Chan, 1986)

Chan elaborated that 20 years ago, the Chinese in all these countries were recent immigrants and preferred Chinese movies, but the new generation, born outside China, had taken up international tastes, or those of the countries in which they resided (Interview, Chan, 1986).

Others discussed their companies' strategies of overseas distribution. For example, Lam (Interview, 1986) said Cinema City was building its own distribution network in Southeast Asia and Taiwan. A first step in that direction occurred in 1985, when Cathay in Singapore and Malaysia signed agreements with Cinema City to be exclusive distributors of its films. The rationale of Cinema City, explained by Lam, is that, 'once you secure a foothold in Taiwan, Hong Kong, Singapore and Malaysia, you're sure to be a winner.' Cinema City has not been very successful distributing in Japan, Lam theorising that, 'Maybe it's because our lead star is not as spectacular as Jackie Chan, or maybe the company we are dealing with in Japan is not doing the best job promoting our films.' He added that it took time to build trust and friendship in the Japan market.

Domestic distribution is concentrated and tends toward monopolisation. As elsewhere in Asia, filmmakers believe distribu-tors have undue control over all aspects of cinema—that they control the industry.

A director said of the system:

'It's the old American monopoly. People who distribute, also own theatres, advertising companies and production houses. It's extremely condensed capitalism—a type you can't find anywhere in the world. We're more capitalistic and cut-throat than the United States. If you survive Hong Kong society, you can survive anywhere.' (Interview, Fong, 1986)

Competition is so severe that companies are forced to make quick decisions as a matter of survival. In the mid-1980s, D and B rented the Shaw theatres, primarily to show their films, but also to ensure that Cinema City and Golden Harvest did not pick them up. In the process, D and B was strapped into producing films at a furious pace and exactly on deadline to fill the theatres (Interview, Li, 1986).

Because of interlocking arrangements and/or ownership, distributors are also producers, or at least, they call the production shots. Producers have been restricted as to the directors and actors they can use and, in some cases, certain stars can be seen only in theatres owned by Golden Harvest. Independents not tied into the distribution circuits have fought for survival, lacking good exhibition slots for their films. But in 1988, a distributor, Newport Entertainment Ltd, was created to cater to the independents. Unlike the other distributors, Newport did not produce films (*Asiaweek* 1988c: 48).

Hong Kong has three major distribution circuits, each with 10–15 theatres, and each tied to a production company. Golden Harvest has Gala Distribution; Cinema City owns Golden Princess and D and B functions also as a distributor. Chan (Interview, 1986) said the limited number of theatres in Hong Kong accounted for the low number of circuits. A fourth, Sil-Metropole, distributes films backed by, or imported from, China.

A film can be seen in as many as 30 theatres simultaneously, but for one to two weeks only, thus not allowing for any warm-up time. One source said no other city of the world had such an arrangement (Interview, Li, 1986). The short run discourages producers from pumping large amounts of money into films, or forces them to seek alternative markets (overseas, video or cable) (Interview, Tobias, 1986).

Box-office receipts are split with distributors and exhibitors (basically the same people) receiving 60 per cent and producers, 40 per cent. More realistically, producers get somewhere around 30–33 per cent after they have paid the costs of advertising, publicity and making prints for 10–15 theatres. As Li (Interview, 1986) reckoned, an average film costs HK $2 million to produce; thus, for its maker to recover costs, the box-office gate must be at least HK $6 million. This, he said, was difficult as the record holder drew only HK $30 million.

High rents and land prices have required theatres to seat 1,200 to 2,000 to be profitable. However, by the mid-1980s, mini-auditoria complexes became popular, when the Hong Kong government changed outmoded building laws and audiences demanded better viewing conditions. United Artists built a six mini-theatre complex; soon after, Golden Harvest, Shaw and Golden Princess also built low-cost mini-theatres.

Construction of new theatres is an indication that movie viewing is still an important leisure activity in Hong Kong. In 1984, for example, US $114 million was spent on 61 million movie tickets. Tobias (Interview, 1986) predicted movie attendance would remain high, despite the effects of videocassettes, because of the nature of the territory. He explained:

'Because of the small flats we live in, we want to go out after a hard day's work. We would not want to watch video or cable TV with six other family members in a tiny room. The concept here is to get out, to have some space, to enjoy free air conditioning in a theatre. Also, people here like to be in masses, with other people, and it's safe to go out at night.'

The same reasons for high theatre attendance were given for the slow development of the videocassette market in Hong Kong. Lam (Interview, 1986), claiming fewer than 20 per cent of the house-holds had VCRs in 1986, said the 'fantastic nightlife' and crowded flats had kept home video down; Chan (Interview, 1986) agreed that uncomfortable living conditions had not favoured video viewing.

In 1986, three or four chains operated about 50 video stores; about an equal number of shops either showed or rented hardcore pornography. (Called 'specialty shops', the latter illegally screened pornographic films at HK $20 a person, and sold videocassettes. 'You buy three cassettes and then exchange them for three more and pay a HK $20 handling fee,' one distributor said.) (Interview, Lam, 1986) A Cinema City official felt that as the Hong Kong population became more affluent, it would seek a wider variety of entertainment, including videocassettes (Interview, Lam, 1986).

By 1987, this prediction was already a reality as more than 400,000 VCR owners existed (compared to 90,000 in 1983), as well as major video store chains, such as KPS Video Rental Shops, with more than 20,000 members, or Fotomax, with 23 outlets as early as 1984. The latter was sold to the Shui On Group of Companies (construction, hotels, food, leisure and entertainment interests) in 1986; KPS was a division of Kam Productions (Tobias 1987c: 548).

Monopolisation is a characteristic of the legitimate video industry as it has been of cinema. By 1988, distributors expressed their anger about video being in the hands of few companies. Fotomax had an exclusive agreement with Golden Harvest to make videocassettes of that company's library, while Jade Video distributed old Shaw Brothers movies and TVB's Jade Channel dramas. Cinema City planned to make its entire catalogue available for video by 1990, releasing seven films a month, but not exclusively to one video company. Although no law or standard exists concerning the lapse of time needed between a film's release in a theatre and on video, in the past it has been about two years.

Foreign distribution of Hong Kong movies has been adversely affected by videocassettes, Chan claiming his company's greatest losses were in overseas Chinatowns. Perplexed as to how to deal with the problem, he said:

'Pirates go into cinemas and photograph our movies. Though of poor quality, the videocassettes then are rented in Chinatowns. When our films are released three months later in Korea, Thailand, Philippines and elsewhere, forget it; the people have already seen them.' (Interview, Chan, 1986)

To counter video-pirating, Golden Harvest has released films concurrently in Taiwan and Southeast Asia to get there before the pirates and has brought lawsuits of copyright infringement against vendors and distributors. Chan (Interview, 1986) acknowledged the magnitude of the problem:

'We have to hire private investigators and it's still hard to find illegal video operators. In the US, we have to register our movies with the Library of Congress to be able to bring a copyright suit. All of this is costing us hundreds of thousands of dollars, and we can't be 100 per cent successful. We just want to suppress the pirating enough to cut our losses to a minimum.'

Cinema City also views the impact of videocassettes upon foreign markets as extremely troublesome. Lam (Interview, 1986) said:

'Video is giving us headaches. We don't know when someone will bring a video camera into a theatre to tape us. It's being done in Malaysia; you can see the heads of the audience in tapes of our films and hear audience laughter. It's done here too at sneak previews. All three major production/distribution companies have a midnight sneak preview of a new movie the Saturday before its Thursday release. Producers and directors watch the audience reaction and maybe make cuts afterwards. And pirates illegally tape some of the previews.

Directing and Scriptwriting

As is often the case, when quality filmmaking is mentioned, a few 'new wave' directors are trotted out for scrutiny. Hong Kong is no exception. Never mind that these directors are so unappreciated they nearly have to beg to get their work produced. Never mind that most of their successful counterparts crank out stereotyped films, uneven in aesthetic and thematic quality. It is an axiom that the attention focuses on the 'new wave' directors.

Hong Kong film critics are wont to divert one's gaze elsewhere, to the mainstream directors, whose cinema is,

> 'stereotyped in every respect. Its staging, design and camera work are all highly standardised, while its acting-styles, approach to characterisation, smart-ass lines and gags are all uniformly hyperbolic.' (Urban Council 1986: 7)

It has been the custom of Hong Kong directors to work in genres, doing very little creative filmmaking but, rather, waiting to cash in on the next film fad (Jarvie 1977: 119, 121).

Kam Ping-Hing (in Urban Council 1986: 11) said contemporary directors make a number of concessions detrimental to quality filmmaking, among which are: shooting on location abroad to provide the crew with a free tour bonus; developing plots to serve the stars' talents; exaggerating and overdoing the acting; filling movies with acrobatic-skill demonstrations; borrowing too many ideas from the West or from old Hong Kong films, and ignoring sound effects and editing, the latter described by Kam as mechanical and lacking in rhythm.

Tobias (Interview, 1986) fondly remembering the 'new wave' directors of the late 1970s, lamented that there were very few important directors in the 1980s. 'Nowadays, anyone can be a director; they are on a trial basis, and if they make it financially, they can go on,' he added. As would be expected, Tobias has his detractors.

Contending his company's directors were different, Peter Lam of Cinema City said that whereas other directors simply reacted to the market, those at Cinema City 'want to do something different, to prove they are the best' (Lam, Interview, 1986). As an example, he said that while 'vampire movies' were box-office successes in Hong Kong, Cinema City resisted doing them. Lam credited Cinema City directors with making the first contemporary movies to capitalise on local comedy, as well as on the public's concerns about Hong Kong after 1997. The latter was reflected in the studio's 1986 blockbuster, *A Better Tomorrow*, directed by John Woo.

Woo's experience did not fit an instant-success formula. According to Lam (Interview, 1986), the first movie Woo made was a flop, as were two others he made while heading Cinema City's Taiwan office. 'He was an emotional and financial wreck. He returned to Hong Kong, and with the help of a friend, put his best effort into making *A Better Tomorrow*,' Lam said.

One of the characteristics sought in directors has been their ability to handle scripts. Because of a shortage of good story materials, directors have been expected to edit outlines and partial scripts into final products. In cases where directors have not had these skills, comedies have been 'brain-stormed' and other movies' plots developed while shooting was going on. 'That is why continuity is strange; different pieces are slapped together,' Tobias (Interview, 1986) said.

Another filmmaker said scriptwriting was weak in Hong Kong because production companies manipulated story ideas. 'Scriptwriters won't initiate a story,' he said. 'If their company only makes comedies, they only make comedies.' (Interview, Law, 1986)

Claiming most of Hong Kong's movie scripts in the 1980s were written by four people (two at Golden Harvest and one each at Shaw and Cinema City), Nansun Shi, Cinema City executive manager, said efforts have been made to enlarge the writing pool. Her studio has gone to the theatre to obtain scriptwriters and has offered a scriptwriting class. 'We advertised for scriptwriters and received 1,000 scripts,' she said. From that number, 20 people were invited to join the class, only one of whom remained for any length of time. Cinema City had two writers in 1986, neither of whom had written a script (Interview, Shi, 1986).

When reviewers and journalists discussed the status of Hong Kong cinema in the late 1980s, they invariably hankered for the films of the so-called 'new wave' directors less than a decade before.

These works, refreshingly realistic and socially conscious, held a mirror to aspects of Hong Kong society that the Shaw and Chow directors had long ignored. They revealed the myth of urban prosperity, the dissatisfaction of youth, the uncertainty about Hong Kong's future and identity, and the myriad problems and societal changes of the Crown Colony. Their characters were often out of the ordinary. As *Asiaweek* (1981a, p. 38) reported:

'If they present a love story, it is likely to involve two retarded youngsters (*Sealed with a Kiss*) or a crippled pornography hawker and a prostitute's daughter (*Cream Soda and Milk*).'

Bicultural, 'new wave' directors preferred stories dealing with international or universal themes, rather than classical or traditional aspects of Chinese culture. As a result, they 'modernised' local film, Li (Interview, 1986) claimed, with adaptations of Western genres. A 'new wave' director characterised himself and his colleagues as,

111

'young people who want to be honest with themselves. They think, "I have this feeling; I want to express myself and get feedback." They are less concerned with genre, with packaging (because they are less experienced), publicity and distribution. They use better technique.' (Interview, Fong, 1986)

Spearheaded by a group of young, trained-abroad directors, most of whom surfaced first on Hong Kong television, the 'new wave' included Alex Cheung Kwok-Min (whose early works were *Cops and Robbers* and *Man on the Brink*), formerly of Shaw, Golden Harvest and then television; Ann Hui (*The Secret*, *The Spooky Bunch* and *The Story of Wu Viet*), trained in London and from RTHK television; and Tsui Hark (*Butterfly Murders* and *Dangerous Encounter of the First Kind*), US-trained with experience at TVB television. Still others were Yin Ho, Tam Ka Ming, Wong Wah Kei, Ronnie Yu, Leung Po-Chi, Rachel Zem, Peter Yung and Clifford Choi.

In their early endeavours, 'new wave' directors attracted finances and the attention of new production outfits (Tobias 1981: 222). However, their situation changed and, by 1986, although some were still employed as directors, most were not. Shi (Interview, 1986) said that of the original 30 to 40 'new wave' directors, only five were still making films, because 'producers did not support their work which did not make hits'.

Li (Interview, 1986) said that 'new wave' directors changed when some of them were absorbed by Cinema City to do big-budget movies. 'Most young directors were successful,' he said, 'and being pragmatic as Hong Kong people are, they made money pictures so they could direct their creative ones.' The trouble was that many stopped making the creative pictures (Interview, Li, 1986).

Major studios continued to employ a few 'new wave' directors in the late 1980s, but with a keener eye on the box office than a decade before. Golden Harvest's Chan (Interview, 1986) explained:

'We give and will continue to give more chances to "new wave" directors. But, we don't want them to do only the artistic. We expect them to combine art and commercial. How do you do that? Work with them on a more commercial topic but use their artistic style. For example, take a theme of a serious divorce problem and convert it to adultery to get more audience.'

A 'new wave' director who continued to work with minimal commercial constraints placed on his work was Allen Fong (Fong Yuk-Ping). After studying film in the US, Fong returned to Hong Kong and assumed the position of assistant director at RTHK. There, he directed outstanding films, including *Below the Lion Rock*. In 1981, he made *Father and Son* with Feng Huang Motion Picture

Company; his other credits include *Ah Ying* and *Just Like Weather*, the latter produced by Sil-Metropole in 1986.

Fong, who makes a movie every two years, talked about the difficulties of retaining his creativity:

> 'My films deal with realism and humanism, no glamorous stars, no sweeping drama—the people play themselves. I will not release a film I'm not personally satisfied with. I just returned from Tokyo where I reshot subtitles. Why Japan? To make any kind of film that does not make big money, I'm forced to reconsider my budget. I can't shoot 35; I have to shoot 16. The blow-up quality is not as good here so I go to Japan to have it done. I treat this project creatively. If I don't have enough money, I'm not slaughtered; I go on.' (Interview, Fong, 1986)

Explaining his financial situation further, Fong said:

> 'All my films are financed by a China-related company. I'm a filmmaker and as long as the producer allows me to do what I want, I'll take the support. It is hard anywhere in the world to get capital for my type of film. We are magicians on how to survive. But I'm saying what is in my heart. I feel very happy when someone in the airport comes up to me and says, "Mr Fong, please make more films." It gives me great satisfaction to know people want me to produce more, faster, but the situation forces me to be slow. I'm barely surviving financially. But, I have a job, don't worry about a roof, or two or three meals a day, and I'm doing what I like. What else can I ask for?' (Interview, Fong, 1986)

Saying that fellow 'new wave' directors had been 'eaten up by the old system', Fong acknowledged that there had to be a compromise between the aesthetic and commercial:

> 'Films are surviving now as a mixture of commercial and new aesthetic work. I don't feel this is a contradiction as we all want to make good films that sell. If directors do everything for money, then there is a problem.' (Interview, Fong, 1986)

Genres and Characteristics
Escapist, imitative and superficial—these are some of the adjectives filmmakers and filmwriters have used to describe Hong Kong cinema.

Perhaps added to these should be circuitous, for popular genres seem to come and go. Just in the past generation, the following have held sway—melodrama, swordplay of ancient times, contemporary unarmed martial arts (kung fu), 'new wave', kung fu comedy and a variant of the latter, farcical comedy, with lots of action. After the spectacular success of *A Better Tomorrow* in 1986, the type of film popular with audiences changed again.

A Better Tomorrow, a production of Film Workshop, a Cinema City satellite, saw the return of the romantic hero, a 'Rambo'-type capable of killing thousands with his machine gun. Li gave four factors accounting for the movie's unexpected success:

'(1)   The film is more like a film, having a story, characters, etc. These virtues have been long absent from films.
(2)   It has violence, not the Jackie Chan spectacular, stunt violence that draws no blood, but violence showing poeple bleeding in slow motion. Stylised violence.
(3)   It is an extremely melodramatic, sentimental story. The typical film jumbles melodrama with comedy and other traits. This one doesn't; it is mainly melodramatic.
(4)   The political climate in Hong Kong is such that the people need a hero, a winner in the theatre. Vicariously, they see the hero killing China.' (Interview, Li, 1986)

Tobias and Lam (Interviews, 1986) saw the film as a trend-setter, ushering in a series dealing with human relationships during trying times. Lam added that *A Better Tomorrow* provided young people with the message of sticking together and fighting, probably against the 1997 take-over of Hong Kong by China.

The type of movies made in the 1980s was affected by the uncertain future of the colony. As one producer explained:

'1997 affects the tastes of the Hong Kong audience. Hong Kong people want a dream factory—bigger-than-life, exaggerated, escapist pictures. If you deal with the more serious topics, your pictures will be flops. Labourers here will not be able to leave in 1997, so they do not want serious pictures; they want escape. Those affluent who can leave also want to escape in motion pictures, as they too are so uncertain as people.' (Interview, Chan, 1986)

Escapism, a universal reason for movie attendance, has been an all-consuming passion of Hong Kong film-goers, whether it be escapism from crowded living conditions, from ideological battles or from the prospect of 1997. The encouraged motion picture, according to Garcia (1985, p. 7), is, therefore, a common denominator type where, 'heroes and villains are clearly identified and where the outcome of the struggle is clear.' Garcia surmised that, 'Perhaps Hong Kong films are the way they are because they want to present an opposite to reality, not its denial, nor its mirror.' (Garcia, 1985: 7)

Tobias (Interview, 1986) thought, in presenting this non-realistic portrayal, Hong Kong film had leaned towards exaggeration. He said:

'Everything is in excess. In the US, it has to be good; here, it has to be excessive. If "Rambo" is big, then we have to out-"Rambo" "Rambo". They do a pint of blood in US movies; we do two pints.'

Fong (Interview, 1986) analysed film types differently. He said they were 'superficial and surface', reflecting the nature of Hong Kong Society, where 'no one thinks about the future, living only for the moment'. He predicted that if the movies changed, there would be a 'different Hong Kong' (Interview, Fong, 1986).

Swordplay, Martial Arts.   This genre really had its boost in Hong Kong after the 1949 Revolution, mainly through Kwan Tak-Hing's portrayal, in nearly 100 films, of the martial arts teacher, Huang Fei Hung. The Kwan films depicted battles between villains and upright village chiefs with martial artists.

In the 1950s-early 1960s' swordplay films, the Confucian code dominated. Plots revolved around filial ties, destruction of which led to violence and revenge, and the master-pupil relationship was important. During the following decade, with directors Chang Cheh and King Hu dominating, martial arts films changed. They were now more action-oriented; the moralistic overtones were replaced by men fighting their way to fame and fortune with deadly weapons, and the aesthetics of kung fu, almost dance-like, prevailed (*Asiaweek* 1980a: 42).

Many of the swordplay films (more than 800 swordplay films were made from the end of World War II through the 1960s, compared with 250 fist/punch movies) were based on pulp novels and classical literature. Wong (1984, p. 16) wrote:

'Filmmakers copied drawings from cheap comics to help choreograph the swordsman's bionic feats and fencing patterns. They also looked to Chinese paintings for scenic settings and scanned history books and folklore for legendary figures to be immortalised in celluloid.'

Among classics of this genre were *Golden Swallow* (1968), *The Wandering Swordsman* (1969), *One-Armed Swordsman* and *Dragon Gate Inn* (1967) (see Urban Council n.d.).

In 1970, *From the Highway* and *The Chinese Boxer* were pioneers in the unarmed martial artist films, on which Raymond Chow catapulted to fame through the talents of Bruce Lee. In his short career, Lee made the internationally known *Fist of Fury*, *Way of the*

Dragon and *Enter the Dragon*; he combined karate with kung fu and returned (although briefly) to fighting for moralistic values.

For a number of reasons, a few of which being Lee's death, a 1,000 per cent increase in production costs over a decade, and the splitting of the martial art form into many types, kung fu lost some of its attraction as a genre in the late 1970s. By that time, kung fu movies had developed into two categories—northern-style martial arts involving hard-to-execute, graceful and acrobatic routines, and kung fu comedy.

A content analysis of kung fu films revealed that more than half of the characters were involved in gangland activities or were depicted as martial arts teachers or students; heroes' primary goals were 'altruistic' and interpersonal (the most frequent goal being revenge for the death of a loved one) and those of villains, political or economic and personal. Narratives were of two types—struggle to achieve and superman. In the former, the hero is helpless in relation to the villain, but trains under a kung fu teacher and defeats his adversary. In the superman narrative, the hero is very powerful from the beginning (Graper 1987: 154–56).

Comedy.   A number of Cantonese comedies appeared in the 1950s and 1960s, characterised as being prosaic and for the lower classes; moralistic and conservative (lacking a sense of satire and protest) and repetitive, derivative and formulaic; tending towards burlesque and exaggeration and centring on the performer (Urban Council 1985: 45).

In the 1970s, the popularity of Cantonese comedy was meshed with kung fu, the first successful movie in this combined genre being *The Good, The Bad and The Loser* (1976). Kung fu comedy, which used fewer fight scenes and more cartoon-like slapstick and con artists, was basically of two types—one where the structure and situations were inherently comical; the other where comic characters and scenes were inserted into the film. (Urban Council n.d.: 36).

A variant of kung fu comedy in the early 1980s was the 'spectacular mega-comedy', described as consisting of 'unrelenting slapstick, spectacular gags (car chases . . . physical stunts), stars whose appeal lies not in their mystique but in their ordinariness and an inconsequential plot' (Garcia 1984: 51). Among these were Cinema City's *Aces Go Places*, followed by a similar series by Golden Harvest, *My Lucky Stars*. *Aces Go Places* was a combination of US spy spoofs and Hong Kong kung fu, whose hero, 'Kodojak', featured 'Kojak's' baldness, 'Colombo's' raincoat and 'Clouseau's' ridiculous mistakes.

Politically and Socially Conscious.   As indicated earlier, in a few cases, the political ramifications of 1997 have found their way into Hong Kong cinema. First to deal with the topic of Hong Kong reverting to China was *Home in Hong Kong* (1983), directed by King Hoi Lam (David King). However, parts of the film were excised by the censors, including a scene where family members discussed immigration plans after Margaret Thatcher's talks with China.

Other films, especially some by 'new wave' directors, dealt with social problems, taking film out of the studios and into the streets. For example, Fong's *Father and Son* (1981) touched upon the housing shortage in Hong Kong; the more recent *Gangs* (1988) showed the redeemable qualities of a juvenile delinquent. But, for the most part, social realism has not been extensive, in-depth or long-lived, because of censorship and 'traditional taboos'. One writer hypothesised that the more sensitive an issue was, the less likely it would obtain a straightforward treatment in film (Jaivin 1988: 46).

It is worth repeating that producers play it safe, treating film as an investment and appealing to the audience. Thus, the function of cinema is limited to entertainment. As one unemployed director observed:

'In the US there are different classes of audiences which support different types of films. In Hong Kong, the number of alternative audiences is not big enough to support alternative cinema.' (Interview, Law, 1986)

Thus, the dozen or fewer experimental filmmakers in Hong Kong find it virtually impossible to exhibit their works.

Regulation

Hong Kong censors do their job with one eye on relations with neighbouring countries and the other on the 1997 issue. This political bent of censorship goes back a number of years but was highlighted in the 1980s by a string of bannings and a new film censorship law.

Officially, the authorities claim movies have been banned because of their potential to upset affairs with neighbouring countries; what they mean is with China. Hong Kong people, being the realists and business people they are, do not criticise China, which has become a chief trading partner. Invariably, films affected come from Taiwan. In 1981, Hong Kong withdrew *The Coldest Winter in Peking*, a multimillion dollar Taiwan production which attacked Chinese communism, and banned *If I Were Real*, also from Taiwan, on the grounds that it was offensive to a friendly country (China). In 1985, *Ah Fu* was withdrawn because it might 'adversely affect relationships with neighbouring countries'. The movie dealt with the 1997 policy.

New film legislation in 1987 resulted partly because of a film that was censored for political reasons. When Hong Kong officials cut *Man Without a Promised Land*, for fear of China's reaction, the *Asian Wall Street Journal* reported that the censorship law used to restrict this film and others for 34 years was not legally binding (Scott 1987: 58).

The new Film Censorship Bill, passed 18 May 1987, drew much ire from a public who feared this was one of the first steps towards erosion of freedom leading up to 1977 (Lau 1987: 12). One of the rationales for the bill was that it would ensure that filmmakers did not use Hong Kong as a propaganda base against China. This fitted in with the previous practice of censors who, in banning 20 movies for political reasons between 1973 and 1987, cut 19 of them for fear of offending China.

Besides setting up a three-tiered classification system, the 1987 law restricted pictures which damage good relationships with other countries; provoke hatred or contempt of the Hong Kong government; encourage public disorder; offend religious bodies or reputable local organisations; provoke hatred in Hong Kong of people of different races and colours; corrupt morals or encourage crime (*Variety* 1987a: 56).

Critics complained that the censors had been so preoccupied with political themes, that sex and violence had usually gone unscathed. For example, in 1980, of the 610 features submitted, the Television and Entertainment Licensing Authority banned only seven because of sex themes (for earlier censorship guidelines, see *Variety* 1977: 58).

Throughout the latter part of the 1980s, discussion took place on obscenity and pornography, often without much resolution. In 1986, after two years of debate, a Control of Obscene and Indecent Articles Bill was proposed. In effect, it would set up a tribunal to deal with publication and importation, and classify works in categories of neither obscene nor indecent; indecent and subject to restrictions on sale and access; and obscene and prohibited. A year later, the Television and Entertainment Licensing Authority warned that those who displayed indecent videocassettes were subject to HK $25,000 fines and twelve months' imprisonment. The regulation did not ban videos, but just made them less accessible to young people (Chadha 1987: 48).

Curiously, a new Film Censorship Ordinance of 10 November 1988, not only allowed more nudity and sex in films but permitted those over 18 years of age to view pornography legally. A result was that distributors scurried about the world looking for soft-porn films.

One film editor, who felt the authorities had not been consistent in their standards, said enforcement would be less lenient and censorship laws stricter because of China's future influence (Interview, Li, 1986).

Professionalism

Best known of all film professionalisation efforts has been the annual Hong Kong International Film Festival, started in 1977. Each year, the festival has screened a full range of foreign, Asian and Hong Kong films, familiarising local audiences with major works. Additionally, the Urban Council, sponsor of the festival, has published a series of bilingual books and pamphlets, increasing the amount of literature available on Asian and Hong Kong cinema.

The festival was started primarily to allow a select audience to see artistic films not generally available in commercial houses, according to programme co-ordinator Li Cheuk-To. Unlike the doomed Manila International Film Festival and the Asian-Pacific Film Festival, Hong Kong's fest has not been competitive. Continued by the Urban Council as long as it is financially successful, the festival, in the late 1980s, had enough revenue to cover direct expenses and, in some cases, to make a small profit. Li said the major problems of the festival had been Hong Kong government censorship; the huge bureaucratic machine of the Urban Councils' Cultural Department; budgetary problems caused by distributors who seek more royalties; and interference by administrators too far removed from film (Interview, Li, 1986).

Hong Kong has had some other professional spin-offs from the festival and its personnel. For example, locating old films has been taken more seriously since they have been needed for the annual retrospectives at the festival. Most have been stored under less than ideal conditions at the two television stations which use them to fill in late-night and early-morning schedules. Others have been saved by private distributors. Li said old movies are getting shorter as they break and the television stations splice them; many are lost through chemical deterioration because of improper storage. He has continually called for an archive but said the Urban Council was not interested because of costs. 'Also, an archive is not as spectacular as a festival,' he added (Interview, Li, 1986).

Film Bi-Weekly, started in 1979 by a group of film critics, is a 52-page Chinese-language periodical offering reviews, interviews, commentary and articles on film and television. 'It is necessary for our survival to include everything, as there is no other serious film magazine in Hong Kong,' the weekly's editor-in-chief said (Interview, Li, 1986). One of its activities has been sponsorship of an annual Hong Kong film award.

In 1985, the Crown Colony's first arts theatre, Columbia Classics, opened its doors. Other film organisations, such as Studio One and Phoenix Cine Club, existed to promote the medium. Phoenix, for a while, organised an annual short film competition.

Training, except for that given on the job, is scarce. No film school exists, although the communication department at Hong Kong Baptist College has maintained a film unit. A local club, Film

119

Cultural Centre, has also offered short courses on filmmaking, film appreciation and scriptwriting, using the services of professionals (Interview, Law, 1986).

Most actors and actresses come into movies through song contests, beauty pageants and talent quests. Trained by a studio, they are occasionally poached by rival producers. A Cinema City official said his company trained through an apprenticeship system. 'The talent moves up; it takes time. Then D and B steals them, offering rosy prospects,' he said (Interview, Lam, 1986).

Once they become popular, stars suffer from over-exposure, making ten films a year, plus concerts and television and personal appearances. Because Hong Kong lacks talent agencies, a set of standards is not applied for the stars to follow (Interview, Tobias, 1986).

NOTES

1   Much uncertainty exists over these beginnings. Tilden (1975, p. 13) called the founder Benjamin Brasky, and the first films, *Revealed by the Pot* and *Stealing the Cooked Ducks*; Armes (1987, p. 137) gave him the surname Brodsky; Tobias (1987b, p. 520) said the first movies were made in Hong Kong in 1898; Sun (1982, p. 41) thought the starting date was 1924, with the appearance of a movie based on a stage drama about an ancient philosopher. Jarvie (1977, p. 5) is the preferred source because he seemed to do the most primary research.
2   Tilden (1975, p. 15) called him Lai Man-Wei.
3   The tragic melodrama (*wenyi pian*) was popular, usually adapted from radio plays. The air-wave novels of Li Wo and Jiang Sheng were favourites. A close relationship between radio and film survived until 1966 when television became more widespread.
4   In 1986 interviews, Hong Kong filmmakers expressed different views on why Shaw quit film production. Allen Fong said the Shaws, being 'true business men' went where the money was, which was in televison; Li Cheuk-To attributed their exit to 'old fashioned production—streamlined, factory-style' which people 'got fed up' with in the late 1970s; Peter Lam claimed the studio was mismanaged and the talent was upset with the studio executive and Law Wai-Ming said Shaw found movie-making too risky among his many other ventures (Interviews, Fong, Li, Lam, Law, 1986).
5   Runme remained in Singapore; at the time of his death in 1985, he managed or chaired 35 companies.
6   Although some writers link swordsman with kung fu, Tilden (1975, p. 135) said they differed markedly in moral and social aspects. Kung fu is based on respect and honour of class; swordsman is oriented to individual honour. Swordsmen roam about looking for wrongs to right, while kung fu boxers stay put and wait to be wronged.
7   Other film personalities joined together to form their production companies. In 1987, Alan and Eric Films Ltd was started by superstar actor-singer Alan Tam and comedian Eric Tsang; the company has a contract with

D and B to produce ten to twelve films to help fill that circuit. Bluebird Films was run by a former actress, Xia Meng. A Golden Harvest vice president saw this trend of actors starting their own companies as a problem. 'The stars are getting so popular that they form their own companies to make pictures; thus, they are not at your disposal.' (Interview, Chan, 1986)

8   Golden Harvest has got round dubbing problems by culturally adapting their films. It takes films meant for Chinese audiences and makes them relevant by recutting, repackaging and reshooting. Often working with a film company in another country, Golden Harvest does not merely translate the sound track, but re-does it, including colloquialisms, etc. Cinema City does similar things. Maintaining a branch in Taiwan, Cinema City produces its films for that market, avoiding topics of sex, politics and violence, but making the films entertaining.

5

SOUTH KOREA

INTRODUCTION

T
he Korean film industry, accustomed to fighting for survival,
waged its fiercest battle ever in 1988, taking on United States
majors over the issue of direct distribution. To fend off the
threat of outside domination of their market, filmmakers united to
persuade exhibitors not to show American movies.

Among their actions were the boycotting of *Fatal Attraction*,
the first film distributed directly by United International Pictures
(distributor of Paramount, Universal and MGM/UA), the closing
for a day of 30 Seoul theatres and the threat to release baskets
of snakes in theatres at screening time. All of this occurred in
September. Earlier, after UIP convinced a small chain of theatres to
show the James Bond movie, *The Living Daylights*, Korean filmmakers threatened to expose to the public, the theatre owner's
involvement in a corrupt loan deal and, to his wife, his extramarital
relationship.

The camps took sides in 1987 when, under pressure from the
US government, direct distribution was permitted. For nearly 35
years, foreign pictures had been brought to Korea under a 'multi-
layered system of Los Angeles-based South Korean buyers, South
Korean-based importers, regional distributors and exhibitors' (Sipe
1988: 50). The 1987 agreement meant UIP by-passed these Korean
middlemen and dealt directly with exhibitors, with whom box-office
receipts were split.

Skirmishes that almost ended in an outright trade war began in
1985, when the Motion Picture Exporters Association of America
(MPEAA), representing the eight largest producers and distributors,
wrote to members of the US Senate Finance Committee stating its
intention to file an unfair trade practice complaint against the
Korean film industry. Particularly piqued that only 14 US films had
been sold to Korea the previous year, the MPEAA listed its
grievances: the ban on US movie company offices in Korea, pro-

hibitive financial burdens brought about by a 1985 law which required importers to deposit US $800,000 with the Motion Picture Promotion Corporation of Korea and to contribute US $170,000 to the same agency for each film imported, the screen quota legislating that at least two-fifths of all screen time in all theatres should be devoted to Korean pictures, restrictions of film-use on home video and television and censorship requirements.

The complaint was dropped after negotiations with the Korean Ambassador in Washington. Six months of further talks were held in 1987, after which US majors were allowed to open offices in Korea, distribute films themselves and collect the rentals. The US invasion was quickly in full force. Within a few months, the number of Korean companies involved in motion picture importation shot to more than 100, US majors earmarked Korea as their second largest Asian market, expecting to pull out US $25 to $40 million a year in film rentals, a California company (Koritain Entertainment) was set up to distribute movies to Korea and the American Film Marketing Association launched a minimarket in Seoul to sell US independent producers' fare (Segers 1988: 32).

Such an onslaught could lead to nothing but doom for the local industry and the reactions were prompt. On 16 September 1988, the MPEAA filed an 'unfair trade complaint' with the US trade representative, charging that Korea had failed to comply with the 1985 agreement, making it impossible for US companies to import and distribute in Seoul. The complaint grew out of a Korean government censorship policy that had the purpose of preventing direct distribution of MPEAA films. The Korean Performance Ethics Committee had ruled that it would not permit any company to have more than one film on its censorship list at the same time. MPEAA realised immediately that because approval of films by the committee took two to three months, a quota of four to six film imports a year was being implemented. The MPEAA said such a policy destroyed the financial viability of US firms which had established Korean offices and the battle was on (*Manila Standard* 1988: 26).

HISTORICAL BACKGROUND

In October 1898[1], a 100ft filmstrip was shown in a Seoul barn to advertise the products of the Anglo-American Tobacco Company. Parrish (n.d., p. 37) claimed the Koreans were offered 2 cents each to watch the strip. Lee (1988: 19) said customers were expected to pay for admission with ten empty cigarette boxes or a piece of nickel. Other filmstrips were shown during the next decade and a half; for example, in 1903, two films were shown in different locations and in

1909, a short Pathe strip was imported from Paris to be shown between acts of live variety shows.

By 1906, Seoul had its first movie house. As the need was felt for domestic production for cultural and nationalistic purposes, the first Korean-made films were shown on 27 October 1919. One, entitled *The Righteous Revenge* (*Asian Messenger* 1980/81b: 38–9)[2], was not a full-length movie, but rather a kino-drama—1,000 feet of location scenes not possible on the regular stage, screened between theatrical scenes to join parts of a play. It was directed by Kim Do-san. The second was *The Landscape of Kyongsong City*, a documentary. Kino-dramas prospered for a short time and paved the way for the first full-length feature, *The Plighted Love Under the Moon*, directed and produced by Yun Baek-nam in 1923[3]. The movie stressed the importance of depositing money in banks. The silent era (1920s to 1935) saw the emergence of many stars, a number of productions each year (between 1926 and 1931, about 80 a year)[4], a number of successful producers and the establishment of the first film corporation, Choson Kinema.

Although the silent films were usually made by cameramen and directors with very little experience, some exemplary work was accomplished, especially after the Association of Motion Picture Arts was founded in 1929 with an aim to develop motion pictures as a medium of national culture. Among successful producers were Lee Pil-u, considered the first cameraman and producer, who made *Tale of Sisters of Janghwa and Hongnyon*; the already-mentioned Yun Baek-nam, who produced *History of Unyong*, and Lee Kyong-son, whose success in the 1920s was attributed to his work with Yun Baek-nam on *Tale of Simchong*. Most of the early films dramatised folk-tales.

Given the most credit for infusing life into the motion picture industry was Na Un-gyu who, during his ten-year career (he died at the age of 36), produced and acted in a number of works, probably the most important of which were *The Bird in Her Cage* and *Arirang*, the latter produced in 1926. *The Bird in Her Cage* described Koreans resisting and fighting the Japanese in underground activities. Na wrote and directed the plot and performed the leading role. *Arirang* also showed the suppressed anger Koreans felt under Japanese occupation.

Another important film of the period was Lee Gyu-hwan's *A Boat Without a Boatman* in 1932. Lee, trained in Japan, returned to Korea at the request of Na to direct the film in which Na played the leading role. One source reported *A Boat Without a Boatman* represented 'national resentment against mechanical civilization as bringing disaster instead of happiness, depicting the tragic end of a boatman who succumbed to his terrible fate amidst life-and-death struggle against the instrusion of civilization', (Ministry of Public Information n.d.: 22). Like its predecessors, this film showed patriotism and resistance against the Japanese (Ahn 1987: 92).

Reminiscing years later, Yoon Bong-choon, who acted in 23 movies between 1927 and 1945, and directed 27 others into the 1960s, described his first movie in 1927:

'The production was almost as sloppy and non-professional as Korea's first commercial movie, where the cameraman's only experience had been as theater projectionist and the director's last job had been drummer in the band marching around Seoul advertising the movie.' (Yoon n.d.: 39)

Yoon said actors in the silent era worked for practically nothing. When the filming was finished, the producer gave each actor the amount of rice he thought his performance deserved. To receive a bag of rice meant the performance was good. Yoon pointed out, as there were six films produced a year, an actor could expect, 'six bags of rice a year if you acted and did a good job in them all! No life of luxury on that salary.' (Yoon n.d.: 39) But, as Yoon indicated, there were other reasons for acting:

'Most actors wanted to be in movies for a completely different reason—to be treated like royalty, to ride to film openings in fine rickshaws, to be entertained after the show with the most beautiful *kiesang* girls (entertainers) in Korea.' (Yoon n.d.: 39)

By the 1930s, the film industry suffered its first significant set-back, as the Japanese occupiers increased censorship and cut the yearly production of films to two or three. According to Yoon, during the Japanese rule, every film had to be seen by a censor first, who also wanted to 'know exactly what we were thinking when we wrote those lines or shot that scene a certain way' (Yoon n.d.: 39).

In 1935, relatively late in comparison with other countries, Korea had its first talkie, *The Story of Chunhyang*, based on a classic Yi Dynasty novel and produced by the Lee brothers, Pil-u and Myong-u. During the next decade, until the Japanese were driven from Korea in 1945, about 50 other pictures followed; to assure their success, many were based on stories already made popular in fiction or silent movies. For example, *Arirang* and *Tale of Sisters Janghwa and Hongnyon* were remade and became successful box-office features. The picture that established the talkies, however, was Lee Gyu-hwan's 1937 *The Man on the Road*, which, like *Arirang* and *A Boat Without a Boatman* had a spirit of resistance.

During World War II, Korean movies were more subjugated than usual, doing 'disgraceful pro-Japanese pictures against the national sentiments' (Ministry of Public Information n.d.: 24). There were about 25 of these Japanese propaganda films. Between 1940 and 1945, the Japanese closed down about ten production companies and all film distributing agencies. Simultaneously, they created a council for motion pictures for central control of all aspects of the industry (see Lee 1969).

With liberation, the industry had another rebirth, although very brief. Some excellent productions appeared—including the first film in colour, *The Diary of a Woman*, in 1949—despite a lack of equipment and the disorganisation of the production companies. Because of a shortage of 35mm cameras, most films between 1946 and 1949 were on 16mm with no sound. The themes were often realistic portrayals of the underground fighting against the Japanese (*Korea Cinema* 1981: 115).

At about the time domestic films were being revived, Korea was again the focus of a war, which started on 25 June 1950. Between 1951 and 1953, the industry produced only eight pictures, none of high quality[5]. A documentary, *March of Justice*, made by the Ministry of National Defence, on the resistance to communist aggression, had limited success. Newsreels became popular during the Korean War, used to promote the war effort and build morale. The government established *Taehan News* to complement *Liberty News*, which had been supplied by the United States Information Service since the late 1940s[6]. The Korean defence authorities made a series of newsreels called *Defense News*.

The approximately 15 years after the Korean War have been dubbed the 'golden age' of Korean films. In 1957, domestic film-makers were exempted from taxation and, shortly after, the number of productions increased sharply (from 20 in 1955 to 40 in 1957 and 100 a year before the end of the decade), as did the number of production companies (to as many as 65) and theatres. A number of new movie-makers appeared, such as Shin Sang-ok[7], Lee Man-hui, Lee Gang-chon, Min Kyong-Sik, Kim Song-min, Yu Hyun-mok and Chong Chang-hwa. Some of these people started their careers in the early 1950s, influenced by European and US directors. Yu Hyun-mok, who later made *The Stray Bullet* (1961), introduced counterpoint and psychological interactions in his films.

By 1957–8, these and other directors helped bring about an unprecedented boom as new films appeared regularly, movie-goers increasingly turned to domestic films and Korean filmmakers 'hitherto supinely passive in their helpless admiration of superior Western products, gained increasing self-confidence.' (Ministry of Public Information n.d.: 26). By 1961, according to Parrish (n.d.: 37–8), Korea had one of the liveliest movie industries in Asia, with 16 movie studios, 402 theatres (81 in Seoul) and huge audiences. Between 1945 and 1961, 472 films were produced in the country, most of which were sentimental love stories and gory 'shoot-em-ups', interlaced with themes of nationalism and freedom. Also in 1961, Seoul hosted the Ninth Asian Film Festival, at which a Korean film, *My Mother and the Boarder*, won best picture; six other Korean pictures won awards. The following year, the Korean government developed its own film recognition system called the Grand Bell Awards.

Generally, Korean productions were not of award-winning quality. Parrish (n.d.: 40) said that in the 1945–61 period—what he called the 'heyday of lowgrade, shoestring productions'—many of the 65 independent production companies that sprang up were financed by speculators (not legitimate film producers) expecting the highest returns in the shortest time and on the smallest investment. Quality suffered artistically and technically for other reasons, including the lack of proper equipment, competent writers and technical know-how and the appeal of foreign films, which had superior techniques, advanced use of colour and exotic subject matter. Parrish (n.d.: 40) reported that in the early 1960s, most motion pictures were made in less than a month and some stars were known to act in five films simultaneously, literally running from set to set. He gave some statistics worth noting: an actor or actress earned up to 4 million won (US $14,800) a year, producers spent up to 7 million won (US $25,900) a film and about 100 million tickets were purchased at theatres every year.

In the early 1960s, the government stepped in, rationalising that high-quality movies would give the world a good image of Korea and earn much-needed foreign currency. The Motion Picture Law[8] was passed on 20 January 1962, 'to contribute to the promotion of national art through the promotion and development of the film industry'. Article 19 stipulated that the 'government may aid the film industry in order to promote the production of quality films as well as development of motion picture culture and international exchange of films.' The first of four amendments to the law, passed on 12 March 1963, required production companies to be equipped with studios and other facilities, to be registered with the government and to be the sole importers of foreign film (Kuroda 1980: 41). By this legislation, which closed financially-unstable firms and tightened licensing criteria for production, the government was able to consolidate 65 filmmaking firms into 17 large companies[9].

In other moves, the government gave grants to these production companies, reduced the import tax on film stock and limited the number of imported films by placing quotas and import duties on them. But some of these regulations were not considered as beneficial to the industry as originally conceived, and on 3 August 1966, the second amendment to the Motion Picture Law was passed. Generally, this amendment relaxed the conditions necessary for the registration of production companies, lowered from 15 to two films the minimum annual production of each company for maintaining registration, obligated the government to assist the film industry and established the Film Credit Union and a quota system for theatres showing imported films.

Perhaps because of this relaxation, by the late 1960s and early

1970s, Korean films reached a pinnacle they have not achieved since. As Ahn (1987, p. 93) wrote:

'Where the films of the 1960s were stepping stones in the aesthetic development of Korean cinema, the films of the 1970s were marked by their commercial aspects . . . Within [this] economic turmoil, the film established its own commercialism. Entertaining mass audiences became the priority of the film industry, and the "aesthetics of economy" was a catch phrase.'

The Motion Picture Promotion Corporation of Korea (MPPC) reported that in 1969, each Korean watched 5.6 films a year (this figure dropped to two per person by 1976) (*Asian Messenger* 1978: 12). The same year, the number of features produced (229) and total film attendance (more than 173 million) established records that remain. Similar records were set in 1971, in the number of films imported each year (82) and the number of cinema houses in operation (717) (*Korea Cinema* 1981: 110).

With the advent of the 1970s, the growing popularity of television sliced significantly into the film market, as did audience apathy, excessive censorship and the relative technological and artistic backwardness of the industry. Again, the government intervened by enacting the third amendment to the Motion Picture Law on 6 August 1970. This law created the Motion Picture Promotion Union and required exporters and importers to be registered with the Ministry of Culture and Information and to produce five films a year.

The Motion Picture Promotion Union, consisting of other organisations, such as the Motion Picture Producers Association of Korea Inc., Film Exporters and Importers Association of Korea Inc., Federation of Theatre Owners of Korea and the Motion Pictures Association of Korea, had among its many aims, to administer export-import films, supervise participation in international film festivals, provide monetary aid and facilities to producers, and generally support the film industry.

The Union, with government backing, set down a specific policy on exports and imports. Article 16 of the Motion Picture Law stated that to qualify for importing a foreign film, a producer had to export a minimum of four domestic films and earn from them at least US $20,000. Also, domestic films which showed for at least 60 days in a foreign market were given cash rewards by the Union. Thus, incentives to produce and export domestic films were built into the policy.

Other stipulations were that the number of films imported should not exceed a third of the domestic films produced each year; applicants had to obtain permission of the Union before they could be recommended for import licences by the government, and films of communist countries, or those that had messages considered anti-government or harmful to social order, could not be imported. Restricted from exportation were films which did not pass government censorship or were barred from public showing, and those which pirated or copied foreign films or presented a threat to Korean interests or images (*Korea Cinema* 1972; see also *Korea Cinema* 1975, *Korea Cinema* 1976).

On 16 February 1973, the fourth amendment to the Motion Picture Law was passed, dissolving the Motion Picture Promotion Union and establishing in its place the Motion Picture Promotion Corporation of Korea (MPPC), a non-profit entity which took charge of all matters for the promotion of film on behalf of the government.

The revised law came on the heels of the Yushin (Revitalising Reform) Constitution of 1972, which emphasised self-awareness and Korean identity. The main objectives of the revisions were to improve quality, rather than quantity, of films; create national and traditional cultures; import films that would implement or support the revitalising reform movement; and export films as propaganda vehicles for Korean culture.

After this fourth revision, the film industry worked under a number of conditions designed to save it. Besides limiting the number of production companies by consolidating inactive units and setting import/export guidelines[10], the legislation required production companies not only to be equipped with prescribed production facilities, but with at least US $100,000 as a production fund. Additionally, the law and its amendments called for the enforcement of more rigid censorship and set new standards for co-productions with foreign producers, helped set up the Motion Picture Distributors Association and the Korean Film Archive Incorporated Foundation (1974), and provided that the Ministry of Culture and Information should issue a general directive concerning the motion picture policy for each year. Included in the directive are stipulations for the year on the number of features to be produced, number of films to be imported (not more than a third of the number of domestic movies) and general rules regarding the promotion of movies, improvement of quality, welfare of film personalities and a screen quota system of four months a year for domestic films.

Such actions were considered warranted by the continuing decline in the industry throughout the 1970s. By 1980, record lows were set in the number of feature films produced (91), number of theatres (447) and total attendance (about 54.5 million). However, total gross receipts that year set an all-time high at nearly 51.5 billion won. In 1978, the lowest number of imported films (31) up to that time was recorded[11].

CONTEMPORARY SCENE

Reasons for the bleak status of the Korean film industry have flowed from the mouths of producers and critics as freely as well-rehearsed lines from the stars of some of the movies. Among reasons given are that directors are more concerned with titles of movies than with contents, that directors give up too easily, that business men do not reinvest film profits into the industry, that admission rates are too expensive, that there are not enough first-class theatres, that television and home video steal the audiences, that harsh censorship hinders the portrayal of favourite themes of sex and violence and that young people are reluctant to have much to do with films. One source added his reasons: after the assassination of President Park Chung-hee in 1979, cinema was more tightly tied to domestic events than usual, the result being the stifling of expression; 'since quotas governing import licences for presumably lucrative foreign films are based on the number of domestic films completed by each company, producers tend to grind out cheap money-losers just to get more import licences, since their better and more expensive efforts are usually not profitable either'; Korean exhibitors have very little sophistication as to which films are likely to draw audiences and importers are saddled with package deals of US distributors, which include mediocre titles of a flop status as conditions for obtaining desirable films (Racketts 1981:256).

Production

Before 1985, when MPEAA pressures changed Korean filmmaking, 20 companies were allowed to operate in Korea, making between 80 and 100 feature-length films a year. For years, the rule was that, to establish a production company, government permission had to be sought under conditions laid down in the Enforcement Ordinance of the Motion Picture Law. The ordinance required a company to have at least one studio of more than 60 square metres, three cameras, other facilities and US $100,000 in production funds. These were in addition to what existed in other agencies and companies in Korea. For example, the government-owned Korean Film Unit and MPPC have facilities, the latter possessing modern sound recording equipment, processing facilities, film archives, editing equipment and special effects studios. MPPC installed its own facilities, which can be rented at cost, after efforts to help producers in the early 1970s failed. MPPC had given loans of US $80,000 to each production company to assist with facilities and equipment, but their financial situations still worsened (Kuroda 1980: 44). Other facilities are available in the country (at least four processing, two sound recording and several small processing and sound recording companies).

The average cost of producing a film nearly doubled in the last half of the 1970s, to at least US \$240,000–\$300,000 (Kuroda 1980: 46). Another source wrote that in 1984, an 'A' film cost \$200,000 to make (Doherty 1984: 843). The MPPC president said the cost of producing a film depended upon its quality, adding that producers were reluctant to give exact figures (Interview, Lee, 1982). To offset the heavy expenses of production, filmmakers have been encouraged to make co-productions with foreign countries. Between 1970, when co-production was approved by the government, and 1977, 69 such movies were made, 50 with Hong Kong, nine with Taiwan and others with the US, Italy, Turkey and the Philippines. Approval of the Korean government is necessary in each production.

Because the government for years did not favour minor companies, a tradition of free-lance producers did not develop, causing concern on the part of one critic who wrote, 'Since the motion picture is a genre of art that can flourish with free ideas and new concepts, it is feared that this rigid government regulation might degrade the quality of film'. (Kuroda 1980: 46)

All this changed in 1985, after which a new crop of producers emerged, some willing to invest in unconventional movies. The number of movie outfits doubled to at least 76 by early 1988, although the number of domestic movies did not shoot up (86 in 1987). The latter figure stabilised because liberalisation of film laws no longer required the shooting of four local movies for every one imported. Most Korean productions continued to lose money. Of the 86 made in 1987, only four attained more than 100,000 viewers, the cut-off number needed to cover costs, and not one was a blockbuster (*Asiaweek* 1988b: 38).

Less stringent foreign exchange and travel controls gave producers more opportunities to invest in films with foreign locations. However, this also meant increases in production costs, already considered too high. Part of the blame for the skyrocketing costs of movie-making were attributed to the economic successes of the Park regime when wages and the standard of living were raised (Doherty 1984: 843). The number of domestic films decreased regularly from the highs of 231 in 1970 and 229 in 1969, to 91 in 1980. Between 1953 and 1961, the average yearly production was 51, compared to 179 between 1962 and 1972 and 110 between 1973 and 1982. Since 1982, the average continues to drop below 90.

Discussing production problems, producer Yu Hyun-mok said the industry was plagued with a lack of modern equipment, shortage of scriptwriters and a village mentality that does not comprehend many of the films. Confident the government, in its desire to improve the industry, would make available better equipment, Yu did not hold out much hope for improvements in scriptwriting:

'This is a very serious problem. With the small investment made in film, we cannot furnish the writers needed to write in short periods of time. Therefore, directors, many of whom have qualifications to amend scripts, usually start a production by revising the script.' (Interview, Yu, 1982)

Yu, anticipating by a few years the opening up of film production to anyone with the creative and financial capabilities, believed the result would be more freedom to create, rather than the previous situation where government favouritism of a selected group of producers led to greed and elitism. 'Creators of films could not do anything without those selected 20 producers, who often chose films solely on the basis of making profits and hired directors who flattered them,' Yu complained (Interview, Yu, 1982). Others concurred (Interviews, Chang, Lee and Han, 1982).

Besides feature film producers, others make documentaries, cultural movies, animation or advertising shorts. The largest is the Korean Film Unit, operated by the government since 1958. Its yearly production of about 100 films includes four types of nationalistic films, weekly newsreels and 26 different types of cultural films and documentaries. The unit makes 150 prints of each cultural film and 60 of each newsreel, which are sent directly to provincial information centres and Seoul theatres free of charge. In 1980, the Ministry of Culture and Information substituted a 15-minute, bi-monthly newsreel, *Camera Sunbo*, for the five-minute, weekly *Taehan News* used previously. The latter had received considerable criticism because of its government propaganda (*Asian Messenger* 1980/1a: 15).

There are 31 other registered cultural film producers making advertising and cultural pictures, including ten animated features (*Korea Cinema* 1981: 105).

Directing, Scriptwriting, Acting

The opening of the domestic market to more producers in the 1980s was expected to be a boost for directors, most of whom had to hustle to make a living. Directors normally make US $8,000 to $10,000 a picture, which requires them to do three or four a year.

Among successful directors, Bae Chang-ho is exceptional because his films make money. Called the Spielberg of Korea, Bae directed six films between 1982 and 1985, four of which were box-office hits. His 1984 works, *Whale Hunting* and *Warm It Was That Winter*, were the number one and three top-grossing movies that year, and *Deep Blue Night* (1985) is the all-time box-office champion. A business administration graduate, Bae worked for Hyundai for two years in Kenya before quitting to try film as an assistant to director Lee Chang-ho.

Bae produces films inexpensively; for example, *Whale Hunting* cost US $100,000 and grossed 15 times that amount. Success at the box office allows him to share in the profits—15 per cent of the distributors' gross in the domestic market and 50 per cent of the sale price if exported (*The Economist* 1985: 87). Bae uses simple, light personal themes in his work. For example, *Warm It Was That Winter* deals with two sisters separated by the Korean War, who, 30 years later, coincidentally fall in love with the same man. The time factor and socio-economic status of the sisters (one is a factory hand, the other a famous concert artiste) stretch credulity, but the audience did not seem to mind.

Among other leading directors are Lee Doo yong, Im Kwon t'aek, Chung Jin-won and Kim Soo-yong. Lee, born in 1942, made more than 70 features in a 17-year period commencing in 1969. His films reflect a personal vision. He first concentrated on dramas that described discord, agony and happiness in human relations, then moved to the theme of the pain of a divided Korea and to historical films describing Korean ways of life and thinking. In the latter, he usually deals with hardship, poverty and suffering of the oppressed (Marshall 1987b: 109).

By the mid-1980s, Im Kwon t'aek had more than 70 titles to his credit, including *Jeung-un* (1973, Witness), *Jokbo* (Genealogy) and *Mandala*. Chung Jin-won, who favours naturalistic patterns, produced and directed more than 50 features, while Kim Soo-yong had more than 100 after his début film, *Gongchoga* (The Henpecked) in 1958. Kim focuses on Korean culture—its people and material environment.

An aspect of Korean filmmaking that has been praised over the years is the photographic technique, although, according to *The Economist* (1985, p. 82), most directors think the camerawork is 'wretched'. Cinemascope frame is not used much because directors find it irksome.

Coming in for severe criticism are musical scores on sound tracks and scriptwriting. One source, in calling the scores 'saccharine', said they were 'generally knocked up for a few won in 10 to 15 days and performed by just a handful of violinists. The result is a constant drizzle of tinkly tunes.' (*The Economist* 1985: 82) Exceptional has been the work of Kim Hee-gap, who composes with an eye to integrating Korean instruments into Western orchestral films.

Time pressures requiring that screen plays be done in a month or less are part of the problem with weak scripts, as is poor pay. Few scriptwriters receive more than US $3,000 a script, necessitating them to turn out too many poor-quality works in a year. Showing these strains, 'many promising scripts fall apart at the end as one melodramatic event is piled on another'; they are also clogged with sentimentality and clichés. *The Economist* (1985, p. 82) opined that, 'A Korean movie in which the heroine is not routinely stripped and ravished by the third reel can be quite refreshing.'

Taking a rather harsh view of Korean film, the same periodical (*The Economist* 1985: 81) said directors and scriptwriters had only a rudimentary grasp of film grammar.

Distribution and Exhibition

All Korean films are distributed through the Korean Motion Picture Distributors Association, created under the Motion Picture Law and consisting mainly of theatre owners. Kuroda said the association's power was 'remarkable,' in that,

> 'no theater can obtain permission for performance without a distribution list made by the association. The authority to issue performance permission belongs to mayors in big cities or the headmen of wards. Theaters, or other organizations and private individuals who want to have a public showing of a motion picture, must submit an application accompanied with a distribution schedule issued by the association.' (Kuroda 1980: 47)

Production companies usually negotiate for distribution directly with the theatres. The contract is often concluded on a percentage basis (55 per cent for the producer and 45 for the theatre) in first- and second-run theatres. A flat fee is charged in lower-level theatres. With foreign films, the theatre used to take up to 50 per cent of the box office (Kuroda 1980: 48). A production company may negotiate with all twelve large Seoul theatres simultaneously, but may not have an exclusive booking with more than two theatres for one film. In cases of direct distribution, producers receive 50 per cent of the net income, from which taxes and other expenses have already been deducted (*Korean Cinema* 1981: 106).

Because movie exhibition is taken very seriously by the government, it is strictly controlled by the Performance Law. Admission fees are set by law, although the National Film Theatres Association has negotiated with the government for the right to determine prices. Ticket prices usually have depended on the production cost of domestic films, and that of importing foreign movies. The average admission fee in 1979 was 1,000 won for national films and 1,500 won for imports. (In 1982, the average increased to 2,000 won, or US $3.) Admission and cultural promotion taxes of 10 per cent each are added, the latter being important for the promotion of Korean culture and arts. For years, each of the 20 selected producers received 300 million won a year from the tax. When theatre owners complained they had not received any of this tax, the government allocated 200 million won to the National Film Theatres Association for improvement of movie house facilities.

Movie theatres have closed regularly since 1971, when the number in operation stood at 717. By 1988, about 370 to 380 remained open; however, with direct distribution, the expectation was that US companies would put up multiplexes, with or without the help of Korean interests. Between 1953 and 1961, the yearly average of movie theatres was 225; between 1962 and 1971, it went to 562, and dropped to 539 between 1972 and 1981.

Taking a specific year for closer scrutiny, in 1979, the number of movie theatres stood at 472—300 of which were in cities, the rest in rural areas. The total attendance at 300 city cinemas was 65,519,000[12] (*Korea Cinema* 1981: 106).

A quota system to protect domestic film production reserved a third of all exhibition days for Korean films. Worked out on a monthly basis, the system required that on 121 days a year, a Korean film had to be shown in each movie house. In 1988, after US film companies won the right to direct distribution, the Korean government invoked a law which required at least 146, not 121, days a year for Korean film exhibition.

Despite the protectionist policy, attendances for domestic films continued to shrink in the 1980s. In 1969–72, when theatre attendances were at their peak (the high being 173,043,272 paid admissions in 1969), 70 to 73 per cent saw Korean films in Seoul. By 1980, the distribution was more equitable—51 per cent domestic, 49 per cent foreign. Total paid admittances in 1980 were only 54,571,679, but total gross receipts were nearly double that of the previous year (*Korea Cinema* 1981:110).

Theatres open at 10.30 a.m. daily and repeat the programme five times. A typical programme includes a short film, newsreels and the feature film. The short films and newsreels are usually the products of the government's Korean Film Unit.

Import and Export

Import and export quotas were used at various times to encourage domestic film production with no definitive verdict concerning their impacts. For a few years into the early 1980s, only production companies were permitted to import, the quotas awarded on the basis of the following qualifications: winner of the Presidential Award in the Grand Bell Award sponsored by the MPPC; winner of the Prime Minister's Award; prize winners in international film contests, and those selected by the Ministry of Culture and Information under the Quality Film Examination System. Foreign-culture films are allowed to be imported without the stipulation of quotas, but these usually do not exceed ten a year.

An earlier policy that allotted import quotas on the basis of the number of local productions meant filmmakers cranked out shoddy 'quickies'. Thus, the market was polluted with lower-quality domestic and foreign movies. For example, in the record year 1971, when 82 films were imported, 202 were made locally.

Equally frustrating was the compensation system of the late

1960s and early 1970s, where a licence to import was given to producers who exported Korean pictures. The end result was that producers, in an effort to obtain the import licence which they saw as their chance to recoup production costs, shipped out large numbers of their films. Korean films were offered at low prices (in 1979, an average of US $4,800 each) and, many times, the exported movies were never released abroad but, instead, were kept in storage (Jang 1984: 73). In 1970, 253 Korean films were exported under these conditions.

Before direct distribution in the late 1980s, 22 or 23 foreign movies were permitted each year, and these had to be top quality works (Interview, Lee, 1982). Yu said quality was assured because of censorship restrictions and because the producers were conscientious and realised that, to make a profit, they had to seek the best from outside, usually winners or runners-up for the US Academy Award. He said a quota certificate was equivalent to about US $300,000 (Interview, Yu, 1982).

The United States was always the main source of foreign films; between 1973 and 1981, an average of 21.7 a year came from Hollywood, down from the 58 in 1962 and 57 in 1966. Other countries that exported to Korea were France, Italy, England, West Germany, Hong Kong, Japan and, to lesser degrees, numerous other Asian countries (Jang 1984: 60).

The long experience of using foreign films to fill theatres, and the lifting of import quotas in 1987, meant bad times for Korean producers. With very limited possibilities of selling their films abroad, they had to expand the domestic market. However, this was nearly an insurmountable task; for instance, more than 70 per cent of the box office receipts in 1987 emanated from screenings of foreign films, and only four domestic works had 100,000 viewers, while five US movies exceeded 300,000 each (Asiaweek 1988b: 38).

South Korean features have not been very popular abroad, despite the efforts of the MPPC, which has maintained branches in Los Angeles and Hong Kong. In the early 1980s, most of the films went to Southeast Asia and a few to Europe (Interview, Lee, 1982). Taiwan and Hong Kong were chief customers for years, importing some Korean movies for as low as $200. In 1976, when Korea earned US $138,601 from exporting 83 features, Hong Kong took 59, the continent of Africa imported seven, Guam six and other parts of Asia five (*AMCB* 1977: 16). Small numbers of films are shipped to the US and Japan for overseas Korean communities.

The possibility of increased overseas markets seems remote, partly because of a lack of aggressive marketing on the part of the industry and MPPC. In the mid-1970s, MPPC hoped to promote foreign marketability through Korean martial arts pictures, but withdrew because taekwando (Korean martial art) did not have the same appeal as the more stylish Hong Kong variety (Doherty 1984: 850).

Always seeking alternatives, Korean filmmakers tried another tactic in 1988. The movie, *Potato*, was screened in Taiwan and Czechoslovakia first in the hope that overseas acclaim would spark box-office success at home (*Asiaweek* 1988b: 38).

Regulation

The aforementioned Motion Picture Law required all film to be submitted for censorship to the Ministry of Culture and Information. On 10 April 1978, this was changed when the Korean Public Performance Ethics Committee was created as a civilian body for censorship. Made up of 13 members named by the Minister of Culture and Information, the committee is autonomous, even though it is subsidised by the Ministry. Under its wings, the Motion Picture Censorship Committee, made up of 20 members, censors both foreign and domestic pictures. These committee members serve terms of one year; more than two-thirds of them must be present to make a decision. Kuroda (1980: 50–1) described the censorship process:

'Article 18 of the Enforcement Ordinance of the Film Law (Motion Picture Law) presents the detailed criteria for censorship. These cover various matters, from politics to violence and sex. These criteria are supposed to reflect the situation that the Republic of Korea now faces. They seem to be very severe . . . When a motion picture company hopes to produce a film, it must pass two obstacles. First, a scenario must be submitted to the Special Scenario Examination Committee for censorship, and then a production application to the Ministry of Culture and Information along with the passed scenario. After the film is finished, it must be screened by the Motion Picture Censorship Committee to obtain permission for public exhibition. The production company is entitled to ask for a re-examination, when it cannot agree to the decision by either of these two committees.'

The Motion Picture Censorship Committee classifies films as suitable or unsuitable for primary school pupils, junior and senior high school students or adults. Theatre owners are punished if they violate this classification system; every theatre has seats reserved for police who regularly check to see that the law is upheld.

One source believed the civilian committee had made a difference, stating that there were 'clear indications that the obstacles to producing films are being eliminated.' He cited the following examples:

(1) The number and variety of themes that can be treated have increased. For example, in recent years, one movie, *Invited People*, showed the persecution of Catholics in Korea, while another, *The*

Small Ball Tossed by a Dwarf, depicted the plight of poor people pushed aside by the rush to modernisation,
(2)   A more realistic and critical attitude in expressing film themes exists. For example, the film, *Two Monks*, depicted religious dogma from the standpoint of humanitarianism,
(3)   Aesthetic expression has been very diversified,
(4)   There have been 'wider and more various elements which can entertain adult audiences'.

He said the easing of restrictions by the government had allowed more variety in movie themes than those of television, and the 'more liberal and more thrilling scenes' were attracting more people to movie houses (Lee 1981: 8–9).

Discussing the government's role in the film industry in 1982, the MPPC president said it sets guidelines and appoints civilians to the censorship board. He specified that:

'Among guidelines the government sets are these: That our traditional culture should be mixed with foreign cultures to create a more brilliant culture; that motion pictures are not for individuals of certain groups but for the public interest and, therefore, they should make everyone happy. In censorship, generally, security of the nation is most important. Second, films should not hurt our cultural heritage. Third, they should not criticise or disregard certain groups in society, such as religious organisations. The trend of movies is toward humanity, emphasising our life in Korea; both good and bad aspects. Joking with the government officials is not important. I'm not saying they are banned, but just saying that we have more important humanity topics to portray than to portray government.'
(Interview, Lee, 1982)

Recognising that recent governments have been much freer than those of Park or Rhee, producer Yu Hyun-mok said that he needed even more freedom, that his 'imagination goes much beyond what is allowed'. He added, almost as if prompted, there must be restrictions because 'night and day we have to be alert to North Korea' (Interview, Yu, 1982).

Political censorship remains stricter than that concerning sexual matters. Film criticism of the national government must be avoided, as well as sympathetic portrayals of communist political systems. If it is to be used, political criticism must deal with individuals, not the entire system. In the mid-1980s, with competition from television, more leniency was shown over the handling of sexual themes in films. Yu said nakedness and provocative bed scenes were allowed in some cases if the film was generally of a very high quality (Interview, Yu, 1982). Foreign films are permitted more explicit portrayals of sexual scenes, but they too are censored (Doherty 1984: 844–5).

When Korean films suffered a downturn in 1988 (because of the showing of more foreign movies, home video and more leisure activities for audiences), the industry made a bold move by asking the government to change the law to allow pornographic movies to be shown in specialised theatres (Shin and Kim 1988: 66).

Censorship is not confined to government bodies; on some occasions, public pressures have stopped film screenings. In 1981, *A Girl Who Came to the City* (1981) was withdrawn from theatres when the Korean Automobile and Transport Workers Union strongly objected to its portrayal of the bus industry. After revisions, it was re-released (Doherty 1984: 844).

To recapitulate, the 1973 film law limited the number of producers of Korean films to 20, who were granted licences to import films if they each produced four of their own. By 1980, new discussions on this law commenced, leading to revisions of 1 July 1985 when filmmaking was divorced from film importing. Companies had to register with the Ministry of Culture and Information to engage in either activity, limits on the numbers of production companies and the films imported were dropped but the total days Korean films had to be shown in each theatre was increased from 121 to 146.

Since 1985, those registering as filmmakers must meet stringent requirements. They must be South Korean nationals capable of showing capital of more than 50 million won and depositing with MPPC an amount equal to the entire budget of a proposed film. Designed to ensure that production funds are up-front, the deposited money is released to the producer as required during the making of the picture. If a company fails to make a film within a year, its registration may be cancelled or it may be ordered out of business for up to six months (*The Economist* 1985: 87).

Genres

The most popular film genres in Korea have been melodrama, action adventure (mainly martial arts), films based on foreign stories, comedies and war films. An analysis of the 106 Korean films of 1979 showed 49 were melodramas, 18 were adaptations from novels, 16 action adventures, seven comedies, four anti-communist dramas, four period themes, one each occult and police story. More recently, Marshall (1987b, p. 108) listed melodramas dealing with love affairs as number one, accounting for more than half of the total, followed by martial arts, serious dramas, comedies and action and crime stories[13].

Describing the ever-popular melodramas, Doherty (1984, p. 845) said they were meant primarily for a female audience ('women's weepies'). The Korean value of *han* (grudge, spite, enmity and resentment) surfaces in many of these melodramas, emanating, for the most part, from the two wars that devastated and split Korean families. Ahn (1987, pp. 94–5), claiming Korean films lacked formal consistency in narrative structure, believed they contained too much sentimentality and 'melodramatic emotionalism'. Perhaps, with television taking the place of film as the purveyor of sentimental themes, and with younger audiences that do not remember the Korean War, film topics will change. Already, university students sarcastically term this genre 'tear gas films'.

Another characteristic of Korean pictures is the ease with which they imitate Hollywood. Doherty (1984, p. 845) wrote of this:

> 'Domestic films that seek to attract a modern audience look to the U.S.—and, more recently, Hong Kong—for direction. The resulting blend of Hollywood narratives and Korean attitudes and locale creates an interesting, if sometimes schizophrenic, result . . . The popular Hollywood film genres and their Korean counterparts crossbreed with amazing ease. Westerns, private eye films, spy adventures, historical costume drama, and the pop musical have all been adopted and put into an indigenous setting.'

Doherty believed the excessive imitation resulted from Korean filmmakers having no cinematic tradition of their own; what was started in the 1920s and 1930s had been lost as those prints no longer existed.

Furthermore, according to Doherty (1984, p. 846), the dividing of the country meant those filmmakers of the South had to define their 'South Koreanness'. Acknowledging the existence of producers and directors who attempt to create a South Korean-type film, Doherty (1984, pp. 846–7) divided them into 'traditionalist' and 'modernist'. The former use an 'imaginative landscape' which draws on values before partition, nostalgic themes and a conservative cinematic style and morality. Among recent films of this type are *The Great King Seijong* (1982), a costume drama, and *Invited People* (1981), which portrayed eighteenth-century Korean martyrdom.

About the 'modernist' type, Doherty (1984, p. 847) said they 'speak to the realities of an acquisitive, changing society at polemical odds with its opposite version in the north'. Doherty further divides 'modernist'. One version warns against political and moral failings, especially because of outside threats (i.e. communism and Western moral corruption). It is exemplified by the most popular film of 1981, *The Free Woman*, the story of a wife ruined by a 'deviant liberal trend' after she became very wealthy. Another 'modernist' subcategory comments on the pressures of modern South Korean society, addressing topics such as prostitution, bureaucratic corruption or the plight of those too westernised. The already described *A Girl Who Came to the City* fits into this category, as well as Lee Chang-ho's *People in Darkness* (1981), the depiction of a country girl who goes to the city, becomes a prostitute and is beaten by pimps while the authorities turn their backs.

This kind of realism, in bold themes unheard of a decade before, became more prominent in the late 1980s. Stories about red-light districts, the lowly life of the barmaid and busgirl or the scepticism of clergy who question their vows, made the Korean big screen.

Strong nationalism and cultural identity in themes of historical events or cultural roots were featured in the works of filmmakers such as Yi Tu-yong and Im Kwon t'aek. Yi's *House of Death* (1980) dealt with shamanism and the rite of death, while *The Spinning Wheel* (1983) showed cruelty to women and women's resistance. Im's *Mandala* (1981) portrayed the 'passage of Nirvana seen through the eyes of a Buddhist Monk,' while *The Village in the Mist* (1982) was about sexual morality in a clan village and *The Daughter of Fire* (1983), about family members' pain because of separation as a result of the Korean War. Others, such as Yi Chang-ho and Bae Chang-ho depicted contemporary life in their work. Showing his concern about societal apathy, Bae made *Tropical Flowers* (1982), *Whale Hunting* (1984), *Deep Blue Night* (1985) and *Hwang Chin-i* (1986) (Ahn 1987: 94). *Deep Blue Night*, with 610,000 viewers in 1985, became the top-grossing Korean film of all time. It was shot in Los Angeles and its environs, using US crews, technology and labs. The story revolved around an illegal immigrant caught in a marriage of convenience scam (*Asiaweek* 1988b: 38).

Professionalism

The government has made a number of moves to improve the professional standards of Korean film personnel. Probably one of the most important was the 1962 establishment of the Grand Bell Awards, Korea's equivalent to Hollywood's Academy Awards. Conducted by MPPC in more recent years, the 21 awards are sought not just for their prestige, but for the financial remuneration they carry. For years, quotas to import foreign films were assigned to producers of the best and 'most excellent' films and about US $100,000 in prize money was given to the other 19 winners. Another US $70,000 in production-encouraging money was subsidised to staff members who produced high quality pictures (*Korea Cinema* 1981: 109). Yu pointed out that, occasionally, winners of some awards do not get wide distribution for their films because they are too artistic and intellectual (Interview, Yu, 1982).

Training has been another area where the government, usually through MPPC, has made a significant contribution. Lee said MPPC has a training scheme (predominantly made up of sending promising people abroad for further studies), but the lack of highly trained personnel still looms as one of the industry's biggest problems (Interview, Lee, 1982). MPPC usually sponsors overseas study tours for one director, scenario writer, cameraman, art director, leading actor and actress who win the annual Golden Bell Awards, as well as a study tour abroad for film processing engineers, and awards scholarships to twelve university and 13 senior high school students (Kuroda 1980: 44). Training is provided in Korea at four-year college courses at Donggook University, Choongang University, Hanyang University and Chung-joo University; a two-year course at Seoul Specialised Arts College and high school courses at Anyang Motion Picture Art School and Geawon Art High School. Approximately 1,300 motion picture students graduate each year despite a very competitive policy that admits only one in 20 applicants. Yu, also a film professor, said there were about ten individual studios or conservatories for the performing arts, as well as lectures and workshops on various aspects of life, sponsored by MPPC (Interview, Yu, 1982). In 1984, MPPC established the Korean Academy of Fine Arts which offered a concentrated one-year course for directors and camera personnel. All of this was a long way from the 1950s, when 'the average South Korean filmmaker had been trained with US help or had seen service in the United States Information Service' (Doherty 1984: 842).

At least two film magazines exist: *Youngwha* (Motion Picture), published with MPPC assistance, and *Film Art*. MPPC also publishes *Korea Cinema*, an annual, and a number of books on film history and techniques.

MPPC has developed a welfare plan which provides an annual pension for 18 movie people, and special bonuses for five others.[14] Other organisations have also contributed to enhancing the professional careers of filmmakers, among them the Motion Pictures Association of Korea, which has committees of directors, technicians, planners, scenarists, actors and actresses, musicians, cameramen and lighting technicians; Motion Picture Producers Association of Korea; Federation of Theatre Owners in Korea; Korea Cultural and Advertising Film Producers Association; Korea Motion Picture Distributors Association; Korea Motion Picture Institute (film professors) and Motion Picture Critics Association.

South Korea, until fairly recently, did not have a tradition of collecting and preserving its old films. Part of the problem resulted from wars' devastation of cultural artefacts, but, in some instances, old movies were thrown away as having no other use. Also, because no more than six prints were made in a film's first run, often not much could be salvaged as the prints were projected until they were almost in shreds. At least Sogang University, which collected old film for more than 20 years to use in courses, and the Korean Film Archive, have tried to preserve the country's cinematic tradition. Developed in 1977, and for five years an arm of MPPC, the Archive acts as a depository. Although producers are not required to deposit their pictures, most co-operate (*The Economist* 1985: 81–2).

BRIEF VIEW OF
NORTH KOREAN FILM

After World War II, a film crew was set up in North Korea to produce documentaries. The National Film Studio of North Korea, created in 1947, produced its first feature, *My Native Place*, two years later. The movie implored people to be patriotic.

During the Korean War, documentaries, such as *Righteous War* and *Announcing to the World*, and feature films, such as *Boy Partisans* (1951), *Again to the Front* (1952) and *Scout* (1953), were produced, most of which were awarded prizes at the international film festivals at Karlovy Vary. As can be guessed from the titles, the pictures depicted soldiers and citizens fighting courageously.

Reconstruction of the studio and the industry in general was necessary after 1953. In November of that year, the Pyongyang University of Cinematics was founded. Production resumed and between 1956 and 1959, a number of films were made, including *Never Can Live Like That* and *The Road of Happiness* (1956), *Orang Village* (1957) and *Love the Future* (1959). In 1959, the Korean February 8 Film Studio opened.

Throughout the 1960s, many films depicted anti-Japanese revolutionary struggles, glorifying Korean bravery, others were on themes of socialist reality.

Among important films of the 1970s was *Star of Korea*, a ten-part feature directed by Om Gil-son. Among other works of Om were *Flames Spreading Over the Land*, *In the First Armed Unit* and *An Jung Gun Shoots Ho Hirobumi*. He has been awarded the 'Order of Kim II Sung', the highest order of the country, and the title of 'labour hero'.

Another important director is Ryu Ho-son, head of Wolmi Island Creation Company of February 8 Feature Film Studio. He has completed more than 40 feature films, including *Far Away from Headquarters* and *Unknown Heroes* (in 20 parts) (see Ryu 1987: 84–5).

In 1986, North Korean Sek Studios received modern equipment from a French production company to work on an animated feature, *Gandahar*, directed by the French.

AFTERWORD

The protests against direct distribution of US films in Korea subsided by November 1988, when agreement was reached between the Korean government and the US film industry.

MPEAA withdrew its unfair trade complaint when the Koreans agreed to allow US film companies 'unencumbered access' to their market. This meant dropping a limitation placed on the number of prints in circulation and guaranteeing that censorship would not be used to restrict the importation of US movies (Harris 1988: 1, 30). (For more on the incidents surrounding the September–October demonstrations and statements issued, see Park (1988, p. 36) and *Variety* (1988, p. 8).)

NOTES

1   Official sources seem to have difficulty in determining when the first film was shown in Korea. The Ministry of Public Information (n.d.) set the date as 1900; another source said it was 1903 (*Korea Cinema* 1981) and Parrish (n.d., pp. 37–41), 1904. Lee (1988, p. 19) seems rather certain the first viewing was in 1898.
2   Probably because of translation problems, another source called this film *Dutiful Fight* (*Korea Cinema* 1981: 114). Lee (1988, p. 26) called it *Loyal Revenge*.
3   Date provided by two sources, *A Handbook of Korea* 1979: 711 and *Korea Cinema* 1981: 114. Again, the Ministry of Public Information (n.d., p. 21) publication disagrees, giving the date as 1921.
4   Parrish (n.d., p. 38) said the number between 1923 and 1935 was 85, while the Ministry of Public Information (n.d., p. 23) claimed about 200 produced between 1921 and 1935.
5   Some motion picture personalities were captured and, along with confiscated equipment, taken to North Korea.
6   The production of Korean news film had begun in 1945 with the showing of *Haebang News* or *Liberation News*. But, this newsreel was not very successful because of insufficient funds, equipment and facilities.
7   Shin Sang-ok was involved in a very mysterious real life thriller later. In fact, some writers said his story would make an exciting screenplay if it were not so far-fetched.
    In 1978, his wife, the famous actress Choe Un-hi was lured to Hong Kong by an offer of a huge film contract, kidnapped and sent by ship to North Korea. Behind this bizarre set of circumstances was Kim Jong-il, son of the head of government and a very influential leader himself.
    Searching for his wife in Hong Kong months later, Shin met the same fate. Less co-operative than Choe, Shin spent four years in prison before being brought to a banquet with Kim in 1983, attended also by Choe. After that, they lived in grand style for the next three years, being given US $3 million a year, as they helped film devotee Kim improve his country's movie business; Shin by directing seven North Korean films, Choe by acting in them. In 1985, Choe was named best actress at the Moscow Film Festival for her role in the North Korean production, *Salt*.
    While in Vienna promoting North Korean film, the duo eluded Kim's intelligence personnel and fled to the US Embassy, where they sought asylum. Later, after a debriefing by the US Central Intelligence Agency, they told the press the above story.
8   Also called Film Law. Kuroda (1980, p. 40) detailed Korean legislation affecting film as: Motion Picture—including the Film Law, Enforcement Ordinance of the Film Law, Regulations Related to the Application of

the Film Law, Ordinance of Licence for Projectionists, Regulations for Controlling Films and Negatives of the Korean Film Unit and Regulations for Aiding the Reproduction of Films for Public Information; Performance —Performance Law, Enforcement Ordinance of Performance Law, Regulations Related to the Application of Performance Law, Regulations for Approval of Limit of Admission Fees, and Regulations Concerning Recommendation of Entertainers for Armed Forces. He said the Film Law regulated production, export, import, censorship and the Motion Picture Promotion Corporation; the Performance Law concerned the exhibition of pictures, cinema theatres and audiences.

9   The growth to 17 was gradual after the reorganisation. In 1964, the following nine production companies were registered with the Ministry of Public Information: Kuktong Production, Hanyang Productions, Hanguk Yonghwa, Shin Films, Hanyuk Yesul, Segi Productions, Tongwon Productions, Taehan Yonhap Productions and Haptong Yonghwa. In 1965, eight were added: Yonbang Productions, Tongyang Yonghwa, Cheil Yonghwa, Taeyang Yonghwa, Asong Yonghwa, Star Film, Taeyong Productions and Chungang Yonghwa.

10   New import requirements were responsible for setting up the National Film Promotion Fund, the principal source of funding for Motion Picture Promotion Corporation. Article 10 of the Motion Picture Law requires a film company which has obtained an import licence to make a contribution to the fund. The fee to be paid to the government by a production company is US $40,000 per film within one month (Kuroda 1980: 43).

11   After 1975, when only 35 foreign films were imported, United States Secretary of Commerce Elliot Richardson reportedly lodged a protest that only 17 came from the US (*Variety* 1976: 4).

12   Another set of figures for the same period showed 484 theatres, 93 of which were first-run. In Seoul, there were 102 (including the twelve first-run), which accounted for 22 per cent of the total in the country. Seating capacity was 311,630 (Kuroda 1982: 47).

13   Producer Yu Hyun-mok said 80 per cent of all films in the early 1980s were melodramas and 10 per cent martial arts (Interview, Yu, 1982). About the same time, Lee (1981, p. 11) claimed melodrama accounted for half, followed by martial arts, which he said were 'nationally unidentified films'. Of course, these differences in figures result from different definitions of genres.

14   In the early 1980s, 1,116 people worked in Korean movies, 127 of whom were directors, 130 scenario writers, 60 cameramen, 549 actors and actresses, 66 producers, 103 engineers and 36 composers.

SOUTHEAST ASIA

6

THE
PHILIPPINES

INTRODUCTION

I f you want to slow down the usually fast-paced and outspoken patter of some Filipino movie people, ask whether the Marcoses were good or bad for the film industry.

They express their ambivalence in a number of ways. On the one hand, the Marcos dictatorship was harsh in its film censorship, using a double standard in favour of foreign movies. On the other, it gave film a relatively high priority because of the patronage of Imelda Marcos, who encouraged the establishment of the international film festival and Experimental Cinema of the Philippines (ECP).

The filmmakers remember all of this very well. Some of them were censored, even jailed; others had their work produced by ECP, helping establish their careers.

National artist Lamberto Avellana, a director for more than 50 years, described Imelda Marcos' contributions as 'some good, some bad', pointing out that she had the Film Centre built, but under circumstances that were not supported by the public. 'Under Marcos, we could do pretty much what we wanted, but we could not step on toes,' Avellana said. Directors such as Lino Brocka 'stepped on toes' by showing the plight of poor people, and their films were banned, he explained (Interview, Avellana, 1986).

Ishmael Bernal, newspaper critic-turned-director, acknowledged that Imelda Marcos had one of his films censored, because it 'portrayed negative aspects of her city', and that he and other directors 'ran up against the authorities all the time'. But, compared with the Aquino government, which he said seemed to have 'a law to ignore us', the Marcos administration did things to organise the industry, even if they were suppressive (Interview, Bernal, 1986).

Peque Gallaga, some of whose directorial work was identified with ECP, does not like the cultural backlash in the country after the dictatorship. Because of the Marcos years, 'you have to prove something every day now' to a clique that has taken over cultural aspects of society, he said. The clique is made up of filmmakers who make social-awareness movies, according to Gallaga, who added that the industry was being put in the hands of those 'who could not make it in martial law'. Gallaga elaborated:

'There is a big move against Regal studio because its owner ("Mother Lily" Monteverde) is of Chinese descent, although she has been a Filipino citizen for 20 to 30 years. The same with me. I'm a third generation Filipino, but because of the colour of my skin, I'm not considered Filipino. I'm from the Spanish land-owning elite. I disassociated myself from my background to get accepted. The current Filipinisation process is hostile to non-Filipinos. If I don't know Tagalog, I'm not accepted. You have to prove you're anti-colonialist—kick a white man today is the attitude (Interview, Gallaga, 1986).

HISTORICAL BACKGROUND

Manila was an active movie centre much earlier than most cities of the world. On 1 January 1897, six brief (not more than 45 seconds) imported films were shown to Filipino patrons who paid 50 centavos for cushioned seats, 30 centavos for benches. By the next year, a Spanish army officer, Antonio Ramos, filmed and showed scenes of Manila as did some Americans during the next few years. Enough production occurred that when Pathe opened an office in the city in June 1909, three studios were launched, antedating even the first ones in Hollywood (de Pedro 1985: 6).

The Philippines were early in other regards. In November 1911, the Board of Censorship for Cinematographic Films was established, immediately countered by the Association of Film Producers and Distributors, set up to fight censorship. In 1915, taxes, the bane of the industry since, were imposed upon films (Deocampo 1985: 11) and, in 1912, two pioneering features were made, released within a day of each other.

Americans Harry Brown and Edward M. Gross produced *La Vida Rizal* (The Life of Rizal), through Rizalina Film Manufacturing Co., and with Gross's wife, Titay Molina, a popular *sarsuwela* (also *zarzuela*, a musical comedy) actress, in the lead. Another American, Albert Yearsly, owner of two Manila theatres, decided to make his own film on the national hero, a 20-minute short which

A scene from Chen Kaige's *Yellow Earth*
(Stills, Posters and Design BFI)

Chen Kaige's *The Big Parade*
(Stills, Posters and Design (BFI)/ICA Projects)

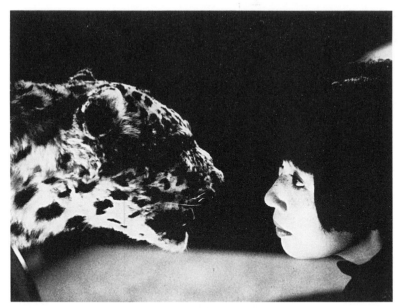

Nabuko Miyamoto in Juzo Itami's *A Taxing Woman*
(Stills, Posters and Design (BFI)/Artificial Eye Film Company)

The "clad in white" gangster (Koji Kakusho) tells the audience how to
appreciate fine cinema and fine cuisine in Juzo Itami's *Tampopo*
(Stills, Posters and Design (BFI)/Jane Balfour Films)

Japanese Director, Juzo Itami
(Stills, Posters and Design (BFI))

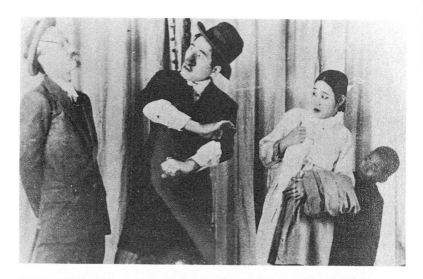

Scenes from two early Korean films; above, Lee Pil-u's *Montongguri* (1926); below, Lee Gyu-sol's *Nongjungjo* (1926)

Hong Kong director, Allen Fong
(John Lent)

Filipino director, Peque Gallaya
(John Lent)

Filipino director, Lino Brocka

Jins Shamsuddin, the Malaysian
founder of the film distribution
organisation, Perfima

A scene from the 1988 Korean film *Adada*, directed by Im Kwon-t'aek

Mira Nair's *Salaam Bombay!*
(Stills, Posters and Design (BFI)/Mitch Epstein)

A scene from *Damul* directed by Prakash Jha with Manohar Singh (left) and Annu Kapoor, first broadcast on Indian television in 1985 *(NFDC, Bombay)*

An Indian street lined with cinemas and gigantic hoardings (*Manjunath Pendakur*)

was screened a day before the Brown/Gross work. In 1913, the first Filipino-produced feature, *La Sombre de la Armada*, appeared.

Movie historian T.D. Agcaoili (1958, pp. 6–8) portrayed movie production in the initial period:

> 'The movies were crude. Theories of filmmaking were not yet formed and the tendency was to photograph scenes from one fixed position, as if the camera was the audience of a stage show or *zarzuela*'

For example, in Gross's film, stage curtains were used for movie sets, props were like those of stage plays, no make-up was worn and actors 'either looked too light or too dark, depending on the ability of the cameraman to use available light' (Agcaoili 1958: 8).

Jose Nepomuceno, an engineer who switched careers to become the nation's most successful owner of a photo studio, fathered the Philippine movie industry. In 1917, Nepomuceno took another chance—he sold his lucrative studio, read up on the movie industry and invested his savings in buying movie equipment from Gross. His Malayan Movies[1] made documentaries before tackling *Dalagang Bukid* (Country Maiden), a *sarsuwela*-based feature considered the first truly Filipino picture (Quirino 1983: 11).

In an interview in 1958, Nepomuceno recalled the movie:

> 'It was a silent picture, for that was the era of silent movies. But one thing peculiar about it was that it was the first musical silent picture. The same orchestra that appeared in the movie appeared in the pit . . . and it played the theme of 'Dalagang Bukid' as the movie was flashed on the screen. Atang de la Rama [a leading actress later named a "national artiste"] herself was there behind the screen. At appropriate moments during the showing, she would sing the songs she sang in the film. No, there was no attempt at all at synchronisation. She simply sang behind the stage to heighten the emotion. The film was filled beyond capacity every day during its ten-day run.' (Dizon 1958: 10–11).

By trial and error, Nepomuceno developed his own style and theory. Because there were not enough foreign films for the half dozen local theatres, Nepomuceno produced his pictures in fast succession; sometimes it took a month, other times only a week. Among his early ventures were *Tatlong Hambog*, *Sampaguita*, *La Mujer Filipina*, *La Venganza de Don Silvestre* and *Un Capullo Marchito*. Before his death in 1961, Nepomuceno made more than 300 films and founded at least Malayan Movies (1917), Malayan Pictures Corporation (1931), Nepomuceno Productions (1932), Nepomuceno-Harris-Tait Partnership (1933), Parlatone Hispano-

Filipino Inc. (1935), X'Otic Films (1938) and Polychrome Motion Picture Corporation (1946) (Salumbides 1952: 7).

The type of equipment used early on left much to be desired, as remembered by Nepomuceno:

> 'In those days, there was not much to talk about in the way of equipment, except the cigar box type camera and the tripod on which it was set. If you were a cameraman in those days, it was necessary for you to have strong and sturdy hands and wrists. For you operated the camera by cranking it with your right hand, not too fast and not too slow, and the cranking had to be steady or the result would be jerky pictures on the screen. With the left hand you manipulated another crank for turning the camera sideways.' (Dizon 1958: 10–11)

Equipment in the theatres was as rudimentary. Because theatres could not afford more than one projector, houselights had be turned on when reels were changed. Projectors, too, were cranked by hand, making for wavy pictures. Nepomuceno said patrons sat on uncushioned, bedbug-ridden benches in theatres where the air was hot and stale.

Eventually, more theatres were built. In the provinces, even the cockpits were temporarily turned into movie houses. 'Some enterprising individuals made good business by travelling from place to place with a portable projector—they used carbide in place of the electric arc light where there was no electricity—and a white blanket for a screen,' Dizon (1958, p. 11) wrote.

As a means of livelihood, the film industry was looked down upon. Movies were considered by some to be a vulgar form of entertainment, and those who performed in them were considered debauched. Thus, recruitment for films was difficult. Nepomuceno's wife and partner, Isabel Acuña, was particularly adept at recruiting, often going from door to door to convince parents to permit their offspring to perform (Quirino 1983: 16).

Nepomuceno's hand was in almost all filmmaking throughout the 1920s and part of the 1930s. His sixteenth film, *Punyal na Ginto* (Golden Dagger, 1933), was among the first Filipino sound productions[2]; his collaboration with nearly all other pioneers was legendary. When Julian Manansala started his film company and produced *Patria Amore*[3], Nepomuceno was technical advisor; when Vicente Salumbides returned from work as an extra in Hollywood, he sought Nepomuceno as camera and laboratory man for his first release in 1925, *Miracles of Love* (Salumbides 1952: 11). Later, in 1937, Nepomuceno helped establish Sampaguita with a group of prominent people, including Rep. Pedro Vera, Sen. Jose O. Vera and Rep. Jose Zulueta, and with George F. Harris, he organised

Filippine Films, responsible for filming the first Filipino movie for world release, *Zamboanga*.

With the advent of the 1930s, a number of significant changes occurred, including the introduction of 'talkies', the star system, big studios and genre movies, all imitative of Hollywood. Stars, 'Caucasian-looking and glamorous' (Tiongson 1986: 4), were developed and retained by the studios, which made them popular among the masses. Even before World War II, magazines and newspapers, such as *Literary Song* and *Philippines Herald*, sponsored contests to choose the most popular actors and actresses.

The stars, as well as directors and technicians, were contracted to the growing list of big studios which dominated: Filippine Films (1934), Parlatone Hispano-Filipino (1935), Excelsior and Sampaguita (1937), LVN (1938) and X'Otic and Salumbides Film Company (1939).[4]

Two companies emerged as the most powerful—Sampaguita and LVN. Sampaguita, started in part by a secession of some artists from Parlatone Hispano-Filipino, and in part by the Vera family, produced 128 movies during its heyday of 1938–50. LVN, which made 150 features and introduced colour cinematography in the same period, was the brain-child of a wealthy industrialist widow, Doña Narcisa Buencamino vda. de Leon, known as Doña Sisang.[5] By 1939, at least eleven film companies with a paid-up capital of P430,000 were in operation, producing 50 films, the fifth highest total in the world. The following year, the number increased to 57 (Lumbrera 1981: 57).

The movies were popular in the country's 345 sound theatres, where a feature costing P50,000 could expect to gross three times that amount. By 1939, directors and stars were highly paid, with some averaging P1,000 a picture. A few years before, stars were paid P36 a month. The most popular genre was exaggerated melodrama, using actresses who could 'cry at the drop of a hanky' (Quirino 1983: 26) and based on stories that came from vernacular magazines, especially *Liwayway* (American Chamber of Commerce *Journal* 1939: 47–8). Other film genres, including comedy, horror and social significance, had been used by early filmmakers such as Nepomuceno, but tear-jerkers were favoured.

Production techniques improved greatly by 1940, prompting Agcaoili (1940, pp. 106–11) to make comparisons with what existed previously:

'Before, the attitude may be best described as willy-nilly. There was no need to see rushes or advance prints . . . There was no need for laborious editing. And the sound technician did not have to worry if there were many disturbing and unintended sound effects in his sound track because . . . the producer didn't worry . . . Sometimes you could see a microphone caught in a frame . . .

But times have changed. Before, anyone's house would do for a set, now nothing less than a studio-built set would be proper . . . Painfully slow scripts were used then . . . [but now, audiences] want timing in their motion pictures.'

Among directors responsible for these improvements was Lamberto Avellana. After having seen a number of pictures, Avellana believed he could do a better job directing, even though he had no knowledge of production techniques. He proved to be correct. Financed by the wealthy Araneta family, Avellana's first effort, *Sakay*, is considered one of the most artistic Philippine films of all time. But it flopped at the box office (Interview, Avellana, 1965).

Describing film's adolescent period, of which he was a part, Avellana (Interview, 1965) said:

'There were many small movie companies in 1925–26. The big companies, however, bred the larger movie stars, who were moving in from vaudeville. In the daytime, stars would do movies; at night, they'd be in their usual vaudeville shows. There were only four or five directors in those days. The stories were fantasies which later developed into more natural tear-jerkers. This sentimental, mawkish story style stayed on well into the 1930s. Movies then were one-way propositions—there were no half-tones as to virtue; either good or bad. There was no technique as to story telling. Then, there was no effort exerted for technical excellence. Both photography and sound were very poor . . . But pre-war movies were of superior quality or even of higher calibre in integrity of manufacture than the bigger and better productions of 1965.'

Avellana believed the largest studios, which had been the benefactor of the industry, became its malefactor by 1941. He said:

'The big studios started to drag their feet . . . and stifled progress. They stopped the production of many movies, and kept creative labour under the thumb of capitalists. There was no expansion possible for the smaller companies because what came to be known as the Big Four controlled the outlets for movies. It was a dictatorship.' (Interview, Avellana, 1965)

The industry grew even more dormant during World War II. Exhibition was limited, partly because the Japanese believed Philippine movies were too attached to the United States. One Japanese writer expressed it this way:

'It may be said that most of the Philippine movies were a shame to the nation . . . and Philippine movies were mesmerized by the skillful manipulation of United States movie men who have lost their standards by which to evaluate life . . . There is not even a single case in which the real life of Manila or of the provinces was ever depicted faithfully.' (Sawamura 1944)

And production was virtually shut down as studios were closed and many actors and technicians joined the underground movement or turned to the stage. The Japanese favoured screening newsreels.

Liberation in 1945 ushered in a plethora of film companies. Sampaguita resumed in June 1945 and, in a short while, 19 production companies existed (Interview, Avellana, 1965). By 1952, the number of producers swelled to at least 40, including Fernando Poe Productions, Manuel Conde Productions, Leopoldo Salcedo Productions, Efren Reyes Productions, Eddie Romero Productions and Padilla Brothers Productions, all headed by actors or directors who turned producers.

Companies which dominated most of the market were Sampaguita, LVN, Lebran and Premiere (the Big Four). Premiere was established by Dr Ciriacio Santiago in 1946. For 15 years, beginning in 1948, the studio benefited from the works of director Gerardo de Leon. A medical doctor by profession, de Leon was coerced to assist a Japanese director during the war, thus beginning his new career. His 75 films exemplified a passion to reproduce Jose Rizal's works and their nationalism, to revise *komiks*[6] and to use sexual symbolism.

Three of these top companies were identified with a specific genre — Sampaguita with melodrama, LVN with comedy and Premiere with action. Together, they released 60 films in 1949 alone.

Although the number of companies mushroomed, fewer made a profit; in fact, only 10 per cent of the companies by 1950. Movies were burdened with high taxes and production costs and an acute scarcity of raw materials. The emergence of more companies resulted in the increased consumption of raw materials, causing shortages. As had been normal, the government did nothing to boost local movies even though it raked in P3.5 million a year in taxes. The industry was the most heavily taxed, paying 28 per cent of its gross earnings to the government (Amigo 1954: 190–3); at the same time, it was unprotected from an onslaught of imports, as many as 460 in 1953. Compounding the problem, the Central Bank of the Philippines permitted 72 per cent of foreign film income to be remitted abroad.

At the same time, producers were criticised for sacrificing 'any factor that makes for excellence to save a few pesos' (*Manila Chronicle* 1948: 75).

The early 1950s saw the Big Four at their peak and the proliferation of independent producers who ultimately changed the industry. Until the end of 1952, the industry depended entirely upon the Big Four, who hired a combined total of 10,000 people.

Organised for the mutual protection and advancement of their four-member studios, the Big Four controlled almost exclusively the production, distribution and exhibition of 90 per cent of Filipino movies.

The arrangement began to disintegrate when employees of Premiere went on strike in 1950. The strike lasted until 1955, with Premiere losing the case in court. During this period, a sister company, People's Pictures, continued making movies and it, along with Premiere, made 30 to 32 a year until they went out of production in 1962. 'We quit producing pictures because our stockholders had been paralysed by the strike outcome', the studio manager of Premiere explained (Interview, Navarro, 1965). Soon afterwards, Lebran also stopped producing features, limiting itself to short advertising films.

A factor which contributed to the Big Four's bargaining power with exhibitors had been its guarantee to supply 72 pictures a year. When Premiere and Lebran, producers of 40 per cent of this total, pulled out of production, this bargaining advantage was lost.

As early as 1953, it was evident the industry had changed, as Deegar Cinema was established to encourage independent producers to borrow money from its production fund, with which they could make movies that were released through Deegar's extensive booking organisation. Using Deegar as financier, top artistic and technical talents bailed out of the Big Four to start their own companies, bringing major stars with them. Independents could offer higher salaries to stars because they did not have the overhead expenses of operating studios. By 1958, about 100 movie companies existed in the Philippines and, within a few years, only Sampaguita of the Big Four was among them (Interview, Avellana, 1965).

A number of incentives to improve production occurred. In 1951, the *Manila Times* instituted the short-lived 'Maria Clara Awards' for filmmakers, and the following year, the Filipino Academy of Movie Arts and Sciences (FAMAS) was formed with its own set of awards. During this decade, directors such as Avellana, de Leon, Ramon Estela, Manuel Conde and Gregorio Fernandez made their best works.

In 1953, the National Media Production Centre began helping filmmakers to make short films for educational and informative purposes and, the same year, the cartoonist, Larry Alcala, experimented with, and taught, animation (Interview, Alcala, 1988). Other efforts to improve production were initiated by producers, including multi-story films and co-productions. Although they still believed a handsome face with no talent was better than a plain one who could act, producers did encourage film people to attend drama and speech clinics. Premiere and Araneta University offered courses for movie people.

Most movie goers of the 1950s and 1960s, as today, went to the theatre to see their favourite stars or to have a good cry. As a result, criticisms continued to pour in on the typical film:

'Dialogues often were tedious, prolonged and unreal; action tended to be either too gruesome, too fantastic, or too sentimental; stories became misshapen before production was over; unforgiveable inconsistencies in plot existed . . . ; sets and locations were not genuine; and the element of truth necessary to many films was missing' (Lent 1971: 120).

Avellana (Interview, 1965) said the industry had the stories and equipment to produce good movies but they were not used. He added, 'here a story is written in two days, shot in eleven and makes money at five days' exhibition, so we make another one just like it.'

In the 1960s, the industry was completely transformed. The Big Four had ceased production; independents dominated, with most in films solely for profits; citizens became indignant about the crime wave and possible links with movie viewing; the content of movies worsened further, providing an orgy of escapism, and the star system was pushed to the limit. With studios not tying them down to contracts, stars could call their shots. As one studio manager said:

'In the Big Four, we were very strict about personal contracts. The independents aren't. Now actors and actresses get P30,000–35,000 per picture for 30 days of shooting. Stars now can make four or five pictures simultaneously.' (Interview, Tecson, 1965)

The studio system had made filming a planned affair where Big Four directors lined up a variety of genres to appeal to a wide audience. But the independents, short on capital, had to get back their investments quickly, which they did by copying the last box-office hit. According to Lumbrera (1981, p. 58):

'The result was a plethora of films that tried to outdo foreign films in their depiction of sex and violence, giving rise to such curiosities as Filipino cowboys, Filipino samurai and kung fu masters, Filipino James Bonds, and, most notorious of them all, the *bomba* queen.'

The *bombas* were bold, sexual movies which featured young starlets who bared all on the screen.

Avellana referred to movie-goers who preferred the slam-bang, blood-and-guts, sex-filled 'quickies' as *bakya*, and a columnist further defined the term:

'The *bakya* crowd is not so much a matter of class distinctions as a certain mentality. The *bakya* mentality advocates conformity, is a zealous practitioner of *pakikisama* (going along with the crowd), and hates what is not of the crowd . . . They watch a *bakbakan* (violent) movie where the hero shoots down seven men with six bullets, seated in a bedbug-ridden, knife-slashed P1.20 seat, their feet on the backrest in front of them, cracking peanuts and repeating loudly every line said on the screen. The rise of the *bakya* masses as the domineering force in our society is a post-war phenomenon. One factor is the population explosion. This country is getting younger, judging by population figures and age brackets. Another factor is the contemporary attitude that demands overt acts of concern for the masses and an over-whelming show of social consciousness. People have an urge to be the champion of the masses.' (Roces 1965)

Most directors continue to see film in terms of the bakya audience, although since the early 1970s, a few others have viewed it as an art form. Young, university-trained and theatre-experienced, these new directors are familiar with the Italian neo-realists and surrealists, French 'new wave' and Japanese art films. They intro-duced a new trend of realism and social consciousness, while experimenting with directorial and acting techniques and developing new talents.

New directors had a banner year in 1976. Several of their films tackled issues about the Filipino's search for identity, among them being labour exploitation, poverty, national identity and US mili-tary bases in the Philippines. Typical of these works were Lino Brocka's *Insiang*, Behn Cervantes' *Sakada*, Lupita Concio's *Minsa'y Isang Gamu-Gamo* (Once There Was a Moth) and Eddie Romero's *Ganito Kami Noon, Paano Kayo Ngayon* (This Is How We Were, How Are You Going To Be Today?). Other later works were Brocka's *Kapit sa Patalim* (Bayan Ko), Ishmael Bernal's *Manila By Night* and Mike de Leon's *Kisapmata* and *Batch '81*.

Some new directors refused to abide by the goals of Marcos' 'New Society', which proclaimed films should show the 'true, good and beautiful'. Many films carried blatant, government-issued propaganda messages; those featuring negative societal charac-teristics had disclaimers that such traits were found in the old Philippines, but not the 'New Society'.

Even with this and other governmental manipulation, some aspects of Philippine movie-making thrived during the Marcos years. Obsessed with extravaganzas, the Marcoses revived the Metro Manila Film Festival in 1975 and, later, established an international festival and the Experimental Cinema of the Philippines.

CONTEMPORARY SCENE

Production

Throughout the 1980s, the Philippines ranked among the top ten film-producing countries of the world, although the industry was beset with many problems and the number of films was down from the 1971 peak of 251. In 1987, total production was 139, a drop from the 151 of the previous year. Forty production companies were in operation.

Increasingly, production was monopolised by three large companies (Regal, Seiko and Viva, together making about 45 films a year) which controlled some distribution-exhibition outlets and tied up stars on a contractual basis. In 1986, ten-year-old Regal signed exclusive contracts with more than three dozen stars, and also with directors, technicians and craftsmen, leading the Philippine Motion Pictures Producers Association (PMPPA) to cry monopoly. PMPPA said Regal's action, which Viva and Seiko emulated, would lead to a shortage of stars for small producers, bloating of talent fees and containment of some contracted stars, meaning they could not compete with other Regal talent.

ACTION (Action Against Movie Monopoly), an organisation made up of small producers, predicted its own number would diminish considerably, not being able to cope with the US $1.5 million Regal spent to corner the major stars. Regal's owner countered that her company had contracted only 5 per cent of the Actor's Guild roster (Dumaual 1986c: 38). One actor said the protest against Regal's monopolisation move gained no headway, because the stars did not sign the contracts under duress and because Regal loaned stars to other producers (Interview, Fabregas, 1986).

Regal was described as operating paternalistically, similar to MGM of years ago. Regal's head Lily Monteverde often assumes the stars' hospital bills, buys them million peso homes, finds them television jobs or gives them interest-free loans against their next role (Interviews, Gallaga and Fabregas, 1986). Seiko, Viva and Poe act similarly.

A common complaint about these large producers, and many of the smaller independents, is that their concern is solely to make money in what is referred to as the 'stench of commercialism'. Del Mundo (1988, pp. 1–2) traced the rampant commercialism to the conception of film as commodity. He said the US colonisation period favoured the dominance of Hollywood cinema and entrenched the notion of film as commodity. This, in turn, led to the current situation where, 'being true to its capitalist goals, the local industry naturally opens itself up to any commodity that spells profit'. Most often, the result is a 'cheap commodity', he added, making the Philippines a 'junk market' for crass commercialism.

There is a plentiful supply of filmmakers anxious to testify to del Mundo's charges. Writing about the previous decade, de Castro (1986b, p. 189), reporting that it took more than US $50,000 to make a quality picture, said most producers, lacking this sum,

'hire sex stars as an insurance for box-office appeal with built-in publicity; they hire quickie directors with a taste for the vulgar and the gross to titillate the audience; and they hire a quickie writer who can concoct sensational if not absurdly illogical plots.'

Another critic said that with the capitalisation required, the favourable conditions given to US films, burdensome taxes and the fact that the film industry was an industry, producers had no other consideration except money. Thus, they resorted to formulas— action pictures with at least 15 fight sequences, river-of-tears melodramas, musicals with colour, movement and song, sex with 'at least six major sexual encounters and preferably showing "pumping" (if possible, penetration) and frontal nudity' (Tiongson 1986: 18).

One director described the attitude of producers as 'scrimp, save and cut quality, yet demand quality'. He said producers expected directors to be magicians able to come up with miracles (Interview, Cinco, 1986).

Because a large part of the formula film's popularity derives from using big stars, leading actors and actresses devour production budgets, sometimes by as much as half. In a typical P3 million (20 pesos to US $1) production, P1,325,000 will go to the cast, P500,000 to promotion and publicity, P450,000 to production staff, P300,000 to raw materials, P100,000 to colour processing and the rest to black/white processing, film equipment rental, food catering, transportation or optical titles (Vertido 1988: 129). Breaking down wage scales, de Castro (1986a, p. 101) gave US $20,000–80,000 for superstars, US $3,500 for a first-rate director and US $1,500 for a top scriptwriter. If a movie does not include superstars, then the total spent on all leading stars is US $21,000, he said.

As an example, Romy Suzara's *Somewhere* cost P3.5 million to make. Out of that, the leading actor took P1 million and the director, P200,000. About a third of the costs went to raw stock, negatives and processing (Interview, Suzara, 1986). Fabregas said big-time actors took 40 per cent of the budget; the two leads made P1.5 million in a P4 million film. Top supporting actors received P50,000 –75,000; others, P35,000–40,000. Editors made P30,000 a picture, but must pay assistants from that, and top cinematographers were paid P60,000 a picture (Interview, Fabregas, 1986). Gallaga pointed out that with the big companies, which have actors/actresses under contract, the salaries were not so far out of proportion. In a P2.5 million Regal film, for example, stars' wages began at

P50,000–80,000 and went up according to a scale (Interview, Gallaga, 1986).

The unstable nature of the country is reflected in the film industry. Numerous coup attempts, civil strife and a depleted economy have kept down investment in movies, while production costs and taxes have spiralled. One handicap of many filmmakers is that a shortage of money has not allowed for updating equipment. Thus, 25-year-old cameras, sound equipment and lights, which one director said belonged in the Smithsonian Institution, are used (Interview, Cinco, 1986).

In recent years, the long-standing, oppressive taxes on the industry have been raised, rather than lowered, as called for by filmmakers. A top scriptwriter said that although there had been moves since the 1960s to lower taxes, they had been raised and more had been added. He said this resulted because, as the 'people's medium, film brings in lots of money and therefore, a lot of taxes' (Interview, Lacaba, 1986). Until 1982, taxes paid by the industry came to about P1 billion a year; in 1986, the figure was P600 million.

At least 17 taxes are levied on film, accounting for about 42 per cent of the industry's gross. A bill in Congress in 1988 advocated a tax reduction (Vertido 1988: 132). Instead, a new value-added tax increased the taxes to 58 per cent of box-office receipts. Among the taxes are cultural, amusement, billings, import, corporate income, censorship, ad valorem, processing, withholding and flood. The uses made of the taxes have raised some eyebrows. Henares (1986, p. 5) said the cultural tax of 25 centavos a ticket was 'exacted from the Nora Aunor fan, and used to subsidize Van Cliburn's performance . . . for the enjoyment of millionaire music lovers'. The flood tax is used to improve drainage.

Competition from foreign films and pirated videocassettes has also adversely affected production. As del Mundo showed, the producer is at a disadvantage to the importer. A viable budget for a local production, he said, was US $100,000, excluding advertising and promotion. On the other hand, the rights to a low-budget US or Hong Kong picture could be obtained for US $50,000, and the importer did not have to endure the production hassles (del Mundo 1988: 5).

The Philippines are unique in Asia for not having placed a quota on foreign films, the result being that the country has become the 'dumping ground for rejects shown in US drive-ins' (Interview, Brocka, 1986). Since the 1960s, efforts to place quotas on imports have failed regularly in the Philippine Congress, because distributors, who also handle the imports, are more powerful than producers, according to one source (Interview, Lacaba, 1986).

Home video has been blamed for a 40 per cent drop in film box-office receipts in its first four years in the Philippines. By the time

Marcos established the Videogram Regulatory Board (VRB) in October 1985, tape renting had become a US $30 million annual business, operating out of 5,000 stores (Giron 1985: 336). VRB required all video retailers to register with the Securities and Exchange Commission and raised by 5000 per cent the penalties for copyright infringements through pirated tapes (see Boyd, Straubhaar and Lent 1989).

Video piracy has been so lucrative and organised that an exposé in 1988 showed the pirates had one of their own people installed on the VRB. Other groups fighting pirated video are the Motion Picture Anti-Film Piracy Council of PMPPA and the US Majors' Philippine Federation Against Copyright Theft (Giron 1987: 41).

Directors are very concerned about pirated video, predicting the death of Philippine films if the pirates are not better controlled. They concur that the major damage done by pirates is in the provinces. One director explained:

'The pirates knock you off in the provinces. We release film slowly here. One print will go to four or five places and will take a month to go to Cebu, even longer to Davao [southern regions]. Thus, the pirates have enough time to copy a print and release it beforehand.' (Interview, Cinco, 1986)

Gallaga said videos for the provinces were more sexually explicit, as producers inserted scenes not permitted for Manila audiences (Interview, Gallaga, 1986).

Besides efforts to reduce film taxation and to control video piracy, the industry has promoted co-productions, Filipino locations for foreign producers, overseas markets and other outlets such as television and legitimate video. None has been particularly earthshaking. Bernal said the co-productions were not significant, being made by half Filipino and half US or Italian crews for US drive-ins (Interview, Bernal, 1986). Regal made films with Italian producers, who used Filipino stars, technicians and locations. In this arrangement, Regal invested in the movies for which it received the Asian rights; all other rights went to the Italians (Interview, Suzara, 1986).

A push was on in the latter half of the 1980s to make the Philippines the major lensing location in the tropics. Among bodies involved were Entertainment Philippines Inc. and Eastern Film Management Corporation. Some major US films attracted to Philippine locations, stars and crews were *Platoon*, *Hamburger Hill*, *Missing in Action III* and *Apocalypse Now*.

Mainly through Entertainment Philippines Inc. and Roadshow Presentation, there have been a 'few weak and ineffectual' attempts to do overseas distribution (Interview, Bernal, 1986). A few films were distributed in San Francisco but not successfully. 'Our films are not marketable in Asia either. It's very strange. We're neighbours but very different from other countries,' Bernal said (Interview, Bernal, 1986). Gallaga, whose *Scorpio Nights* was marketed in Hong Kong and Singapore, said the Philippine industry was aiming for the ASEAN market, putting something in for each country (Interview, Gallaga, 1986).

Television and legitimate video have become increasingly important as secondary outlets for Filipino movies. Among top-rated shows on the five main television networks are re-runs of movies, e.g. 'Regal Presents' or 'FPJ sa GMA'. Networks have agreed not to show any movie until one year after its first theatre engagement. Regal, Viva and Seiko have viewed television as more than a secondary market, producing sitcoms and drama series using their contracted stars (Vertido 1988: 130). Some producers have made videocassettes of their movies for the 2.5 million Filipinos abroad.

Distribution and Exhibition

The familiar refrain that distributors control the industry resounds among Filipino filmmakers, and for the same reason as elsewhere in Asia: 'They have direct contact with the money,' actor Jimmy Fabregas explained (Interview, 1986).

Two circuits exist in Metro Manila and that both are owned by Filipino Chinese does not bode well with prevalent nationalistic sentiments. One director confidentially compared the situation with Malaysia a generation back, when, he said, the Chinese split the circuits among themselves. But another director, who thinks he is victimised by the nationalism, was satisfied that the Chinese handled distribution very well, claiming any other sector would 'botch up the job' (Interview, Gallaga, 1986).

Listening to other movie people, however, one gets the impression distribution is already a mess, especially as it benefits producers and directors. Avellana said distributors, with 'their finger on the pulse of the audience', determine themes and actors for pictures (Interview, Avellana, 1986); scriptwriter Ricky Lee agreed. Lee described the situation at Regal, the studio for which he writes:

> 'Many producers consult distributors first. At Regal, "Mother Lily" [Monteverde] is told by the distributor that certain stars should be in a movie. Distributors have a monopoly, so producers have to set up their own movie houses. "Mother Lily" owns some theatres.' (Interview, Lee, 1986)

Director Manuel 'Fyke' Cinco added that although anti-trust laws prohibit distributors from investing in productions, they do so nevertheless (Interview, Cinco, 1986). In 1978, the two rival exhibition organisations, Greater Metro Manila Theatres Association and Metro Manila Theatres Association, joined together with the aim of entering production. Filmmakers such as Joseph Estrada were alarmed. He warned that such a monopoly by 'alien' theatre owners-producers would eliminate play dates for other producers (Henares 1986: 5).

Although producers are promised a third of the box-office profits (with another third each going to distributors-exhibitors and the government), they are often shy of this target; the system is designed to defraud them.

More realistically, the distributor gets 40 to 60 per cent of the net film share. Lee pointed out that a rating system which provided a 50 per cent rebate for 'A' films and 25 per cent for 'B', was ineffective because distributors did not comply (Interview, Lee, 1986); Fabregas said that theatre owners bribed attendance checkers to underestimate the figure, so that 'people can be lined up for a block to see a movie, and the producer will still lose money' (Interview, Fabregas, 1986).

At one point in 1979, the plight of producers had become so bad that, as a group, they threatened to boycott all Metro Manila theatres if exhibitors did not give them a 'fair deal'. They campaigned for income-sharing terms and asked that they should not be made to pay for the production of newspaper movie guides and lobby and outdoor advertisements, nor suffer unreasonable delays in remittances.

Corruption has played a key role in distribution-exhibition, according to Sazon (1986 pp. 115–18). Detailing problems of distributors, he included the usual ones of taxes, ultraconservative censors and pressure groups, government ignorance of the industry and limited theatre circuits. But, distributors, and ultimately producers, also endure delinquent remittances from theatres, fraudulent practices in ticket selling (e.g. tellers who recycle already sold tickets), illegal exhibitors, dishonest checkers and bookers and burdensome and unfair terms from established distributors (e.g. 70 per cent of the box office) (Sazon 1986: 115–18).

Theatre owners have their own difficulties, among which are taxes, harassment from city inspectors, corruption in the periodic inspection process, overcrowding and littering, vandalism and theft (Sazon 1986: 117–8).

Movies have been booked in two ways—locked date, meaning that specific play-dates are agreed upon; and holdover, where films play as long as attendance remains at a certain level. The locked date system predominates in major theatres, because exhibitors want a change of films each week (del Mundo 1988: 4), with the abundant supply that exists. Some very good films are extended to a second week.

Films are released slowly, according to Cinco, to maximise the audience in one region before marketing in the next. If he had his way, Cinco would simultaneously distribute films in Manila and the provinces, as well as extend the number of showing days (Interview, Cinco, 1986).

The stiff competition in getting movies booked through the two circuits results in smaller producers folding, resorting to making bomba or skipping the Manila big houses in favour of fringe theatres and those in the provinces. But, success is usually determined by a film's showing in Manila. According to one director, for a movie to recoup its investment, its take in the provinces must double that of Metro Manila. Some do not retrieve their Metro Manila slice (Interview, Cinco, 1986). Another source claimed that for a film to capture the Metro Manila audience before heading for the provinces on an eight-to-ten month, 250–350 theatre tour, it has to recover 40 per cent of investment (Vertido 1988: 128–9).

In some ways, the distribution system is antiquated. Called *lagare* (saw), the system operates on the principle that producers rotate a limited number of prints of a film to service many theatres where it is showing. Scriptwriter Jose 'Pete' Lacaba described lagare:

'For example, to show your film in 40 theatres at one time, you produce ten prints. The distributor starts one film in three houses in Cubao [a district] at 9 a.m., then takes the same first reel to another series of houses at 9.15 a.m. A bicyclist then moves the reels from house to house. As a result, movie houses open at staggered 15-minute intervals.' (Interview, Lacaba, 1986)

Numerous complaints of delays in screenings are voiced when bicyclists are stopped by the police or have accidents.

Theatres, which range from first- to third-run and total 1,200 in the Philippines, have had financial problems in recent years as maintenance cost has shot up, and attendance has dropped because of other diversions, i.e. home video and television. Still, seven out of ten people in Metro Manila attend the theatres regularly (Vertido 1988: 131); nation-wide, there are about 600 million theatre viewers annually (Tiongson 1986: 10). In Manila, movie-goers pay an average cost of US 40 cents. A new showing occurs every two hours from 9 a.m. to the last which begins at 10 p.m.

Directing, Acting and Scriptwriting

Directors have two major spaces in which to work, according to del Mundo (1988, p. 6)—either inside or outside the system.

Working outside the system are experimental, documentary and animation filmmakers such as Kidlat Tahimik (Eric de Guia), Raymond Red and others connected to some universities. About as free as a director can be, Tahimik operates on his 'cup of gasoline' approach: 'I compare myself to someone driving a car and I have a cup of gasoline. Then I scrounge around for the next cup of gasoline, and on and on until I get it all together.' (del Mundo 1988: 9)

However, the economics of movie-making does not allow for many directors to work outside the sytem. Instead, they make serious movies which have the 'guise of box-office entertainment' and feature superstars (Interview, Bernal, 1986), or they alternate commercially-successful films with their favourite projects, the latter often money losers.

Of 147 members of the directors' guild, only 20 to 25 made two or three movies in 1986; the rest were lucky if they had one film (Interview, Cinco, 1986). At that time, famous 'new wave' directors, such as Bernal, Brocka and Marilou Diaz Abaya, were without film contracts. Bernal (Interview, 1986) said if things got worse, he would go to New York; scriptwriter Lee claimed the top ten directors had already moved into television. Lee felt 'new wave' directors were jobless because they were too artistic, quoting the Regal's owner as saying what she did not want were 'art-art and strikes' (Interview, Lee, 1986).

Perhaps what had happened was that the directors (especially socially relevant 'new wave' ones) had been demoted in the film schema from their peak in the late 1970s and early 1980s, when, according to Fabregas (Interview, 1986), the public began thinking of directors (not just superstars) as important. 'Now, film is not just a star vehicle, but also a director and script vehicle,' he said.

Most prominent of the group of new directors is Brocka, a controversial and complex figure who works within the confines of the industry. He had tried his own production company, Cine Manila, which went bankrupt. Armes (1987, p. 153) pointed out the contradictory works Brocka had made—*Bona* (1980), which used stars to attack the excesses of the star system; *Kontrobersyal* (1980), which is pornography, as well as a denunciation of porn, and *Angela Markado* (1980), which attacked rape in the form of a vigilante-style revenge movie. He added that Brocka offered a 'cleaned-up version of poverty' and maintained 'complicity with the worlds the films ostensibly denounce' (Armes 1987: 153). Francia (in Downing 1987: 213) said Brocka's camera, in films such as *Jaguar* (1979), *Insiang* (1976), *Manila in the Claws of Neon* (1975) and *Bona*, gave a view from below, warts and all.

Because they have dealt with slums and poverty, among other negative aspects of society, Brocka's films have suffered from government scissors and proclamations. 'I can't count how many of my films have been banned or censored,' Brocka said (Interview, 1986). His *Ang Bayan Ko* (My Country) was disavowed as the Philippine entry in the Cannes Film Festival in 1984, unless Brocka excised scenes of protest rallies and labelled the movie 'for adults only'. Instead, the director filed a suit with the Supreme Court. In 1985, he and fellow director, Behn Cervantes, were arrested for incitement to sedition as they participated in a *jeepney* (converted jeeps used for mass transit) drivers' strike. Brocka served three weeks in jail. He also led the Free-the-Artist Movement and Concerned Artists of the Philippines and was an appointed delegate to the Constitutional Commission, from which he resigned in protest after helping to secure some freedom for the arts.

His 'more than 70' films (Brocka's estimate), starting in 1970, have included a number of award winners and entries in the Cannes and other international festivals. Yet, Brocka is not internationally known, according to Domingo (1984, p. 44), because of the reluctance of major film companies to distribute risky Third World movies and Brocka's refusal to work for financially well-endowed producers with formularistic policies.

Discussing his emphasis on characters, Brocka said:

'I still love movies. The reason my films are melodramas, film noir, is because I love them, and film noir seems to me to be close to the social reality of the Philippines. I have always been in love with characters. They are terminal people . . . they have nowhere to go. But they don't give up. They turn around, away from the wall. They make a choice. They're strong. They fight back.' (Hodel 1984: 35)

Brocka, as well as numerous other directors, came from the theatre—in his case, the Philippine Educational Theatre Association (PETA), an effort at a national theatre in the Filipino language. When PETA produced a television show on the format of 'Play-house' in the US, Brocka was one of its four directors. He made his first movie, *Wanted: A Perfect Mother* in 1970 (Interview, Brocka, 1986).

'The movie industry was a closed system then—like a big family, and those with a college background were anathema', because the old directors thought they would make boring art films, he said (Interview, Brocka, 1986). After a producer saw Brocka's work and asked him to make his first movie, *Manila Chronicle* critic Ishmael Bernal was also asked to be a director in 1971. 'There was a fad then to allow young college-educated people in as directors,' Brocka explained (Interview, 1986).

Pointing out that before his productions, only the bakya crowd attended Filipino films, Brocka said he changed that by combining commercial appeals with a touch of art. He said he closely studied US works, the gangster movies of John Garfield, as well as other formula films, such as *Tarzan* and Astaire and Rogers. 'I was a film fanatic,' Brocka said. 'I decided I would make this type of film but technically better than the norm in the Philippines.' His philosophy was:

'I would not alienate the audience; I'd show something familiar but a little bit different. The audiences came and opened the door for this type of film. They were box-office successes, and producers only understood box office; they were very happy about this mixture. It was like a tug of war: to make some movies I like to make, I'd make one that would be a sure box-office success. Then the next one would be with new actors and would be more artful. I'd make one based on komiks, then one on an original script. When I made five a year, four would be commercial and one that Marcos would not like, that would enrage Imelda.' (Interview, Brocka, 1986)

Also making social relevance types of films was Bernal, who concentrated on 'the underground, subterranean, marginal people of Manila; on modern Filipinos in the city' (Interview, Bernal, 1986). Some of his notable films are *Pagdating sa Dulo* (At the Top), his first; *Himala* (Miracle); *Nunal sa Tubig* (Mole in the Water) and *Manila by Night*. Because the latter dealt with the seamier side of Manila's nightlife, Imelda Marcos had the title changed to *City by Night*, claiming that what was portrayed in the film could not have been shot in Manila.

Bernal's work is noted for witty, amusing satires, as well as a number of traits listed by de Castro (1986b, p. 193) as,

'urbane and intelligent dialogue, fast-paced story development, ironic situations which reveal the true feelings of his bourgeois characters, upper middle-class settings, symbolic imagery and emotional control which . . . develops into alienation.'

Obviously directors of socially relevant films represent a minority in the industry; more prevalent are filmmakers such as Peque Gallaga, Romy Suzara and Manuel 'Fyke' Cinco.

Gallaga, whose work was very popular in the mid-1980s, received his break from the Marcos-conceived ECP. 'It stank and was rotten, but I owe my career to ECP,' Gallaga said. He believed some older directors were improved by ECP, which 'shook them up' with the question, 'are you going to do good work for a change?' (Interview, Gallaga, 1986).

After about six years of theatre and television work, Gallaga directed his first film in 1971. When martial law was declared the following year, he returned to his home province, where he remained for four years. Upon his return to Manila, Gallaga worked under Bernal, who taught him 'to be a director, not just to direct'. Making the distinction, he said to direct was a technique, while to be a director was 'a social thing'. The latter, according to Gallaga, involved the 'way you treat the press, the formalities, the Asian way of doing things' (Interview, Gallaga, 1986).

Criticising what he termed as the 'Cannes school of filmmaking', Gallaga said Filipino directors had to do movies for the public, 'not just for personal expression' or for entry in Cannes. Attributing much of the change in the director's role to Brocka, Gallaga said the role should be to ask questions, not to have all the answers (Interview, Gallaga, 1986).

At first identified with period films, Gallaga is now comfortable with all genres. Among his films are *Oro, Plata, Mata* (Gold, Silver, Death), an award winner which described the decline of the autocracy after World War II, and *Scorpio Nights* which, in 1985, broke box-office records.

Suzara, who has directed about 40 films of all types (comedy, drama, mystery, horror, action and bold), came up through the system. After he left high school, he worked as an extra, supporting actor, assistant director and production manager, before going to New York, where he studied and worked. In 1972, a producer in Manila gave him a break and he began directing (Interview, Suzara, 1986). Suzara was named best director in 1983 for his *Uod at Rosas* (Worm and Roses).

Cinco, a director of more than 50 movies, at least five of which earned him FAMAS' best picture or best director nominations, also progressed within the ranks. Starting out as a sound technician for Premiere, he advanced to scriptwriter, assistant director and, after 1968, director. He directs three to five films a year including comedy, action, drama and bold (Interview, Cinco, 1986).

Looking at directors by the way they tell stories, Lee identified three types—those of the 1950s and 1960s, who came to film from broadcasting, used plots and stories with beginnings, middles and ends and portrayed characters in black or white terms; those of the 'first wave', such as Brocka and Bernal, who leaned about half-way to something different, and those of the 'second wave', such as Gallaga. He said the latter types told stories in unconventional ways. For example, Bernal's *Manila by Night* had no plot and the city of Manila was a character in itself. In previous movies, each character had to be motivated, but 'second wave' directors thought there could be cinematic motivations. They also used irony and sarcasm with audiences who were more mature than those of a generation before, and they began to think of the old stories as naive. Lee said they were more professionally aware and cosmopolitan, having attended workshops and studied foreign classics (Interview, Lee, 1986).

As indicated, Philippine movies are based on stars who are 'hot'; in some cases, stories are built around a star, rather than the star being cast in a role. As one writer said, 'People come to watch their favourite stars who happen to be in the film, not the character in a story which happens to be played by their favourite star.' (Vertido 1988: 129)

The stress on commercialisation and monopolisation has had debilitating effects upon the profession. Shortages of trained actors and actresses exist; the criteria for starring roles are often based on actresses undressing and actors 'sending female hearts fluttering' (de Castro 1986b: 195). The high fees paid to superstars deplete budgets and have the tendency to make some actors lazy and indifferent. One actor explained:

'Producers just want money to come in and continue to make commercial movies. Thus, if a bold (bomba) picture is successful, there will be 15 more in a week. This affects acting. For example, I work at Regal. "Mother Lily" has a stable of actors which she uses in one fantasy and bomba picture after another. This does not leave room for improvement of the craft. There is no preparation at all, and some actors are in four films at one time. No matter how good an actor you are, in such cases, you can't have time to work on roles, and you become lazy. It's like an assembly line. Some bomba stars don't feel they have to work at roles, just show boobs and some pubic.' (Interview, Fabregas, 1986)

Sex films are less expensive to produce, partly because they depend on young talent willing to forego huge salaries in order to get a start. As Brocka said:

'The producers get a young girl willing to undress. Then they name her. First, they were giving the girls rich people's names, then they used soft drinks ('Sarsi', 'Pepsi'); now they use hard liquor names ('Brandy', 'Vodka Zobel'). The naming is a tongue-in-cheek, get-back-at-society gimmick.' (Interview, Brocka, 1986)

Some older stars are enshrined in roles which they repeat almost by rote. Since the February 1986 revolution, some veteran actors and actresses have been stigmatised by the nationalistic fervour. Gallaga (Interview, 1986) said they were discriminated against because of politics. 'They are not considered for what they are, but for what they stand for. The box office is down for some, accused of letting Marcos use them,' he added.

In some circles, maturation of acting skills occurred in the 1980s. The actors' guild ran workshops built around group dynamics, and the concept of training spread into other areas of filmmaking, such as scriptwriting and cinematography. Gallaga believed a strong sense of professionalism resulted with actors looking at themselves as 'individuals, not competitors'. The workshops were successful, according to him, because actors 'do not want a year of training, but if you put it into six days, they will attend' (Interview, Gallaga, 1986).

Resurgence of the big studio system has perpetuated the monopolisation of the services of stars. In 1986, when Regal signed 39 stars to one- or two-year contracts, each to do eight to nine films, Viva followed. Monopolising stars is an old problem. In 1977, for example, Fernando Poe, jr, as president of PMPPA, called for a 'democratisation of the superstar system', whereby top stars would make themselves available to small producers at lower rates (de Castro 1986b: 195).

If superstars are overpaid, at the other extreme are the script-writers, who see themselves as exploited by the industry. They complain of being underpaid, having requested minima in 1977 (US $1,340 a script) and a decade later (US $375 and then US $1,000); being both ignored and interfered with by producers and directors; working on a seasonal basis and having their scripts mangled and changed. They agree that a prerequisite for writing scripts is the ability to compromise—to self-censor for the sake of box-office receipts or producers' whims.

Although the industry has advanced past the 'matchbox school of scriptwriting',[7] at least one writer, Clodualdo del Mundo jr, worries about a return to the days when directors shot without seeing a script. His fear stems from the Board of Censors' decision no longer to require a script, just the treatment of the film. Del Mundo, who has written scripts for de Leon, Brocka and others, said a writer could break into the film industry if he was willing to do everything the producer wanted (Interview, del Mundo, 1988).

The road to a scriptwriting career takes many paths. Del Mundo, a filmmaker himself, had been a college teacher, whereas others came out of the journalistic ranks. Lacaba, a film reviewer and political writer before being detained for two years under Marcos, resumed movie reporting upon his release from prison. On assignment to interview Bernal, the director, he ended up writing a script for him. 'Bernal said instead of me interviewing him, I should help him write a script,' Lacaba said. Averaging a script a year, Lacaba has also edited *Mid-Week Magazine* since 1985 (Interview, Lacaba, 1986).

Highest paid of the approximately 80–100 screenwriters is Ricky Lee, a short-story writer who was imprisoned for one year under martial law. Although he averages three or four scripts a year now (seven in 1983) at about US $1,000 each, and works with the finest directors, Lee had a dislike for scriptwriting in the 1970s. 'I got into scriptwriting by accident,' he said. When he was released from prison jobless, in 1975, Lee was introduced to some film people, for whom he wrote a script. He 'dropped out' after his initial film because, 'there were so many people telling me what to do, so many physical things to do, such as meetings and negotiations'. Lee said he became a film reviewer until 1979, when it was 'more exciting and safer to enter movies as there was the new wave of Brocka and Bernal' (Interview, Lee, 1986).

Most scriptwriters are free-lancers because studios do not retain in-house writers. Usually, a studio hires the director who, in turn, brings in his favourite writer. In some rare cases, a producer will go directly to the writer with a story idea. The writer then provides a synopsis of the story, and perhaps a sequence guide, after which the producer brings in a director to make the film. Lacaba said sometimes a producer had only a title and asked the writer to develop a story around it; other times, the writer was implored to come up with a story for a particular star (Interview, Lacaba, 1986).

The scriptwriter's position is not an enviable one, often suspended between the director and producer. Lee gave examples:

> 'The director will ask for a script for a star. After it is written, the director can say yes or no about using it. If the answer is yes, maybe the star will back out, or the producer will change his mind. If the producer says you need action in a script, a director will say don't listen to the producer. The director does what he wants to do. With my producer, you finish a first draft and she might want a new director, so you have to change the whole script. I don't know a single film project that is not a compromise.' (Interview, Lee, 1986)

Describing his writing for Regal, under 'Mother Lily' Monteverde, Lee said:

> 'She only wants to do fantasy—"Horsey Horsey, the Flying Horse"—and melodrama. She puts everything in a fantasy or melodrama perspective. Doing a script for her goes like this: "Mother Lily" tells you her life story and you are to put her story into the film. Her own drama gets into her films, her own anecdotes. She will think of a title (she was obsessed with English-language songs, and her films were titled *Til We Meet Again*, and such names) and then get the stars. Directors and scriptwriters are given the title from which they must develop a story.' (Interview, Lee, 1986)

Lee said she then retreats, allowing the story to be written, but with the first rushes, she interferes again, demanding that certain things be inserted.

The following anecdote, provided by Lee depicts the scriptwriter's frustration:

> 'Three years ago, "Mother Lily" heard I had a story about a twelve-year-old blind girl. She called, and I started the script. A week later, she called again and asked, "Who is the leading man?" I said she has no leading man; she is twelve and kills people in revenge for being an abused child. She says, "No, Ricky, you have to have a love theme." I said, "Blind girl is too busy killing, can't have boy friend." "Mother Lily" said, "Okay, no leading man, but have twelve men in the script." I said, "But, she won't kill twelve

men." Then, "Mother Lily" did not like the title, *Bulag* [blind]. She substituted *Memories*.' (Interview, Lee, 1986)

In addition, there are the problems of producers' reluctance to experiment; the self-censorship of scriptwriters (not for fear of censors, but of the box office); and the difficulty of doing scripts when everything in real life is more interesting than film stories.

The main sources of many Philippine movies (30–40 per cent of big studios' scripts) are the komiks, the popular weekly magazines often called the Philippine national book. Komiks make successful films because they have pre-sold audiences accustomed to that type of script.

Different approaches are taken in adapting komiks to movies. At Regal and other studios, film people monitor komiks to see which stories sell the best, or they go through back issues of komiks for story ideas (Interview, Fabregas, 1986). In other cases (almost half of the komiks movies), a producer sells an idea to the komiks publisher who brings it out in printed form. During the last few weeks of the komiks serialisation, the movie version appears with a climax that may or may not be the same as the magazine (Interview, Gallaga, 1986). Some producers make komiks characters look like movie stars, who then play the screen role.

Director Suzara said if a director wanted a box-office hit, he had to get the story from komiks or the radio. 'About 10 per cent of all scripts are from the komiks,' he said, adding,

'We monitor komiks regularly, and we do not wait until serialisation is over. As long as the komiks has a good sell, we get the story. We buy the story directly from the writer, and sometimes from the publisher.' (Interview, Suzara, 1986)

The impact of komiks is felt by all scriptwriters and directors. Brocka admitted the first movie he made was based on a komik that had been serialised for two years. He does not think komiks are bad for the film industry, although the stories have convoluted plots of ' "Dallas", "Dynasty", rapes, abortions, catastrophes and accidents all rolled into one' (Interview, Brocka, 1986). Lacaba, who gave 50 per cent as the number of films adapted from komiks, said the magazines had an impact on scriptwriting, with some writers specialising in adapting komiks to the screen, while all others were forced to use their story formula (Interview, Lacaba, 1986). Most of the scripts used by Seiko and Viva studios came from komiks, as did almost all action and drama stories (Interview, Fabregas, 1986).

Genres

Melodrama and action, preferably pre-sold in the komiks, and bomba have been the most popular genres during the past generation. The same types predominate today, but as audiences are more aware of the difference between good and bad films, they are better produced (Interviews, Lacaba and Fabregas, 1986). Scriptwriter Lee added formularistic slapstick comedy and fantasy to the list. He said that on some occasions, producers (especially 'Mother Lily') combined all five genres into one big fantasy (Interview, Lee, 1986).

In the late 1980s, genres were very imitative of those of the 1950s, including many melodramas based on the shop-worn theme of rich boy meets poor girl, with liberal doses of crying thrown in. Bernal believed the retrogression to escapist melodrama, action and bomba resulted because the '1980s does not have any more Lino Brockas really' (Interview, Bernal, 1986).

Facing some uncertainty in the post-Marcos era were the bomba, as the Aquino administration deputised provincial fiscals as arms of the censors' board, with the power to close theatres and prosecute their owners. The concern was with provincial theatres because they often insert explicit 'pene' (penetration) segments into films (Interview, Cinco, 1986).

Filmmakers had varying views of bomba, although, at one time or another, most had worked in the genre since its start in 1968. Cinco (Interview, 1986) was concerned about their competitive edge, pointing out a director would spend US $250,000 to make an action film and then 'get knocked off' by a bomba, starring bar girls, that would cost one-fifth as much. Others worried about the censorship of bomba. Bernal (Interview, 1986), predicting more cuts of bold movies, said the more they were censored the more ways their producers would devise to titillate, which he thought was 'more irritating than frank brutality' (see Lanot 1982: 18–22, for analysis of portrayal of women in bomba.)

Gallaga (Interview, 1986), who said he made more money from directing bomba than other genres, thought their popularity had already dwindled by 1986, because they were not done well and there were too many (as many as 70 per cent of all movies). 'Now bomba will go underground and people will pay more to see a little snatch,' he predicted, 'because Filipino males like the sensual.' Fabregas (Interview, 1986), predicting the survival of bomba, thought the Aquino government would not do anything more than the Marcos censors, who were tougher with social relevance, than with bold films. He said if bold movies were left alone, the public would tire of them, adding, 'the average Filipino goes to see bold because it is illegal'.

Avellana (Interview, 1986) attributed the growth of bold films to the Philippines' becoming a selling society in post-World War II. At first, he said,

'People were into selling jeeps. Selling a used jeep was just as good as selling a 17-year-old body and soon Filipinos did not know what they were selling. In film too. The thinking was why sell jeeps when you can sell film sex and have more fun?'

Avellana saw no let-up in the production and exhibition of bomba.

A big year for bomba was 1971, when most of the 251 Filipino movies were sex-oriented. But frontal nudity was still taboo. The ECP, exempt from censorship, showed bomba movies in the latter years of the Marcos era (*Asiaweek* 1985: 55).

Of the major genres, action films have remained the most popular in the Philippines, accounting for 47 per cent of the total during 1978–82. Melodramas of a soap opera type made up 32.8 per cent and comedy, 20.2 per cent in this categorisation scheme (Tiongson 1986: 8).

Tracing its origins to early theatrical forms (see Tiongson 1980: 61–2), the action film includes a strict form of morality, idealism of the code of honour and a set of traditional values. The hero of an action film is therefore always virtuous, patient, protective of the weak and a one-woman man. Other statements that can be made of action films are: violence is never a gratuitous act, blood money is not acceptable, the mother is the centre of the family, the church offers salvation to the wayward, only a virginal woman can become the wife of a hero and social institutions serve only the rich and powerful (Sotto 1987: 9–12).

In the first years of Philippine movies, action movies pitted patriots against the Spaniards; and after World War II, guerrilla fighters against the Japanese. In the 1950s and 1960s, Philippine westerns were created for action stars such as Fernando Poe jr, and a Filipino original—the illiterate champ of the masses whose only capital is his guts—for Joseph Estrada. The criminal became the action hero of the 1970s. Stars such as Ramon Revilla and Rudy Fernandez portrayed the life stories of real criminals, often poor, victimised people, who, after seeking help from the law, take matters into their own hands (Sotto 1987: 6).

The socially relevant topics were less frequently used by the mid-1980s, according to Avellana (Interview, 1986), as audiences increasingly turned to escapist fare. But the nationalistic fervour in the Philippines after 1986 was likely to turn the tide again. Gallaga (Interview, 1986) believed directors had been plagued with nationalistic calls to be socially relevant, even though they often did not fully understand the term. A scriptwriter said that since 1976, he wrote more in Filipino than English; he explained that the nationalist movement from 1976 onwards generated an interest in film serving the masses (Interview, Lacaba, 1986).

Government and Film

Film has been restricted for various reasons in the Philippines, depending on the type of government in power. All through the US

occupation, communist-related and anti-commonwealth government movies were banned, while during World War II, those
favouring the US were stopped by the Japanese. The Marcos regime
censored or banned some films which did not promote Mrs Marcos'
ideology of 'what is true, what is good, and what is beautiful'.

A Code of Motion Picture Censorship, adopted on 1 April
1947, served the industry for years. It disapproved of immoral,
obscene, indecent, lewd and lascivious scenes, as well as those that
were vulgar, tended to create disrespect for the law, incited to crime,
or offended racial or religious sensitivities.

In 1962, Republic Act 3060 was approved, proclaiming,
among other things, that 'no film or motion picture intended for
exhibition at movie houses . . . or on television shall be disapproved
by reason of its topic, theme, or subject matter, but upon the merits
of each picture considered in its entirety.' The Board of Censors
created by the same Act, succeeded partly because of the number of
movies it reviewed and also because it encouraged producers to
censor their own works.

Among the provisions of the law on censorship were: crime
shall not be presented to sympathise with the criminal against law
and justice, or to drive others to imitate it; methods of crime shall
not be explicitly presented so as to glamorise crime; action showing
the taking of human life should be minimised; suicide, as a solution
to problems, is to be discouraged; excessive flaunting of weapons by
criminals shall not be permitted; and no scenes shall show law
enforcement officers dying at the hands of criminals unless these
scenes are vital to the plot.

During the Marcos decades, the authorities played roles of
restricting, regulating and facilitating cinema.

For example, between 1975 and 1980, the Philippine government cracked down on films encouraging subversion, violence,
pornography and crime; revamped the censorship board and told
producers to redefine industry guidelines to support Philippine
values. But, the government also encouraged the showing of
Filipino movies, through support of the Manila Film Festival.

Some recommendations during this time were frightening.
In 1977, the government announced plans to license producers,
directors and scriptwriters and to subsidise local films which
hastened economic development and improved the cultural heritage.
Two years later, a Batasan (Parliament-like body) committee
recommended nationalisation of the industry within five years,
stipulating also that the number of imports be dropped from 300 to
150 and that cross-ownership between exhibitors and producers
cease. This came on the heels of the Motion Picture Industry
Act (Lumauig Bill) introduced to Batasan in 1978, which proposed
a gradual cut-back of imports, granting of subsidies and other
incentives to local producers and abolishment of monopolies, thus

allowing producers to exhibit in the maximum number of theatres.

The Lumauig Bill, which also favoured a Commission on Motion Pictures to oversee the industry, followed the route to defeat of previous bills meant to strengthen local film. Among these were a 1962 bill to limit imports and at least four others (before martial law in 1972) that would have increased tariffs on foreign films or lowered taxes on local ones (Hernando 1986: 201–2).

Censorship was tightened in 1977 when the Interim Board of Censors for Motion Pictures declared that story lines should be read by a committee of three; that films should be submitted for censorship earlier than before, and that all movies should be approved for general patronage only. As mentioned above, the board also licensed film personnel.

Government involvement escalated in the waning years of Marcos. In 1981, Marcos signed an Executive Order creating the Motion Picture Development Board to oversee four major bodies: Film Fund, which would offer loans of up to US $190,000 to deserving projects; Film Academy, which would integrate the guilds, train and give awards; and Film Archives and the Board of Standards, the latter to replace the Board of Censors.

Initially, the Development Board was allocated US $6 million. Sotto (1982, p. 249) said this was the industry's first solid success after 20 years of lobbying; others saw the board's role differently, claiming it could control more scripts. Mrs Marcos, the human settlements minister, said she would raise US $6.7 million to help producers upgrade film, but that they had to 'enhance the identity, dignity and humanity of the Filipino people'.

Brocka described Mrs Marcos' meaning of the latter terms:

'My films were outrages to Imelda. I'd show the slums of Tondo; she'd say, "It's not true Tondo people are poor" explaining, people in Tondo are smiling when you go there. "If they are smiling, they're not poor," she'd say. "What's wrong with your point of view, Lino; they may be poor in material goods, but rich in spirit," Imelda said. I told her I was not making films for tourism industry.' (Interview, Brocka, 1986).

Another Marcos action of 1981 had a more far-reaching impact. Presidential Decree 868, which strengthened the censors' powers, included objectionable rulings such as the annual licensing of all artists, permanent relinquishing to the board of all master negatives and board approval of all story lines before actual film production. In response, Brocka formed an artists' coalition called Free-the-Artist Movement, which demonstratd until PD 868 was withdrawn. The movement itself was broadened into the Concerned Artists of the Philippines in 1983.

Fear of nationalisation of the industry surfaced again in 1982 when the government formed ECP, which was involved in production, distribution, exhibition and importation. Its taxation and censorship exemptions, as well as the truisms that it was headed by Imee Marcos, daughter of the President, and its films were exhibited at the Film Centre, Imelda Marcos' project, made film people have second thoughts. ECP had much leverage, with power to construct alternative theatre and forge linkages with the private sector (see Dumaual 1985a and b). Executive Order 1051 of 1985, which appeared to be for ECP's abolishment, in reality made it a privately funded body.

By 1982, the censoring agency, earlier named the Board of Review for Motion Pictures and Television (BRMPT)[8], was again beefed up with Sen. Maria Kalaw Katigbak as its tough chief. During her administration, charges of arbitrary censorship were levelled at the board. Films which were not true, good and beautiful were subject to censorship on subversion charges: for example, the depictions of a girl being raped by a man in a uniform in *Boy Kondenado* and of the wife in *Moral*, who tells her New People's Army (communist group) husband that she was 'savaged' by the military. Even portrayals of poverty in the Philippines were termed subversive.

By an executive order of 12 June 1982, the Film Ratings Board was established to grant tax rebates of 50 per cent to films rated 'A' and 25 per cent to those rated 'B'. The board judged by the following criteria: technical and artistic qualities, 40 per cent each, and scope and purpose, 20 per cent.

The Marcos years were noted for creating many new film organisations or renaming old ones. In late 1985, BRMPT was succeeded by the Movie and Television Review and Classification Board (MTRCB), established by Presidential Decree 1986. This new agency, thought to be more liberal, asked producers how they wanted their films classified. If they said 'for general patronage', they were told to expect cuts; if 'for adults only', a few or no cuts. If the majority of the board felt a film was unfit, they rated it 'X' and banned it from commercial screening (*Malaya* 1985: 7). The board was forced to approve or disapprove, rather than cut films. However, the rules specified banning of films for the usual reasons of being libellous, subversive, rebellious, racially or religiously offensive, etc. Anyone involved with any aspect of film had to register with the board for a two-year period ('Rules and Regulations of the Movie and Television Review and Classification Board' 1985).

A few months after this newest change, Marcos fled during the February 1986 revolution. At that time, the following government film agencies functioned: MTRCB, Videogram Regulatory Board, Film Development Foundation of the Philippines, Film Archives and Film Ratings Board.

The new president, Corazon Aquino, could not move quickly enough for the filmmakers. Despite the myriad national problems she inherited and a number of actions she did take concerning film, Aquino was criticised for not making the arts a priority. Avellana, Brocka, Gallaga, Bernal, Suzara and Lacaba (Interviews, 1986) all roundly chided Aquino, only six months after she assumed power.

Gallaga said individuals who had been abroad during the Marcos years, or who otherwise lost touch with the situation, were put into high positions affecting the film industry. He added, 'Cory has snubbed local film, which is of no importance to her, and cabinet members are not letting her know that it could be a priority.' (Interview, Gallaga, 1986) Others, including Gallaga, said that under Marcos they knew the limitations, but these were not clear in 1986.

Brocka, appointed by Aquino to be the arts' representative on the Constitutional Commission, said:

'During the Marcos administration, we were regulated to the point of being used. We must give the new government a chance as 'democratic space' is so precious. Cory's advisors say film (the arts generally) is not a priority. This is unfortunate because film can shape national development.' (Interview, Brocka, 1986)

Shortly after assuming office, in March 1986, Aquino appointed the Government Task Force on Film, meant to take charge of all government-related film bodies. Representing the industry on the force were Brocka and Lacaba. After a two-month investigation, the task force recommended a National Film Commission and a reorientation of government policies. Generally, it saw its roles as ensuring freedom of expression, formulating policies and co-ordinating activities, upgrading the art of film, preserving the film heritage, making available services and facilities required by film-makers, overseeing public film structures and curbing infringement of intellectual property (Giron 1986c: 6; also Francia 1986a: 49). The task force survived much infighting and threats of walk-outs by Brocka, over many sore issues, including the appointment of Marcos loyalists (Dumaual 1986a: 36).

Brocka described some problems faced by task force members:

'Lacaba and I fought for a Film Commission to oversee all film groups, but not like in the Marcos administration. But we were criticised by the Chinese bookers and distributors who don't want the unearthing of the industry's corrupt practices.' (Interview, Brocka, 1986)

The other film member of the task force said none of the recommendations he and Brocka made for the board of censors was approved (Interview, Lacaba, 1986).

Among other actions taken by the Aquino government in its first four months in office were the sequestration of some government-subsidised film entities and the closure of others. The Presidential Commission on Good Government sequestered at least Vicor-Viva film group for its close connections to the previous administration[9] (Miranda 1986: 20). Abolished were the government-aided Entertainment Philippines and the Film Development Foundation, including its subsidiaries: the ratings board, Film Fund and alternative cinema. Those that survived Marcos, although stripped of government subsidies, were the Film Archives, MOWELFUND and Film Academy of the Philippines. The controversial Film Centre was also closed (Giron 1986b: 5).

Filmmakers joined other artists in the Alliance of Artists to push for a larger role for culture proposing, as early as 19 March 1986, a separate Ministry of Culture. The government turned down the proposal on the basis of shortage of funds. However, a year later, Aquino signed Executive Order 1180 which created the Philippine Commission on Culture and the Arts (PCCA). The National Film Committee was one of 14 subcommissions of PCCA. In 1988, a bill was filed to form a National Commission for Culture and the Arts from the existing PCCA (see Fernandez 1988).

Brocka (Interview, 1986) gave his version of the Alliance's activities:

'We formed an alliance to recommend a separate Ministry of Art and Culture and even told how to finance it in these financially bad times. The government took no action; actually side-tracked it so that now, we'd settle just for the Film Commission if we could get it.'

Concerning film laws, Aquino announced in April 1986 that those of the Marcos years would remain. In 1988, a new body, Movie and Television Review and Classification Board, tried to examine legislation amid much controversy over the board's inconsistencies in the implementation of policies (Vertido 1988: 130).

Governments of the Philippines, especially that of Marcos and his wife, have made use of film. During the 14 years of the 'Imelda cult', the First Lady used her patronage

'of art and culture as glitter and whitewash, for personal gratification and aggrandizement in the eyes of the media and foreign friends, to dazzle the people as part of her "bread and circuses" largesse, and to perpetuate the regime.' (Fernandez 1988: 1)

That change should be expected just because a new government is in power raises false hopes, if we are to believe an article in the organ of MOWELFUND:

'It [Philippine cinema] bowed down to the whips of censors, succumbed to the banal imagination of capitalists, and prostituted itself to ignominy. In each change of government came the obligatory facelift in cinema accompanied by a sudden rush and flourish of powers.' (*Movement* 1986: 2)

Professionalism

In 1982, amid much controversy, the Philippines hosted the first Manila International Film Festival. A pet project of Imelda Marcos, the festival was meant to make Manila the film capital of Asia. No costs were spared with even a US $30 million Film Centre constructed to house the event. At least 30 workers' lives were lost in the haste to finish the building on time.

Domestically, criticism was voiced about the disregard of workers' safety and the extravagant costs, at a time when poverty was rampant. Some European filmmakers boycotted the event because of the deaths and the oppression of the Marcos regime, but it was still a success with 200 movies shown from 40 countries.

The following year, in what seemed like a tug-of-war between Marcos and his wife, the President cut off the Festival's budget a few days before its opening. Claiming she recognised the need for economic belt tightening, Mrs Marcos obtained the necessary US $1.2 million from theatre owners in yet another controversial move. Each of 141 Manila theatres was allowed to screen uncensored festival films (pornographic movies called 'flying fish') to draw patrons. The President was reportedly upset, and the World Bank accused the Philippines of spending money frivolously. The 1984 festival was cancelled for economic reasons after Marcos announced he was imposing austerity measures.

In a left-handed way, the Marcoses were good for Philippine cinema. They established the ECP, which produced some films, provided training and housed the National Film Archives from 1982 to 1985. But ECP, with its tax exemption and freedom to show uncensored films, became a threat to the rest of the industry. In 1985, Marcos abolished ECP as a government entity and converted it into a private enterprise; the archives were turned over to the board of censors. In 1984, the government required all producers to turn over master negatives of all films to the archives for preservation. But, government aid in professionalisation came at heavy costs to freedom of expression for some filmmakers.

Previously, Filipino filmmakers had worked on professionalism without the patronage of the Marcoses. In 1952, the Filipino Academy of Movie Arts and Sciences (FAMAS) was created with its annual awards; two years later, Filipino artists entered their works in the Asian Film Festival, with favourable results for Avellana and others. In 1966, the Citizens Council for Better Motion Pictures awards were instituted, as was the annual Manila Film Festival, the latter designed to build audiences for Filipino movies. The previous year, Ben Pinga established the Film Institute of the Philippines to provide film education. Pinga also launched, in 1970, one of the first departments to offer film courses, the Department of Cinema and Television at Pamantasan ng Lungsod ng Maynila.

Other efforts were made at education and training. The University of the Philippines (UP) which, through its Institute of Mass Communication, has offered a bachelor's degree in film since 1984, was involved even earlier. In 1968, in a broadcasting documentary course, students worked with super-8 cameras; four years later, Cartoonist Larry Alcala offered an animation course and in 1974, a university film club initiated cinema-as-art workshops which evolved into the UP Film Centre. The First Manila Short Film Festival was sponsored by UP in 1981.

Ateneo de Manila University and Movie Workers Welfare Foundation (MOWELFUND) had a short-lived degree programme in 1982 and, in the 1970s, Clodualdo del Mundo jr taught film at De La Salle College. By the mid-1980s, at least twelve academic units promoted film in various ways; some of them formed the Film School Board of the Philippines in 1984.

For professionals who cannot take off long periods for training, workshops exist. The Actors Workshop Foundation offers highly personalised, formal acting courses, usually six days long, on topics such as 'being' or 'believing', and Lee uses his home as a base to instruct about 50 new scriptwriters in two-month long programmes. Lee's Writer's Studio, in existence since 1983, provides intensive instruction every Sunday, 9 a.m. to 6 p.m.

The welfare of movie personnel has been put in the hands of MOWELFUND, a non-profit organisation started by Joseph Estrada in 1974. Designed to help film workers with hospitalisation, life insurance, emergency assistance and overseas and local training, MOWELFUND received its funds after 1975, from the Metro Manila Film Festival, an expansion of the Manila Film Festival. Initially, Presidential Proclamation 1459 requested local governments to donate their ten-day amusement taxes from the festival to MOWELFUND. When not much repsonse was forthcoming, Mrs Marcos, as governor of Metro Manila, gave MOWELFUND authority to manage the festival and share 50 per cent of the P4 million tax proceeds.

MOWELFUND Film Institute was created in 1979, the only such training programme in Southeast Asia; a bimonthly periodical, *Movement*, started in 1985 and, with the Independent Cinema Movement, an Independent Film and Video Festival began in 1986.

Directors such as Suzara and Cinco, who called MOWELFUND an insurance company for employees, worried about its future under the Aquino government (Interviews, Suzara and Cinco, 1986). In mid-1986, when the Metro Manila Commission was given management of the festival, MOWELFUND lost its major source of income. Simultaneously, the government thought of sequestering the organisation because of its previous support of Marcos. Estrada, as chair, denied the charges and resigned to allow MOWELFUND to survive (Calderon 1986: 12). However, the problem of finding funds to pay insurance and death benefits to its members still existed (Dumaual 1986b: 12).

Rival professional groups kept the industry lively in the mid-1980s. In 1981, the Film Academy of the Philippines was started; two years later, it sponsored awards to counter those of the then-31-year-old FAMAS. Immersed in scandal, FAMAS was accused of vote-buying and crass campaigning, to the degree that in one year, a father and son won best actor and best child performer and a mother and daughter, best actress and best supporting actress. They were sarcastically referred to as the Mamas and Papas Awards that year.

Also in the mid-1980s, movie journalists launched Makinilya, a group to fight physical abuse by actors after one star punched a scribe. The acting community responded with its association, Dangal, to defend against character assassination by mass media.

By 1988, the Film Academy seemed to be dominant, although, as Bernal (Interview, 1986) pointed out, no organisation seemed strong enough to hold the industry together. Cinco (Interview, 1986) earlier had indicated the Academy was in limbo, although it serves as an umrella of twelve guilds, such as PMPPA, Integrated Movie Producers, Importers and Distributors of the Philippines, MOWELFUND and those made up of screenwriters, production designers, directors, actors and actresses, cinematographers, editors, film musicians and sound technicians.

The Film Academy bestows awards in 14 categories each year. In 1986, the competing awards given were FAMAS, Urian, Catholic Mass Media and Star. The Urian awards have some prestige; they are given by Manunuri ng Pelikulang Pilipino (Critics of Philippine Cinema), a group formed in 1976 to act as a consumer guide for moviegoers and to upgrade films.

NOTES

1   Pilar (1978, p. 2473) reported that two short-lived movie companies preceded Malayan Movies—Manila Film Company and Sirena Films Company.
2   George P. Musser, proprietor of Manila Talkatone, produced the first

'talkie', *Ang Aswang*, in 1932, but its sound was very poor. Nepomuceno's 1933 movie was more technically advanced.

3   This 1929 movie had the distinction of being the first Filipino work to be the subject of a court action. The Spanish community attempted to have *Patria Amore* banned because it dealt with the Philippine rebellion against Spain.

4   Salumbides (1952, p. 27) listed other lesser companies of pre-World War II as Del Monte Productions, Cervantina Filipina, Manila Films, Waling-Waling Pictures and Acuña Zaldariaga Productions. Quirino (1983, p. 76) also included J. Amado Araneta Productions.

5   Doña Sisang was not the first woman in a film managerial role. In 1930, Carmen Concha became the first woman producer when she made the King of Balagtasan into a star in her *Oriental Blood*. Concha also wrote and directed some of her movies. In 1939, Aurora Quezon, wife of President Manuel Quezon, joined in a limited partnership with Vicente Salumbides and his wife to form Salumbides Film Co. Ltd (see, Salumbides 1952: 27; Quirino 1983: 26).

6   *Komiks* is the term for Philippine comic magazines.

7   Where the director jots down ideas concerning the day's shooting on the back of a matchbox.

8   Previous bodies were Board of Censorship for Moving Pictures in 1929; Board of Review for Moving Pictures, 1938; Board of Censors for Motion Pictures, 1961.

9   Before the Revolution, other film groups boasted close government affiliations—Cine Suerte had placements made by 'Bong Bong' Marcos, the President's son, or General Fabian Ver; Regal was tied to Benjamin Romualdez, Imelda's brother, and Gryk Ortaleza had top military personnel as 'godfathers'.

7

MALAYSIA AND SINGAPORE

INTRODUCTION

Lakshmana Krishnan had been important enough to the Malaysian film industry for the government to confer the honorific title 'dato' upon him. When interviewed in November 1986, he was so pessimistic about the industry that had served him well, one would have thought the title was given for film criticism.

Dato Krishnan himself had long since abandoned feature films in favour of television documentaries, serials and commercials. Not many features were produced, he said, and those that were, did not have export or domestic markets. Video and other leisure-time activities carved away audiences, as did the easy flow of foreign films into Malaysia and audience preferences for Chinese-, Tamil- or English-language movies, according to their ethnic affiliations.

The type of film needed to lure back movie-goers, according to Dato Krishnan, was the 'extravaganza, the super film', but, stopping in mid-sentence, he explained those were not possible on the US $100,000 film budgets given to producers. 'One gadget in a super film could cost that much,' he said. Quality pictures were not the answer either, he added, because the public wanted only good stories, not sophisticated technique.

What about revitalising the efforts of the National Film Development Corporation (FINAS)? Dato Krishnan was against the FINAS training facility, reasoning 'if you don't have films to make, why train technicians?' Send them abroad for training, he said, 'it's less expensive.' The proposed FINAS film script bank, where writers would be encouraged to deposit scripts for future use met with the same scepticism. 'It won't work. Some scripts will stay in the bank and not be used', thus discouraging already underpaid writers, he explained.

As for the future of the 'already moribund' Malay film, the veteran producer did not believe it would be prosperous 'unless FINAS comes up with a magic wand', adding, 'and that stops that notion'.

Perhaps a look at the historical development of Malaysian film can offer clues to why a filmmaker would become so sour about his profession.

HISTORICAL BACKGROUND

The cinema, promoted as a variety theatre and amusement park novelty, was introduced to the then-Federated Malay States and Singapore at the turn of the century. By the 1910s, cinema halls—most owned by the Chinese—existed in larger towns, and travelling shows took the medium to the more accessible rural areas. As early as 1898, newspapers mentioned the public viewing of movies in Kuala Lumpur, one of the first films showing the golden jubilee of Queen Victoria. Press reports indicated that the first films had unusual effects upon audiences; for example, some viewers 'had to be restrained from going behind the screen to find out how the "new wonder worked".' Many other people thought the projectionist had magic powers and for days after, they went to him to solve thefts and to give advice on their misfortunes (Davies 1973).

Almost from the beginning, British authorities in the Federated Malay States were wary of the medium's effects; by the mid-1920s, their apprehension turned to the Hollywood-dominated cinema, feared as a threat because of its educative role. Critics, one of the most vocal being Sir Hesketh Bell who toured Malaya in 1926, thought that the film controls were inadequate, that Hollywood-originated movies spread communist propaganda and undermined the prestige of the white people and colonial rule (Stevenson 1974: 209). They claimed that United States cinema showed Asians the weaker aspects of white people, and that the European woman's wanton image as reflected on the screen was in marked contrast to traditional ideals in Asia about the role and status of women. Some of the criticisms Bell and others raised are still heard throughout the world today: most notably that cinema boosts crime rates and promotes interracial sexual relationships.

Stricter controls were called for by numerous officials, and King George V, after reading Bell's articles, instructed his secretary to enquire if anything could be done about the 'deplorable effect of cinema pictures on the prestige of the European in the Far East' (Stevenson 1974: 212). The result was the passage of The Cinematograph Films (Control) Enactment 1927, empowering the official censor to inspect every film and every picture photograph, poster or figure advertising a film, and to ban any of these. Fines of up to US $500 were levied when films did not meet the censor's approval. The law also allowed any police official to enter and search without warrant any premises that were suspected of exhibiting unauthorised films, and to arrest those involved in the exhibition. The enactment provided for an appeal committee appointed by the Federated Malay States chief secretary, but appeals were acted upon favourably only if they supported additional censorship. In other words, the committee could reverse a censor's decision if the complaint stated that there was not enough censorship; it could not change a decision if a complaint was made of excessive censorship.

Even before the 1927 enactment, cinema control in the Federated Malay States was rigorous. The Theatres Enactment of 1910, for example, required cinemas to be licensed and films to be passed by local authorities. In 1923, the Straits Settlements (Penang, Singapore and Malacca) government promulgated Ordinance No. 200 (Cinematograph Film), which established the official censor of film and provided him with numerous powers. Police staffed the official censor's office in Singapore and screened all films entering the Straits Settlements, the Federated Malay States and Johore. Thus, in 1925, 12 per cent of all films entering what are now Malaysia and Singapore were prohibited, while objectionable portions were censored from 90 per cent of all others. The official censor in October 1927 reported that his office, during the previous eight months, banned 128 films considered 'harmful to Eastern audiences'. The censor expressed concern about the 'immodest dress of Western women' in the films, the portrayal of gambling and criminal methods (the censor said he had 'definite evidence' that some Chinese in Singapore had successfully used methods adopted from the screen) and the showing of intimate interracial marriages and attachments. The censor was especially fearful that Western films might promote the intimate mingling of whites and nationals, resulting in the Asians lacking respect for Europeans. This legislation was mainly aimed at US movies; in 1926, for instance, an unsuccessful attempt was made to put a quota on the importation of foreign films, stipulating that at least 30 per cent should be British-originated.

Despite such restrictions, the cinema flourished, so that by the end of the 1930s, there were 30 to 40 permanent theatres in Singapore and the Federated Malay States, with an almost equal number of mobile booths. The larger theatres were open seven days a week and averaged 48 performances a month. Attendance figures were high, partly because cinemas and racecourses were the two places in colonial society where all classes of people met. By the 1950s, it was estimated that the per capita rate of film attendance in Malaya was probably the highest in the world (Stevenson 1974: 219).

The first locally produced picture was *Laila Majnun*, based on popular Persian folklore and dealing with two ill-fated lovers. It was produced in 1933 by Chisty and directed by B.S. Rajhaus, Indians with rudimentary film knowledge who had just arrived in Malaya. Actors were recruited for this and other early films from the *bangsawan* (Malay opera), a wise move on the producers' part as their fame preceded them (Latif 1987: 98). When the Shaw Brothers, Run Run and Runme, set up their Singapore film unit in the 1930s, they too employed players from bangsawan.

By the mid-1930s, Loke Wan Tho founded the Cathay Productions, based on a nucleus of theatres in Kuala Lumpur and Singapore. Like Shaw, Cathay branched out into film distribution and production, as well as other interests.

Although efforts at using film for propaganda existed as early as 1926, when the Federal Health Department produced a film on the work of the Kuala Lumpur Infant Welfare Centre, it was really the Japanese occupation of the 1940s that brought out the full potential of the medium. By November 1943, the Japanese had abolished British and American films and substituted their own movies to promote 'Nippon consciousness'. The Bunka Eiga Gekijio (government propaganda body) showed only newsreels and educational movies. As one writer said of the movies of the period:

'It is undeniable that these shows were fairly good, and that they possessed propaganda value. The films were designed to emphasise the rare qualities of the Japanese spirit, the thoroughness of Japanese patriotism, the supremacy of the Japanese Armed Forces, the efficiency of Japanese light and heavy industries, the vastness of Japanese material resources, the capabilities of Japanese organising skill, the quickness of reconstruction in conquered regions, the willing co-operation of the "freed peoples" of Dai Toa . . . Other picture-houses screened "culture films" whose themes were calculated to bring out the excellence of Japanese family life, the harmony of the Japanese social system, the "modernness" of Japanese civilisation without the sacrifice of the finer points of ancient culture, the fine qualities of Japanese art and music, the nobility of filial devotion and the greater nobility of devotion to the Nation and the Emperor.' (Onn 1946: 151).

The development of an indigenous film industry in Malaya occurred after World War II. The authorities set up a film production organisation that was probably an outgrowth of the Army Film and Photography Unit which came to Malaya with Mountbatten's forces after the Japanese surrender. When the British Military

Administration was in power, a Crown Film Unit[1] emerged which was taken over by government authorities during the Emergency (1948–60) to produce propaganda films aimed at stopping the growing threat of communism to Malaya. By 1952, the unit (by then known as Malayan Film Unit) was the centre of all government information programmes (Interview, Nettleton, 1973).

The 1950s were the growth years for the Malay-language feature film industry. Indigenously produced movies in Malaya before World War II often employed Indian and Chinese languages; however, in the 1950s, Shaw Brothers, which had set up Malay Film Production Ltd in 1947, hired a number of directors from India to establish the Malay feature film market. Usually, the Indian directors just translated Indian scripts into Malay, the result being that the films had all the Indian nuances, cultural idiosyncracies and mannerisms, and very little that was truly Malay (Moraes 1972: 12).

The Shaws' Malay Film Production was quickly joined by Cathay-Keris Productions, a merger of Keris Film Productions (formerly Rimau Productions, a merger itself of Nusantara and Keris) and Cathay Productions. The first picture of Cathay-Keris was *Buluh Perindu* (1951).

Each production house issued a new film a month, starring actors and actresses who made the 1950s the peak years for the industry: P. Ramlee, Zaiton, Kasma Booty, Jins Shamsuddin, Saloma, Sarimah Zulkiflee, Ahmad Mahmud, Mustapha Maarof, Wahid Satay or Nordin Ahmad. Many of these movies were exported to Indonesia (Ng 1972a: 11). The industry was rather profitable, and the two studios even built 'resettlement colonies' for their top contract stars (Latif 1987: 99). In December 1960, Lakshmana Krishnan, apparently with Ho Ah Loke, started Studio Merdeka in Kuala Lumpur. Later, when the Shaws closed down in Singapore, they increased production at Merdeka, which they partly owned (Interview, Krishnan, 1986).

But, for economic and political reasons, Malaysia's film industry went into a skid in the 1960s. Attendances dropped, production costs increased and quality suffered. Krishnan said the advent of television and the 'choosy' nature of a more educated public hastened the demise of the industry (Interview, Krishnan, 1986). Other factors were also responsible:

(1) A confrontation between Malaya and Indonesia in the early 1960s which nearly led to war between the two nations, and the development of an Indonesian film industry, all but killed the marketability of Malaysia's films in Indonesia.

(2) Malay-language films failed to adjust to societal changes, still using techniques the Indian filmmakers brought to the industry. As one writer said, the Malay films of the 1960s and 1970s were influenced by the style of a generation before — 'where

a song is sung whenever the hero feels sad or happy, at a marriage or a funeral'. (see Khoo 1973).

(3) The 1963 inauguration of television in Malaya took some of the audience.

(4) The government did not lend the industry the type of support needed to pull it out of the doldrums. Critics point out that whereas the Indonesian government gave filmmakers credit up to 80 per cent of the total costs of producing a film, this type of help was not offered in Malaysia[2].

Shaw Brothers, after facing labour difficulties, closed its Singapore studios in October 1967, and Cathay-Keris followed suit in 1972. With production drastically cut, to not many more than the seven made each year by Merdeka, in 1972, hundreds of filmmakers were out of work. Those who continued to work for Merdeka were contracted by the film; top artists were paid a few thousand dollars for a movie that took three months; supporting artists received US $160. There were numerous instances in the late 1960s and early 1970s of movie stars working in stores, or as cabaret girls, models or taxi drivers, or acting or dubbing on television between pictures. By 1972, the situation was desperate enough to warrant this statement: 'There is no Malay film industry to speak of, only one film company making Malay films' (Ng 1972b: 10).

Merdeka, the existing production company, enticed the top money-earning star in Singapore, P. Ramlee, to join its ranks in 1963. During most of the next decade, the studio prospered on the strength of this one individual's acting and directing. Ramlee, born Teuku Zakariah bin Teuku Nyak Putih, began his career at 19 as a background singer in Singapore films. In the next 25 years, he acted in more than 100 films, some of which won him prestigious awards at the Asian Film Festival and elsewhere. He also directed 34 films, the first being *Penarik Beca*, (The Trishaw Man, 1956), wrote and sang musical scores and did comedy and theatre work[3].

By 1972, the film industry of Malaysia was in particularly dire straits. The number of productions was at a low point; the films the few remaining studios made were criticised on nearly every count. The movies were unrealistic, uninspiring and lacking a social conscience; the studios lacked talented stars, appropriate scenery, colour technology, adequate equipment and qualified technicians. In numerous cases, the movies suffered in quality because the producers were making them almost single-handedly. For example, script writers were in short supply because they were paid only US $120 a story; as a result, producers and directors—some of whom had lost touch with their public—resorted to writing their own scripts (Ng 1972a: 11). P. Ramlee told of instances where he wrote the script, composed the musical score and songs, directed and starred in the film, handled the cameras and carried out editing, dubbing and recording duties (Ng 1972a: 11).

The difficulty of obtaining the services of talented movie personnel was not that they did not exist in Malaysia; they were not offered enough money to return to movie careers. Malay star of the 1940s and 1950s, Kasma Booty said she felt 'ashamed to say how much they offered me' to perform in films in the 1970s (Ng 1972b: 10). The actors willing to accept the relatively low salaries were mediocre, partly because, as one writer said, they 'have to struggle with an office job, modelling or operating a boutique for a living', and cannot devote their full time to filmmaking (see Khoo 1973). The lack of money hindered efforts to use foreign co-stars and local young talent; therefore, the audiences, in addition to seeing the same old scenes, saw the same old faces.

Inadequate facilities and equipment also stood in the way of quality production. For example, Merdeka restricted shooting to a ten-mile radius of its studios so that the same scenes appeared in all of its films—the zoo, surrounding jungle and even the same furniture. One director said that he was forced to delete a seaside scene because there was not a sea within ten miles of the studios; on another occasion, a script called for a scene where the hero returned home by plane, but there was not an airport nearby. Instead, the hero arrived at the doorstep of his *kampong* (village) home in a taxi.

Recognising the dilemma of the industry in 1972–3, the Malaysian government and some filmmakers attempted to provide remedies. New studios were created; by 1974, Sari Artists Film Productions was active, and Malaysian Film Industries, more commonly known as Perfima (Perusahaan Filem Malaysia), and Rumpun Melayu were in development stages. Other companies given 'pioneer' status, meaning they were owned by *bumiputras* (Malays), were Yusari Film Sdn. Bhd., Sabah Film and Pura Mas.

Perfima, established by several top Malay stars such as Ramlee and Jins Shamsuddin, was meant to 'meet the rising expectations of the people' who had been imbued with foreign-type films, to allow locals to participate in the distribution of films and to assure that an 'equal balance be achieved to develop the recently revived Malay film industry' (see *Straits Times*, 24 October and 5 November 1972; H'ng 1972: 9; Henderson 1970: 377). The organisation was set up with US $2 million in 1972. Perfima planned to build theatres throughout the nation and to produce colour films for foreign and domestic markets. In its first year of operation, it concentrated on boosting the showing of Indonesian films which used colour and cinemascope techniques not available in Malaysian movies. By May 1973, Perfima succeeded in importing 60 Indonesian films. Rumpun Melayu was formed in 1973 by Ramlee after he left Perfima; the company did not succeed in accomplishing much because Ramlee died that year.

During this same period, politicians urged Pernas, the government trading corporation, to break the show business monopoly of Cathay and Shaw Brothers (see Ratnam 1972: 11; Noordin Sopiee 1972), by establishing independent cinemas, by obtaining overseas contracts from film companies for distribution to independent theatres in Malaysia and by forming a local film production company.

In 1972–3, government ministers insisted that cinemas should be set up in every state to screen Perfima films (*Straits Times*, 5 November 1972). Other ministers called on local filmmakers and writers to produce movies comparable to foreign counterparts, but without the detrimental social influences (*Star*, 30 August 1973, p. 6) and to suggest that local film producers attune their products to the concept of a multiracial society.

In an address to the 1973 ASEAN Film Festival, the then-Deputy Prime Minister, Hussein Onn, said there were too many film companies in the nation giving rise to unnecessary competition and duplication. Because filmmaking is expensive, he felt all studios should merge to form one or two large companies (Bernama News Agency dispatch, 7 November 1973).

In 1975, Malaysian filmmakers thought they saw designs by the government to implement some of Hussein Onn's guidelines. That autumn, 60 film companies formed the Malaysian Chamber of Film Companies to safeguard local interests and build the private film industry. The move came at the same time that Parliament considered the formation of a National Film Corporation (NFC) to undertake certain aspects of the film trade. The private entrepreneurs feared a state take-over in the distribution and exhibition of films, certainly hinted at previously, but made more forceful in a 1975 speech in Parliament by the Trade and Industry Minister, who criticised the monopolisation of production, distribution and exhibition by a few large companies; said he was unhappy with the nation's heavy reliance on foreign films (2,000 imported each year, costing US \$30.8 million) and hoped the NFC would pursue local film production goals.

The proposal for the NFC arose when the government cabinet established a committee to study commercial competition within the industry (Koh 1975: 39). Besides being the policy body for the industry, the NFC was being designed to build cinemas, provide marketing and technical services, lease out equipment, provide loans and make pictures (*Malaysian Business* 1975: 9). The proposing of this corporation, coupled with the strengthening of the propaganda aims of the governmental Filem Negara and the revising of the movie censorship codes, seemd to fit the pattern of control Malaysian authorities had laid down on other mass media in the early 1970s. Filem Negara, the film department of the Ministry of Information and Broadcasting, aimed to provide information on government policy and to project the image of Malaysia through educational and documentary films for use by 257 mobile units of the Information Department, by Television Malaysia and by private commercial exhibitors such as cinemas.

MALAYSIANISING THE INDUSTRY

During the decade 1975–85, the government increasingly involved itself in the film industry. In 1976, it ruled, to the chagrin of distributors and the pleasure of exhibitors, that all non-Malay feature films, filmlets and commercials should carry Bahasa Malaysia (national language) subtitles. Government ministers explained the move was an attempt to 'ensure that the film industry made its contribution towards national unity and nation-building efforts' (*New Straits Times* 1976: 1). Later, when a number of films were dubbed, problems resulted because of the shortage of dubbers—25 active in the country who also worked on television and radio shows.

The main concerns of the government related to the stranglehold non-Malays, especially Shaw Brothers, had on production and distribution and the domination by foreign films. From at least 1974, when the task force that proposed NFC was formed, deliberations took place concerning ways to boost Malay cinema, simultaneously assuring that at least 30 per cent of the business must be in bumiputra hands, as guaranteed under the government's New Economic Policy.

By 1977, the task force presented its proposals for parliamentary consideration. It recommended the establishment of a national film board; controls on imports though advanced screening of scripts even before reels arrived; forced closure of Shaw Brothers and Cathay; limits on the extent of foreign film distribution and the length of each run; and the formation of a training academy and a new chain of theatres.

The report showed the existence of a shortage of Malay films, claiming Chinese movies took up 53.9 per cent of screening time, English 21 per cent, Indian 12.2 per cent and Malay 12.1 per cent. The poor showing was attributed partly to the lack of Malay films; only seven were produced in 1976 (*Asiaweek* 1977a: 16–17).

Fears of government interference stalled the implementation of these proposals until 1981, when Parliament passed a bill that created the National Film Development Corporation (FINAS). Many of FINAS' goals were in line with the earlier recommendations— stimulate local production with an influx of Malay participation, wrest distribution from outside agencies and set up professional and training institutes. From the outset, FINAS was criticised because none of its members hailed from the film business. But fears of the government monopolising film production were allayed by top officials, including the prime minister-designate. In fact, the parliamentary bill that created FINAS assured that no corporation, public or private, could swallow up the industry by stipulating film companies could undertake only one of these activities: producing and distributing; distributing and screening; or producing and screening (*Malaysian Digest* 1981: 5). Among FINAS' first actions were the lifting of film stock duties and co-operation with the Indonesian film body in continued film exchange.

Production, Distribution and Exhibition

Discussing production problems in 1979, one critic (Mazlan Nordin 1979: 50) cited those familiar throughout Asia—shoe-string budgets, a 25 per cent tax, lack of adequate access to outside markets (particularly Indonesia) and insufficiently trained directors. One difference from some other Asian film industries was the low percentage of production costs given top stars, who usually received US $4,000 in a typical film budget of US $115,000–150,000.

Although many problems persisted, some of those mentioned by Mazlan Nordin were not as serious by 1988. A Malaysian Film Academy, which recruited its first group of students in 1988, was expected to train directors, as well as actors and technicians[4]; the co-operation with Indonesia was consolidated and a new wave of directors changed the nature of film. Budgets changed, but not in the direction producers would have liked (average cost for each film was US $80,000), and the split of receipts still favoured exhibitors, who took 60 per cent in larger cities and 70 per cent in smaller towns. Theatre ownership remained a monopoly, 216 being under Cathay or Golden Communications.

Malaysian filmmakers always dreamed of expanding their markets, mainly by shipping more work to Indonesia, over ten times larger in population and the country with which Malaysia has closest cultural and linguistic ties. When, in 1982, Malaysia's FINAS signed an agreement with the National Film Council of Indonesia, each country waiving import restrictions on ten films a year (see *Asiaweek* 1982: 40), this was the most encouragement for a more open policy since the mid-1960s. At about the same time, Malaysia and Indonesia agreed to co-produce two films at a cost of US $435,000.

The big shake-up of Malaysian films in the 1980s resulted, as in Taiwan, Hong Kong, the Philippines and elsewhere, from the incursion of 'new-wave' directors, such as Rahim Razali, Nasir Jani and Hafsham (Othman Samsuddin). Realism, rather than melodrama, is their forte, as is the use of new techniques in editing and camerawork[5] and themes that deal with social issues, such as child abuse, corruption, music piracy, family relationships of *nouveau riche* Malays, religious and ethnic problems and the culture shock experienced by returning Malays, who studied or worked abroad.

Rahim in his *Puteri* (Princess, 1987), portrays a young woman who leaves her inherited land to reside in Kuala Lumpur, while his *Tsu-Feh Sofiah* (1985) explores religious and ethnic issues, showing how a recent Chinese convert to Islam is better morally than some born-in-the-faith kampong folk. Hafsham's *Mekanik* (Mechanic, 1983), a realistic mix of Malay, Tamil, Chinese and English dialogue, deals with a mechanic who finds some loot and becomes involved with a 'gang-moll decoy and a female undercover cop' (*Asiaweek* 1988a: 34), and Nasir's *Kembara Seniman Jalanan* (The Travelling Artiste, 1985) depicts record piracy, a topic very close to the director's heart who believes he has been robbed by film pirates.

Despite these inroads, the old melodramatic, formula pictures continued to dominate, often creating a tension between the two types of directors. Also popular were youth-oriented movies, examples in the late 1980s being *Ali Setan*, *Gila-Gila* and *Jejaka Perasan*.

Film critic Anwardi Jamil, a partner in R.J. Studio with his parents Rosnani and Jamil Sulong, both directors, worried that the schism between old and new directors could tear apart an industry not well glued together. He told *Asiaweek* (1988a, p. 36): 'Instead of working with the older generation, they are attacking them and saying their talents are not needed anymore. But by doing this, they are attacking the producers and their source of funding.'

Whatever the philosophy behind them, Malaysian films continued to wage a hard fight into the late 1980s. The popularity of home video compounded long-entrenched problems and forced filmmakers to find alternative ways to attract audiences. Figures from Survey Research Malaysia indicated that between 1984 and 1987, film attendance dropped from more than one million to 300,000, while advertising expenditure for cinema shrank from 8.5 per cent of the nation's advertising budget to 0.2 per cent. The number of theatres was down to fewer than 200 from earlier highs of more than 400[6].

Among the ways exhibitors—spearheaded by Cathay Organisation, the largest chain with 27 theatres—hoped to rejuvenate the industry were refurbishing cinema halls, bringing in appealing films, mostly comedies and action-packed thrillers, and promoting the movies. Promotional gimmicks abounded, including a joint television advertising campaign with a cigarette company and an arm-wrestling contest in conjunction with *Over the Top*, a story about arm-wrestlers.

Regulation

At the time the task force on film was created in 1974, a number of changes had recently been implemented in regulation. In the midst of an 1972–3 campaign against sex and violence portrayals in film, amendments were made to the Cinematograph Films (Censorship)

Act 1952, chief of which was a call for the establishment of two censoring bodies—a new Film Censorship Board and an Assessment Committee. The Assessment Committee, chaired by the secretary-general of the Ministry of Home Affairs, was made up of at least one psychologist, sociologist, educationalist, dramatist, youth and police representatives and members of Muslim, Christian, Buddhist and Hindu faiths. Under the new amendments, the Film Censorship Board included a chief censor, his deputy and eight other members, all of whom had to be born in Malaysia, 'have high morality and integrity', and know local customs (*Straits Echo*, 5 November 1973). They must be reasonably educated, widely-read, responsible, upright, conscientious, knowledgeable, intelligent, analytical, perceptive, critical and able to siphon the good from the bad, the essence from the dregs. Members of the board are appointed by the King on the recommendation of the Ministry of Home Affairs.

The Parliamentary Select Committee on Controversial Films was also instrumental in obtaining the vote in the House in mid-1973 for the banning of crime, violence and sex films. Sex films were allowed to enter the country in March 1972 when the Ministry of Home Affairs directed the Film Censorship Board to issue pink certificates for the exhibition of these movies to persons 18 years old or older. But, during 1972–3, youth, religious and political groups successfully lobbied for a total ban on these films, and the Parliamentary Select Committee, in its report, recommended that 'sex films which serve no educational purpose and films which emphasise violence should be banned where they are likely to lead to a lowering of public morals, affect racial harmony or disturb the security of the country' (*Straits Times*. 13 July 1973).

The Malaysian press, strongly guided by, and highly supportive of, most governmental campaigns, could not contain itself in its praise for the actions of the Parliamentary Select Committee. Editorials, news stories and reports of parliamentary speeches blasted sex films as the causes of public love-making, crime, venereal disease, orgies and the creation of sex maniacs. Coverage of the issue was very biased. For example, a *Straits Echo* (20 July 1972) article, headed 'Most Penangites in Favour of Sex Film Ban', determined 'most' by interviewing four people in the streets; the *Straits Times* (3 December 1973) polled the public on sex films and described the one person who thought sex films were all right as a 'long-haired, 19-year-old HSC drop-out.' The same *Straits Times* story told of a man who was in court because he had 'embraced a housewife [while] under the influence of Sex films.' Other headlines included: 'Lord Gore, Lady Smut'; 'Of Skin Flicks and VD Menace'; 'Away with Excessive Film Violence'; 'Better Films Please'; 'Sex Films Ban Welcomed by All'; 'Thumbs Down on Sex Films' and 'I See Uncut X-Film'.

A look at some of the guidelines under which censors have

operated shows that all this outcry was unnecessary, as sexual themes, as well as those on race, religion, politics, crime, violence, brutality and horror, have usually been treated with care in this multi-ethnic, multi-religious country. The projection of any racial theme portraying the domination of one race over another had been censored and, in other instances, banning or censorship took place because negative film depictions of other nationalities could prove detrimental to Malaysia's foreign policy of neutrality. Also, films condemning or showing disrespect for any religion were traditionally banned or censored, as well as political themes glorifying communism or the triumph of communism over democracy. For example, in one Tamil movie, even posters of prominent leaders of the Indian Communist Party visible in the background were censored in Malaysia.

Crime films have been viewed by censors to check if they are criminally instructive, encouraging or inspiring, and if the criminal methods used are easily applicable to local circumstances. Censors have screened these films with the following criteria in mind: themes should show that crime does not pay, step-by-step criminal procedures should be deleted, criminals should not be glamorised, police tactics (not those of criminals) should be emphasised and scenes of the apprehending of criminals should be lengthened.

Of course, with the prevalence of home video in Malaysia, these guidelines are not very effective in curbing what people view. The percentages of homes with videocassette players in Malaysia, Brunei and Singapore are among the highest in the non-Western world. In at least Malaysia and Singapore, governments have acted since the mid-1980s to curb piracy and circulation of illegal videocassettes. Usually, this has involved stepping up raids of pornographic and other illegal video parlours and shops, increasing the amounts and terms of penalties and beefing up sometimes-outmoded licensing, copyright and censorship laws (see Lent in Boyd, Straubhaar and Lent 1989).

By the mid-1980s, the government was able to loosen the grip of Shaw Brothers and Cathay, by legislation which required such companies to dispose of at least 30 per cent of their holdings. The two companies sold off more than the minimum required. Shaw Brothers sold 70 per cent to Perlis Plantations and United Estates Projects, but retained management of the company. Shaw also sold its Malaysian studio to FINAS. Cathay sold all of its holdings (including 60 theatres) to Borneo Film Company.

SINGAPORE

Except in the historical perspective above, Singapore has not come in for much discussion, mainly because feature film production has all but ceased.

Dreams of returning to the pre-1960s split of Malaysia and Singapore when Cathay and Shaw Brothers churned out movies each month, sometimes fill the heads of film people. For example, government-owned Radio Television Singapore, in the late 1970s, envisioned a film training school with the possibility of restarting feature film production and, in 1986, the distributor, Motion Picture Marketing, announced its intention to make an initial crop of four Singapore films.

As late as 1977, four local outfits brought out eight films, chief of which was Chong Gay, which made three. Other producers that year were Singapore Feature Productions, Malaysian Film Distributors and Cinema Centre Productions.

Although production has virtually halted since then, the island-state continues to have one of the highest *per capita* film attendance in the world. Singaporeans see films in theatres owned by mainly three companies—Shaw Brothers (26 halls), Cathay (20) and Chong Gay.

These distributor-exhibitors changed viewing venues in the late 1970s, as they built theatres in or near apartment houses of the satellite towns that sprouted in the suburbs. They have also pushed to change admission prices. An early attempt in 1976 to raise prices was rejected by the government, even though the distributors pointed out that the prices remained almost unchanged for three decades. Other price increase proposals were sent to the authorities in at least 1979 and 1984. At times, distributors have not thought the government very sympathetic to their goals. Box-office taxes are considered high at 35 per cent. Distributors also pay another 16 per cent on rental revenues.

Singapore participated in regional and international film festivals in recent years, usually with locally produced documentaries. In 1979, the government hosted the annual Asian Film Festival, while in 1987, the First Singapore International Film Festival was held.

Singapore's government, noted for taking tough stands on freedom of expression, did not spare film. The Board of Film Censors, under the Ministry of Culture, has exerted varying degrees of pressure upon the industry. In 1972, for example, the board totally banned sex and violence from films shown in Singapore. A group of distributors that year went to Hong Kong to persuade producers to cut the violence. Yet, in 1981, on the premise Singaporeans had become a 'more discriminate' audience, the government created a six-member review committee to consider letting up on censorship. The committee believed the board could become less rigid, but the changes had to be gradual and carried out with caution.

Rationalising Singapore's strict policies, at the same time pointing out liberalisation trends, the Parliamentary Secretary for Culture, in a 1980 address, concluded:

'We are basically an Asian society. Most Singaporeans still regard sex as very private and personal . . . In fact, many thinking Singaporeans are concerned that the Western liberal values and permissiveness . . . will erode our traditional values and bring about a decline of morality . . . The Ministry of Culture therefore cannot be expected to change or liberalise to a large extent our censorship policy, and release undesirable publications, films and videotapes indiscriminately.' (Singapore Government press release 15 August 1980)

In 1981, the Films Act was passed by Parliament. Among many other stipulations, it provided for setting up the board, the licensing of film personnel and the censorship of all movies. A Committee of Appeal, made up of nine persons appointed by the Minister of Culture, was established. Shortly afterwards, the government came up with a series of acts to bring more control to the burgeoning videocassette industry. By 1987, survey research showed three out of four Singaporean homes had videocassette recorders.

NOTES

1   In the early 1950s, the name of the unit was changed to Seladang Studios, later to Malayan Film Unit, and finally to Filem Negara.
2   For clarification, Malaya became known as Malaysia with the development, in 1963, of the federation, which included West Malaysia, Sabah, Sarawak and Singapore. Singapore left the federation in 1965 to become an independent state.
3   Books have been written in the 1980s on Ramlee's career. Also, Banks (1985), studying how Ramlee portrayed women in five films he directed, said, they were in minor roles, subservient to men and self-sacrificing.
4   The Academy, which offers a three-month short course, a one-year certificate programme and a three-year diploma, is staffed by local industry professionals and occasional foreign film crews and lecturers.
5   Hafsham said today's filmmakers were influenced by techniques and special effects in foreign movies. The new directors had stayed away from the 'Hindustani' film traits of 'wide angles, static shots, overacting, verbose scripts and song-and-dance numbers' (*Asiaweek* 1988a: 35).
6   The figure of 400 might be conservative. One source reported that in 1977, Shaw Brothers had more than 400 theatres, including 42 first-run

theatres in eight cities and Cathay Organisation, more than 300, with 32 first-run halls in eight cities. Another 300 independent theatres existed, to give a total of more than 1,000. The same source claimed there were 21 registered, independent film distributors, only four of which were active (Cacnio 1977: 37).

8

INDONESIA, THAILAND AND BURMA

INTRODUCTION

A mong the contrasts of Southeast Asian cinema is that of how nationals accepted the movies. In Indonesia, the first film roles had to be performed by local Dutch or Chinese as Indonesians found film work to be degrading.

But not in Thailand, where for years, princes (even to a second generation) served as directors or producers, and famous publisher-journalist-politician, M.R. Kukrit Pramaj, played the role he was to assume in real life a generation later—that of the Prime Minister—opposite Marlon Brando in *The Ugly American*. Kukrit, who was Prime Minister of Thailand in the early 1970s, never forgot his indebtedness to Hollywood for the international fame, and throughout the 1970s and 1980s, used his popular *Siam Rath* column to promote the import demands of the Motion Picture Export Association of America.

Neither did Cambodian royalty shy from film; in fact, the country's movies were launched by the Chief of State, a playboy who cast himself in romantic roles.

Prince Norodom Sihanouk had made eight full-length features, six of which were released, by the time Cambodia was catapulted into a generation of war, genocide and occupation. Sihanouk's films, which represented Cambodia in the early Asian film festivals, were nearly one-man shows. For example, the credits for his major production, *Shadow over Angkor*, listed the prince as producer, director, leading actor, scenarist and music director. His leading lady was his Swiss-Eurasian wife, Monique. Sihanouk's hobby of film-making led him to organise the World Festival of Film in Phnom Penh in 1968[1].

201

But, as has been seen with other parts of Asia, just as there are contrasts, there are similarities within Southeast Asian cinema.

INDONESIA

HISTORICAL BACKGROUND

The history of Indonesian films is fraught with many of the problems that faced other countries—a public view that film acting was degrading, a sharp dichotomy between film as art and as business, the use of movies for propaganda by Japanese occupation and post-independence governments and the necessity to wrest film from a colonial mentality.

Indonesian film history is a bit different because it includes a chapter on the use of movies for fighting an ideological battle which had ramifications for the entire nation. What developed in the late 1950s and 1960s was laid at the feet of President Sukarno and his 'Manifesto Politik'. The President had said that society must fight against the evils of liberalism so that Indonesians can live according to the 1945 Constitution and *Pancasila* (national ideology). Leaders of the Indonesian Communist Party used the manifesto to whip up anti-Americanism and a boycott of US films was put into effect by a group called PAPFIAS (Action Committee for the Boycott of Imperialist American films) (Djarot 1987: 53).

The Indonesian film world was already weakened in 1957, because of a heavy influx of Indian pictures; a rejection of ten points presented by film representatives to Sukarno, who retorted he had not seen an Indonesian film reflecting the national spirit and culture; general neglect of the industry by a government beset by other problems and an inability to obtain suitable screenings for local movies.

After an organisation that promoted Indonesian films (PPFI) announced, in April 1957, that all its members were ceasing film activities[2] because of the undue competition and governmental slight, the Communist Party chose film as its first target. The PPFI stoppage was used to attack the Communists' major opponents, Usmar Ismail and Djamaluddin Malik, film kingpins who had started production houses earlier and a cultural organisation, LESBUMI, to offset that of the Communists, LEKRA. Usmar was branded a US agent and 'prostitute', especially after he made a few lighter movies to try to save the industry (see Misbach ca 1982: 38–41; Buruma 1983a: 40).

The battle had its casualties. Djamaluddin was jailed between

1957 and 1959 for siding with a rebellion and his production company, PERSARI, collapsed. The careers of others were ruined, including the leading LEKRA producer and director, Bachtiar Siagian. (Bachtiar, whose theme was often humanitarian love, had done quality work with *Pisau Surit* (1960), *Baja Membara* (White-Hot Steel, 1961) and *Dilereng Gunung Kawi* (On Mount Kawi, 1962).) A 1964 government decision to place film under the Ministry of Information failed to be implemented because of communist opposition, but was finally carried out in 1966–7, and LEKRA bowed out of the cultural scene with the failed coup of 30 September 1965.

Some of the rest of the history is familiar: The first feature produced in Indonesia, *Lutang Kasarung*, was an adaptation of a folk-tale (West Javanese), made by Europeans, G. Kruger and L. Heuveldorp; the actors were always local Dutch, and the 1928 entry of the Wong brothers into film commenced Chinese control of the industry.

Movies of the Wongs and other Chinese businessmen, such as Tan Khoen Hian (Tan's Film, 1929) and The Teng Chun[3] (Cino Motion Picture Corporation, 1931), were usually in Chinese dialects with all-Chinese casts. Sometimes Javanese songs were inserted but, for the most part, these films attracted the Chinese community (Misbach ca 1982: 21).

Authentic Indonesian movies made their début in the 1930s, through the efforts of two other Europeans. With borrowed money and very basic knowledge of film gleaned from books, Albert Balink, a journalist of Dutch-Indonesian descent, collaborated with the Wongs to make *Pareh*. With the help of the Dutch domumentary maker, Mannus Franken, Balink produced a meticulously detailed and costly movie which attracted a large audience but sent Balink and the Wongs into bankruptcy. *Pareh* attempted to do more than make money; it hoped to show Indonesian culture.

After establishing ANIF (Algameen Nederlands Indische Film Syndicaat), Balink, again with Franken and the Wongs, brought out the first feature in Malay, *Moonlight*, in 1937. The film, starring Roekiah and Raden Mochtar, became a model for new companies that emerged in the late 1930s. One writer described it as a 'hybrid',

'based on a kind of musical theatre, hugely popular among the Chinese, called Opera Stambul: stories of fantastic kings and queens in fictitious lands, incorporating elements from Bali, the Philippines, India, China, Arabia and even Hawaii.' (Buruma 1983a: 40)

Success that it was, *Moonlight* spelled the end of Balink's career. Stockholders of ANIF felt betrayed and bailed out, claiming they were led to believe the company was to make documentaries about Indonesia for a Dutch market.

Appeals to gain a middle-class audience before World War II were mostly in vain, the thinking being that stage people in films were undereducated, immoral, anti-social and given to adventurism. Furthermore, the middle class was a hard group to please as it took its standards from imported films and from other Indonesian art forms. As a result filmmakers decided to seek the patronage of the less-demanding lower class (Misbach ca 1982: 27).

With the Japanese occupation of Indonesia, all movie facilities were confiscated. The movie policy put into effect was that of Japan in the 1930s (closely copied from that of Hitler's Germany). It incorporated the 'Outline for Film Propaganda in Southern Areas (September 1942)', which aimed at a unified movie policy for all of occupied Southeast Asia. In these countries, movie industry management was to be entrusted to Nichi'ei (Japan Motion Picture Company) and Eihai (Motion Picture Distributing Company), both with head offices in Tokyo.

The Japanese replaced US and European imports with their own and local films. All movies featured friendship between Japan and Asia; exaltation of patriotism, military operations and the strength of the Japanese military; the evil of Western countries; morals based on Japanese virtues and increased production and other wartime campaigns (Kurasawa 1988: 4). An average of 52 Japanese films and newsreels were brought into Indonesia each year. A decision was made to import 32 Chinese and six Axis countries' movies, but this was probably not carried out (Kurasawa 1987: 68).

Encouragement was given to large-scale domestic production, and Jawa Eiga Kosha (Java Motion Picture Corporation) was created in late 1942 to make documentaries, culture films and newsreels. After Nichi'ei was assigned as the monopoly company for Southeast Asia, it took over movie making in Java. The office to supervise the entire region was in Singapore, with a Jakarta branch developed in April 1943. The latter was enlarged into Jakarta Seisakujo (Jakarta Movie Producing Unit), one of two Southeast Asian units engaged in filmmaking. (The other was in Manila.) The six other Southeast Asian branches (one each in the Indonesian cities of Medan and Makassar) operated as liaison offices and shot news films.

Feature films came later, the first being *Kemakmoeran* (Prosperity) in January 1944. Limited in number, their themes were dictated by the propaganda bureau of the military government. They were in Indonesian, used actors recruited from among the Indonesians and were less concerned with entertainemnt than with instruction.

With limited staff and facilities, the Japanese made many films of a variety of types in wartime Java. Kurasawa (1988, p. 6) believed the Japanese improved the film length and quality over that of pre-war Indonesia.

During Indonesia's struggle for independence (1945–47), film activity was at a standstill. A number of stage and film personalities joined the fight for independence or entertained troops. Among these was Usmar Ismail, who formed a drama group (Maya), at the same time as serving in the national army and heading a daily and a cultural periodical. Upon becoming interested in film, Usmar closely studied US and other works shown in Indonesia, and when he was arrested by the Dutch he was involved in some of their film projects.

In 1948, South Pacific Film Corporation (SPFC) was started as a subsidiary of N.V. Multi (formerly ANIF), its purpose being to make documentaries. Usmar became assistant to the director, Andjar Asmara and, when the latter left, Usmar was made director. Usmar's first title was *Tjitra* (1949), followed by *Harta Karun* (Treasure).

SPFC, after its first production in 1948, was joined by a new company, Tan and Wong Brothers, set up by the pioneering Wong brothers and Tan Khoen Hian, and The Teng Chun also reappeared as a producer.

Usmar established the first film company owned by a native Indonesian, PERFINI (National Film Corporation), in March 1950, vowing not to compromise with commercialism. Though made under primitive circumstances, Usmar's films were realistic, 'cultural vehicles that clearly reflect through their touch of fine sentiments, inner depth, and meditative atmosphere the manner of thought and feeling of typically Eastern societies' (Djarot 1987: 52). Among Usmar's early important works were *Darah dan Do'a* (Long March, 1951), *Krisis* (1953) and *Tamu Agung* (The Honourable Guest, 1955).

A few weeks after the start of PERFINI, Djamaluddin Malik launched another native production house, PERSARI (Indonesian Film Arts Company), which made mainly entertainment films.

The public was not enamoured of many of the indigenous movies. The middle classes, particularly severe in their criticisms, favoured imported fare from the West, and then from Malaya, the Philippines and India, thus denying the film renaissance of which Usmar and others dreamed. In 1950, 863 films were imported, 660 from the US, with others from Hong Kong, India, Malaya and the Philippines. Only 13 Indonesian movies were made that year.

After unsuccessfully seeking government intervention concerning the abundance of imports, Usmar and Djamaluddin established PPFI in 1954, with the objectives of restricting Malayan film exhibition, pressuring first class theatres into showing domestic movies, and preparing Indonesian movies for entry in the Asian Film Festival. A partial solution was forthcoming when the Jakarta mayor ruled that all first class theatres should show at least one Indonesian movie every six months. But, except for Usmar's *Krisis*, most were not successful in the top theatres, some only lasting through one showing (Misbach ca 1982: 36).

Early 1950s' films, such as *Si Pincang* (The Limp, 1952), *Harimau Tjampa* (Tiger from Champa, 1953), and others by Djamaluddin, were in line with cultural congresses which stated Indonesia was in a state of cultural confusion resulting from colonialism, capitalism and rapid social change (Djarot 1987: 53).

After the 1965 coup attempt, the Indonesian film industry was in bad shape. Few filmmakers were left, and capital was in short supply, equipment in disarray and the market very narrow. Anxious to get theatres operating again as a source of tax revenue, the Government opened the gates wide on imported films, swooping in a number with blatant sex or violence themes. The impact upon local films was devastating, to the extent that the National Film Production Council (DPFN), founded in 1968 to set an example by producing high quality work, could not fulfil its task because of competition offered by explicit imports.

In 1970, domestic filmmakers requested and received the same relaxed atmosphere from censors afforded to foreign films, as a result of which, new faces entered the business and capital came in droves. But the open policy lasted only briefly; by 1971, sections of Indonesian society criticised the moral standards of local pictures and, the followig year, the censor board tightened regulations.

Some noteworthy work came out of this period. Wim Umboh's *Sembilan* (Nine, 1967) was the first colour film to be shot in cinemascope, and DPFN's first production, *Apa Yang Kau Cari Palupi?* (What Are You Searching for, Palupi? 1969) captured best feature honours at the Asian Film Festival. *Bima Kroda* (1967), directed by D. Djayakusuma, was adapted from *wayang* (Javanese mythology) and performed by a traditional theatre group, which saved money from its nightly stage shows to meet production costs. *Bernapas dalam Lumpur* (The Longest Dark, 1970), in its exploitation of sex, was a box-office hit, lending confidence to the idea that domestic films could beat imported ones.

The Government increasingly looked at protectionist policies for the industry. In 1969, a US $540 fee was levied on each imported film, the proceeds intended to finance DPFN. Indonesian producers could apply for credits from this board of up to US $18,000. In 1973, a quota restriction was placed on foreign films—700 in 1973, followed by 500 in 1974 and lowered by 100 a year until 1978, after which the Government would allow in only selected films.

In other protectionist moves, the Government in 1976, required that importers also become producers of local films. For every five films (reduced to three) brought in, the importer had to produce one Indonesian movie. However, within a year, this ruling was abolished because too many 'quickies' were made solely to obtain the import permit.

Also in 1976, the authorities unsuccesfully tried to organise all importers into the Federation of Indonesian Film Importers, Producers and Distributors, with the purpose of bringing more order and less competition to the business. Instead, four consortia were created: one for Mandarin films with an import quota of 73; two others for US and European films with a quota of 72, and a fourth for non-Mandarin, Asian films with a quota of 79. By 1987, when 205 imports were allowed, 125 were US-European, 50 Mandarin and 30 non-Mandarin Asian.

Indonesian film production increased sharply immediately after some of this legislation (to a high of 134 in 1977, many of which were 'quickies') but, by 1978, it was down again. The government then asked all importers to contribute US $7,500 for each movie imported to a film development fund, made loans available and placed high taxes on imported films (D'Cruz 1978: 11). Because of a need to fill screening time in theatres, the annual film quota was raised to 260, with six (rather than three as before) prints of each.

CONTEMPORARY SCENE

Production

The 1970s were a strange time for Indonesian film—a time when nearly as many films (573 between 1969 and 1978) were produced as in more than four decades previously (613 between 1926 and 1968), yet theatres complained of a shortage; a time when organisations were created to spur higher-quality work, yet the Indonesian Film Festival refused to give a best feature award in 1977 because of shoddy work; in short, a time of experimenting to lift the level of national cinema.

Among other 'experiments' were the creation of the National Film Council and the Government Film Unit, both in 1979. The council, made up of 49 representatives of social institutions, the film industry and the government and other prominent figures, was designed to help the Information Minister to define government policy on the development of a national film.

The film unit was to become more involved in production, especially of documentaries, but also of features. Through its subsidiary, Pusat Produksi Filem Negara, the unit produced four features in 1979, at an average cost of US $41,667. The rationale for doing features was that the government could produce them less expensively, because its performers would be non-professionals recruited and trained by the government-owned and -operated acting school, and because colour processing would be handled by the government's new laboratory.

Eventually, this thinking proved correct. In 1986, the government was the country's largest film producer through its State Film

Production Centre, making 70–90 documentaries, 156 television episodes and some feature films each year.

The industry itself suffered a down-swing in the late 1980s. The number of local productions inched downward year by year—from 71 in 1983, to 54 in 1987, and up to 82 in 1988, and the number of unemployed film workers shot upward. In 1987, 965 professionals (599 actors among them) could not find work on a production; and only 41 of 95 film directors had a movie.

Producing films remained a big gamble. Of about 100 production companies registered with the Association of Indonesian Film Companies, only 20 were active in 1987 (Anwar 1988: 134). Reasons given for the plight of the industry at that time were an economic recession, distributors who obstructed a regular and fair flow of income to producers and the impact of videocassettes.

Producers blamed video for many of their problems, unlike four years earlier, when they thought it helped them. In 1983, they said that since video piracy usually dealt with imported film, the resultant drop-off at the box office for US-European films would give Indonesian movies a clear shot at audiences. Indonesian television does not pose much of a threat to local film because only five million of the 170 million population have receivers. Some concern was expressed about the television of neighbouring countries which spilled over into Indonesia, such as TV-3 of Malaysia which shows popular Indian movies.

At least one producer of the 1980s knew the formula for successful production. At a time when only one in four Indonesian films recouped their losses, 99 per cent of the 180 features made by Ali Hassan of Inem Films (1976–86) recorded at least a modest profit. The 10–12 features he makes a year are pitched to lower-class audiences, cost US $100,000 to 125,000 without much attention to quality and are sold to sub-distributors on an outright basis.

The return on these films is calculated on the assumption that they play in most of Indonesia's 1,700 'C' category theatres, where they are retained for about two days. Each theatre is expected to gross US $40 a day for a total of US $136,000. Additionally, Hassan's films are marketed in Malaysia, Singapore and Brunei at the rate of US $2,000 a title.

Operating on a conveyor belt principle, Hassan keeps two films each in preparation, editing, shooting and dubbing at any one time. The average shooting schedule is 30 days, and films are released within 14 weeks. Hassan has 120 employees, hired on a casual picture-to-picture basis, and 15 directors. He does not advertise and provides distributors with only a set of stills and one poster (*Variety* 1986d: 442).

Distribution and Exhibition

Distribution of films in Indonesia was likened by Anwar (1988,

p. 135) to a 'jungle where there are no rules, where everyone has to fend for himself'.

Many groups handle distribution, often making for an unwieldly situation full of conflicting interests. For example, distributors are also importers tied to the four consortia representing US, European, Mandarin and non-Mandarin Asian films; they also own chains of theatres. Therefore, they are in positions where they can control what is shown.

To counter such discrimination, the government, in the mid-1970s, made it obligatory for at least two Indonesian movies to be shown each month in every theatre. To implement the policy, PT Perfin (Indonesian Film Distributors Company) was formed to determine distribution schedules and allocate Indonesian movies to central film distributors, who distributed them directly to Jakarta theatres and to regional film distributors. The latter, who worked solely in one of 15 distribution regions, handled the release of films outside Jakarta (Department of Information ca 1981: 9). Anwar (1988, pp. 135–6) said Perfin was successful only in Jakarta; provincial distributors and theatres paid no attention to its policies.

Cinema owners are organised as Gabungan Pengusaha Bioskop Seluruh Indonesia (GPBSI). To ensure a regular supply of films for their theatres, exhibitors deal with bookers who negotiate with the association of film importers and producers on the price of each film. Films in Indonesia are sold, not rented. Bookers have become powerful, according to Anwar (1988, p. 136), dictating the price of films to the detriment of producers. They are often closely connected with importers or act as financiers of productions and, in this regard, they can influence producers on the types of films made and the stars employed. Thus, producers have little choice in the type of film they make, and cinema owners not much say in the films they exhibit.

Obviously, the job is one that is sought, for Indonesia has more than enough bookers (about 100), causing fragmentation and chaos in distribution channels. Anwar (1988, p. 136) said bookers have other businesses they maintain, employ a huckster mentality and are noted for not paying producers on time.

Attendance figures in the more than 2,100 theatres (251 in Jakarta) continue to rise. By 1987, there were more than 180 million movie-goers in Indonesia, 10.87 million of which were in six key cities. Jakarta has an annual film audience of more than 2.65 million. Most movie-goers are categorised as 'middle class-below' and in the 15–25-year age group.

Three grades of theatres exist. The top category, where the government-approved admission price is about US \$4.50, shows only major releases, while in the middle-range theatres, second-run engagements are booked. The playing time in any theatre is a maximum of one week; films which do not break even must be retained for at least two days. Some producers target their films for the lowest-grade theatres ('C'), and if they qualify for an 'A' or 'B' that is a bonus. Tickets in 'C' theatres, which change films every two days, cost US 20 cents (*Variety* 1986c: 443).

Directors and Their Films

Indonesia has had its share of dedicated directors, individuals who overcome the odds to make quality, interesting films, while keeping an eye on the box office.

Foremost among these is Teguh Karya, who, like fellow directors Wim Umboh and the late Syumandjaja, graduated from the Moscow Film School. In his films, which helped bring about a renaissance of film in the late 1960s and early 1970s, Teguh succeeds where many Third World filmmakers cannot; he makes quality films that are profitable without too much compromise to commercialism.

Teguh, as with a number of directors, came from theatre—the National Academy of Theatre Indonesia. He also returns to theatre from time to time and maintains his own theatre troupe. In 1981, after two years with a drama group, he made the film *Age 18*. His first film in 1971 was *Wajah Seorang Lelaki* (A Man's Face), which gave Indonesian films a distinctive character, but it was not successful. Next, he made *Cinta Pertama* (First Love) in 1973, a story about a teenager's love, followed by *Ranjang Pengatin* (The Bride's Bed) in 1974 and *Kawin Lari* (Elopement) in 1975.

Other Teguh films are *November 1828*, made with the huge budget of US $480,000 in 1979 and *Mementos* (1986), winner of the best picture award at the Asian Film Festival. Teguh's works probe behind the façade of family life, have a strong Indonesian flavour and are very artistic and technically skilful.

Wim Umboh was known for his love stories of people in high society until he filmed a story about the lower classes, *Pengemis dan Tukang Becak* (The Beggar and the Becak Driver), in 1975. After being out for a couple of years because of a serious illness, he returned to films in 1981 with *When Love Breaks Through*.

Another theatre artist (and writer) who entered films in the 1970s is Arifin C. Noer. His first work, *Suci Sang Primadona* (Suci the Primadona) in 1976, was well received, while his next, *Petualang-Petualang* (The Wanderers) in 1977, was banned for eight years for criticising growing government corruption. Apparently to redeem himself in the government's eyes, he finished two movies for the state-owned film company, in one of which, President Suharto figures prominently. His *Yuyun, a Patient in a Mental Hospital* received accolades in foreign festivals of the early 1980s.

The late Syumandjaja epitomised the philosophy of some of these directors, making cinematic personal statements about the poor and underprivileged and compromising between themes of realism and escapism to stay afloat. Among Syumandjaja films are *Lewat Jam Malam* (After the Curfew, 1971), *Si Mamad* (1973), *Si*

Doel Anak Modern (Doel, a Modern Kid, 1976), *Kabut Sutera Ungu* (Mist of Purple Silk, 1980), *Bukan Sandiwara* (It's Not a Play, 1981), *Kerikil-Kerikil Tajam* (Sharp Rocks, 1984) and *Opera Jakarta* (1985).

The 1980s saw a re-awakening of nationalism in films as some of the above-named and a new crop of directors identified with transformations of Indonesian culture and society. They were concerned about the same societal dilemma that became the theme of other Asian 'new' directors—the tension between modern urban life and that of the traditional village. Straightforward films, such as *Desa di Kaki Bukit* (The Village at the Foot of the Hills) and *Putri Giok* (The Jade Princess) dealt with village isolation broken by modernisation and inter-ethnic relationships, respectively.

Among the new directors was Slamet Rahardjo of the National Academy of Theatre Indonesia, who had acted in Teguh's plays and films. His first movie was *Rembulan dan Matahari* (The Moon and the Sun, 1980), followed by *Seputih Hatinya Semerah Bibirnya* (White Is Her Heart, Red Are Her Lips, 1981) and *Ponirah Terpidana* (Ponirah for Justice, 1983). Although his films won awards, they often failed at the box office.

The first film by new director Eros Djarot, the brother of Slamet Rahardjo, was considered the beginning of a new era in Indonesian films in 1989. *Tjoet Nia Dhien*, which swept most awards at the 1989 Indonesian Film Festival, joined *Peluru dan Wanita* (Bullets and Women) in an attempt to introduce Indonesian films to the world. Both had large budgets, *Tjoet Nia Dhien*, US $800,000; *Peluru dan Wanita*, US $1.5 milion. The latter was the country's first major co-production with Hollywood (Vatikiotis 1989: 66).

The commercial successes popular with the 'middle class-below' audiences did not carry social relevance themes. Usually they were comedies, youth movies, soap operas, romantic melodramas or 'mystical' films based on old Javanese legends, spiced with as much sex (a bit only) and violence (a great deal) as the censors allowed. Many of the crowd-pleasers were imitative of Hollywood, Hong Kong and Indian movies.

Religious, social and government pressures often determine the make-up of movies. For instance, in the late 1970s, professional groups, such as that of the nurses, protested if depicted negatively in films, so directors began to use 'safe films' featuring prostitutes who were not yet organised into a pressure group. All films must acquire government permits, granted after they have been examined and evaluated by the Film Censor Board under the Department of Information. The board's guidelines focus on theme, religion, sociocultural affairs, politics and public order. Films which often pass scrutiny in Jakarta are banned in other parts of Indonesia.

Directors repeat that they can make whatever film they want, but they *are* restricted. They cannot produce films about communism, that comment on the contemporary political situation or portray police, military or civil servants negatively.

Professionalism

In 1954, Indonesia was anxious to enter its cinematic efforts in the First Asian Film Festival, held in Tokyo. Because Japan and Indonesia had not yet ironed out their differences, Indonesia did not participate. Instead, the following year, Indonesia sponsored its own festival, repeated in 1960, 1967 and each year since 1973. The Indonesian Film Festival is held on a rotation basis in a different provincial capital each year, to allow various publics to pay their respects to the stars. The Citra Awards are given in 13 categories.

Other professional activities, revolving around education and training, film preservation and the social welfare of filmmakers, are carried out by at least 15 film organisations. For instance, registered film workers are organised in Ikatan Karyawan Film dan Televisi (Association of Film and Television Workers) and artists in Persatuan Artis Film Indonesia (Indonesian Film Artists Union).

A film library, a pioneering archival effort in Southeast Asia, was established in 1975 by the municipal governor of Jakarta. By 1983, the library was in financial distress when a new city government abandoned it. The Film Artists' Foundation (YAF) was another joint venture, between the industry and Jakarta's regional government. Intended to work for members' social welfare, after 1977, the organisation focused on improving skills through courses. Also into training is the Academy of Cinematography in Jakarta. Supported by the Kino Workshop, under the management of the Jakarta Institute of Art Education, the academy offers a five-year curriculum in film theory and practice. In the first six semesters, students receive basic education in all aspects of film; during their final four terms, they choose a cinematic field in which to specialise.

THAILAND

HISTORICAL BACKGROUND

Without experiencing the colonialism forced upon its neighbours, Thailand had their same bifurcated film history, complete with a double set of 'firsts', those achieved by foreigners and those by Thais. The first films imported into Thailand were brought by Japanese military and business men at the beginning of the century; the first film import company set up by a Thai business man was in 1916

(Boonyaketmala 1982: 39). The first film produced in Thailand, *Suvarna of Siam*, was made by an American, Henry McRay, in 1922; the first by a Thai was *Choke Song Chan* (Double Luck), made by Sri Krung Film Company in 1927 (Soongnarata 1977:1).

Sri Krung Films, formed by the Wasuvati family, was not the first production company; one made up of artists with the patronage of the King existed a few months earlier. The Thai film industry was different from those of other Asian countries in that it did not face public ostracism; in fact, members of noble families and high-ranking government officials were often used in starring roles. For example, in 1940, Pridi Panomyong, one of the nation's most influential politicians, directed *The King of the White Elephants*. Noble families also owned main film companies, such as Patanakorn Company during the reign of Rama VI (Vajiravudh) or Charoenkrung Company during the time of Rama VII (Pradathipok) (Blanc-Szanton 1989: 11).

Sound was introduced by Sri Krung in 1931 but, throughout the next two decades, many producers found it less expensive to maintain dubbers live at the theatres, often behind the projectors (Sukwonga 1987: 116). Later, dubbers found employment with foreign films. Thailand produced about 20 films a year in the 1930s and 1940s.

After World War II (during which film was replaced by drama and stage), the industry stayed in a state of flux for about a decade. The demand for films was there, but not the supply of talented stars, good scriptwriters, experienced technicians, suitable novels and other material for scripts and government support. The quality of the films was poor—sometimes almost worn out—because so few copies were made with the shortage of materials. Teams of dubbers accompanied the films as an economic measure to avoid the costs of sound production. To survive, producers imitated, down to copying titles of movies that had made money. They also leaned heavily on plots taken from popular radio dramas or magazine short stories.

The birth of the star system and emergence of several independent producers between 1945 and 1955 meant more studios and more productions. (In the 1950s, Thailand produced 25 movies a year.) Stars appeared in 20 to 30 films simultaneously, some made by new studios such as Hanumarn Films, Asawin Films and Lawo Films. The latter two companies were started by Prince Bhanu and his brother, Prince Anusorn, respectively.

In the mid-1960s, the Thai film business received a boost from the box-office success of love story musicals. The popularity of top singers in these films matched that of the leading stars, especially in the provinces, and any folk vocalist could become popular despite a lack of acting ability. Films were full of songs—more than 30 in some cases, many of which were hardly relevant to the story. This genre remained the most popular until 1970 and included *Mon Rak*

Luk Tung (Love Story of Our Farmland), the highest grossing film up to that time.

By the mid-1960s, Thai films changed from 35mm to 16mm and, in 1966, and for a short time after, annual production was 260. But, throughout this period, the foreign films dominated, being shown in two-thirds of the total exhibitions.

Disruptive political events and numerous changes of government in the 1970s affected the film industry. For example, the National Executive Council disbanded the film censor board in 1972 and appointed a much more restrictive one, made up entirely of police and headed by the military son of the Prime Minister. After martial law in October 1976, a curfew hurt movie attendance and lowered the number of daily shows. Legislation passed included a 1977 control act which banned those 18 years of age or under from X-rated films and a 1978 copyright law which protected Thai and foreign films. At least four attempts to organise a government body to control and represent the film industry failed during the decade.

CONTEMPORARY SCENE

Production

Between 1983 and 1987, Thailand produced 626 feature films, an average of 125 a year. (The total for 1927–87 was about 3,000.) The number peaked at 141 in 1984 and was down to 114 in 1987, partly because of the national economic situation and the intrusion of videocassettes.

What is encouraging about these figures, which rank Thailand twelfth among the world's leading film producers, is that such prodigious production was accomplished despite high production costs, customs duties and taxes; poor equipment; fierce competition from foreign movies; an unprofessional approach to filmmaking; and film censorship.

Three levels of production budgets exist in Thailand—films that cost US $120,000 or more to make (about 40 per cent of all films), those that take US $40,000–$120,000 (30 per cent) and those that require less than US $40,000 (30 per cent). But these figures do not stand up well as nearly all films exceed budget because of unforeseen difficulties, such as the necessity of renting equipment, or bad weather and flooding which delay shooting (Suwunpukdee 1988: 166).

Eating into these budgets are relatively high acting salaries which have increased substantially over the years, as well as exorbitant advertising and promotion costs. The star system's salary scales fluctuate wildly with the economy, changes in the movie industry and the number of stars appearing in a picture. For example, when oil prices increased in the mid-1970s, stars' salaries went up at least

15 per cent; some doubled. A star such as Sombat Metanee made US $7,500 in 1977; if he appeared with another major star, the salary nearly doubled. The rationale was that the more stars in a picture, the more money a producer could expect, especially from provincial distributors, thus the more that should be shared with the stars. In other ways, stars had producers in strangleholds; because some actors appeared in a dozen or more films at the same time, any schedule deviation on their part (such as travel abroad) could suspend work on a number of productions (Soongnarata 1977: 7).

Inordinately large advertising budgets plague the producers; some, while facing bankruptcy, have squandered US $50,000 or more to advertise a picture. Often, advertising costs range from 33 to 100 per cent of the cost of production, and independent producers usually cannot afford newspaper and prime-time television advertisements.

High taxes at fixed rates and customs duties on imported film and equipment also take heavy tolls. Between 1983 and 1985, the Government collected at least US $1,666,000 from duties on film and equipment, plus another US $476,000 in taxes. A source in 1984 said the Government took 35 per cent of the ticket admission price in taxes, the rest was divided among the producer, director and cinema owner, with the latter likely to take 50 per cent (Sananchit 1984: 63). Still another source earlier reported the government's take at 55 per cent, including indirect taxes (Soongnarata 1977: 7).

A 1988 survey found that 42 per cent of the producers owned their own equipment, 2 per cent owned some but rented the rest and 56 per cent rented everything. Much of the equipment is old, over-used or inadequate. In the same study, charges were made about the unprofessional approach to filmmaking that results from insufficient training. A conclusion was that although filmmakers loved their work, they did not know the rudiments of the profession. Of all producers and directors, 20 per cent were university graduates, while the rest had high school or vocational school educations. Forty-three per cent learned film on the job, 30 per cent by reading books and self-study, 17 per cent by consulting with other people and 1 per cent by majoring in film at a film school (Suwunpukdee 1988: 165).

Possibilities for film education exist in seven universities which have film departments and in two acting schools. Most of these programmes are new with small numbers of graduates—about a total of 150 a year. So far, the film industry does not seem to be attracting the graduates. These programmes require 24–30 credits; however, technicians must enrol in more courses.

Incentives for good film work have been available since at least 1977 when the annual Thai Tukatatong Awards were given. After a three-year hiatus, two sets of awards were available in 1980—Tukatatong and Suphannahong Committee Awards and, by

1985, the Suraswadee Awards (considered the local 'Oscars') were given, amid controversy over the choice of best actress. Criticism was voiced about the manner in which awards were chosen earlier in 1980, when top officials of the Suphannahong Committee were charged with entering their own works and garnering the prizes.

Imported films have provided keen competition for decades. In the 1950s, when Columbia, MGM, Twentieth Century Fox, Paramount, United Artists, Universal, Warner Brothers and Disney set up offices in Bangkok, the US became the best organised film importer, although Hong Kong and Taiwan were also major film suppliers after Shaw Brothers connected with Union-Odeon and Golden Harvest with Saha Mongkon. Other foreign films imported at significant levels were those from India, Japan and Italy.

Between 1961 and 1976, of the total 9,068 films exhibited in Thailand, those from the US accounted for 32.37 per cent, followed by Hong Kong and Taiwan, 21.85 per cent; Thailand, 12.37 per cent; India, 7.28 per cent; Japan, 6.48 per cent and Italy, 5.38 per cent. Other figures point out the preponderance of foreign movies: about 62.5 per cent of all foreign exchange for film in any year was paid to the eight US companies in Thailand; in 1971, Western films earned 44 per cent of the total revenues from films, followed by those from Hong Kong, Taiwan, Japan and India with 40 per cent and Thailand, 16 per cent (Boonyaketmala 1982: 40–1).

This favourable role for the importers was side-tracked in December 1976, when the Tanin government increased the tax per metre of imported film by 1400 per cent. The government recognised the potential revenues to be made from film, noting that in 1974, of the US $81.8 million in gross receipts, US $26.95 million ended up in the state treasury through taxes. It also knew that 85 per cent of total screen time was in the hands of transnational corporations and that an average of US $25 million a year in royalties and profits was sent out of Thailand by foreign film distributors and television networks.

Tanin's move was calculated to claim more of this revenue and to placate the Thai Motion Picture Producers Association (TMPPA), which had pushed for a limit on the number of foreign pictures. Tanin helped local pictures in other ways, by reducing admission taxes from 50 per cent to 40 or 10 per cent, depending on the price of the tickets, and by developing the Thai Film Industry Promotion Committee which, however, was never very effective.

The fourteenfold tax increase had immediate effects, temporarily drying up Chinese film exhibition and cutting the number of imports overall by about a third. Within a year, Chinese films recaptured part of the market by bringing in movies in negative, rather than positive, form, a less expensive process. The tax also stimulated more local productions (from 80 in 1975 to 140 a year later), made Thai films the top grossing by early 1978 and encouraged more Thai filmmakers to use foreign locations. What it did not do, though, was spur producers into making better quality films.

While many film entrepreneurs learned to co-exist with the tax rule, the Motion Picture Exporters Association of America (MPEAA) vengefully boycotted all US imports to Thailand. The MPEAA argued that it feared a snowball effect; if it accepted these terms in Thailand, ultimata would also be issued by other countries.

Tanin was out of office by October 1977, and succeeding coalition governments regularly received MPEAA lobbyists. In 1980, Prime Minister Kriangsak Chomanan ordered a 50 per cent reduction of the import tax (to 75 cents per metre), hoping to encourage the showing of better foreign films in Thailand and to augment the quality of local movies through competition. Local filmmakers expressed their dismay, pointing out that fully-booked theatres could not handle the extra films. Kriangsak did not last out the year in office, and the four coalition governments of Prem (February 1980–December 1983) had very little interest in film except as a generator of money for the state treasury.

Finally, in May 1981, the MPEAA, realising the tax per metre of film was to stay and acknowledging the growing importance of the Thai market, lifted its boycott. Of course, annual double-digit inflation in Thailand had undermined the severity of the tax anyway. Between 1983 and 1985, Thailand spent more than US $14 million on importing 723 movies (349 US, 336 Chinese, 19 Indian, 6 Japanese, 13 from other countries).

As the 1980s ended, many independent producers had to close or find other alternatives. In 1985 alone, 60 per cent of the producers quit and called for government help, particularly in combating video piracy[4].

Producers tried to cope in the 1970s and 1980s by co-producing with other countries, such as the United States (1976), Hong Kong and South Korea (1977), Japan (1979) and others; by pandering to less-sophisticated rural audiences with formularistic, Hollywood-type and unimaginative movies (Buruma 1983b: 53–4), and by increasingly throwing themselves at the mercy of distributors.

Distributors have meddled in production matters throughout the past two decades, partly to control the types and numbers of films to fill their theatres. For example, Union-Odeon, a circuit controlling five Bangkok and three up-country theatres, took minority stakes in up to 30 films a year by 1977; at the same time others set up their own production houses. By 1980, independent producers were forced to join these new production companies, among which were Apex, the production arm of Pyramid Entertainment Group (largest first-run circuit with twelve theatres), and Go Brothers Films, managed by the Petchrama-Metro-MacKenna theatre chain.

The number of producers dwindled, from about 200 in 1977 to about six or seven in 1980. Within another short span, the production boiled down to four companies—Apex, Go Brothers, New Five Stars and Saha/Mongkon, all Sino-Thai operations that monopolised the industry.

Writing in 1984, Sananchit (p. 63) noted the power distributors had over the types of films shown. Sananchit said that all producers had to submit their film proposals to one of the five distributors (representing five geographical areas), listing the names of the director and leading actors/actresses and providing an outline of the plot. When this was approved, the distributor invested in the film.

Distribution and Exhibition

Because of many of the above-mentioned problems, a number of theatres closed or were converted into cocktail lounges, skating rinks or mini-theatres. Yet, in 1986, 1,014 theatres survived, offering 577,179 seats for a population of more than 49.5 million (Suwunpukdee 1988: 165).

Thai film distribution originates with the producer providing prints directly to Bangkok theatres and to distributing agents. The latter release the films to sub-agents, who, in turn, give them to theatres outside Bangkok. Thailand, for distribution purposes, is divided into parts (e.g. north, south, northeast, central and suburb) with sub-agents assigned to each. Sub-agents distribute the films to theatres and can rent them to television stations and individuals, as long as the activity is confined to their regions. A simple financial arrangement operates. For films distributed directly to Bangkok theatres, the producer and exhibitor split ticket sales. In transactions between the producer and distributing agent, the latter receives 5 to 7 per cent of the ticket receipts, and in dealings between distributing agent and sub-agent, the rate varies according to ticket sales (Suwunpukdee 1988: 167).

Thai theatres average about 20 showings a week. Most theatres are considered modern and have been referred to as 'palaces of the common people' (Boonyaketmala 1982: 40). In 1988, there was a mushrooming of mini-theatres in Bangkok department stores and shopping complexes, because they take up less space in the crowded city and are more inexpensive to build than those with 1,000 seats. Despite the urban mini-theatres, though, 80 per cent of the viewers remain up-country, in the provinces, and it is at this audience that large production companies aim (Buruma 1983b: 53).

Circuit owners have tremendous clout in the Thai film industry, perhaps because they have the largest capital investment (as much as 83 per cent of the industry's total). As early as the mid-1970s, the major circuit owners alone were solidly entrenched in business, having swallowed up smaller exhibitors. They could dictate their terms to distributors and producers alike as they determined whether a film was seen in their theatres. For example, taxes levied on admissions are charged back to the producers and distributors, rather than coming out of the theatre owners' take. They and distributors have been credited with keeping some stars popular, while rejecting new ones, and with deciding whether a film is to be top grossing by its placement in theatres. In fact, in 1978 20 or more disgruntled independent producers, tired of not being able to get their movies into first-run theatres, opened instead in second-run ones.

Theatre owners, thinking of only profits, have looked askance at some government actions designed to bail out the industry. After the 1976 fourteenfold tax increase on foreign films, exhibitors sided with the MPEAA, lobbying for a slice of the tax money or calling for the ruling's repeal. Circuit owners said that as imports fell because of the tax, local productions would not be plentiful enough to fill their theatres. They also claimed the livelihood of 400 dubbers would be affected.

The lot of the dubber was interesting, not to mention lucrative. Dubbers made about US $1,500 a month. Additionally, they could tape their dubbing and charge exhibitors US $25 each time the tape was used. Usually, two to four dubbers were required for a showing although many did all the voices in a film. They were well known for spicing up films, often inserting references to local events familiar to the audience.

Directing and Acting

Commercialism has been the end result of the tie-ins of producers, distributors and exhibitors, and the key to financial success is through signing up the biggest stars. In the 1980s, these top-liners were Sorapon Chatri and Jarunee Sukswadee; the previous decade, they were Sombat Metanee, Krung Srivilai and Aranya Namwong. Thai movie-goers could expect to see one or more of these actors in eight out of every ten movies.

Such exposure means some actors and actresses are overworked, shooting scores of movies each year and two and three scenes from different films on the same day. Sukwonga (1987, p. 117) wrote that, 'producers queue up to catch them, delaying or staggering shooting schedules to match their frantic pace. Here, actors don't learn their lines, studio voice-overs are the rule.' The voice-overs are done by highly paid stand-ins.

When Sombat appeared in 80 per cent of all movies, directors were forced to shoot all of his scenes in a few days, because in a given month, he might appear in 60 productions. In the 1970s, if Sombat was not top-lined, it was not considered a safe film.

Heavy dependence upon two or three major talents makes for sleepless nights for directors. If anything happens to the star—which used to be even more likely because they did their own stunts until the 1980s—the production has to be seriously altered, or even scrapped. For example, a blow was dealt to the film industry in 1973 when popular actress Petchara Chaowaray stepped down at the age of 30 because of a cataract. In her short career, Petchara had more than 300 starring roles.

Audience preference for a few established stars means directors are wary of introducing new talents. Directors such as Piak Poster and Cherd Songsri took chances with new stars between 1978 and 1980 and found success in films such as *Wai Olawon* (Only Sixteen) and *Pae Kao* (The Scar), respectively (Cacnio 1980: 449), but these may be exceptions.

Despite the concentration upon box-office receipts, some directors do get above the mediocre, among them being Cherd Songsri, Vichit Kounavudhi, Prince Chatri Chalerm Yukol, Paimpol Cheyaroon, Piak Poster and Dokdin Kanyaman. On occasions, each of these directors has made films almost as one-man shows, doing everything, including producing, directing, writing, lensing, editing and starring. Whereas more commercially oriented directors make as many as three or four movies a year, those seeking higher quality rarely make more than one.

Vichit Kounavudhi, for example, produces a film every two years and, although he seeks quality (acknowledged by the 24 Thai 'Oscars' he has received), he is careful not to make commercially-unsuccessful movies. Kounavudhi began his career as a journalist, and later became a scriptwriter. He is one of the very few directors who are permitted to make the films they want.

Cherd Songsri's success was partly attributed to *The Scar*, a story about a doomed love affair that became a masterpiece at the same time as it set a box-office record of US $17.5 million. His *Puen Paeng* was more commercially done. Prince Chatri Chalerm, son of another filmmaker, Prince Anusorn, studied archaeology and cinematography in the US before returning to his homeland to become the first Thai director to shoot with synchronised sound. Prince Chatri focuses on poverty, prostitution and violent crime in his films, the best known of which is *The Citizen*, a story describing the fate of a taxi driver whose car is stolen by a gang.

A former movie poster artist[5], Piak Poster tried to change the way Thai films were made with his 1970 work, *Thon*. A departure from the norm, *Thon* was made carefully, with precise camera movements and other pioneering efforts. Piak Poster works on the principle that there are mass and well-educated audiences and, to survive, one must cater to the former while maintaining certain standards demanded by the latter (Soongnarata 1977: 7).

Other directors have innovated. Payuth Ngaokrachang, for example, made the first full-length animated feature, *Sudsakorn*, in 1978, while a young Supravat Jongsiri (known as Supaksorn) found success by introducing the student comedy genre to Thailand in the 1980s.

BURMA

HISTORICAL BACKGROUND

British films were shown in Rangoon's Edison Carnival Tent as early as 1910 and, within the decade, local productions appeared. Burma's first films are credited to U Ohn Maung, an employee of a film equipment store who opened his own photography studio in 1915. Persuaded by Mohd Auzam, manager of a cinema house, U Ohn Maung shot a two-reel documentary on the funeral of a Burmese politician, which earned him the paltry sum of Rs 200.

A member of a merchant family, U Nyi Pu, went into partnership with U Ohn Maung to form Burma Film Company, their first production being *Myitta Hnit Thura*. After six other films, the partners went separate ways, U Nyi Pu setting up Maha Sway Film Company, whose first feature was a 36 reeler, *Yadanabo*, and U Ohn Maung establishing London Art Films, whose initial work was *Taw Myaing Soon*. About the same time (1923), another entrepreneur, U Nyunt, formed British Burma Film Company (Sudan 1985: 113–4).

Burmese cinema traced some of its thematic and stylistic roots to theatrical forms, such as *zat* (drama), *yoke thay* (marionettes) and *pwe*. Early features reflected Burmese societal traits of *arnarde* (regard for others' feelings), freedom of Burmese womanhood, filial piety and respect for elders. Some were historical fantasies or stories from Burmese Buddhist mythology, while others were adaptations of all types of Western films, featuring local counterparts of Rudolph Valentino or Richard Talmadge (Maung 1947: 24).

By 1930, the industry was well established with a number of cinema halls, most owned by foreigners, and production companies. Animation had been attempted in 1927, and 'talkies' came in with the new decade, through works by A-1 Film Company, British Burma Film Company and Imperial Company. By the 1930s, British Burma Film Company had already built the first Burmese-owned cinema hall and had evolved as the leading producer.

Maha Sway Film Company, managed by U Nyi Pu's brothers, U Tin Nwe and U Tin Maung, changed its name to A-1 Film Company in 1933. U Nyi Pu[6] gave his attention to creating still another production company, Maha Vizzadhor Films. These two pioneering companies, as well as British Burma (renamed Nyunt Myanma Film Company) existed in the late 1980s, when Burma had only eight independent producers left from the 80 of pre-World War II days.

After the virtual shutdown of the industry with Japan's occupation in 1942, a number of changes occurred in the post-war period. Production costs soared, more producers emerged, the star system evolved and, by 1957, silent films were completely replaced by those with sound. The government provided support by reducing entertainment taxes and requiring theatres to show local movies 60 days a year. In 1952, the first film awards were given and, the following year, additional categories were honoured.

The government and ruling Burma Socialist Programme Party intervened at other times in the 1960s and 1970s. After the Revolutionary Council took over in a 1962 coup, it helped set up the Film Council (in August), the purpose of which was to work for the best interests of the industry through consultation with the State Film Promotion Board. One of the new stipulations provided for the licensing of producers, and only those registered were permitted to make films. Of 118 producers licensed in 1962, only 78 remained five years later. In 1968, the State Film Promotion Board invited applications for new registration from persons involved in the industry. At the same time, it encouraged partnerships of at least five people involved in a film. The new government of Ne Win also banned night clubs, Western dances, 'fleshy' movies and other 'decadence.'

As the 1970s began, a crisis developed because of a sudden increase in raw stock prices, high salaries demanded by superstars, restricted screening times and lowered profits resulting in part from an increase in entertainment taxes. The problems peaked in 1975 when the Film Council fell apart because of internal strife. The Burma Socialist Programme Party stepped in and helped form the Motion Picture Council Organisation Committee (MPCOC) in 1977. One of the MPCOC's objectives was to do something about the star system. The superstars ensured 60 to 65 per cent hit productions a year, but their high wages, coupled with limited box-office earnings, required the use of new talents. Thus, MPCOC established the country's first training course for actors, actresses and directors in 1979. The course, taught by volunteer professionals, was successful enough to warrant a second one in 1984.

Just as Burma produced films without sound for longer than most countries, it continued to use black-and-white film into the 1980s. Many of the 70 films a year still are not in colour because of the high costs and lack of local processing facilities.

CONTEMPORARY SCENE

Despite these and other problems, Burmese films are in better shape than those of neighbouring states. A few reasons may account for this: films are subsidised by the Ministry of Culture; they are less expensive to make (average US $45,000 in 1983) because they are processed in government film laboratories; they remain popular in a state closed to many outside entertainment diversions and they are protected by import restrictions.

In 1983, Burma imported 31 movies, one-third each from Japan, the United States, and India and other countries. In 1986, only 20 foreign films entered Burma legally (Marshall 1984: 89; 1987a: 77).

However, much like other closed societies, Burma was not able to escape the threat of video. By 1981, the underground film network was already in place. Rangoon had 15 to 20 underground cinemas, each holding about 40 customers; others existed in at least Mandalay and Moulmein. Television and VCR sets used in these theatres are usually brought in by sailors working abroad. Screenings, from 5.30 p.m. until dawn, can bring in US $215 or more a night, based on the admission price of US $2.15. Although this is twice the price of the best seat in a registered theatre, it is willingly paid by those eager to view otherwise censored, often pornographic, fare (*Asiaweek* 1981c).

During raids on the underground theatres, patrons can be fined US $7, while theatre owners can receive up to two-month jail terms. Additionally, projectors and video machines can be impounded. But not many raids are successful as police are given bribes to look the other way, and video owners pay people in the ruling People's Councils to warn them of raids. Home video is not prevalent among Burma's 33 million people, because television itself is a new medium in the country, and receivers are still expensive.

Rigid censorship stayed in place through most of the 1980s, during which sex and violence topics and scenes were taboo. More suited to the market were action and family comedy movies. Films passed by the censor are given longer exposure than in some other Asian countries—a minimum of three, and sometimes up to 20, weeks in Rangoon theatres. Burma has about 400 theatres, all owned by the state and most very old.

Burma's closed-door policy until 1988 isolated the film industry from the rest of the world. Fearing ridicule, Burmese officials generally shied away from showing their features abroad; only documentaries were exhibited for foreign audiences. An exception was the 1983 Asian Film Festival where two works of septuagenarian U Tu Kha (*Spinning Gold and Silver Threads in a Loom*, 1976, and *Equal Love*, 1979) were shown (Tobias 1982: 30).

AFTERWORD

An attempt to initiate a new era in Indonesian film (mentioned earlier under 'Directors and Their Films') saw some fruition in 1989 with the box office and Citra Awards success of Eros Djarot's *Tjoet Nia Dhien*.

The movie, a tribute to a Sumatran war heroine of the nineteenth century, captured eight awards in 1989, unprecedented in the history of the ceremony. More unusual was the fact the film stayed on the circuit in Jakarta for a month, a seldom-matched feat.

Eros Djarot proved what he set out to show—that a quality movie could succeed. But, it was not an easy task, as he gathered the best local talent, avoided the dictates of popular taste and the studios by launching a fund-raising campaign that netted US $840,000, and showed up at theatres throughout Indonesia to make sure the film was shown. His presence was necessary at these showings, according to *Asiaweek* (1989b, p. 43),

> 'to ensure the showing of the film by often unscrupulous theatre owners. Since theatres can stop showing a movie unless a certain number of tickets are sold, cinema owners can easily sabotage the film by showing it earlier than scheduled or allocating insufficient time for ticket sales. Pressure from importers to show their movies instead also figures prominently in the problem . . .'

Concurrently, Thai films changed somewhat in recent years in genres and topics. Still very popular are melodramas traditionally featuring actors wearing fancy clothing, story lines which are circular and endings which are happy. Today, although actors still wear extravagant clothing, the melodramas have different themes, sometimes dealing with poor people as the oppressed, the plight of women relative to polygamy, prostitution and marriages of Thai women to servicemen. Other themes abound with religious and moral overtones.

Simultaneously, a batch of more realistic pictures has been made by a new generation of university trained filmmakers, whose work resembles the art cinema of India. A major difference is that the Thai works have been box-office hits in the countryside, a tribute to the augmented sophistication of those audiences (Blanc-Szanton 1989: 27).

NOTES

1   After Sihanouk's productions, there was not much activity in the Cambodian film industry. Ti Loon made his successful *The Snake Man*, based on a very famous folk legend, and its sequel, *The Marvellous Snake Man*. The former, released in 1972, was distributed throughout Asia and other parts of the world by Hong Kong's Golden Harvest. Although not part of the local industry, a Cambodian medical doctor, Haing S. Ngor, captured world attention for his prize-winning role in *The Killing Fields*. This author met Haing Ngor on a set in Taipei, where he was performing in 1986.

Throughout the 1980s, Cambodian theatres showed films mostly from India or the Soviet Union. Western films were smuggled in from Thailand and shown in video shops.

2   Within a few weeks, after the government finally met with the film people and agreed to put film under one ministry with the purpose of building it, the PPFI withdrew its statement and film people went back to work.

3   Following the careers of some of these pioneers: Kruger became a cameraman for Tan's Film; Tan got out of the business in the 1930s, afraid of US competition and the Wongs and The continued to work. In 1926, The changed his company's name to Java Industrial Film, involved his three brothers in the company and turned film into an industry for the first time (Misbach ca 1982: 22).

4   By 1984, video already caused the closure of at least 19 of 37 theatres in two provinces, and Bangkok theatres claimed a loss of 50 per cent of their audiences. At least 300 video rental outlets functioned in Bangkok, another 200 up-country.

5   Thai film posters are artistic marvels. Often towering several storeys and measuring 164 feet in length, they are done by painters who usually have not seen the films, but draw from stills. As Warren (1983, p. 35) wrote, 'They supplement this raw material with vivid touches drawn from their own imaginations, sometimes grossly misrepresenting what audiences finally see on the screen.' The artistic level of posters often surpass [sic] that of the film. Describing one poster in which the artists tried to include something for everyone, Warren (1983, p. 35) said:

'A gigantic effort for a typical Thai film several years ago showed 40-foot representations of the hero and heroine, a Golden-eyed cat with blood dripping from fangs and claws, a seminude girl talking on a telephone, a comic couple having a spat, a man fighting with what looks like a bear, another man beating up a woman, and a ghostly female with a bloody face.'

6   One source claimed U Nyi Pu, and some other producers, left for Japan in 1937 to study cinematography. There, they filmed *A Daughter of Japan*, with a Burmese and a Japanese actor. The film was meant to strengthen relations between the two countries. This film began a trend towards political themes which persisted throughout the rest of the 1930s and after World War II (Maung 1947: 24).

SOUTH ASIA

9

INDIA

*Manjunath Pendakur**

INTRODUCTION

For nearly 50 years, cinema in India has been the dominant form of popular entertainment. Its mass appeal has rested on delivering pleasure on a grand scale to millions by using bigger-than-life sets, locations, stars, fights, songs, dances and melodramatic storytelling techniques. Films have been so central to Indian culture that film music and songs pervade various ceremonies from birth to death, and even political gatherings.

While the images of the stars occupy large street-side hoardings and decorate homes, star power has often translated into political power. Political parties often court stars to be their candidates and new parties are organised around a major star. In the last 20 years, two male superstars have been elected as heads of states, and the central government has appointed some stars to the Parliament's Upper House. In the shadows of this star-studded industry, an avant-garde movement, often called the 'new cinema' or 'parallel cinema', swept in like a storm around 1969–70, but apppears to have lost much of its steam and is being drawn into the newly arrived mass medium—television. This chapter will examine the economic and political aspects of the Indian film industry and probe the current trends in filmmaking.

INDUSTRY

Systematic data on the feature film industry are not gathered by any industry or government agency but available statistics clearly suggest its importance. It is the ninth largest industry in the country, employing some 2.25 million people in production, distribution and exhibition. The total estimated investment in all sectors of the industry for 1981 was 8,000 million rupees (15 rupees = US $1).

*This chapter © 1990 Manjunath Pendakur

229

An estimated 13 million tickets are sold every day in the approximately 13,000 theatres nation-wide (see Table 3). Unique to India are the touring cinemas, temporary structures with bamboo walls and thatched roofs, which are located in rural areas. They make up about a third of the total theatres and operate only in the off-rain season. Given that India's population is about 800 million, its seating capacity—roughly seven seats per thousand people—is one of the lowest even in Asia. Despite the popularity of cinema with the masses, rural people still have to travel several miles on bullock carts to see a movie. As 80 per cent of the population still live in rural areas, it is safe to assume that millions of potential viewers are still not served by the existing cinemas.

Lack of theatres in rural areas is attributable to three reasons: poor transport, energy and communication infrastructure; shortage of investment; and cumbersome state regulations governing theatre construction. Small towns with populations of fewer than 10,000 are still underdeveloped in electrification, roads, transport and communication facilities. Parts of the country can be reached only by foot. Investors are scared off by such economic conditions and the area may not be profitable enough for investment in theatre construction, when alternative ventures such as liquor production and distribution may be more lucrative. Additionally, the licensing process to construct theatres, maintenance and inspection—all set up to ensure public safety and order—have generally been subjected to corruption by the bureaucracy, which can be daunting to an investor without the necessary political clout and/or cleverness.

India's prolific film output is in the range of 750 to 800 features a year which exceeds that of any country in the world. Studios in Bombay, Bangalore, Bhubaneswar, Calcutta, Hyderabad, Mysore and Trivandrum contribute to that total in the 16 officially recognised languages, as well as in the others. As Table 1 indicates, 63 per cent of the total pictures are, however, produced in the four major languages of southern India, a consistent pattern for the last 20 years. A key determining factor may be the various schemes created by the southern states to encourage film production in the local languages.

Since the introduction of 'talkies', Indian audiences have desired motion pictures in their own languages and dialects. The result is clearly seen in the Table. Features are produced even in languages spoken by relatively small numbers of people limited to parts of a state (Bodo, Harynavi, for instance). From 1984 to 1988 there were nine features in English as well. This characteristic makes Indian cinema uniquely regional which, in cultural terms, has worked like a shield over the years, thereby making Indian films very competitive to imported films. The phenomenon of dependence on foreign, particularly American, films found in some other parts of the world is not the case with Indian movie-going audiences. The result is, historically speaking, an estimated 93 per cent of screen time is occupied by regional-language films.

What is noteworthy is that the Hindi-language films, which make up about 20 per cent of the total production and are known for their commercial formulas, have captured the all-India market, while regional-language films remain confined largely to their own linguistic communities and geographic areas. Furthermore, the new cinema, despite its success at international film festivals, has not touched the mass audiences nation-wide. For instance, even Satyajit Ray's films, made primarily in Bengali, which are circulated in the West through international film festivals and alternative distribution networks, are seldom screened in regular theatres outside Calcutta[1]. Commercial cinema in various languages has had the stranglehold on the limited playing time in theatres. The recently expanded television network, however, may be changing that situation somewhat—to which we will return later.

Production costs in the 1980s have escalated considerably. In 1970, the average Hindi film was produced for under Rs 1 million, a star-studded film for about Rs 5 million and a low budget film for Rs 150,000. In the late 1980s, the average Hindi film costs about Rs 7.5 million, while a star-studded film may cost between Rs 20 and Rs 30 million. A low budget film may be priced pretty close to Rs 2.5 million (Burra 1985: 7). While costs of all inputs, such as

Table 1: *Feature films produced by language and year, 1984–88*

Language	1984	1985	1986	1987	1988	Total
Telugu	170	198	192	163	162	885
Hindi	165	187	159	150	182	843
Tamil	148	190	154	167	152	811
Malayalam	121	137	130	103	83	574
Kannada	81	69	59	88	67	364
Bengali	35	28	47	35	37	182
Gujarati	30	22	13	11	6	82
Marathi	25	16	17	27	23	108
Punjabi	10	8	7	8	6	39
Oriya	14	17	17	9	16	73
Bhojpuri	9	6	19	14	8	56
Assamese	5	10	11	8	7	41
Rajasthani	2	3	–	4	7	16
Urdu	1	2	1	1	3	8
Manipuri	2	–	1	–	1	4
Nepali	4	4	–	6	2	16
English	2	1	–	1	5	9
Haryanvi	4	10	7	6	5	32
Bodo	–	–	2	–	–	2
Others	5	4	4	5	1	19
Total	833	912	840	806	773	4,164

Source: National Film Development Corporation, Bombay.

sets, equipment rental, and the salaries of technical personnel, have gone up, the significant rise has been in stars' salaries, raw stock and print and publicity costs. Despite some efforts in the 1960s to manufacture raw stock in collaboration with East Germany, India is still dependent on Kodak for colour negative and positive stock, which has to be paid for in hard currency[2]. In the same period, the value of Indian currency against the US dollar has taken a dive, from Rs 7.5 in the 1970s to Rs 12–15 in the 1980s, thereby doubling the cost of colour raw film.

Table 2 provides a comparison of major items and their costs for the years 1975 and 1985 for a Hindi film producer. In talking to various industry people in other language areas, I found their economic situation similar to that of Hindi film producers (Author's Notes, 1985–86 & 1988). Superstar salaries have gone up by 400 per cent, top directors cost 300 per cent more, and other principal items have doubled or more in the ten-year period. While a small number of people have such huge incomes, available data suggest that the less visible workers (grips, set decorators, assistants to various other technical directors) and minor actors/actresses may not have benefited much.

Aside from the high living of the stars and producers, all the indications are that the living conditions of the workers are generally poor and unworthy of a major industry in the country. Of the estimated 2.25 million people employed in the industry, it is not known how many of them live solely on income derived from their film-related employment. The President of the Film Employees Federation of South India, Mohan Gandhiraman, said in 1985 that there was no collective bargaining, no fixed minimum wages, no guaranteed social security benefits for the members of the 24 craft unions his Federation represented. All too often the crew members, including the director, were not paid fully and had to pester the producer to meet the obligations of the contract, even after the picture had been released. The Federation had fought for

Table 2: *Comparative costs of Hindi film, 1975, 1985 (in Rs.)*

	1975	1985
Raw film negative stock 1,000 feet	2,000	4,000
Superstar cost	1,500,000	6,000,000
Top director	1,000,000	3,000,000
Top music director	400,000	800,000
Fight composer	15,000	100,000
Dance composer (per song)	3,000	10,000
Cost of one print for a three-hour movie	25,000	40,000
All-India publicity for a big budget film	1,200,000	3,000,000
Extra (per day)	22	37

Source: Mitra (1985: 167).

some decent housing for its members, which, by 1985, yielded 68 houses built with government aid in the city of Madras (Interview, Gandhiraman, 1985).

Within the commercial cinema, the rate of success is quite limited. Unlike in the US film industry, where supply is controlled by nine firms, hundreds of Indian producers contribute to this huge annual output of nearly 800 features. Some vertically integrated production-distribution companies, all privately held from the pre-World War II period (AVM, Prasad, Navketan), do make films, but they may not distribute their own pictures nation-wide because of the high costs involved. A major release consisting of 300 prints is estimated to cost approximately Rs 6 million in print costs (at Rs 20,000 a print) and an equal amount in publicity expenses (Interview, Shetty, 1985). Given the enormity of risks in film distribution, national distribution companies do not exist, but territorial ones are common. As the bulk of the films are made by fly-by-night operators, they simply look for a quick sale to a territorial distributor to recoup their investment.

Films are typically sold on a flat sale, percentge deal or pre-sale basis with an advance towards the box-office gross. The big budget Hindi films command the highest price, currently around Rs 12 million for each of the six territories in India (Tripathi 1989: 85). Foreign markets are an additional source. As banks generally have been reluctant to invest in film production, producers often rely on pre-sale to distributors to raise finance, thereby indirectly handing over the creative control of a production to the distributor. In cases where such pre-sale cannot be arranged, a producer may borrow funds at usurious rates of interest (often at 40–60 per cent) to complete a film.

This system of production has two important consequences. Pre-production planning takes a back seat, and production is characterised by chaotic conditions, where it is all too typical to find a director shooting a scene (by improving it as s/he goes along), while the next scene is being written in the back of the set. A popular star may be signed up by 20 producers at one time. Juggling for shooting dates around the star's availability, or shooting at a hurricane speed as the star may not be available for another six months, have become common experiences.

The abundant supply of film often means that theatres in key markets charge an inordinate sum of money as house rent. In the city of Madras, which had 85 theatres in 1985, weekly rent ranged from Rs 12,000 to Rs 21,000. Seating capacity and the grossing power of theatres were supposedly used as variables to fix theatre rent. Theatres with 800-seat capacity charged about Rs 16,000 a week and those with seat capacities of 1,000 or more in the centre of the city charged about Rs 21,000 a week (Interview, Anandan, 1985). To recoup its investment, a big budget production, sold, let us say, at Rs 12 million a territory, must attract 75 per cent of potential revenue for at least eight weeks, if it is to become a success. In other words, it has to fill 75 per cent of all the seats in the theatres where it is running.

National statistics are not available to analyse how many of the films released in a year reach that level of success. A film is also considered a hit if it runs for more than 100 days in a given theatre, filling at least 75 per cent of the seats. In 1985, out of 170 features released in Madras, a key city, only 14 (8 per cent) ran for 100 days and only six (4 per cent) pictures had longer runs. That appears consistent with industry wisdom that, on the average, 10 per cent of the releases break even and about 2 or 3 per cent are super box-office hits. Recently, a big budget film, *Ganga, Jamuna, Saraswati* (1988), starring Amitabh Bachan, who has dominated the Hindi cinema for nearly 15 years, flopped after a week's run. It was sold at Rs 7.5 million a territory and the print and publicity expenses brought the total of the distributor's investment to Rs 12 million a territory. The film ran to 95 per cent capacity during the first week of its release in Bombay, demonstrating the star's power to draw audiences into the theatre but, during the second week, revenues dropped between 28 and 40 per cent (Tripathi 1989: 85). The producer-director, Manmohan Desai, who had packed the film with action, drama, songs, fights and chases—all usual ingredients of the Bombay film formula—had declared to the press: 'We have a regular clientele that comes for the action scenes.' Obviously the film could not sustain the audience support, another indication of the fragility of a formula.

A critical factor affecting a distributor's share of the box office is taxes levied by the government at the time of sale, i.e. on each ticket. Film entertainment comes under the jurisdiction of the states, which have capitalised on the film patrons to collect huge sums of money in the form of entertainment and other taxes. On the average, entertainment tax amounts to about 50 per cent of the ticket price, and theatres keep about 50 per cent of the net box-office as rent (Interview, Broca, 1985). Additionally, a surcharge of 10 per cent, imposed as a temporary 'relief measure' to support the war-torn economy of Bangladesh in 1974, has become permanent. In some states, such as Maharastra, the state levies the surcharge on the price of ticket, adds up the two, and levies entertainment and surcharge on that total, which amounts to a tax-on-tax[3]. In 1983, out of a total of Rs 9,840 million in box-office revenue, the state governments claimed about 50.5 per cent, or Rs 4,970 million[4]. The Central government also took out another Rs 80.5 million in the form of excise and other duties on prints (Mitra 1985: 168). Such taxation is onerous, to say the least. Theatre owners took away about 65 per cent of the rest of the revenues, which left approximately Rs 1,700 million for the producers. Coupled with the vagaries of audience taste, recoupment of producers' investment is a dream. Of the 132 Hindi films made in 1983, only 17 managed to recover their costs (Mitra 1985: 166).

Such net loss of revenue to the industry aside, the dominant trend in the theatrical industry is growth, as Table 3 indicates. Between 1980 and 1987, both the number of theatres and total box-office revenue (after tax) have shown a considerable increase, although the figures are not adjusted for inflation. These box-office statistics should be read as rough estimates, since theatre operators, especially in small towns, cheat regularly by reselling the same tickets to evade taxes and to under-represent the revenues to distributors, especially if they have to pay them a percentage of the gross.

Revenues from ancillary markets (videocassette, television, etc.) may also be growing. Desai, who made *Ganga, Jamuna, Saraswati*, was reported to have sold the video rights of the film for an estimated Rs 4 million, and some 50,000 cassettes were released in India while the film played in theatres. Indian producers have hesitated to exploit the new markets, especially video, believing that they would keep the audiences at home. Given that the cost of a videocassette recorder is still too high for most families in India, only upper-middle-class audiences, primarily in urban areas, have them. As pirate copies of the new releases circulate, no matter what, Desai's strategy to take in as much revenue up-front from the video market appears correct. If that becomes a trend in the coming years, overall growth in revenue for the feature film will be even more striking.

Failures at the box office may signal changes to producers in content, casting, etc., but audience demand for entertainment does not appear to be diminishing in any way. In many cases of box-office disaster, as Mitra points out (1985, p. 166), 'the men involved have gone bankrupt, pawned the last piece of their wives' jewellery, attempted suicide, gone insane or found refuge in the bottle', but new producers keep arriving. An important factor that seems to drive new investment in film is the underground economy in India,

Table 3: *Total number of theatres and after-tax box-office revenue, 1980–87*

Year	No. of theatres	After tax B.O. (Rs million)
1980	10,894	3350.00
1981	11,239	3860.00
1982	11,766	4010.48
1983	12,284	4510.79
1984	12,448	5130.67
1985	12,701	5580.66
1986	12,790	5850.83
1987	13,183	6300.74

Source: National Film Development Corporation, Bombay.

which some claim is as large as the regular economy. New entrepreneurs may be attracted to the glamour and possible fame of being involved in film production, but the opportunity to wash their 'black money' by burying it in filmmaking may be particularly compelling. Stars and others are usually paid half of their salary in 'white' and half in 'black', thereby legalising half the total investment which was earned originally by evading taxes in some other business. It is widely acknowledged now that the post-war profits made by Indian capitalists, by evading taxes as a matter of their patriotic duty to oppose British rule, found their way into the film industry and changed the nature and character of production entirely, whereby the haphazardly put-together *masala* film became the industrial norm.

Government's Role

The Government of India's intervention in the film industry, until the end of British colonial rule in 1947, was limited primarily to censorship of films in order to prevent the nationalists from employing the power of cinema to mobilise the masses. When political power passed to the Indian rulers, censorship was kept intact and, under the rubric of development of indigenous arts, the Central and state governments have expanded their powers over the film industry. Documentary and newsreel production are monopolised by the Central and state governments and theatre owners are compelled under the law to exhibit them[5]. Furthermore, when the country was reorganised into states based on language groupings in the early 1950s, it gave rise to language chauvinism on the one hand, but on the other, helped promote local languages and various art forms, including cinema.

Several state governments have assisted in developing their own regional film production by way of low-interest loans and subsidies to eligible entrepreneurs for infrastructure such as studios, labs, recording and dubbing facilities, etc. Many states have also instituted cash awards to meritorious films.

In Karnataka, a southern state, which offered the best support scheme in 1985, an art film producer was entitled to a cheque of Rs 300,000 for a colour feature film, if principal photography was done in that state and if s/he obtained a censor certificate (Mysore Math 1985: 1). Commercial films also made within the state were awarded a subsidy of Rs 150,000 for a black-and-white feature and Rs 250,000 for a colour film. All films made within the state were further supported by a 50 per cent reduction in the entertainment tax charged on every ticket. The subsidy, first offered in 1967, clearly has boosted production in the state over a 20 year period; feature film production went up from 26 in 1967 to 88 in 1987. A total of 612 feature films had been subsidised between 1967 and 1984 (Subba Rao 1984: 94).

Available data suggest, however, that Karnataka was spending a small portion of what it collected from taxation on tickets. In the eight years between 1977 and 1984, the state's entertainment revenue amounted to Rs 1,471.3 million, whereas it paid out only Rs 40.47 million, which amounted to about 2.7 per cent (Subba Rao 1984: 94). While this policy may have assisted low budget filmmakers and generally supported overall development of the infrastructure of the industry in the state, the government appears to be the biggest beneficiary as the taxes from the film industry go directly into the general treasury.

National Film Development Corporation. In the last 20 years, the central government has played major roles at the national level in the film industry. These include financing, distribution, promotion of films at home and abroad; subsidies for theatre construction; censorship; taxation; limiting entry to foreign companies; and giving awards to filmmakers. The institutional mechanism to institute the central government policy is the National Film Development Corporation (NFDC), which was organised in 1980, amalgamating two earlier institutions—the Film Finance Corporation and the Film Export Corporation. The government initially set up the NFDC as a tool to develop 'good cinema' as opposed to the commercial fare. NFDC's powers and activities have, over the years, grown considerably. They include nearly all the important activities of filmmaking and marketing at home and abroad. NFDC's screening, subtitling, duplicating and other facilities, which have been added in the last ten years, are impressive.

The NFDC encourages good scriptwriting by holding national competitions and helps produce the chosen few, either by co-financing or fully financing them. In less than nine years since its inception, NFDC has co-financed more than 200 feature films and some documentaries. Its productions include Satyajit Ray's *Ghare Bhaire* (1985) and *Ganashatru* (in production), and many other award winners, such as Ketan Mehta's *Mirch Masala* (1988) and Utpalendu Chakravorty's *Debshishu* (1987). It is not possible to assess how many of these feature films have actually returned their investment or made a profit, because those data are not available. The NFDC has provided 'interim' financing to filmmakers who have already made substantial investments to complete their films, charging them interest on the loans. The loans are advanced on the basis of a collateral, just as a bank operates. Since 1984, it has started to finance fully a few pictures a year. As the banks have been reluctant to get involved in financing movies, the NFDC's role, even as a co-financier, is crucial to many filmmakers.

The NFDC has also become involved in the international co-production of features and television programmes, most notably *Gandhi* (1984) and *Salam Bombay* (1988), both of which brought many prestigious awards. The latter was directed by Mira Nair,

Table 4: *Theatres completed under NFDC's theatre financing scheme, 1988*

State	No. of theatres	Seating capacity
Andhra Pradesh	11	8,446
Assam	2	2,010
Bihar	1	772
Gujarat	2	1,724
Karnataka	10	7,183
Kerala	7	6,098
Madhya Pradesh	12	10,708
Maharastra	5	4,187
Manipur	1	1,326
Orissa	6	4,756
Pondicherry	1	971
Rajasthan	1	1,163
Tamilnadu	8	6,256
Uttar Pradesh	11	6,286
West Bengal	4	3,915
Total	82	65,801

Source: *NFDC News*, October–November, 1988, p.6.

winning her the famed Camera d'or at Cannes in 1988. NFDC has started to collaborate with India's television network, Doordarshan, in making TV movies.

Under its theatre financing scheme, where private entrepreneurs receive low-interest loans and a subsidy, the NFDC has financed 127 theatres, of which 82 are operational in 15 states of India, thereby adding a total of 65,801 seats (see Table 4). This policy helps alleviate the shortage of theatres in general, although it is hard to tell whether it has resulted in building theatres in rural towns with populations under 50,000, where such entertainment facilities are sorely needed.

The NFDC acts as a distributor and exhibitor. It imports about 50 to 60 films a year, a wide variety coming from different parts of the world to be screened in the few non-commercial theatres in various cities (Chandran 1989). It claims to have first option on playing time at the theatres built with its assistance; however, it is not known to what extent that has been used. Generally speaking, theatre owners are not enthusiastic about providing playing time to off-beat films, because they claim that audiences are not interested in such films. However, there are many examples of successes, once given access to theatres. Govind Nihalani's *Ardh Satya* (1983), produced at a cost of Rs 1.6 million, grossed at least double that in its theatrical release. In 1985, Amol Palekar's *Ankahee*, not an NFDC production, ran for more than 13 weeks in three theatres in Bombay (Interview, Palekar, 1985). Despite those 'hits', the overall performance of the off-beat film has been poor in attracting audiences and building a base. The NFDC's efforts to expand the domestic markets for India's new cinema appear discouraging.

Some filmmakers have complained that their films have not been promoted well by the NFDC, as it tends to concentrate its efforts on one or two big name directors, such as Satyajit Ray (Interview, Palekar, 1985). That controversy aside, participation by Indian filmmakers at international film festivals appears to have grown.

Indian films have historically been popular in various parts of the Middle East, Africa, Asia, USSR and Latin America. These markets expanded throughout the 1970s, along with the rise in the number of Indians living abroad. Gross revenues from export of feature films grew from Rs 55 million in 1973 to Rs 150 million in the peak year of 1980, after which they started to decline[6]. The NFDC has grappled with this problem by setting up a regional office in London and by organising film bazaars during various international film festivals, as well as the New Delhi International Film Festival. In 1987–8, a total of 48 countries imported 823 Indian features and the gross revenue from those sales amounted to Rs 73 million, as Table 5 indicates. Although video piracy is blamed as the main cause for the decline in export revenues, between 1981 and 1988, for which data were available, the sale of video rights through the NFDC grew considerably. That, however, did not offset the losses incurred by the decline in the sale of the theatrical and television rights of films. That point is made dramatically if the total revenues in 1981 and 1988 are compared, showing an overall decline of more than 50 per cent.

Table 5: *Revenue from foreign markets, 1979–February 1989 (Rs thousand)*

Year	Theatrical/ TV rights	Video rights	Recorded videocassettes from Seepz*	Total
1979–80	1214.64	–	–	1214.64
1980–81	1507.43	–	–	1507.43
1981–82	1454.98	16.25	889.00	2360.23
1982–83	1150.70	103.00	736.00	1989.70
1983–84	967.67	185.07	387.00	1539.74
1984–85	693.85	155.76	386.00	1235.61
1985–86	618.28	99.58	445.00	1162.86
1986–87	572.18	146.24	332.00	1050.42
1987–88	730.68	176.06	221.00	1127.74
1988–89	606.44	298.19	232.51	1137.14

*Tax free export zone
Note: These figures represent only the revenues channelled through the NFDC and do not include the illegal sale of theatrical/television/video rights sold abroad.

Source: NFDC, Bombay

Table 6: *Number of films sold and revenue from key export markets for Indian films, 1988*

Country	No. of films	Revenue (Rs)
Arabian Gulf	179	24,349,000
USSR	18	9,811,000
Indonesia	41	9,484,000
Sri Lanka	30	2,588,000
Burma	17	2,463,000
UK & Ireland	67	2,286,000
Morocco	36	2,031,000
Jordan	28	1,814,000
Fiji Islands	29	1,785,000
Singapore	27	1,642,000
Mauritius	61	1,632,000
Sudan	31	1,288,000
Tanzania	28	1,281,000
Maldives	27	1,214,000
Kenya	22	1,086,000
Malaysia	33	808,000
Yemen, Djibouti, Sanna	13	761,000
West Indies	13	590,000
South/Latin America	12	524,000
Gambia	11	536,000
Nigeria	10	451,000
Liberia	10	331,000

Source: NFDC, Bombay.

The NFDC appears to be concentrating on the traditional markets for Indian films abroad to increase sales. Table 6 lists the major foreign territories, number of films sold, and revenue from each of those markets. The Arabian Gulf, the USSR and Indonesia were the biggest markets in total revenue. In the Gulf countries and in many parts of Africa, video markets are probably larger than theatrical and television broadcast markets. Video piracy, however, makes it difficult for the copyright holder to gain much from that growing market. The NFDC has not been very successful in exploiting the North American market. It has been planning to open a regional office in New York to have a presence in this most important but tough market, hoping to promote and sell Indian films to various kinds of markets in the US and Canada, including art cinema houses, video outlets and non-theatrical markets, such as the universities and colleges. Indians living abroad who might be interested in better quality tapes have not yet been tapped.

Importation of films. Foreign imports enter the Indian market through four legal channels:

(1) Motion Picture Export Association of America (MPEAA),
(2) Sovexport Film,

(3)   NFDC, and
(4)   non-resident Indian importers.

Pirate versions of foreign film/video materials circulate widely, although clandestinely, coming into the country probably through the Gulf countries of the Middle East. It is estimated that the American majors alone lose an estimated US $10–15 million a year because of video piracy in India (MPEAA 1989).

Foreign distributing companies are not allowed into India without an operating agreement with the NFDC. Because of foreign exchange shortages, the government has historically used this policy to limit the number of imports into the country and, thereby, the earnings of foreign distributors. It has also attempted to impose limits on remittances of hard currency by those companies, as well as on the uses of non-repatriated earnings (Pendakur 1985). The MPEAA and the Sovexport Film each have bilateral agreements to operate in India. Under the terms of the present agreement, the MPEAA is allowed to import about 100 titles and the Sovexport Film, 20 titles a year (Chandran 1989). The MPEAA members, who together earn about US $5 million a year from India, may not remit more than US $700,000 in 1989, US $1 million in 1990, and US $1.4 million in 1991.

Foreign corporations licensed as importers must pay the NFDC a canalising fee of 15 per cent on the cost of prints, insurance and freight of films, trailers, stills, etc., brought into the country. This may not amount to a great deal, given the quota of about 120 films in all. However, it is a guaranteed source of revenue in hard currency to the NFDC. Soviet imports do not receive as wide a release as the MPEAA imports, which are shown in about 100 theatres in large and medium size cities (Pendakur 1986). In the last few years, the government licensed Indian entrepreneurs who are living abroad— popularly known as non-resident Indians (NRI)—to import foreign films into India. The NRI importer pays a canalising fee of US $15,000 for each film up-front. They are not subjected to any quota as other importers have been. Some 15 to 20 companies have been licensed, which have brought in mostly martial arts and sexploitation films, thereby creating a controversy about the double standards applied by the government to foreign versus NRI companies.

In the home video distribution market, all but the MPEAA companies are restricted to sell and distribute their titles through the NFDC, which runs the only film-to-tape transfer and video duplicating technology centre in the country. The NFDC claims that it has acquired the rights to more than 100 'good' films from all over the world and has released high quality cassettes (NFDC 1988). Although technically not barred from the home video market, the MPEAA companies have run into a clever rule devised by the Government to limit their profits. For all the titles the MPEAA companies imported into India before 1 August 1988, videocassettes must be imported through the NFDC (MPEAA 1989). This policy effectively gives the NFDC a monopoly on the Hollywood majors' large libraries of film titles in the Indian market. The MPEAA argues that without sufficient quantities of previously released titles, its member companies cannot operate profitably.

Censorship. While the US film industry avoided government censorship by imposing self-censorship in the 1920s, the British colonial administration institutionalised censorship in India and the national government has continued that tradition[7]. The Central Board of Film Certification administers the Cinematograph Act through regional boards of censors located in Bombay, Madras and Calcutta[8]. These boards have the power to recommend cuts, as well as ban a film outright. A producer may appeal against their decision through the higher authority vested in appeals committees, and eventually the Ministry of Human Resources Development in New Delhi. If all that fails, the decision can be contested in a court of law.

While the 'no kissing' policy has been widely publicised in the Western media, implementation of censorship policy in general is uneven at best. For instance, the board is supposed to ensure that 'anti-social activities such as violence are not glorified or justified', 'the *modus operandi* of criminals or other visuals or words likely to incite the commission of any offence are not depicted' and 'pointless or avoidable scenes of violence, cruelty and horror are now shown'. Not only vulgarity and obscenity are forbidden but 'visuals or words depicting women in ignoble servility to man or glorifying such servility as a praiseworthy quality in women are not presented' (Chandran 1989).

Commercial cinema is replete with violations of the above guidelines as producers with political clout in the capital have been able to stretch the regulations. Amjad Khan, an actor-director, who was frustrated in his efforts to get censor clearance for his film, *Chor Police*, noted emphatically, 'If I am influential enough to know the right man at the right place, I can get things done in ten minutes.' (Ramachandran 1985: 542). Filmmakers in Calcutta have, for a long time, complained that their regional censor office applied the regulations much more strictly compared with the ones in Bombay and Madras. Raj Kapoor, a major producer-director who died in 1988, could get away with a lot more sexual imagery in his films, allegedly because of his loyalty to the ruling Congress Party[9].

Despite rules and guidelines, suggestive dialogue, crude sexual exhibition, rape and other violence against women are common ingredients in the popular cinema. Several filmmakers have been able to push the limits of what is allowable by providing morally acceptable endings to the film. For instance, I.V. Shashi's *Her Nights*, the story of a prostitute, contained explicit sex and went on to become a box office hit. He was allowed to release the film only after he agreed to change the ending to a happy one.

In another Malayalam blockbuster, *Dream Nights*, a pubescent heroine seduces a 15-year-old boy. They are seen passionately making love behind a temple. In a twist, probably provided to appease the censors, she is killed by a snake bite in divine retribution.

In some cases, where the Censor Board ordered the deletion of certain scenes, the producers put them back into the release print after obtaining the clearance. This has come to be known as 'interpolation'. A Kannada film, *Antha* (1985), consisted of extremely violent scenes where a pregnant woman was kicked in her stomach. It drew huge audiences in Bangalore, and the press focused on how such a film could obtain the censor certificate. The board's response was that it had not permitted those scenes, but the producer had interpolated them later. There are some instances when audiences have been totally shocked (or delighted) to find an explicitly sexual scene, clearly put back in the film after it had passed through the Censor Board.

Besides such gratuitous sex and violence, the overall impact of censorship on Indian cinema is distorted treatment of sexuality. Adult themes are seldom tackled in a mature way, i.e. where sex is treated as a basic human need and how it cannot be fulfilled in a society where young couples have seldom the space, privacy or cultural tolerance for it. While the larger society remains puritanical, the larger-than-life images of sexuality in cinema are highly exaggerated ones, simply fuelling fantasy for millions of young people. One wonders whether any of these fantasies ever come true and whether the Indian movie-goer's psyche is a bank of frustrations.

Censorship has had serious consequences on the political use of cinema. For instance, no filmmaker is allowed to name and criticise the party in power (the Nehru/Gandhi family) and to deal with controversial topics, such as the Naxalbari revolutionary movement or the recent scandalous arms deal with the Swedish firm, Bofors. M.S. Satyu's *Garm Hava* (1974), which went on to win the national award, was held up for nearly a year. It was the first time a filmmaker touched the topic of how a Muslim family felt during the time of India's partition in 1947.

In the following year, marked by a national emergency, the political film, *Kissa Kursi Ka*, created history when it was denied censorship and its negative and all the prints mysteriously vanished[10]. It is alleged that the negative and all the prints of the film were burned at the behest of Sanjay Gandhi, the then-Prime Minister's son, as it was critical of the ruling party. A film entitled *Naxalites* (1980), written and directed by the well-known K.A. Abbas, was held up for 102 days before receiving the censor certificate. Anand Patwardhan's documentary film, *Bombay Our City* (1984), which dealt with the suffering heaped on Bombay tenement dwellers by the city government and the rich who want to beautify the city, was detained by the censors until a public uproar caused them to give in. One Bengali producer-director, Biplab Ray Chaudhuri, told me that his film, *Yeh Kahani Nahin* (1985), dealing with the conflict between the caste Hindus and untouchables, was unacceptable to the censors unless he accepted 64 cuts. They were all dialogue scenes where the high caste characters revealed their feelings towards the untouchables; without them, there was no story left. He fought the case in court and eventually won after accepting to delete four scenes.

The consequence of such legal battles often damages a film's distribution and thereby its profitability. Shyam Benegal, another major director, who has had his share of problems with censors, put it bluntly:

'Litigation could be suicidal for the producer with all his money locked up in the film. The way the economics of the industry works, it is imperative for any producer to get his film released without delay. He cannot afford to take the Censor Board to court.' (*India Today* 1980: 71)

Any delay in releasing a film is costly, especially if the producer had borrowed completion money at usurious rates of interest, as is common. Even getting an 'A' certificate, as opposed to a 'U' certificate, could make a big difference to the producer's profitability[11]. In the particular instance of Ray Chaudhury's film, it could not compete for the national award, thereby affecting its future marketability and profits.

Censorship is inherently coercive and limits artistic and political expression in Indian cinema. The producers often guess what may be allowed and construct ideas and scenes around those conceptions. The net result is a dampening effect on the filmmakers and the exclusion of certain themes which might be considered risky by the investors. The government's role in India's cinema is clearly that of a patron and police. One cannot help noticing how close it is to that of a feudal overlord, who patronised art and, at the same time, set serious limits on it.

Members of various boards, who are appointed by the government, are largely regarded with contempt by the industry and its critics. G.D. Khosla, former justice who chaired the 1969 Enquiry Committee on Film Censorship, made the following observation about the board members:

'Censorship should be exercised by those who do not live in ivory towers. The films, in the first instance, are shown to a group of morons—the so-called panel advisors on the Censor Board—who are nominated not because they are qualified but because they have influence in the right quarters. They grab the offer to sit on

Censor panels so that they may have the thrill of uncensored films free of charge.' (Ramachandran 1985: 540)

At best, the panel members reflect the conflicting tastes and moral standards of a multicultural society, giving rise to differences in the way the guidelines are applied to various films. Besides, when confronted with a politically risqué film, they worry about the consequences if they displease the politicians in New Delhi. Patronage often works in subtle ways to reinforce the power of the state as the ultimate arbiter of taste, morality and the boundaries of political discourse in Indian cinema.

Between Film and Television: Shifting Axis

Indian television is a monopoly of the central government and has grown from an insignificant experimental operation in Delhi and Bombay to a nation-wide delivery system by 1985, using the most advanced communication-satellite technology. From half a million television sets in the country at the beginning of the decade, India now has about 13 million sets, most of which are located in affluent urban upper- and middle-income homes (Chandran 1989). With the introduction of sponsored programming in 1985, the government has made it very attractive for large national (Tata, Godrej) and international corporations (Colgate, Lever Bros) to reach a nation-wide audience at relatively low cost.

The clear indication of that fact is in the dramatic increases of revenue earned by the government from advertising and sponsorship fees, which went up from 0.64 million rupees in 1976, when Doordarshan started to accept commercial messages, to 51.92 million rupees in 1985 (Government of India 1985). Table 7 lists the major advertisers and the amount of money they spent on television.

As sponsors entered television production, advertising agencies which provide the necessary expertise, have grown in size and importance. Market research and public opinion polling have gained prominence by probing into the tastes and preferences of the consumers as well as their voting behaviour. Table 8 lists the major advertising agencies in India and the dramatic growth in their revenues, which coincides with the commercialisation of television.

One immediate result of the influence of advertisers and their agencies is the wholesale importation of programme formats from the US and, in some cases, entire story ideas. For instance, 'Dynasty' became 'Khandan'. Half-hour serials, quickly shot with single- or two-camera set-ups—some entirely on location—have flooded the TV schedules. Commercial messages for all kinds of consumer goods are piped into the television homes[12].

Faced with criticism by the press and intellectuals over the commercialisation of television, the government began two impor-

Table 7: *Major sponsors/advertisers on Indian television, 1985*

No.	Name of advertiser	Amount spent (Rs)
1.	Colgate Palmolive	3,401,500
2.	Food Specialities Ltd.	3,885,000
3.	Hindustan Lever	2,310,000
4.	Khaitan Fans	770,000
5.	Vicco Lab	2,555,000
6.	Parle Exports	840,000
7.	M/S Prima Marketing	490,000
8.	Gujarat Cooperatives	2,555,000
9.	Tata Oil Mills	1,785,000
10.	Richardson Hindustan Ltd	750,000
11.	Ponds	765,000
12.	Dabur	590,000
13.	Godrej	3,075,000
14.	Mayur Pan	910,000
15.	Geoffrey Manners	1,925,000
16.	Cadbury (P) Ltd	1,680,000
17.	VIP Champion	105,000
18.	Reliance Textile	770,000
19.	Bombay Oil Mills	1,540,000
20.	Bajaj	1,855,000
21.	Others	7,430,000

Source: *Screen*, 6 December 1985, pp. 1, 2.

tant programmes that have deeply affected the film industry. It first began to court eminent filmmakers, who had won national and international awards, to make films for television. Satyajit Ray was commissioned to make *Sadgati*, a TV movie, which was aired on the network in 1985, thereby starting a new trend. In the next four years, major filmmakers who had principally worked in the parallel cinema, have made television serials. Govind Nihalani, whose films, *Akrosh* and *Ardh Satya*, won him wide acclaim, made a mini-series entitled, *Tamas*, which probed the reasons for the Hindu-Muslim violence that heaped misery on millions of people during the partition of India in 1947. The series touched a raw nerve among Hindu politicians, who called for its ban. In 1988, Shyam Benegal co-produced with the USSR a TV series on Jawaharlal Nehru, the first Prime Minister of India. Many other parallel cinema directors, including Saeed Mirza, Muzaffar Ali, Ketan Mehta and Sai Paranjpe, have made TV series. It appears as though their failure to reach a wider audience through the theatrical markets has been rectified through sponsored television going out to 13 million homes, a number no avant-garde filmmaker ever hoped to reach in India.

The government offered Rs 800,000 for telecasting any Indian film winning a national award and set up a tiered system of fees to other noteworthy films. Prakash Jha's *Damul*, an award winning exposé of feudal relations in Bihar, was telecast in 1985, reaching a

Table 8: *Gross billings of major advertising agencies, 1982–87 (Rs million)*

Company	1982	1983	1984	1985	1986	1987
Adv. & Sales Promo.	72.5	86.0	100.3	110.4	121.5	131.2
Chaitra Adv.	76.5	110.8	–	119.5	163.3	180.6
Clarion Adv. Services	160.2	193.5	–	–	–	297.1
Contract Advertising	–	–	–	26.5	100.7	168.7
Creative Unit	–	–	–	45.2	49.9	64.4
daCunha	–	–	46.0	59.7	80.2	108.0
Everest	83.6	–	95.3	130.0	199.4	282.0
Grant, Kenyon, & Eckhardt	58.8	61.6	60.8	–	–	–
Hindustan Thompson	272.7	275.3	317.9	363.8	444.1	644.4
Jaisons Adv.	61.8	71.2	94.9	–	109.6	–
Lintas India	158.4	216.3	237.3	283.1	396.8	656.2
Nat'l Adv. Service	21.3	27.6	–	–	45.0	–
Ogilvy, Benson & Mather	100.0	125.5	146.8	178.2	245.2	307.0
Rediffusion	–	–	124.0	181.4	–	–
R.K. Swamy	–	–	100.0	145.0	180.0	250.0
Shilpi	47.3	64.7	–	–	83.3	–
Sistas Pvt. Ltd.	–	–	–	100.0	128.8	–
Ulka Adv. Pvt. Ltd.	82.5	90.0	110.0	135.0	–	254.9

Source: *Advertising Age*, various.

wide audience who would not have seen that film in a theatre. This policy has become another important source of support to many parallel filmmakers who could not rely on theatrical markets for recouping their investment and expanding their audience base. Additionally, every Sunday, a regional-language film with subtitles is shown on the national network, thereby increasing the exposure to regional cinema.

Television audiences are certain to grow as India's middle class expands from its estimated 20 per cent of the total population and as prices for television sets begin to fall. Major commercial film producers and directors have staked out their claims on television after the phenomenal success of *Ramayan*, a series directed by Ramanand Sagar, a commercial director, based on an epic story. This does not, however, mean that films meant to be shown in theatres are going to disappear. Given the inegalitarian nature of the Indian economy, there will be a large enough cinema audience, especially in rural towns, where the people cannot afford to buy a television set. But the axis has begun to shift away from theatrical- to television-based entertainment.

The still-developing video industry has the potential for another major outlet for all kinds of filmed entertainment. According to one newspaper report (*Prajavani* 1986), the video market consisted of an estimated 40,000 retail outlets, 15,000 buses equipped with video, 20,000 video parlours and 11,000 hotels with video. The estimated turn-over in this business was around Rs 1,500 million, 99 per cent of which was earned in illegal trading. The general response of the film industry associations has been one of asking for stricter policing to eliminate piracy, rather than figuring out how to extract more revenue out of this emerging business. As stated earlier, the NFDC has started to market good-quality videos of 'serious films' from all over the world, a much-needed step with Satyajit Ray's *Apu Trilogy*.

The Indian film landscape has changed greatly in the 1980s. What is outstanding about it all is that there are significantly more opportunities to make one's first film in India now than 20 years ago. The avenues to seek profits, although not guaranteed, have also expanded considerably, especially given the arrival of the new technologies of television and video.

An Indian Aesthetic?

The dominant trend in Indian cinema in the last 20 years has been the dichotomy between the commercial and the new cinema, the roots of which lie in Italian neo-realism. The new cinema is usually credited with social responsibility, because it attempts to call the viewers' attention to the nation's economic-social-political problems. On the other hand, the commercial cinema's principal motivation is said to be profits and the often ruinous chase for the blockbuster. The new cinema's other principal pre-occupation has been to shun the genres and formulas that are common to the commercial cinema, which in itself is admirable, but also a sure way to lose audience empathy.

State intervention, in the name of supporting 'good cinema', may have widened the gulf between the commercial and 'art' cinemas of India. What the State has pursued is a policy to seek out prestige abroad by encouraging artists who can compete in major inter-national film festivals, such as Venice, Berlin or Cannes, and to cultivate a certain arrogance on the part of the filmmakers who are not subjected to the market test within India.

The cinema, of all the major twentieth-century arts, is charac-terised by the struggle between art and commerce, because of the dominance of entrepreneurial capital, often in large quantities, and film's search to please a wide range of audiences. The tension one sees in India's commercial-versus-new cinema is a product of that basic tendency. That tension is compounded by the fact that India is so vastly diverse as a society. To speak to those various groups of people and their differing tastes and priorities, the commercial filmmakers have employed a strategy of seeking the widest appeal possible.

This process is certainly not new to India. Probably because of that tendency, formulas that have succeeded don't change easily. For instance, rich boy meets poor girl, falls in love, wants to marry her, is an old story-line repeated over and over again. The challenge to the new cinema directors has been to break out of that mould but still tell their stories compellingly so that their audiences are not turned off. Some have had great success in that: Shyam Benegal's *Bhoomika*, the story of a poor girl rising to stardom and seeking out a female identity in a male-dominated world; and Govind Nihalani's *Akrosh*, a depiction of the oppression of the *adivasis* (indigenous people) of India.

Melodrama, as a communicative strategy, is also resisted as too common to commercial cinema by the new cinema directors. India's performing arts tradition, which goes back several centuries, is rich with melodrama and is popular with the viewers. Instead of making intelligent use of it, as many creative directors of the 1940s and 1950s did (Shantaram in Hindi, B.N. Reddy in Telugu, for example), the new cinema directors typically stayed away from melodrama and their cinematic representation became too flat, thereby almost unfeeling and unmoving. This antipathy towards established cultural traditions is also tinged with a good deal of arrogance, and it has resulted in sterile representations of 'realism'. Much vitality has been lost in the process.

Currently, one of the most promising directors is Ketan Mehta, who works primarily in the Hindi language. He has made a total of four feature films since venturing into direction with *Bhavni Bhavai* (1980), a film about untouchability. That and his third film, *Mirch Masala* (1986), have been recognised for synthesising certain formal traditions in indigenous folk-art forms, as well as in Indian 'talkies' themselves. Mehta talked about working for a synthesis of form and style based on Indian ethos and tradition in these two films:

'Both films look to tradition for vital elements which are then used in contemporary synthesis. In *Bhavni Bhavai*, the attempt was to synthesise the earlier folk traditions of Gujarat. In *Mirch Masala*, the attempt is to regain some of the vital elements of the early talkies. There was a very interesting phase in the cultural history of India in the late 30 and 40s and, I think, the gains of those developments were never really consolidated. There were interesting experiments with form and content done at that time, to arrive at new syntheses based on the Indian ethos, without any elements taken from outside'[13].

Music and songs which are so central to the Indian film tradition were largely shunned by the new cinema directors as formulaic. Mehta has tried to synthesise musical forms as he did with visual forms in *Mirch Masala*:

'The attempt is three fold. One is to arrive at the genesis of Indian popular music. All the three songs selected were, in their way, the advance guard of Indian popular music. Second, there is very authentic folk music sung by folk singers from Gujarat and Rajasthan, written by them, and using authentic folk instruments. The third is a layer of background music which really seeks to transform sound effects into music. This is the three-fold pattern which I have tried to weave in.' (Masud and Chandran 1986)

Mehta's ideas about colour, its cultural specificity to Indians and its usage in *Mirch Masala* are worth noting:

'Here the basic division has been in terms of the muted colors of the earth, of the walls, and in this monochromatic kind of world, we have sudden bursts of color. As the song goes, "Mat manav man bana oob gayo kirtar/Mirch masala dale rang diyo sansar." Our reaction to color, our sensibility to color, is very different from the European or Western sensibility. Our usage is very different, the light is very different. In folk theatre forms, you see how color becomes a vital, integral part of the entire structure of the performance, and I thought that kind of boldness was necessary in terms of the usage of color and in terms of the volume of color.' (Masud and Chandran 1986)

Mehta's latest film, *Hero Hiralal* (1988), is a fairy-tale rendition of a small town auto-rickshaw driver, whose addiction to the Hindi commercial film has transformed him into a typical hero. Brilliantly played by Naseeruddin Shaw, one of the new cinema's leading actors, it is a playful, fantastic parody of India's culture industry (advertising, cinema, television and all its various trappings). The protagonist, Hiralal, has all the virtues that are endowed in the Hindi cinema heroes—romanticism, chivalry, street smartness, ability to triumph over immense odds, including the physically abusive thugs on the streets, and conviction to certain basic ideals of goodness and honesty. A film crew visits his town for a shoot, which brings Hiralal in contact with the film world, not on the screen but in flesh and blood. The crew consists of a hero, but in real life, that actor has all the characteristics of a Hindi film villain. He is Westernised, egotistical, lecherous and drinks like a pig. He even attempts to rape the actress who plays the heroine.

Mehta's hero, the common man of India who is in love with Hindi cinema, is contrasted with the real people who play these idealised characters that are the basic stuff of Hindi cinema. This cleverly constucted idea to demystify and to expand on the reality of Hindi cinema's effect on popular consciousness is pushed to the limit in the film, when the protagonist is ready to make the ultimate sacrifice, i.e. to give his life to win over the actress he is in love with, just as the Hindi film heroes do, day in and day out.

The film is formalistically conceived exactly like a commercial Hindi film: from the first dramatic entry of the rickshaw driver through a film hoarding to beat the thugs with his handkerchief—mimicking the many fights that are common ingredients of the popular cinema—to him falling in love with the star of a movie unit, and through to the suspense-filled end. The irony is delicious and the drama unfolds in the second half just as most formulaic cinema in India does.

What Mehta has accomplished in his work is the wiping out of the artificial dichotomy between form and content that seems to have plagued much of the new cinema of the last 20 years. Each of his films represents innovation at both levels. Particular content matter is explored in a particular style because of its suitability. If this becomes the trend with the current filmmakers, it will have rich possibilities for the future survival of the new cinema.

One important aspect of India's new cinema is that it has lacked a coherently expressed ideology. Perhaps that is also its strength as it could encompass highly divergent kinds of films, from Mrinal Sen's didactic films of the 1970s, to the lyrical realism of Satyajit Ray, Girish Kasaravalli and the political films of Goutam Ghose. Given such breadth, and lacking any institutional umbrella, such as the Cinemathèque Française in Paris, it became a ward of the state for all kinds of patronage. There is no organisation of filmmakers to unify them on their own terms, to chalk out new ideas and effectively to turn this whole cultural production and dissemination process into a national movement. Perhaps new directors, such as Ketan Mehta in Bombay, and the older ones, such as Adoor Gopalakrishnan in Trivandrum, will not only work towards the synthesis of form and content but push the creative energy of the new cinema into a national movement in the 1990s.

NOTES

1   Ray's pictures may get a Sunday morning show at a regular theatre in large cities. His *Shatranj Ke Khilari*, made in Hindi, was an exception. While it was released in many northern cities, it was reported that audiences in some cities were so enraged by the seemingly endless manoeuvres with the chess pieces that they smashed up theatre furniture (Mitra 1985: 168).
2   For various problems within the Hindustan Photo Films, a central government-operated factory, see Gopalan (1980, pp. 1–2).

3   According to the Theatre Owners Association in Bombay, on a ticket of Rs 7, for example, Rs 0.70 is added as surcharge and then entertainment and surcharge are imposed. It then works out at Rs 4.88 as taxes and the after-tax revenue to the industry from each ticket is Rs 2.82 (see Kuka 1979: 2).

4   This figure differs from the one in Table 3, the reasons for which could not be ascertained. What is important is to recognise how the total box-office revenue is divided up and how the state gets the lion's share.

5   The consequences of such state control over documentary production have not been studied well. Independent filmmakers who want to produce documentaries have to raise their own finances, and their films may not get screen time at all, as the state monopolises that time. To get government finance, they have to be included in a roster of producers and can make only approved films. The few independents who work outside this system of production rely principally on exposure at foreign film festivals and sales abroad.

6   These data were compiled from different sources: for 1973–76 see Dharap (1979); for 1977–80 see *India Today*, 16–31 July 1981, p. 63.

7   The Cinematograph Act of 1918, the first such law to deal with cinema, licensed the safety of theatres and certified films that were suitable for public exhibition. Boards of film censors were set up in Bombay, Calcutta, Madras and Rangoon in 1920, whose decisions were valid throughout British India, but could be suspended by a provincial authority. General principles governing censorship were borrowed from the British Board of Film Censors in England. Provincial boards of censors had all the power to license films for exhibition, which meant a film allowed in one area of India could be banned in another. This system, cumbersome and costly for filmmakers, was changed by the Cinematograph Act of 1949, when censorship was centralised (Ministry of Information & Broadcasting 1978: 2–3).

8   Voluntary censorship along the lines of the Hays Office's Production Code Authority was recommended by a government-instituted Film Inquiry Committee in 1952. It had support from the Indian Motion Picture Producers' Association. Those recommendations have never been implemented (Ministry of Information & Broadcasting 1978: 2–3).

9   In *Mera Nam Joker* (1970) and in *Satyam Shivam Sundaram* (1978), he presented his heroines in the nude and convinced the Censor Board to allow those scenes. Before the latter film was released, he declared the market value of female nudity, without mincing any words: 'Let people come to see Zeenat's tits, they'll go out remembering the film.' (*India Today* 1980: 66)

10   For an analysis of the Emergency's effect on India's mass media and the political scandal surrounding this film, see Pendakur (1988a).

11   Producers fear they would lose about 30 per cent of revenues if their film is assigned an 'A' certificate. To avoid it, they may agree to re-shoot, delete the scenes found objectionable by the censors, etc.

12   For an analysis of the twists and turns in India's national policy towards the use of television (from educational to commercial), see Pendakur (1988b).

13   Mehta says there were three reasons, 'One is the post-war changes in the entire set-up of the culture industry; secondly, it was the kind of vehemence with which the government came down on the left wing immediately after the war; and thirdly, by that time a process of lumpenisation had been inadvertently already started' (Masud and Chandran 1986).

10

PAKISTAN, BANGLADESH, AND SRI LANKA

INTRODUCTION

'The story: he and she loved each other very much since they were about six years old. He is the son of a rich peasant. She is an orphan and a bad omen to superstitious villagers. The twain shall never meet, decrees his father. She cries a lot. He cries a lot. He (now nearly twenty-five) is strung up to a pole for being so naughty and she is sent off to another village. He sings a heart breaking song and cries a river. She listens to the song from the other village and cries a river. Then he gets leprosy on his wedding day. She hears about it on her wedding day. He is exiled from his village. The twain meet in the middle of no where.'
(Kabir 1979: 32)

Bangladesh's critic-turned-director Alamgir Kabir wrote that description of a Bengali film in the late 1960s. More than 20 years later, it holds up fairly well in depicting much of South Asian cinema, where filmmakers of Pakistan, Bangladesh and Sri Lanka imitate, and plagiarise, the Indian model of music, dance, action and difficult-to-obtain-and-retain romantic situations.

In that, South Asian film industries have a commonality. There are others. All countries, newly independent since World War II, have young film industries; all have the same basic regulatory structure laid down by the British in the Cinematograph Act of 1918; all have been large production centres at various times and all have been plagued by similar problems—disruptive civil wars, the lure of Indian films and the disastrous impacts of television and videocassettes.

The Indian influence permeated two other South Asian film

industries, those of Afghanistan and Nepal. The first film with a semblance of Afghan identification was Reshid Latif's *Ishq wa dosti* (Love and Friendship), shot in India in 1946, with the help of an Indian filmmaker. Because it was always easier and more profitable to import from India and Iran, the Afghans brought out only six films by 1978, four by the government-owned Afghan Films. The 1973 coup, after which film distribution was nationalised, limited supplies of capital, raw stock and equipment, and the war and occupation of the 1980's prevented the development of Afghan cinema.

Nepal's first film, *Raja Harishchandra* (1950), featured the combined talents of Indian and Nepalese artists and was produced in India. The first movie made in Nepal appeared in 1961, when Heera Singh, assigned to making Nepalese films by King Mahendra Bir Bikram Shah Dev, produced a newsreel for the occasion of the King's birthday. Singh also made features, such as *Aama* (1963), *Hijo Aaj Bholi* (1966) and *Parivartan* (1968).

However, not until the first six years of the 1980s did the Nepalese industry become organised, when the Royal Nepal Film Corporation and private producers made about a dozen features. By the middle of the decade, Nepalese films were recognised at an annual film awards ceremony. By then, the trend was towards co-productions with India, Bangladesh and Pakistan.

PAKISTAN

HISTORICAL BACKGROUND

Before its partition from India in 1947, Pakistan had a film centre in Lahore, where, as early as the 1920s, silent movies were made. Responsible for much of the development of Lahore's filmmaking was D.M. Pancholi, whose studio was managed by Diwan Sardari Lal when Pancholi left for Bombay in the late 1940s. It was Lal who made the first film in the new country of Pakistan. Released in 1948, *Teri Yaad* flopped at the box office (Ali 1964: 42; Ijaz 1987: 102).

Filmmakers were apparently not deterred by the failure of the inaugural film, nor the uninhibited importation of Indian cinema. In the next two years, some Indian film people (including Shaukat Hussain Rizvi) migrated from Bombay to work in Lahore; new studios were established (i.e. Shahnoor, Federal, Quaisar and Karachi) in Lahore, Karachi and, finally, Dacca in East Pakistan; technical facilities were set up; production increased to a total of 13 movies by 1950 and the Ministry of Information and Broadcasting began making documentaries and newsreels.

During the 1950s, the industry established its footing by recognising and tackling some serious problems and developing its infrastructure. The most vexing problems were those caused by the free import of Indian films and producers' heavy dependence upon distributors. In 1952, an economic crisis, partially generated by the free import of Indian films, led to demonstrations and the picketing of an Indian film. The government reacted by stopping the free import licences and imposing a fee of Rs 1 per foot for any film permitted to be imported (Ali 1964: 46). Later, Indian films were totally banned.

The problem of the distributors' power was much more elusive. Insufficient capital meant that distributors often bought up a film while it was in production, making themselves financier-distributors or co-producers. Years later, in 1966, producers were still dependent upon distributors who required that films follow a set box-office formula—i.e. to cater to every type of audience by including all the appealing ingredients of music, fights, comedy, melodrama, sentiment, dance and as many stars as possible (Ahmad 1966: 24)[1].

Among the infrastructure changes of the decade were the establishment of the Film Finance Corporation in East Pakistan, as well as a processing company; the liberalisation of imports of equipment and new raw film; the arrangement to exhibit Pakistani films in first-class theatres; and the setting up of the First Pakistan Film Festival and annual Presidential Awards in film[2].

The pay-offs were attempts to make Pakistani film, using a native formula and local settings; the development of local talents in directors such as Khalil Qaiser (*Clerk*, *Shaheed* and *Farangi*), Anwar Kamal (*Gumnam*), Khurshid Anwar and G.A. Gul (*Qatil* and *Dulla Bhatti*); and increased production. In 1956, 31 films were released, eleven of which were silver jubilees'[3], six were relatively successful and 13 failures (Ali 1964: 48). The following year, Pakistan had 15 film production companies, five studios and 50 distributing companies. But, by 1957, filmmakers, having reached creative exhaustion and bankruptcy, reverted to outright plagiarism, a characteristic of Pakistani cinema to this day. In 1961, of 38 films released, only five were profitable.

The 1960s saw a number of other changes. In 1962, Indian films were again banned, this time for five years. The following year, a court nullified the ban ruling, to which the government reacted by passing the Censorship of Films Act of 1963, requiring every theatre to screen Pakistani films 85 per cent of the playing time. Punjabi-language films, which had a slump earlier, were the rage by the mid-1960s, as were those about fighting in the Wild West and among gangsters in the United States and gladiators in Ancient Rome. Some fleshy and sexy films were also hits.

Because of the recommendations of some advisory groups, including the Film Fact Finding Commission, a film academy and a pilot studio were created for training purposes; more theatres were built; a film export company was set up to seek markets; and the Central Advisory Council was made responsible for co-ordinating all film industry matters and promoting the production of better films. The council, chaired by the Minister and Secretary of the Ministry of Information and Broadcasting, had complete powers to deal with film (Ijaz 1987: 103).

After nearly 20 years (by 1966), the industry had grown to nine studios—in Lahore (five), Karachi (three) and Dacca (one)—which had 100 films in production at any given time. The largest studios worked on 40 to 50 concurrently in four shifts a day. Additionally, 140 distributors (15 of whom were branches of foreign film distributors) rented to 515 permanent and 30 touring theatres, taking 55 per cent of the total receipts of each showing. Nearly 80 per cent of all theatres were in West Pakistan (Ijaz 1987: 103).

The 1970s dawned with another rejuvenation of the film industry, but when the decade ended, filmmaking was in turbulent straits. In 1973, the government established the National Film Development Corporation (NAFDEC) to regulate the trade. NAFDEC stepped up co-productions, tried to control imports and produced a few films itself.

Throughout most of the decade, the number of films remained high, although the same could not be said about quality. The chances of films making profits were slim—because of increased production costs, higher taxes or the limited number of theatres—yet, in 1976, 107 films were released, and about 600 were in different stages of development. The annual production average was more than 100. The secret of financial success lay in directors and stars working on more than one film at a time and in producers investing in regional-language movies, which constituted half of the production total. Usually, 50 per cent of non-Urdu pictures recovered their costs and there was no shortage of money for them (Khan 1977: 448).

The more than 200 filmmakers continued to churn out the basic formula of romance, dance and song, more often than not plagiarised from Indian and Western movies. One Western observer in 1976 wrote that Pakistani film's claim to fame was the 'scale and impertinence of its plagiarisation', adding that there was 'not a hit out of Bombay that is not copied in details' (Woollacott 1976: 35).

Each month, Pakistani producers and directors drove or flew to Kabul to watch the latest Indian pictures and then purchase the ones they later copied frame by frame in their Pakistan studios.

The worsening political events of 1977 sent the industry into a tail-spin. During fighting in the early part of the year, about three dozen theatres were badly burned or damaged by demonstrators, after which theatres, as well as studios, closed down temporarily. One supporter of the Bhutto government, matinée idol Mohammad Ali, was especially targeted. Anti-Bhutto forces threatened to burn theatres showing his films.

The military junta led by Zia Ul Huq, which deposed Bhutto in July, had deep ideological and religious biases which affected film. With a goal of the quick Islamisation of the country, Zia imposed bans on liquor, horse-racing, night-clubs and gambling, as well as on the exhibition of movies dealing with these topics and with sex, crime and violence generally. A number of directors had to reshoot films already in production because of the bans. In 1980–1, the government applied even more stringent censorship laws when it reconstituted the Central Board of Film Censors and ordered it to be more vigilant. All filmmakers were required to be licensed with the Ministry of Culture; those without 'solid' educational backgrounds and supporters of Bhutto were not registered.

Required registration and governmental crack-downs on income tax evasion sent a number of filmmakers into exile or scurrying for other jobs. Of the first batch of 300 applicants, only 40 were registered, and these only after six months' delay. For years, film people were among the nation's biggest tax dodgers. With the clamp-down, the authorities confiscated equipment and other property of directors and stars, some of which was auctioned off, some returned after negotiations. For nearly the first 18 months of the 1980s, the robust film industry ground to a crawl, with studios closed for a while and actors out of work.

Zia also began an inquiry into NAFDEC in 1977. Allegations of misappropriations, misuse of funds and favouritism plagued the state-owned body. A 1979 White Paper claimed NAFDEC had lost more than US $21 million and had introduced a new type of violence to Pakistani screens with imported kung fu. By 1980, a reorganised NAFDEC restricted itself to title approval only of foreign films.

CONTEMPORARY SCENE

For most of a working day in July 1984, President Zia addressed a delegation of film people. The marathon session was historic because it served as a pep rally for a winless industry. President Zia traded concessions for a number of government expectations. He said film would be accorded status as a fully fledged industry, assuring it the same privileges in importation of equipment and other areas as given to other industries. Further, the government would sponsor an annual film festival, convention and awards ceremony[4], encourage the production of more Sindhi films, make sure Indian films were not imported, instruct Pakistan television to resume a slot for the showing of local films and set up a committee to investigate the psychological impact of cinema.

Claiming the industry was almost without direction in its first 37 years, Zia offered guidance. Movies should help the public's morality and have a healthy impact on the economy, culture and ideology; film people had a moral obligation to pay their income taxes and film halls could not show 'blue' movies under penalty of being demolished, he said. Zia warned that filmmakers who reinserted censored parts into films after they were approved by the censors[5] would be dealt with severely. But, he was much less decisive on the 'video menace', admitting, 'I do not have a solution. Meanwhile, I would like someone to suggest a solution.' (Samdani 1984: 8, also *Morning News* 16 July 1984: 12; *Muslim* 16 July 1984: 1).

An editorial in the daily *Dawn* (18 July 1984) explained that Zia's granting such a long session meant that film was important to him. Although the industry produced quantity, much dissatisfaction was voiced about film quality, the editorial continued, warning that:

'Unless a way is found to ensure that the socially responsible filmmaker can survive side by side with the mercenary, that the distribution of box-office returns is equitable, and that intelligent boys and girls are attracted to film studios, no significant advancement of the cinema is possible.'

The government provided figures on the quantity of films at the meeting. Between 1980 and 1983, 395 pictures were made, 120 of these in 1983. Of the total, 194 were in Punjabi, 104 in Pashto and 94 in Urdu. Pakistan had 632 cinemas in 1983, compared with 496 in 1970. The authorities also reported that 78 producers had their registrations cancelled in 1983, because they had not made a film in two years.

Production

In addition to the impact of ideological censorship and required registration, Pakistani producers faced sharp increases in production costs and the incisive inroads made by television and videocassettes.

By the mid-1980s, the cost of producing a colour feature had risen to US $150,000. Films in regional languages cost US $100,000, thus accounting for their increased numbers. In 1985, Urdu films were already overtaken by Punjabi 'blood and guts' action pictures where it was not unusual for the hero to knock off 200–300 opponents in ten minutes (Rasheed 1986: 51). Such action films demand comparatively high budgets of US $90,361 to $150,000 or more. Usually a third each is allocated for the cast and film stock, another 20 per cent for the music and the rest for everything else. Scripts are nearly non-existent in action films, thus saving that expense. Stars are told the idea of the picture which they ad lib.

Financially, the government has not been very helpful. Taxes are high, including a 100 per cent admissions fee, and all imported film stock is controlled by the government NAFDEC, which takes a commission on raw stock and a 57 per cent commission on imported foreign films. The high taxation means that for a US $100,000 movie to recover its investment, gross revenue must total US $750,000 (Khan 1977: 448).

As intimated earlier, Pakistani producers carry on in spite of adversities, finding alternative ways to bring out their work. By the mid-1980s co-productions were almost a necessity (with Nepal, Sri Lanka, Bangladesh and Turkey), especially for Urdu pictures, and foreign locations and actors were in vogue. In 1985 more than a dozen Pakistani films were shot abroad (Ijaz 1985: 78) and, by the following year, Pakistani releases were up to 90 a year from the low of 58 in 1980.

The 'video menace' President Zia alluded to in 1984 was noticeable much earlier. When theatres closed during the 1977 strife, smuggled videocassettes were being shown in privately arranged screenings. As the film industry became bleaker in the next five years, more than 100 private illegal exhibition places showed Indian and US films for an admission fee of US $1. The result was that video took away middle-class or gentry film audiences, who preferred the uncensored films available very quickly on video-cassette (Interview, Arif Nizami, 1984). As a government media official explained, 'Why go to the movies when 15 days after *Time* magazine reviews a film in the US, you can rent it here?' He said the government admitted defeat by lowering the import duty on videocassette recorders from 125 to 85 per cent. 'Because Pakistan makes videos for Pakistanis working in the Gulf States, the government cannot complain very vociferously about video imperialism,' he added (Interview, Muzaffar Abbas, 1984).

An Indian television station at Amritsar, less than 100 miles across the border from Lahore, also affected domestic film-going. On the four or five nights a week Indian films were shown, attendance at Pakistani theatres in the vicinity dropped sharply. As one writer observed, Pakistanis now could see the original movies from which their own were plagiarised (Cowie 1978: 262).

Distribution and Exhibition

Pakistan, for years, has been divided into three main distribution circuits—Punjab-NWFP and Sind-Baluchistan, both domestic, and one for overseas distribution. Punjab-NWFP has handled as many as 60 per cent of all theatres.

Foreign distribution has never been very lucrative, despite ready markets where Pakistanis immigrated, such as England, Canada and the Middle East; where Urdu was known, such as parts of East

Africa and Asia; and where Indian films had already made inroads. In 1977, filmmakers expressed dissatisfaction with the State Film Authority and NAFDEC, the agencies in charge of exports, because only 30 per cent of the Pakistani films found foreign markets. Apparently the situation worsened by the early 1980s, partly because of a lack of marketing knowledge. For example, NAFDEC does not supply foreign distributors with new prints, English-language scripts or dubbing.

Exhibitors tried shut-down ploys in 1983 and 1985 to protect their deplorable state. The 100 per cent tax on admissions, one of the highest in the world, plus 32 other taxes exhibitors pay, have kept them fighting mad. In 1983, exhibitors went on strike nationally when the admission tax in Punjab went to 150 per cent; two years later, they and distributors closed temporarily, insisting on a tax reduction to 12½ per cent and a complete ban on video. Neither demand was met.

Efforts to avoid the entertainment tax, among other illegal activities such as the black marketing of admission prices and showing of uncensored films, were blocked in 1979, when the government ordered all exhibitors to join the Pakistan Film Exhibitors Association. Theatres are classified as 'A', with 800 seats; 'B', with 500 and 'C', with 200.

Many theatre owners in the 1980s closed down or converted their buildings into warehouses or markets, rather than continue their struggles.

Directing and Acting

Films have plunged in quality because directors and actors depend too much on trial-and-error techniques and are overworked. In 1984, it was said that there were directors who did not know the number of films they were engaged in, and some who cast people in films without knowing their sex beforehand. Many top stars have multiple roles. When one actor died young in the 1970s, he was in 50 or more unreleased films; when an actress eloped in 1982, she was in at least 30 films.

The most popular and highly paid star of the mid-1980s, Babra Sharif, has been outspoken about the drastic drop in acting standards. At the top of her profession since a producer hired her after an appearance in a televised soap powder advertisement in the early 1970s, Babra starred in recent blockbusters, such as *Miss Colombo*, *Miss Hongkong* and *Miss Singapore*.

Discussing the industry in 1986, Babra said:

'Now there is only one type of film—action. So they want me to do karate and judo and make up to three dress changes during a single song but they don't want me to act anymore. It is not the directors' fault. Serious directors who want to make human drama films find that their films flop. They get depressed and give up. Films are no longer made by directors but by the special-effects people.' (Rasheed 1986: 53)

Scripts are no longer written down, she said, rhetorically asking, 'how can you write down one fight after another?' For each film, Babra must learn new 'gimmicks', such as skating, break-dancing or hanging from a helicopter. Regretting that the gentry no longer attend films, she said, 'The whole cultural climate is now so depressing that you cannot just attack the film industry for bucking under. It is doing the best it can under the circumstances.' (Rasheed 1986: 53).

Regulation
Film regulation has been beefed up considerably, especially in line with further Islamisation. Under the Ali Bhutto government, the State Film Authority was established with powers to register film-makers and scrutinise scripts; the censorship code was revised; the central and regional censor boards were reconstituted and a ceiling was fixed on feature film length (12,000 feet, revised to 14,000 after protests) to save precious raw stock. All this occurred in 1976.

Although the new code was more liberal, with the government accepting filmmakers' rights to express themselves artistically within national cultural perceptions and sensitivities, the censor boards themselves were hard-nosed (Khan 1977: 448).

In its attempt to cleanse local pictures of Western sex and violence, the Zia government pushed through the Motion Picture Ordinance 1979, which reinforced the Cinematograph Act 1918 and Film Censorship Act 1963. The new law made the censoring board omnipotent. It can deny a censorship certificate to any film without providing a reason, and no appeal of convictions under the ordinance can be brought before any court.

Revised censorship codes, standardised for foreign and domestic films, stated that pictures cannot do harm to the nation or portray sex, violence or kissing. Violations under the 1979 ordinance draw penalties of three years' imprisonment and a US $10,000 fine. If some Islamic zealots had their way, the industry would have been disbanded (both production and exhibition) or nationalised to produce documentaries and propaganda movies.

By 1986, the censorship was so frequent and strict that the few scripts that existed were reduced to banality. The army, police or government cannot be criticised; there cannot be any hints of corruption or bribery; officials must be shown in a favourable light; a 'mother cannot hug her son, lovers cannot even touch, let alone kiss' and newspapers cannot show 'sexy' pictures of movie stars or indulge in film gossip. Rasheed (1986, p. 51) mentioned other restraints:

261

'Heroes and heroines must abstain from singing and dancing on a rocking boat or in a rain storm. The hero should not abduct "two female artistes at one and the same time", and villains cannot be shown to escape from police custody or beaten by police.'

BANGLADESH

HISTORICAL BACKGROUND

If it is kept separate from those of India and Pakistan, the film industry of Bangladesh has had a very brief history—since national liberation in 1971. However, history cannot be divided that neatly, especially in a partitioned region such as South Asia; thus, this treatment analyses filmmaking in the geographical territory now known as Bangladesh, which was East Bengal before 1947, and East Pakistan after partition.

Apparently a Western film was shown in Dhaka in 1898, and members of the Nawak family of that city produced a four-reel silent picture in the late 1920s (Azam 1987: 75). However, before 1947, only one, unsuccessful, feature was made by a Bengali Muslim, and that was Obaidul Huq's *Dukhey Jader Jibon Gora* (Misery Is Their Lot), released in 1946. Obaidal Huq, with some cash, a script he wrote about the 1943 Bengal Famine and some government connections, went to Calcutta the year before in search of a producer[6].

The next step in the evolution of Bangladeshi film was a 1953 meeting Dr Abdus Sadeq, director of statistics of East Bengal, called of film distributors and exhibitors, where he asked if anyone wanted to make films. Abdul Jabbar Khan, a stage actor with no film experience, accepted the challenge and, with two partners, established the province's first successful production company, Iqbal Films. In 1956, Iqbal produced *Mukh-o-Mukhosh*, based on Jabbar Khan's stage play, using a borrowed household tape recorder for sound, a paltry Rs 64,000 for capital and the free services of artistes. Initially, distributors were reluctant to promote the feature, fearful it would not be profitable and that their theatres would be damaged if they released a Muslim movie. Upon its eventual release, *Mukh-o-Mukhosh* was successful because it was the first (Kabir 1979: 23).

In 1958, the Film Development Corporation (FDC) was put into place in East Pakistan, with 51 per cent of the capital staked by the government. FDC, which became the nucleus of the film industry, was filled with Calcutta-trained staff and excellent production facilities. Before its creation, private capital made no attempts to indigenise film for the more than 100 theatres of East Pakistan. Instead, the 33 distributors favoured importing from Calcutta (Ali 1964: 51).

In 1958–9, three films were in production, the first released being *Akash-ar-Mati*. Also in 1959, *Jago Hua Savera* (Day Shall Dawn), made in East Pakistan by a Lahore studio, was brought out to some acclaim. Early on, audiences returned to Indian or West Pakistan fare, partly because their own directors lacked cinematic time- and speed-sense.

Different language and genre approaches were tried during FDC's first decade, most for short-lived runs. Early attempts to make realistic pictures were rejected, as was the tendency to incorporate basic components of successful Urdu cinema, common until 1962. After Ehtesham's *Chanda*, an Urdu film made in Dhaka in 1962, drew large audiences, the switch was from Bengali- to Urdu-language use.

That lasted only briefly, to be replaced by popular folklore themes, after Salahuddin directed a successful film version of a village operetta, *Roopha*. For a short time, all directors used these folk themes and the traditional stage style of entrance-dialogue-exit. The result was that Bengali productions increased from five in 1965 to 25 in 1968. When there was not enough folklore to fill screen time, scriptwriters busied themselves 'inventing' it. Again, audiences tired of this genre, especially when they realised films used faked folk-tales (Kabir 1979: 29).

In the years closest to the 1971 war with West Pakistan, the favourite type of film revolved around contemporary, urban themes. Some of these were the first Bengali 'social' movies involving political content. One example was the 1970 release, *Jibon Thekey Neya* (Glimpses from Life), directed by Zahir Raihan, which epitomised the dictatorship of Ayub Khan, and expressed on film, for the first time, the rising tide of nationalism. The movie was an exception in the dismal years of 1969–70, when 71 features were released, most of which were uninspired amateur work or plagiarisms.

Kabir (1979, pp 36–7) makes the point that in the early days, East Pakistan had numerous opportunities to excel in filmmaking, but threw most of them away. For example, production financiers were unusually liberal in film financing policy, so that almost all of the 28 features of Dacca Studio between 1959 and 1965 were based on contemporary, serious themes. But, most failed because of crude filmmaking, with directors incorrectly establishing times and situations and taking their audiences for granted.

POST-LIBERATION PERIOD

Filmmaking virtually halted during 1971, with the non-co-operation movement and war with West Pakistan. Only one feature and four propagandistic documentaries on the war were released.

Although production was almost non-existent, something that would have been more important to the future of the industry was developing. Filmmakers under Zahir Raihan's direction formulated a scheme to nationalise the industry, hoping to bring about quality production, guaranteed work for directors and more equitable distribution of theatre receipts. The plan died when Zahir Raihan disappeared while searching for his brother, who had been kidnapped by Pakistani collaborators (Kabir 1979: 51).

Uncertainty ruled at the end of the war in December 1971. Producers hesitated in releasing films until they knew whether the Bangladesh government planned to grant concessions to Indian films as a tribute to that country for its help in the war. When it was apparent the government had no such plans and, in fact, banned all imports, film productivity moved faster than any other sector of the economy. Kabir (1979, p. 53) cites these reasons for the spurt of activity:

'a) Because of the war and general state of lawlessness prevailing in the country a handful of people had accumulated massive wealth. Film industry was considered by them the most suitable sector to invest their "capital" as no other sector would offer such easy immunity from possible official censure. It also offered a golden opportunity to make "black" money "white".
b) This is the only industry that could guarantee not only a quick return of the investment but, with a bit of luck, also a fat profit.'

The good times did not last long. A number of factors, including a rise in the amusement tax by more than 125 per cent in two years, curtailed profits, while improved relations with India, leading to easier plagiarism of Indian films, led to quality degeneration. The quantity stayed somewhat consistent, fluctuating between 28 and 44 in 1972–78. A total 240 films (only three in Urdu, the rest in Bengali) were unreeled in that period.

Production, Distribution, Exhibition

The seven FDC and four privately owned studios of Bangladesh released about 60 features a year in the mid-1980s. Many of the films were produced at FDC, where about 200 were in production each year. Local productions consumed more than 95 per cent of the exhibition time in more than 400 theatres in Bangladesh.

In Bangladesh, a producer is merely a financier, usually a

successful business man with undeclared 'black' money. Most major actors, actresses and technicians engage in 'black' transactions, demanding a substantial part of their fees in money under the table.

Very few producers are able to provide the entire capital investment needed for a film[7]. About halfway through the shooting schedule, funds are usually exhausted, at which time, distributors put up cash in exchange for the film's 'exploitation' rights for three to ten years. The transaction favours the distributor, who, according to Kabir (1979, p. 79), '[B]y a peculiar logic . . ., gains the right to adjust his own investment first in addition to his exorbitant commission amounting to anything from 20 to 40 percent while the firstcomer, producer, has to wait for his turn which usually never comes.'

Economic practices are even more unfair to the producer, because distributors make agreements with exhibitors to under-receipt a film rental, often for up to 80 per cent, in lieu of a lower rate. Thus, the producer is shown no more than 25–30 per cent of the actual earnings, the result being that, 'If a film draws slightly less than "super-hit" crowds, it is doomed so far as the producer is concerned.' (Kabir 1979: 80)

Distributors benefit further in that the money they invest in production is not from their own pockets. Because Bangladesh's protected market requires a steady supply of films for the more than 400-theatre network, cinema houses compete in booking films right from their production stages. Distributors sometimes collect advance money from theatre owners to ensure they receive the films. Kabir (1979, p. 80), being in the movie business for decades, documented other unethical, if not illegal, practices. He said, 'Most seasoned directors prefer to deal with a large number of films of both "hit" and "flop" categories. "Flop" films help to fix the books on "hit" films to dupe income-tax people. For the distributor, thus, any film is useful.'

Bangladesh's four major exhibition circuits are in Dhaka, Chittagong, Rajshahi and Khulna, cities which contain about 80 per cent of the nation's theatres. The advance booking of films while still in production, common among these theatres, is done by 'third-party bookers'. Their 5 per cent commission also comes out of the producer's paltry share of the box-office take.

Ticket prices have risen considerably with both the government tax department and exhibitors pushing them up. During the decade of the 1970s, ticket prices nearly tripled. A survey in the late 1970s showed that 62 per cent of the box office gross went to taxes, 19 per cent to exhibitors, 17 per cent to distributors and 2 per cent to producers. Exhibitors had increased their share of profits by tacking on an air-conditioning surcharge, although often the theatres were not air-conditioned or, if they were, the system was often not turned on.

Types of Films
In its first 20 years, Bangladeshi film concentrated on various topics: the idealistic life, a theme brought over from the Calcutta studios; realistic portrayals of Bangladesh; social messages; folk *jotra* and political issues. After 1971, war was a main theme, especially cheap commercialisations of war tragedies such as rape.

Analysing the 183 movies produced between 1972 and 1976, Kabir (1979, p. 57) categorised them into plagiarised (125 titles), non-plagiarised (25), off-beat (eight) and war (five). Popular among non-plagiarised movies were those that were merely 'camera theatre', ranging in themes from that of a friend 'sacrificing not only his girl for his bosom friend but also . . . one of his eyes', to those that depicted post-liberation decay. Most of these films exploited the religious beliefs of Bangladesh's majority.

Kabir (1979, p. 61) reported that in this five-year span, 70 per cent of the movies were plagiarised. Some were copied from Pakistani hits which themselves had been plagiarisms of Indian features. Although the Board of Film Censors forbids plagiarism, it has not enforced the ruling. As a result, producers and directors go to Calcutta, watch many Bengali or Hindi hits and tape-record their entire sound tracks. Back in Bangladesh, writers use the sound tracks to create 'screenplays', usually by picking the best scenes from several films and putting them together. In other cases, directors buy footage of scenes and splice it to their own film (Kabir 1979: 62–3).

One feature common to almost all Bengali films is the penchant for introducing in the first half all kinds of complications that must be solved in the second half. When it is difficult for the scriptwriter otherwise to solve the problems he has created, a miracle is introduced. Interestingly, the religious miracle solution serves a second function, assuaging the guilt of theatre-goers for their attendance at 'sinful' film showings (Kabir 1979: 34).

Regulation and Professionalism
The Bangladesh Censorship of Film Rules, 1972, are rather comprehensive. General principles of the code specify that filmmakers should consider whether their works impair moral standards, extenuate vice, deprecate social values, offend any sector of society, adversely affect children under twelve years of age or impair national ideology.

Specifically, films should not ridicule Bangladesh or its people, portray sedition, anarchy or violence with political motive, satirise or ridicule any aspect of national ideology, propagate racial or religious hatred, reveal military or other official secrets, bring into contempt the military or police, maliciously portray incidents prejudicial to any people, race or nation, attack any religion, exhibit cruelty to animals, show how crimes are committed, plagiarise other movies, show 'science as a means of acquiring devilish powers by master criminals' or display dowry, except to condemn it.

Professionalisation of the industry has taken a number of forms. In the 1970s, awards were instituted to upgrade film quality, including the Bangladesh National Film Awards given out in 20 categories by the government since 1975; Cine Journalists Association Awards, given in similar categories as the government ones since 1972; *Uttaran* Film Award since 1972; Bangladesh Film-makers Association Film Awards since 1977 and the Film Critic's Award. Also in the 1970s, a film archive and FDC training schemes were established.

The country's producers, directors, film artistes, distributors, editors, exhibitors and cine journalists have their own organisations, some of which are active in upgrading the profession. By 1986, the Bangladesh Better Cinema Front was busy, providing direct production and post-production assistance to filmmakers. The main purpose of the Front is to initiate a free-length and free-gauge cinema in direct opposition to the lengths and formulas demanded by commercial exhibitors.

SRI LANKA

HISTORICAL BACKGROUND

Almost all early Sri Lankan film activity was in the distribution and exhibition of foreign pictures. An Indian company, Madan Theatres, opened cinema halls in Colombo after the first public screening of a movie there in 1901. (The first local cinema house was opened in 1903.) The Indians controlled exhibition until Ceylon Theatres Ltd, an import, distribution and exhibition firm, was founded by Chittampalam A. Gardiner and Associates in 1928. Ceylon Theatres monopolised the market until competitors came along about two decades later (de Silva and Siriwardene n.d.: 40–1).

Because showing foreign movies was a successful endeavour — despite outcries from some nationalists that the movies constituted an 'inferior and morally subversive medium' — there were not many attempts at making local films. In 1925, A.G. Noorbhai produced *Royal Adventure*, but it was destroyed by fire in an overseas screening and was never shown in Sri Lanka.

When Sinhala films were finally made, they either adapted local drama, particularly traditional plays (*naadagam*) to the screen, or copied South Indian cinema formulas. The first local films were merely cinematic reproductions of B.A.W. Jayamanne's popular plays, composed of satirical themes about middle- and upper-class life and melodramatic plots.

Jayamanne, and those pioneers who followed his lead, did not see the enormous possibilities of camera work or editing. Cameras were static, and nearly all the bad features of the plays were carried over to cinema. Writing about the first of these, *Kadawunu Poronduwa* (Broken Promise), released in 1947, one writer said it was nothing more than a stage play reproduced in moving pictures, and that the only requirement of the actors was to go 'through their phases declaiming and crying, singing and dancing' (Gunasinghe 1968: 98). The actors in the early films were Jayamanne's brother, Eddie Jayamanne, who played the comic hero role, and the latter's wife, Rukmani Devi, who performed as a tragedienne.

When plays were not available for conversion, novels were recast as plays and shot on the screen, resulting in what one critic in 1950 described as 'thread-bare themes, re-orchestrated from film to film' (Ariyadasa 1977: 3). Studios did not exist in Sri Lanka so the films were shot entirely in South India, using Indian technicians, musicians and, sometimes, directors.

Despite their many imperfections, these movies were important and successful because they created the local cinema artiste and gave the public their first productions in the local language.

Rather quickly, Sri Lankan filmmakers surmised the big business potential of the industry. Budgets increased; the star system and technical sophistication came about and extravaganzas appeared. Investors saw no reason to risk their money in original Sinhala films when they could copy Indian ones. One writer said that when the first Sinhala movie was made in 1947, Indian cinema, already in twelve languages, found another tongue (Armes 1987: 128), while Amunugama (1971, p. 33) reported, 'Some [directors], leaving nothing to chance, even mixed up sequences from several Indian films in one Sinhala production!'

In these films, actors and actresses imitated Indian stars, even down to the jewellery they wore. The movies were melodramatic, but also moralistic, with villains brought to justice (Savarimutti 1977: 24).

Among some of the early producers were S.M. Nayagam and Sirisena Wimalaweera. Nayagam, who produced *Kadawunu Poronduwa*, hired South Indian directors of Tamil-language movies to work in his Sundara Sound Studio. He also directed some films himself, including *Podiputha* (1965), a story of a father's love for his son and the cruel fate that befalls him (Jayatilaka 1987: 111). Wimalaweera opened the first local studio in 1951, followed by that of Ceylon Theatres Ltd in 1956.

Importation and exhibition remained the prerogative of Ceylon Theatres Ltd, joined by Ceylon Entertainments in 1946 and

Cinemas Ltd in 1949. These three companies strengthened their monopoly by various agreements among themselves.

In 1948, the Government Film Unit was established, with encouragement and help from two Italians, Gulio Petroni and Federico Serra. Initially, GFU owned only two 35mm movie cameras salvaged from the surplus stocks of the British Army. Processing had to be done in Madras (*Ceylon Today* Sept.–Oct. 1968: 22–3). It is ironic that GFU, started by foreigners, set up a scheme in the early 1980s, to invite well-known filmmakers to Sri Lanka to produce its movies. The unit, since renamed the Films Division of the Department of Information, produces most of the country's documentaries regularly screened in theatres and schools.

Sinhala Cinema moved into another realm in 1956, when Lester J. Peries produced *Rekawa*, the first film entirely shot in Sri Lanka. Peries brought realism to the film, making maximum use of local colour, background and players, and taking the camera outdoors. Amunugama (1971, p. 34) said Peries introduced a new genre as the filmmaker moved to the village and studied social relationships there: 'It is the Sinhalese village which provided a refuge to the talented Sinhalese film director from the cliches and banalities of the South Indian stereotype.' Peries' *Rekawa* was considered a big breakthrough as it drew the attention of the intelligentsia, set a model for young filmmakers and challenged the Indian formula film. But, as will be seen later, it was not an overnight success.

The demand for national and serious Sinhala film accelerated after *Rekawa*'s release, thanks to growing audience sophistication, competition among formula film producers and the bad quality of Indian copies. Other changes were in the offing when agitation about the monopoly in the industry led to the government-appointed Commission of Inquiry into the Film Industry, 1962.

In its 1964 report, the commission recognised the monopolisation: three of the five circuits operated by the principal distributors controlled all but 13 of Sri Lanka's 274 cinemas[8], most of the imports and much of the production, the latter in the studios of Ceylon Theatres Ltd and Cinemas Ltd and through the financing of independent producers. Monopoly control was not good for the industry, the commission found, because it exploited the independent producer and favoured money-making foreign films and the film formula of Bombay or Madras.

Among its recommendations, the commission called for the establishment of a national film corporation to undertake the importing and distributing of films and the operating of a studio. The latter was to provide facilities and produce documentaries and children's films. Through the National Film Corporation, importing and distributing were to be taken out of private hands, loans were to be made available to producers and the number of imports was to be restricted. However, the change of government in 1965 led to a five-year shelving of the report.

When new elections were called for 1970, the future of the film industry was a campaign issue of the victorious United Front. The new government established the State Film Corporation (SFC) which, by 1976, took over the total importation and distribution of films. A year later, SFC initiated a loan scheme, subject to its approval of scripts and the establishment of its own studio; created a script bank and registered technicians and directors to ensure their professionalism. The credit scheme had a snag in that selection of producers was based entirely on the personal choice of SFC officials[9], and the script bank was not used much as producers preferred well-known writers. But, almost immediately after SFC's formation, more films earned larger profits (in 1976–7, 14 of 30 films released had gross earnings of Rs 1 million each) and a greater variety of imports was available, not just those from the United States and England (Warnasiri 1977: 5–6).

From the outset, the SFC was put in a difficult position; at the same time as it was to approach film as more than just a commercial commodity, it had to be financially viable, i.e. make a profit. When Junius Jayewardene assumed power in 1977, he retained the SFC under his purview. In 1981, it was renamed National Film Corporation, by amendment to an act introduced to Parliament by the Prime Minister and, by 1988, NFC started its own colour laboratory, studio complex and the National Film Institute. Simultaneously, one director, Amarnath Jayatilaka, criticised NFC for being lethargically mismanaged, incompetent and corrupt.

CONTEMPORARY SCENE

Production, Distribution, Exhibition

The problems of Sri Lankan filmmakers, distributors and exhibitors are not very different from those in most of Asia—television and home video threats, antiquated equipment and limited talent pools, among others.

Perhaps unique to Sri Lanka is the amount of time that elapses between the production and the release of films. With 25 to 30 films produced each year and a limited number of theatres, it was not uncommon for finished films to lie idle in the can for three years. Once in the theatre, they could expect three weeks of exhibition, no matter their popularity, before being put back into the can and shelved.

It was an unhappy situation all round. Investors were extremely reluctant to tie up money that long without seeing rewards; producers who had taken out loans paid long-term interest without any assurance of a return on their work and exhibitors took risks to keep long-awaited films around a bit longer. Anura Goonsekera, former director-general of national television and a long-time observer of the film scene, explained the latter point:

'If I am an exhibitor, I do not want an unpopular film. Knowing that if 50 per cent of the seats are not filled, the film will be pulled, I will buy the tickets myself to keep it in my theatre. This is common; it happens regularly. Usually the idea is to retain the film until the weekend or a holiday.' (Interview, Goonsekera, 1986)

A partial remedy to the delayed releases came about at the end of the 1970s with the creation of the fifth circuit. Politics was the motivator of this development. A powerful politician who had made a film was not willing to wait three years for its release, and the rules were set aside to accommodate him. In the process, the fifth circuit was established, with the selection of quality films to be released in it left to the decision of a committee. In the 1980s two other circuits were added. Although the number of films produced had dropped to about ten a year, there was still a backlog from previous years to make seven circuits feasible.

Local production has now shrunk considerably. First, it has not been in the best interests of the National Film Corporation to encourage it. NFC, which was not doing well by the late 1980s, receives its revenues mainly from the importation and exhibition of foreign pictures, where it takes 55 per cent of all proceeds, the rest going to exhibitors. With local films, the producers also take a slice. Goonsekera said it was 'very profitable' for NFC to bring in foreign movies; in his view, the 'more local quality films, the less profits of NFC' (Interview, Goonsekera, 1986).

A second reason for the drop in production relates to television and home video. Television was introduced to Sri Lanka only in 1982, with the development of Rupavahini. Obviously, film people have not yet learned how to live with it. Giving evidence to a film committee created in the mid-1980s by President Jayewardene, Goonsekera said he proposed that:

'filmmakers market their films by advertising them on television. The few times they had, the number of people who went to cinemas increased tremendously. In time, people will get used to TV and go back to the cinema. TV is still a novelty.' (Interview, Goonsekera, 1986)

As home video became readily available in the 1980s, the film industry felt its impact. By late 1986, there were only about 20,000 sets in a country of around 15 million people, confined mainly to the affluent. But, home viewing was expected to become more available

271

among the blue collar ranks as prices of videocassette recorders dropped. At the beginning of 1987, a complete VCR cost about US $370. Cassettes could be rented at less than US 50 cents each in shops that had US $20–37 refundable membership fees.

Illegal video halls, where 20 to 30 people can watch a film, are prominent anywhere electricity exists. Hindi movies and those banned in Sri Lanka, including pornographic, are shown. In the mid-1980s, when some enterprising individuals thought of opening video cinemas that would hold 200–300 people, filmmakers lobbied the government for a decision to prohibit them. However, as is the case worldwide, home video is almost uncontrollable because of rampant smuggling and piracy and outmoded legislation.

Goonsekera is wary of governmental inquiries and controls on video because of the chance of unexpected repercussions and the forcing of it underground. He feared:

'History is repeating itself. The old film commission report of the 1960s was meant to help the film industry, but actually brought about a monopoly situation. It was not at all helpful to the artistes or the industry and gave rise to a number of productions we did not need or could not accommodate. Why should a small country like Sri Lanka make 30 films yearly? An unintended result of controls they did not bargain for. The same will happen if restrictive policies are applied to video. The reality is that police will be taking bribes, etc. It is far better to legalise video so film people can make a living from it (Interview, Goonsekera, 1986).'

Despite Goonsekera's concerns, the government of Junius Jayewardene set up a committee to investigate film, looking at imports of South Indian films, the impact of television and video and the long queue of productions waiting to be released. The results of the inquiry were not quickly disseminated.

Importation of South Indian (and Western) films caused much consternation over the years. The free import of films was first stopped in 1958 and, until SFC became the sole importer-distributor in the mid-1970s, a quota system was determined by the controller of imports and controller of exchange. However, the quota system continued to favour the large importers-distributors (Warnasiri 1977: 6).

Thus, complaints continued into the present decade. In 1975, SFC was looked down upon as it spent Rs 2 million a year to import Western movies for only 15 per cent of the filmgoing public. On the other hand, SFC spent only half that amount to import Asian pictures for 65 per cent of the audience. In 1976–7, the SFC reported that imports were based on quality, not quantity, and that the corporation preserved its foreign exchange allocation to buy a variety of films (Warnasiri 1977: 6)[10]. In 1978, the complaint was that the large number of Hindi films screened tied up theatres that could be used for local productions.

The government in 1982 ordered SFC to cut the number of imports, thus making local movies more marketable. At the time, SFC imported 80 dubbed, English-language productions a year, but a larger number of imports came from South India, partly because they were preferred by the Tamil-speaking minority of Sri Lanka. In 1979, to recapture the Tamil audience, the new SFC head, at the instigation of President Jayewardene, brought in South Indian stars to perform in movies, with the stipulation that other roles and duties had to be given to locals (*Variety* 1982: 35).

Directing, Acting

A new generation of directors—called 'new wave' by some—dotted the Sri Lankan movie landscape by the late 1970s. The problems their films explored were very real, such as ethnic and religious strife, a corrupt legal system or the unemployed youth. Because these directors broke the rules of formula films, they had great difficulty in enticing audiences.

First to break away was Lester James Peries, considered the foremost Sri Lankan director. Peries' success came the hard way; it took him at least a decade to find an audience, and after two decades and seven films which 'probed the fabric of Sinhalese social life with such depth and sensitivity', Peries could not find work much of the time (Amunugama 1971: 38). A scriptwriter for theatre and radio during World War II, Peries became interested in film through a meeting with British photographer Lionel Wendt. While in Great Britain in the late 1940s, he experimented with film, producing three shorts. He returned to Sri Lanka in 1952, influenced by British documentary, Italian post-war neo-realism and international film trends.

Rekava, one of the first films to break with South Indian models, was not an immediate success, and Peries had to wait four years for his next film, *Sandesaya* (The Message). It made money but, again, four years elapsed before the next Peries' production, *Gamperaliya*. Considered one of his best works, *Gamperaliya* broke many of the rules: it did not use a single song and was shot on location (Siriwardene 1977: 35). Other works of Peries include *Beddegama*, *Kaliyugaya* and *Yuganthaya*.

These, and most of his other important films, were edited by his wife, Sumitra Peries, a famous director herself. Her films dealt with a range of emotions and experiences of women and included *Gahanu Lamai*, *Yahalu Yeheli* and *Sagarayake Jalaya*.

Peries' forte is his sensitivity to the interplay of human emotions. Some of his work has a recurring theme of survival; all of it is richly Sri Lankan in content but international in appeal. Interviewed in the late 1970s, Peries described problems besetting him as the lack of recognition in Sri Lanka; inadequate equipment with some 'museum pieces' more than 20 years old; a dearth of talent making it difficult to pull together a crew; and an inability to make much money even though many theatres showed his films (Siriwardene 1977: 35).

Other directors experimented with non-Indian formulas in the 1970s. Dharmasena Pathiraja, in his first production in 1974 (*Ahas Gawwa*, A League of Sky), probed the lives of lower middle-class, urban youth—unemployed and adrift. The film, which avoided making slogans, was an example of social radicalism. His third film, *Bambaru Avith* (The Wasps Are Here), was also considered 'new wave'. Vasantha Obeysekera's *Valmathwuvo* (The Lost) also depicted unemployed youth, but was a box-office loser.

A few others have ignored the box office in favour of making quality film, including Mahagama Sekera, Siri Gunasinghe, Dharmasiri Bandaranayake and Gamini Fonseka.

Fonseka had acted in more than 100 movies before turning to directing in the mid-1960s. His first film, *Parasathumal*, omitted the staple diet of song and dance, sentimental story and the theme of rich bad guys and poor good guys. Fonseka said he started directing by making bad movies for money and graduated to making good ones for nothing. Among the latter are the controversial *Sarungale* (Kite, 1979), probably the first movie to tackle the problems between Buddhist Sinhalese and Hindu Tamils. His *Uthumaneni* (Your Honour) showed the British-bequeathed legal system in Sri Lanka as corrupt and inefficient.

The veteran director said the major hurdle he faced was the importation of foreign films which took up most of Sri Lanka's screen time. Fonseka added, 'Films already made and in production will fill all available screen time for local films for the next seven years.' (*Asiaweek* 1981b: 12)

Topics

As indicated before, Sri Lankan films have incorporated many new themes in those borrowed from India, other parts of Asia and the West. The latter are still there in abundance: the Indian 'dream' formula of boy meets girl, ten songs and five dances; the Hong Kong martial arts action picture and the explicit portrayal of sex, commonly identified with the West.

Sri Lanka was not unlike other South Asian countries in its hesitancy to produce films with sexually oriented themes. In fact, as Amunugama (1971) wrote, a double standard existed concerning local and Western movies, in that,

'While frontal nudity in Western films is winked at by the censors the Sinhala and Tamil film producer is obliged to put his actresses under a waterfall with monotonous regularity to emphasise their curves!'

However, changes were made in the 1970s, when the first screen kiss was allowed, actress Geetha Kumarasinghe appeared topless in a film and Tissa Abeyasekera and Vasantha Obeyasekera directed *Karumakkarayo* (The Unlucky Ones) and *Palangetiyo* (Grasshoppers), respectively. Both films explored morally dubious relationships.

Other breakthroughs in topic treatment occurred in the 1980s. Political satire was featured in Gamini Fonseka's 1981 movie, *Sagarayak Meda* (In the Middle of an Ocean), based on charges of corruption filed against Minister of Justice Felix Bandaranaike and his aunt, the former Prime Minister. Bandaranaike attempted to have the movie banned, but after being viewed by a government agency and the courts, it was allowed to be shown. The victory meant that films could make political and social comments.

Some films have touched upon communal strife between Tamils and Sinhalese, such as *Sarungale* (1978) and *Adara Kathawa* (1984), the latter a portrayal of ethnic and religious differences yielding to young love. Peries has dealt with class divisions and family life in a changing society in some of his movies.

Despite these innovations, many of Sri Lanka's pictures are splashy and sentimental, appealing to mass audiences. Peries, master that he has been, realised as early as the mid-1970s, that he occasionally must follow the 'cheap' trend, the formula of love, crime, action, comedy, song and dance. But he also lamented, 'Any kind of serious cinema is dependent on non-commercial reasons for existence. And in this country it has been an empty dream.' (Ranawake 1976: 15)

AFTERWORD

Looking at more recent film in one South Asian country—Pakistan —it was obvious that not much had changed for the better.

The staple fare of Pakistani cinema in 1989 consisted of 'a sensuous heroine draped in a clinging wet sari, a dastardly villain, a liberal dose of melodrama and action at full throttle', but themes were still 'hackneyed', romance 'stylised' and scripts 'unimaginative' (*Asiaweek* 1989a: 35). Most films continued to be remakes of the last big hit, so that in 1988, of 34 made in Punjabi, one was a comedy, the others were action movies with revenge themes. Very few of the 50 films in Pashto, Sindhi and Urdu deviated from that plot.

But the action theme, or any other theme for that matter, could not help the box office. One producer claimed 1988 was the champion money-losing year of the industry; it was also the year when 15 theatres were destroyed or closed. Among factors blamed for the malaise were escalating real estate prices that made it profitable to replace theatres with other business places; the popularity of home video, and political instability in some regions, which closed theatres temporarily or kept people off the streets at night (*Asiaweek* 1989a: 35).

With the ascent to power of Benazir Bhutto in November 1988, film personnel expected a more creative and tolerant attitude towards film. Movies with sensuous scenes were allowed, and efforts at co-productions with Nepal, Sri Lanka and Bangladesh attempted.

But the situation looked so dismal for Pakistani film in early 1989, that one distributor direly said, 'From the look of things, we could well be watching the last reel. Things are that bad.' (*Asiaweek* 1989a: 35).

NOTES

1   Early Pakistani films used a theatrical style of quick exchanges of dialogue, 'quips and pat replies of a passionate and romantic nature' and situations involving surprise and coincidence, which were either very touching or very romantic, heroic or terrifying. All of these traits drew upon *rehes*, or folk-plays, seen in country fairs and later used by legitimate theatre. Rehes and old theatre were operatic, employing much dialogue in verse and constant bursts of song and music. Film used this theatricality because audiences enjoyed it and because the early scriptwriters and directors developed their skills on the stage (Ali 1964: 44–5).

2   The Presidential awards, initiated in 1956, were stopped the following year and revived in 1960. In the interim, a Karachi film magazine started the *Nigar* awards.

3   A 'silver jubilee' picture has been a box-office success for 25 weeks, a 'golden jubilee', for 50 weeks.

4   Earlier, there had been film awards and a festival. In 1978, the Pakistan Film Institute, an autonomous body, sponsored its first international festival of film classics, a 21 day affair held in five major cities. Two years later, at President Zia's urging, the National Film Festival in Lahore became an annual event to encourage quality filmmaking.

Zia's 1984 promises were met on an annual basis. For example, at the Third Annual National Film Awards in 1986–7, cash prizes were given to movies in 14 categories.

5   These films are called *tota*, meaning slice. In such films, slices of hard pornography entirely unrelated to the story are spliced in at intervals.

6   Obaidul Huq had to assume a Hindu name for this production. Except for one Muslim actor, the rest of the cast was Hindu. One reason for this was that for centuries, Muslims did not participate in the performing arts, thus, there was a dearth of actors and actresses (Kabir 1979: 15).

7   In 1979, a black-and-white movie cost US $25,000–$61,500 to produce. An additional 30–40 per cent was required for colour productions (Kabir 1979: 79).

8   Ceylon Theatres, 108; Cinemas Ltd, 125; Ceylon Entertainments, 28.

9   The government guaranteed the loans at regular commercial-interest rates. Previously, banks were reluctant to approve loans to film people.

The SFC graded film scripts as 'A', 'B' or 'C', and a film had to have at least a 'B' rating to receive a loan. With the very few 'A' scripts, SFC itself advanced the money, which was a considerably larger sum (Interview, Goonsekera, 1986).
10   As an example of the variety of languages of film imports, in 1974, there were 144 in English, 38 in Sinhala, 28 in Tamil, nine in Urdu, six in Hindi and three in other languages.

REFERENCES

Agcaoili, T.D. (1940) 'Filippine Movies Today', *Philippine Yearbook*, September, pp. 106–11.

Agcaoili, T.D. (1958) 'History of Philippine Movies', *Chronicle Magazine*, 20 April, pp. 6–8.

Ahmad, S. (1966) 'Development of Pakistan's Film Industry', *Pakistan Review*, August, pp. 23–5.

Ahn, B.S. (1987) 'Humor in Korean Cinema', *East-West Film Journal*, December, pp. 90–8.

Ali, S.A. (1964) 'Rise of Film Making in Pakistan', *Pakistan Quarterly*, Spring, pp. 41–55.

AMCB (*Asian Mass Communication Bulletin*) (1977) ' 'Korean Films', September/December, p. 16.

Amercian Chamber of Commerce *Journal* (1939) 'Philippines Fifth in Movie Making', September, pp. 47–8.

Amigo, C. (1954) 'The Movie Industry—Is It Flourishing or Dying?' *Progress 1954*, pp. 190–3.

Amunugama, S.L.B. (1971) 'The Cinema in Ceylon', *Ceylon Today*, March–April, pp. 30–41.

Anderson, J.L. and D. Richie (1982) *The Japanese Film: Art and Industry*, Expanded Edition, Princeton University Press, Princeton, N.J.

Anwar, R. (1978) 'State of the Indonesian Film Industry', *Media Asia*, 5: 3, pp. 159, 164, 170.

Anwar, R. (1988) 'The Indonesian Film Industry', *Media Asia*, 15: 3, pp.134–7, 176.

Ariyadasa, E. (1977) 'Thirty Years of Sinhala Cinema,' issued on the occasion of the OCIC Salutation '76, Sri Lanka Foundation, Colombo.

Armes, R. (1987) *Third World Film Making and the West*, University of California Press, Berkeley.

Asian Messenger (1978) 'Films Recovering', Spring, p. 12.

Asian Messenger (1980/81a) 'News Film', Winter/Spring, p. 15.

Asian Messenger (1980/81b) '60 Years of Korean Moviedom', Winter/Spring, p. 39.

Asiaweek (1977a) 'Malay Film: Enter the Government', 26 August, pp. 16–17.

Asiaweek (1977b) 'The Cash Flows in the Dream Business', 8 July, pp. 40–1.

Asiaweek (1979a) 'Breaking the Love Mould', 1 June, p. 22.

Asiaweek (1979b) 'Kung Fu Films. The Second Coming', 27 July, pp. 32–7.

Asiaweek (1980a) 'The Advance of Kung Fu', 9 May, p. 42.

Asiaweek (1980b) 'The Sex Surge', 23 May, pp. 20–4.

Asiaweek (1981a) 'A Flourish of Fresh Talent', 31 July, pp. 38–9.

Asiaweek (1981b) 'A Victory for Satirical Freedom', 6 March, p. 12.

Asiaweek (1981c) 'Rangoon's Racy Underground Cinema', 11 September, p. 40.

Asiaweek (1982) 'Indonesia and Malaysia: The Doors Open', 1 October, p. 40.

Asiaweek (1983a) '*Ah Ying*: The Fish Seller and the Camera', 9 December, p. 30.

Asiaweek (1983b) 'Hongkong Film-Makers: Outward Bound', 4 March, pp. 31–4.

Asiaweek (1983c) 'Towards an Asian Identity', 22 April, pp. 23–5.

Asiaweek (1984) 'A Coming of Age in Taiwan', 25 May, pp. 48–9.

Asiaweek (1985) 'Hot and Getting Hotter', 25 October, pp. 55, 60, 66.

Asiaweek (1987) '5th Generation Excitement', 10 May, p. 47.

Asiaweek (1988a) 'Malaysia's Brave New World', 29 January, pp. 34–6.

Asiaweek (1988b) 'Seoul's New Drive and Imagination', 8 April, p. 38.

Asiaweek (1988c) 'Spotlight on the Independents', 22 April, p. 48.

Asiaweek (1989a) 'In Pakistan, a Losing Game', 10 March, p. 35.

Asiaweek (1989b) 'Making History with History', 14 April, p. 43.

Azam, S. (1987) 'The Cinema in Bangladesh', *Cinema India-International*, 1, pp. 75–7.

Banks, A.S. (1985) 'Film and Change: The Portrayal of Women in Malay Film', paper presented at film symposium, East-West Center, Honolulu, Hawaii, 26–30 November.

Benedicto, C.M. (1987) 'Film Festivals Big in Taiwan Where Flicks are Viewed as Cultural Windows to the World', *Free China Journal*, 2 November, p. 3.

Benedicto, C.M. (1988a) 'Directors Have "Responsibility" for Good Films', *Free China Journal*, 31 October, p.6.

Benedicto, C.M. (1988b) 'Taipei Film Exhibition Ripe for Full Festival?' *Free China Journal*, 21 November, p. 6.

Benedicto, C.M. (1988c) 'Taiwan's Antonioni Sets the Scene for a Future of Quality Filmmaking', *ROC Roundup in Pictures* of *Central Daily News*, 9 October.

Bernama News Agency (1973) Dispatch No. 125, 7 November.

Binford, M. (1987) 'India's Two Cinemas' in J.D.H. Downing (ed.), *Film and Politics in the Third World*, Praeger, New York, pp. 145–66.

Blanc-Szanton, C. (1989) 'Forms of Resistance in Films of the Last Two Decades in Thailand: "Art Cinema" Versus "Third Cinema" ', paper presented at Association for Asian Studies, Washington, D.C., 17–19 March.

Block, A.B. (1974) *The Legend of Bruce Lee*, Dell, New York.

Bobb, D. (1978) 'Kissa Kursi Ka, The Case of the Missing Film', *India Today*, 1–15 June.

Boonyaketmala, B. (1982) 'Case Studies: Thailand and Argentina' in T. Guback et al. (eds.), *Transnational Communication and Cultural Industries*, UNESCO, Paris, pp. 38–44.

Bornoff, N. (1989) 'The King of Comedy', *Far Eastern Economic Review*, 4 May, p. 60.

Borsuk, R. (1976) 'Jakarta Bans Film Import After 1978', *Media*, November, p. 25.

Boyd, D.A., J.D. Straubhaar and J.A. Lent (1989) *Videocassette Recorders in the Third World*, Longman, New York.

Burra, R. (ed.) (1985) *Indian Cinema 1980–1985*, The Directorate of Film Festivals and the National Film Development Corporation, New Delhi.

Buruma, I. (1983a) 'A Formula in Focus', *Far Eastern Economic Review*, 11 August, pp. 40–1.

Buruma, I. (1983b) 'Thailand's Film-makers Sink in a Morass of Money vs Artistry', *Far Eastern Economic Review*, 27 October, pp. 53–4.

Buruma, I. (1984) 'The Fatter the Country, the Thinner the Stars', *Far Eastern Economic Review*, 3 May, pp. 45, 71.

Buruma, I. (1986) 'Slapstick and Gore Displace Small Oases of Talent', *Far Eastern Economic Review*, 29 May, p. 94.

Buruma, I. (1987) 'The Eye of the Camera Crosses National Borders', *Far Eastern Economic Review*, 26 March, pp. 40–1.

Caagusan, F. (1982) 'Interview: Ricky Lee', *Diliman Review*, November–December, pp. 23–8.

Cacnio, P. (1977) 'Biz in Big Malaysian Cities Key to Film's Click in Rest of Mkt.', *Variety*, 1 June, p. 37.

Cacnio, P. (1980) 'Stars Shine Bright in Bangkok; Producers Groom Newcomers', *Variety*, 7 May, p. 449.

Calderon, R. (1986) 'Joseph Estrada Talks on MMC Takeover of the Metro Filmfest', *Manila Times*, 25 August, p. 12.

Ceylon Today (1968) 'Twenty Years of the Government Film Unit', September–October, pp. 22–27.

Chadha, K.K. (1987) 'New Porn Rules Could Confuse Homevid Industry in Hong Kong', *Variety*, 2 September, p. 48.

Chadha, K.K. (1988) 'Top 3 Film Outfits Led Hong Kong Biz to $96-Mil Total', *Variety*, 27 January, p. 31.

Chalkley, A. (1974) 'The Selling Saga of Kung-fu', *Media*, April, pp. 14–19.

Chandran, M. (1989) *Documents*, National Film Development Corporation, Promotion and Public Relations, Bombay.

Chang, W. (1988) 'Life Becomes Art on Taiwan Director's Film', *Free China Journal*, 5 September, p. 6.

Clark, P. (1987) *Chinese Cinema: Culture and Politics Since 1949*, Cambridge University Press, Cambridge.

Cowie, P. (ed.) (1978) *International Film Guide 1978*, A.S. Barnes and Co., New York.

da Cunha, U. (ed.) (1984) *Indian Cinema 83/84*, The Directorate of Film Festivals and the National Film Development Corporation, New Delhi.

Dadamcah, S.A. (1972) 'Hong Kong's Booming Movie Business', *Penang (Malaysia) Star*, 2 August, p. 13.

David, J. (1987) 'Film Education Comes of Age', *Midweek*, 16 September, pp. 31–3.

Davies, D. (1973) 'Looking Back with Donald Davies', *Sunday Gazette* (Penang), 24 June.

Dawn (1984) 'Film Industry's Problems', 18 July.

D'Cruz, F. (1978) 'Mass Communication in Indonesia', *AMCB*, June, pp. 8–11.

de Castro, P. III (1986a) 'How Much Does It Cost To Produce a Dream Movie' in C. del Mundo, jr (ed.) *Philippine Mass Media: A Book of Readings*, Communication Foundation of Asia, Manila, pp. 104–8.

de Castro, P. III (1986b) 'Philippine Cinema (1976–1978)' in C. del Mundo, jr (ed.) *Philippine Mass Media: A Book of Readings*, Communication Foundation of Asia, Manila, pp. 187–200.

de Pedro, E. (1985) 'A Historical View of Philippine Cinema', *Movement*, September–October, pp. 6–7.

del Mundo, C. jr (ed.) (1986) *Philippine Mass Media: A Book of Readings*, Communication Foundation of Asia, Manila.

del Mundo, C. jr (1988) 'Production, Distribution, Exhibition: Notes Toward the Development of Philippine Cinema', paper presented at First Asian Cinema Conference, Athens, Ohio, October.

Deocampo, N. (1985) *Short Film. Emergence of a New Philippine Cinema*, Communication Foundation for Asia, Manila.

Department of Information, Indonesia (1970) *The XVI Film Festival in Asia. 15–19 June 1970, Djakarta*, Jakarta.

Department of Information, Indonesia (ca 1981) *Report on Indonesian Cinema*, Jakarta.

de Silva, M.A. and R. Siriwardene (n.d.) 'The Film in Sri Lanka' in *Communication Policies in Sri Lanka*, UNESCO, Paris.

Desser, D. (1988) *Eros Plus Massacre: An Introduction to the Japanese New Wave Cinema*, Indiana University Press, Bloomington.

Dharap, B.V. (1979) *Indian Films 1977 and 1978*, Motion Picture Enterprises, Pune.

Dissanayake, W. (ed.) (1988) *Cinema and Cultural Identity, Reflections on Films from Japan, India and China*, University Press of America, Lanham, Md.

Dizon, D. (1958) 'Jose Nepomuceno', *This Week*, 20 April, pp. 10–11.

Djarot, E. (1987) 'Film as Medium for Cultural Expression'. *Solidarity*, July–August, pp. 50–58.

Doherty, T. (1984) 'Creating a National Cinema', *Asian Survey*, August, pp. 840–51.

Domingo, A.G. (1984) 'Brocka Comes to America', *Bridge*, 9:3/4, pp. 42–3.

Downing, J.D.H. (ed.) (1987) *Film and Politics in the Third World*, Praeger, New York.

Dumaual, M.V. (1985a) 'ECP "Abolition" Scaring Movie Folk', *Malaya*, 6 September, p. 11.

Dumaual, M.V. (1985b) 'EO 1051 Did Not Really Abolish ECP', *Malaya*, 30 August, p.11.

Dumaual, M.V. (1986a) 'Like a "B" Movie', *Midweek*, 23 April, pp. 36–7.

Dumaual, M.V. (1986b) 'Mowelfund Loses Gov't Subsidy', *Malaya*, 23 August, p. 12.

Dumaual, M.V. (1986c) 'Outcry Against Regal', *Midweek*, 20 August, pp. 38–9.

The Economist, (1985) 'South Korean Films Set to Make a Splash by 1988', 13–19 July, pp. 79–87.

Eichenberger, A. (1986) 'Southeast Asia: A Cinematographic Growth Region?' *Movement*, April-June, pp. 14–16.

Evan-Jones, M. (1981) 'Raymond Chow's Bid for the Big Time', *Insight*,

April, pp. 21–30.

Feria, M. (1988) 'A Kidlat Tahimik Retrospective', *Kultura*, 1:1, pp. 33–36.

Fernandez, D.G. (1988) 'The Paths of Policy: Art and Culture in the Aquino Government', paper presented at Association for Asian Studies, 25–27 March, San Francisco, Ca.

Film Comment (1969) 'Films in Vietnam', pp. 46–85.

Findlay, I. (1983) 'Hong Kong's Cinema Survives, Despite Soaring Production Costs', *Far Eastern Economic Review*, 20 October, p. 62.

Francia, L.H. (1986a) 'Film-Makers Battle with Sex, Laws and Indifference', *Far Eastern Economic Review*, 25 September, pp. 48–9.

Francia, L.H. (1986b) 'Right-wing vs. Left-wing', *Manila Chronicle*, 25 June, p. 14.

Free China Journal (1984) 'Soong Rejuvenates Film Industry with a Professional, Artistic Format', 9 September, p. 3.

Froilan, V.S. (1985) *Manual on Media Education*, Communication Foundation of Asia, Manila, pp. 71–85.

Garcia, R. (1984) 'The Exciting Films Come from the Industry's Fringes', *Far Eastern Economic Review*, 3 May, pp. 50–3.

Garcia, R. (1985) 'On the Eighth Day', *Hong Kong Professionals* 1:3, pp. 4–9.

Giron, M.V. (1980) 'Roundup on Filipino Pic Biz; Attendance Booming but Costs, Censors Hurt', *Variety*, 7 May, p. 446.

Giron, M.V. (1982) 'Many Filipino Industry Changes; Some Fear a "Nationalization"', *Variety*, 26 May, p. 39.

Giron, M.V. (1984) 'Political & Economic Woes Push Filipino Pic Ills into Back Seat; Gripes about Video and Censor', *Variety*, 9 May, p. 433.

Giron, M.V. (1985) 'Marcos Plucks Censor Thorn After Filipino Trade Tirade', *Variety*, 16 October, pp. 336, 413.

Giron, M.V. (1986a) 'Aquino To Keep Marcos Pic Laws', *Variety*, 2 April, pp. 1, 35.

Giron, M.V. (1986b) 'Philippines Film and TV Industries Impatient for Clear Govt. Policies', *Variety*, 16 July, p. 5.

Giron, M.V. (1986c) 'Philippines Task Force's Report Recommends Natl. Film Commish', *Variety*, 9 April, p. 6.

Giron, M.V. (1987) 'Manila Pic Dropoff To Be Felt Widely; Govt. Strife Hurts', *Variety*, 14 October, pp. 41, 44.

Gopalan, T.N. (1980) 'Lid Off Hindustan Photo Films. Doings, Undoings of "Gang of Four"', *Screen* (Bombay), 25 July.

Government Information Office (1978) *China Cinema. Republic of China*, Taipei.

Government Information Office (1980) *Cinema in the Republic of China Year Book*, Taipei.

Government Information Office (1984) 'The Motion Picture Law', Taipei.

Government Information Office (1985) 'Bylaws Governing the Execution of the Motion Picture Law', Taipei.

Government of India (1985) *Television in India*, Audience Research Unit, Doordarshan Kendra, New Delhi.

Graper, D.J. (1987) 'The Kung Fu Movie Genre: A Functionalist Perspective' in S. Thomas (ed.) *Culture and Communication*, Ablex, Norwood, N.J., pp. 153–58.

Gunasinghe, S. (1968) 'The Sinhala Cinema', *Ceylon Today*, February–April, pp. 95–99.

Hachimori, M. (1988) 'Jushosha Intabyu' (Interviews with Award-Winners), *Kinema Jumpo*, No. 979 (February), pp. 107–15.

Handbook of Korea, A (1979) Seoul.

Harris, P. (1988) 'Korea Will Allow U.S. Distribs Free Access to Market', *Variety*, 2 November, pp. 1, 30.

Henares, H.M. jr (1986) 'Fading Shadows on the Wall', *Philippine Inquirer*, 24 August, p. 5.

Henderson, J.W., et al. (1970) *Area Handbook for Malaysia*, US Government Printing Office, Washington, DC.

Hernando, M. (1977) 'The New Golden Age of Philippine Movies', *Ningas-Cogon*, February, pp. 18–19.

Hernando, M.A. (1986) 'Against All Odds: The Story of the Filipino Film Industry (1978–1982)' in C. del Mundo, jr (ed.), *Philippine Mass Media: A Book of Readings*, Communication Foundation of Asia, Manila, pp. 201–16.

Hitchens, G. (1969) 'Filmmaking under the Bomb', *Film Comment*, Spring, pp. 86–7.

H'ng, H.Y. (1972) 'In Search of the Real Ramlee', *Straits Times* (Kuala Lumpur), 1 November, p. 9.

Hodel, R. (1984) 'Acts of Civil Disobedience', *Bridge* 9: 3/4, pp. 31–5.

Hosillos, L. (1986) 'Movies in a Third World Country', *Movement*, April–June, pp. 17–20.

Hosillos, L. and N. Deocampo (1987) 'The Cinema in Philippines', *Cinema India-International*, 1, pp. 105–7.

Hou, J. and H. Xia (1989) Unpublished paper, presented at Society for Cinema Studies, Iowa City, Iowa, 13 April.

Ijaz, G. (1985) 'Thriving Coproductions', *Cinema India-International*, July–September, p. 78.

Ijaz, G. (1987) 'The Cinema in Pakistan', *Cinema India-International*, 1, pp. 102–4.

India Today (1980) 'Films. Who's Afraid of Censorship!' 1–15 October, pp. 66–71.

India Today (1981), 16–31 July.

Jaivin, L. (1988) 'From *The Orphan* to *Gangs*, Hong Kong Loses Innocence', *Far Eastern Economic Review*, 12 May, pp. 45–6.

Jang, H.K. (1984) 'Protectionist Policy and Mass Media Development: Film Industry in Korea', Masters thesis, University of Pennsylvania.

Jarvie, I.C. (1977) *Window on Hong Kong: A Sociological Study of the Hong Kong Film Industry and Its Audience*, Centre of Asian Studies, University of Hong Kong, Hong Kong.

Jayatilaka, A. (1982) 'Sri Lanka', in P. Cowie, (ed.) *International Film Guide*, A.S. Barnes, New York, pp. 276–8.

Jayatilaka, A. (1987) 'The Cinema in Sri Lanka', *Cinema India-International*, 1, pp. 111–2.

Kabir, A. (1979) *Film in Bangladesh*, Vintage Publications for Bangla Academy, Dacca.

Kakeo, Y. (ed.) (1985) *Omoide no Morita Yoshimitsu: Remembering Yoshimitsu Morita*, Kinema Jumpo, Tokyo.

Khan, J.A. (1957) 'The Film Industry in Pakistan', *Pakistan Quarterly*, Summer, pp. 56–64.

Khan, M.A. (1977) 'Pakistan Pix Flood Home Mart; Seek Expansion of Export Coin', *Variety*, 11 May, p. 448.

Khoo, G. (1973) 'Are Our Film Stars Paid Enough?' *Straits Times* (Kuala Lumpur), 2 December.

Kim, T-S. (1973) 'The Pro-Governmental Films and Popularity', *Dong-A Yearbook*, Dong-A Newspaper Company, Seoul.

Kinema Jumpo (1988) 'Hachijunana-nen Eigakai Judainyuusu Senshutsu' (Ten Big Events in the 87 Film Industry), No. 979 (February), pp. 216–7.

Koh, E. (1975) '60 Malaysian Film Cos. Form Chamber To Fight Govt. Moves', 5 November, p. 1.

Korea Cinema (1972) Motion Picture Promotion Corporation, Seoul, Part II.

Korea Cinema (1975) Motion Picture Promotion Corporation, Seoul.

Korea Cinema (1976) Motion Picture Promotion Corporation, Seoul.

Korea Cinema (1981) 'Present Status of Korean Motion Picture Industry', Motion Picture Promotion Corporation, Seoul.

Kuka, E. (1979) 'Distress of Cinema Theatres', *Letter* submitted to the Secretary to the Government of Maharashtra, Bombay, 8 August.

Kulkarni, V.G. (1976) 'A Mixture of Brilliance and Mindlessness', *Media*, February, pp. 8–9.

Kurasawa, A. (1987) 'Propaganda Media on Java under the Japanese 1942–1945', *Indonesia*, No. 44, pp. 59–116.

Kurasawa, A. (1988) 'Cinema in Indonesia During the Japanese Period 1942–1945', paper presented at Association for Asian Studies, San Francisco, 25 March.

Kuroda, T. (1980) 'A Survey of the Korean Film Industry', *Asian and Pacific Quarterly*, Autumn.

Ladrido, R.C. (1988) 'Eric de Guia: On Being Kidlat Tahimik', *Kultura*, 1:1, pp. 37–42.

Lanot, M.P. (1982) 'The Absentee Woman in Local Cinema', *Diliman Review*, November-December, pp. 1, 18–22.

Latif, B.A. (1987) 'The Cinema in Malaysia', *Cinema India-International*, 1, pp. 98–9.

Lau, E. (1987) 'Sense and Censorship', *Far Eastern Economic Review*, 23 July, p. 12.

Lee, Y-I. (1969) *History of Korean Film*, Korean Film Association, Seoul.

Lee, Y-I. (1981) 'Changing Trend', *Korea Cinema '81*, Motion Picture Promotion Corporation, Seoul.

Lee, Y-I. (1988) *The History of Korean Cinema: Main Currents of Korean Cinema*, Motion Picture Promotion Corporation, Seoul.

Lent, J.A. (1971) *Philippine Mass Communications: Before 1811, After 1966*, Philippine Press Institute, Manila.

Lent, J.A. (1976) 'The Motion Picture in Malaysia: History and Problems', *CILECT*, 9, pp. 19–25.

Lent, J.A. (1983a) 'Heyday of the Indian Studio System: The 1930s', *Asian Profile*, October, pp. 465–74.

Lent, J.A. (1983b) 'History and Problems of Film in Korea. Part I', *CILECT Newsletter*, June, pp. 7–15.

Lent, J.A. (1983c) 'History and Problems of Film in Korea. Part II', *CILECT Newsletter*, December, pp. 5–13.

Lent, J.A. (1984a) 'Asian Cinema: A Selected International Bibliography. Part I. East Asia, Featuring Japan', *Journal of Film and Video*, Summer, pp. 75–84.

Lent, J.A. (1984b) 'Films and Governments of the ASEAN', *Asian Cultural Quarterly*, Winter, pp. 37–49.

Lent, J.A. (1985) 'Asian Cinema: A Selected International Bibliography—Part II: Southeast and South Asia, Plus Taiwan and Korea', *Journal of Film and Video*, Summer, pp. 76–82.

Lent, J.A. (1986) 'Malaysian Film: A Brief Literature Review', *Jurnal Kewartawanan Malaysia*, April/May/June, pp. 37–8.

Leonardia, A. (1987) 'Fundamentals of Film' in C. Maslog (ed.), *Philippine Communication: An Introduction*, PACE, Laguna, pp. 238–47.

Li, Laura (1987) 'Taiwan's "New Cinema" After the Vogue', *Sinorama*, November, pp. 96–101.

Li, Li (1989) 'Speral Report on 1988 Chinese Film', *People's Daily, Overseas Edition*, 10, 11, 16 January.

Lin, N-T. (1979) 'Some Trends in the Development of the Post-War Hong Kong Cinema' in the Third Hong Kong International Film Festival, *Hong Kong Cinema Survey 1946–1968*, The Urban Council, Hong Kong, pp. 15–25.

Liu, B. (1988) 'Wang Wen-ching Sole Taiwan Golden Horse Winner', *Free China Journal*, 10 November, p. 6.

Liu, B. and E. Chow (1988) 'MTV Video Clubs Catering to Teenage Sub-Culture', *Free China Journal*, 28 November, p. 6.

Liu, W. (1987) 'Emei Film Studio: Film Production Team' in G.S. Semsel (ed.), *Chinese Film: The State of the Art in the People's Republic*, Praeger, New York, pp. 159–64.

Luhr, W. (ed.) (n.d.) *World Cinema Since 1945*. New York, Ungar.

Lumbrera, B. (1981) 'Problems in Philippine Film History', *Diliman Review*, July–August, pp. 56–61.

Luo, Y. (1989) Unpublished essay, Beijing.

Ma Van Cuong (1969) 'Newsreel and Documentary Photography in North Vietnam', *Film Comment*, Spring, p. 88.

Malaya (1985) 'Why Dan Alvaro's Solo Film Was Banned', 28 December, p. 7.

Malaysian Business (1975) 'It's Time To Share the Film Distribution Network', December, p. 9.

Malaysian Digest (1981) 'Corporation To Help Local Film Industry', 31 March, p. 5.

Malcolm, D. (1983) 'Taiwan', *Sight & Sound*, Spring, p. 81.

Manila Chronicle (1948) 'Better Pictures Will Solve Present Crisis in Local Movies', 21 April, p. 75.

Manila Standard (1988) 'US Film Group Files Complaint Against South Korea', 28 September, p. 26.

Marchant, G. (1976) 'Film Industry Is World's Second Largest', *The Times*, London, 29 September, p. viii.

Marchetti, G. (1988) ' "Four Hundred Years in a Convent, Fifty in Hollywood": Sexual Identity and Dissent in Contemporary Philippine Cinema', *East-West Film Journal*, June, pp. 24–48.

Marshall, F. (1984) 'Cinema in Burma Today', *Cinema India-International*, July–September, pp. 89, 111.

Marshall, F. (1985) 'Brocka Puts Philippines on World Film Map', *Cinema India-International*, March, p. 126.

Marshall, F. (1987a) 'The Cinema in Burma', *Cinema India-International*, 1, p. 77.

Marshall, F. (1987b) 'The Cinema in the Republic of Korea', *Cinema India-International*, 1, pp. 108–9.

Masud, I. and M. Chandran (1986) 'Women as Catalysts of Change', *NFDC News* (Bombay), May-June.

Matsushima, T. (1986) 'Ichiya ni Shite: Gendai no Shinwa' in T. Shimaji (ed.), *Eiga Yonjunen Zenkiroku*, Kinema Jumpo, Tokyo.

Maung, M.S. (1947) 'Notes on the Burmese Cinema', in *Burmese Culture*, Indian Council of World Affairs, New Delhi, pp. 23–4.

Mazlan Nordin (1979) 'A Chance for Malay Films', *Asiaweek*, 9 February, p. 50.

Ministry of Information and Broadcasting (1978) *Film Censorship in India* (A Reference Paper), National Documentation Centre on Mass Communication, Research and Reference Division, New Delhi, 16 June.

Ministry of Public Information, Korea (n.d., ca 1967) 'Mass Communications', Korea Series No. 6, Seoul.

Miranda, O. (1986) 'Running Wild, Running Scared (Others Are Simply Running)', *Philippine Daily Inquirer*, 17 May, p. 20.

Misbach, Y.B. (ca 1982) *Indonesian Cinema: A Glance of History*, P.T. Perfin Pusat Jakarta, Jakarta.

Mitra, S. (1985) 'Cinema, The Fading Glitter', *India Today*, 31 December.

Mohd. Hamdan Adnan (1988) 'Malaysian Films: Survival or Revival', *Media Asia*, 15: 3, pp. 155–64.

Moraes, D. (1971) 'The Flesh Films', *Asia*, 7 November, pp. 9–11.

Moraes, D. (1972) 'The Film Star's Chauffeur Who Became a Movie Mogul', *Asia Magazine*, 30 April, p. 12.

Morii, M. (1989) 'Senkyuhyakuhachijuhachinendo Bideo-gyokai Kessan' (Video Industry in 1988: Summary), *Kinema Jumpo*, No. 1003 (February), pp. 275–81.

Morning News (1984) 'Cinemas Showing Blue Films Will Cease To Exist: Zia', 16 July, p. 12.

Moses, C. and C. Maslog (1978) *Mass Communication in Asia: A Brief History*, Asian Mass Communication Research and Information Centre, Singapore.

The Motion Picture Code of Ethics (1960) Eirin Sustaining Committee, Tokyo.

Motion Picture Export Association of America (MPEAA) (1989) *Report to the United States Trade Representative: International Trade Restrictions Facing MPEAA Member Companies*, Washington, D.C., March.

Movement (1986) 'Film and Politics', April–June, p. 2.

Muslim (1984) 'Zia Promises All Help To Bolster Film Industry', 16 July, p. 1.

Myers, H. (1982) 'Rivals of Shaw, Chow: Bang Bang, CC, Century, Feng Huang and Seasonal', *Variety*, 12 May, p. 319.

Mysore Math, S.G. (1985) 'Liberal Incentives To Boost Kannada Cinema', *Screen*, 9 August.

National Film Development Corporation of India (NFDC) (1988) *NFDC News* (Bombay), October–November.

New Straits Times (1976) 'Subtitles in Bahasa for All Films', 26 May, p. 1.

Ng, P.T. (1972a) 'Flicker of Hope on the Screen', *Straits Times* (Kuala Lumpur), 9 October, p. 11.

Ng, P.T. (1972b) 'What Went Wrong with the Smash Hits of the 50s', *Sunday Times* (Kuala Lumpur), 8 October, p. 10.

287

Nguyen H. (1978) 'Erasing Vietnam's Past', *Index on Censorship*, November–December, pp. 18–20.

Nguyen T. (1987) 'The Cinema in Vietnam', *Cinema India-International*, 1, pp. 118–9.

Noordin S. (1972) 'Sex, Violence and the Jelak (Fed Up) Principle', *Straits Times* (Kuala Lumpur), 1 October.

Nukumizu, Y. (1981) *'No Yo na Mono' (Something Like Yoshiwara*: Interview with Morita), *Kinema Jumpo*, No. 823 (October), pp. 107–09.

Ocampo, S. (1982) 'Hollywood Revisited', *Far Eastern Economic Review*, 5 February, p. 12.

O'Leary, D.M. (1976) 'A Mixture of Brilliance and Mindlessness', *Media*, February, pp. 3–15.

Onn, C.K. (1946) *Malaya Upside Down*, Jitts and Co., Singapore.

Park, S-H. (1988) 'Korean Directors, Writers Stage Protest Against Yank Releases', *Variety*, 5 October, p. 36.

Parrish, F. (n.d. ca 1966) 'Korea's Motion Picture Industry', *Free World*, 16:8, pp. 37–41.

Pendakur, M. (1985) 'Dynamics of Cultural Policy Making: The U.S. Film Industry in India', *Journal of Communication*, Autumn, pp. 52–72.

Pendakur, M. (1988a) 'Mass Media During the 1975 National Emergency in India', *Canadian Journal of Communication*, December, pp. 32–48.

Pendakur, M. (1988b) 'Indian Television Comes of Age. Liberalization and the Rise of Consumer Culture', *Communication*, 11:1, Summer.

Philippine Times (1979) 'RP Cinema Still a Profitable Venture', 20 August, p. 8.

Pilar, S.A. (1978) 'The American Colonial Period (1900–1941): The Old Movie Melons and Lemons' in *Filipino Heritage: The Making of a Nation*, Lahing Pilipino Publishing, Manila, pp. 2470–2477.

Pomery, C. (1985) 'Raymond Chow Movie King', *Asia Magazine*, 17 November, pp. 25–9.

Prajavani (1986) (Bangalore) 31 January.

Quirino, J. (1983) *Don Jose and Early Philippine Cinema*, Phoenix, Quezon City.

Racketts, A. (1981) 'So. Korea Loses Film Theatres; Tense Political Year a Drag; Fans Unpredictable', *Variety*, 13 May, p. 256.

Ramachandran, T.M. (ed.) (1985) *70 Years of Indian Cinema (1913–1983)*, Cinema India-International, Bombay.

Ranawake, E. (1976) 'Sri Lanka: Fruits of Nationalisation', *Media*, February, p. 15.

Rasheed, J. (1986) 'Formula for Mediocrity', *Far Eastern Economic Review*, 17 June, pp. 51–53.

Ratnam, R. (1972) 'The Ever-Growing Enterprise in Southeast Asia—Shaw Brothers', *Straits Echo* (Penang), 31 July, p. 11.

Reyes, E.A. (1986) '1984: Towards the Development of a Nationalist Cinema' in C. del Mundo, jr (ed.), *Philippine Mass Media: A Book of Readings*, Communication Foundation of Asia, Manila, pp. 217–26.

Richie, D. (1983) 'Notes on Mitsuo Yanagimachi—A New Japanese Director', *Film Criticism*, 8, No. 1 (Fall), pp. 7–11.

Roces, A. (1965) 'The Bakya Mentality', *Manila Times*, 12 March.

Ryu, I-S. (1987) 'The Cinema in the Democratic Republic of Korea', *Cinema India-International*, 1, pp. 84–5.

Salumbides, V. (1952) *Motion Pictures in the Philippines*, Author, Manila.

Samdani, Z. (1984) 'Full-fledged Status To Be Accorded to Film Industry: Zia', *Dawn*, 16 July, p. 8.

Sananchit, B.(1984) 'A Bleak Future for Good Films', *Far Eastern Economic Review*, 3 May, pp. 63–4.

Savarimutti, R. (1977) *Development of Sinhala Cinema 1947–1967*, OCIC Publications, Colombo.

Sawamura, T. (1944) 'For the Glory of Philippine Movies', *Philippine Review*, March, pp. 53–56; April, pp. 50–53.

Sazon, E. (1986) 'Film Distribution and Exhibition' in C. del Mundo, jr (ed.), *Philippine Mass Media: A Book of Readings*, Communication Foundation of Asia, Manila, pp. 113–20.

Schlender, B.R. (1985) 'Hong Kong Film Makers Look Abroad', *Asian Wall Street Journal*, 28 February, pp. 1, 7.

Scott, M. (1986) 'Strict Censors Make for Good Neighbours', *Far Eastern Economic Review*, 25 September, p. 50.

Scott, M. (1987) 'The Good Neighbour Steps Outside the Law', *Far Eastern Economic Review*, 14 May, p. 58.

Screen (1985) 6 December.

The Sea and Poison (1986) English Programme Note, Herald, Tokyo.

Segers, F. (1988) 'Americans Go for the Gold in South Korea', *Variety*, 8 June, p. 32.

Segers, F. (1989a) 'Japan in '88 Appeared to Ready a Showbiz "Takeover" ', *Variety*, 11–17 January, p. 78.

Segers, F. (1989b) ' "Last Emperor" Stood Tall in Japan, But Foreign Pix Did Slack Biz Overall', *Variety*, 25–31 January, p. 22.

Semsel, G.S. (ed.) (1987) *Chinese Film: The State of the Art in the People's Republic*, Praeger, New York.

Shahini, C.R. (1988) 'Is the (Philippine) Commission on Culture a Good Idea?' *Philippine Studies Newsletter*, March, pp. 19–25.

Shao, M. (1984) 'Summary of Casual Thinking on Film Aesthetics', *Film Art*, November.

Shinoda, Y. (1986) 'ATG no Yume to Genjutsu' (ATG: Dream and Reality) in T. Shimaji (ed.), *Eiga Yonjunen no Kiroku: The Complete Data Book of Motion Picture*, Kinema Jumpo, Tokyo.

Shin, S.S. and M.W. Kim (1988) 'Sex on the Screen in Seoul?' *Asiaweek*, 19 February, p. 66.

Sipe, J. (1988) 'A Venomous Flap Over Film Distribution Rights', *Far Eastern Economic Review*, 6 October, p. 50.

Siriwardene, R. (1977) 'Film-makers Look for an Audience', *Far Eastern Economic Review*, 14 January, p. 35.

Soongnarata, T. (1977) 'Brief Background in Film Productions, Thailand', presented at AMIC seminar on Some Aspects of the Multi-Media Approach to Mass Communication, Bangkok, 4–6 November.

Sotto, A. (1982) 'Philippines' in P. Cowie (ed.), *International Film Guide 1982*, A.S. Barnes, New York, pp. 249–51.

Sotto, A.L. (1987) 'Notes on the Filipino Action Film', *East-West Film Journal*, June, pp. 1–14.

Specter, M. (1983) 'Kung fu Loses the Cinematic Fight to a New Wave of Realism', *Far Eastern Economic Review*, 22 December, pp. 82–3.

Stevenson, R. (1974) 'Cinemas and Censorship in Colonial Malaya', *Journal of Southeast Asian Studies*, September, pp. 209–24.

Straits Echo (1973) 'Most Penangites in Favour of Sex Film Ban', 20 July.

Straits Echo (1973) 'Three Film Censorship Agencies for Malaysia', 5 November.

Straits Times (1972) 'Film Stars Set Up $5 Mil. Company', 24 October.

Straits Times (1972) 'Govt Is Urged To Set Up Cinemas in the States', 5 November, p. 1.

Straits Times (1972) 'Enough!—Cry Sex Film Goers', 3 December, p. 1.

Straits Times (1973) 'Film Censorship', 13 July. p. 4.

Subba Rao, V.N. (1984) *Kannada Talkies Golden Jubilee, 1934–1984*, Government of Karnataka and Karnataka Film Chamber of Commerce, Bangalore.

Sudan, I.M. (1985) 'Origin and Growth of Cinema in Burma', *Cinema India-International*, January-March, pp. 113–15.

Sukwonga, D. and K. Kounavudhi (1987) 'The Cinema in Thailand', *Cinema India-International*, 1, pp. 116–17.

Sun, S. (1982) 'A Hong Kong Formula for Hollywood Success', *Asia*, November-December, pp. 38–43.

Suwunpukdee, P. (1988) 'Thai Films: Survival or Revival', *Media Asia*, 15: 3, pp. 165–8.

Takahashi, S. (1989) 'Senkyuhyakuhachijuhachinendo Kessan Tokushu: Nihon Eigo' (Japanese Film in 1988: Summary), *Kinema Jumpo*, No. 1003 (February), pp. 102–5.

Tang, B.B. (1975) 'Cinema in the Republic of China', Masters thesis, California State University, Northridge.

Tayama, R. (1988) 'Senkyuhyakuhachijunana-nendo Kessan Tokushu 1: Nihon Eiga' (Japanese Cinema in 1987: Summary), *Kinema Jumpo*, No. 979 (February) pp. 110–13.

Teneze, I. (1983) 'Le Cinema en Malaisie', *La Revue du Cinema*, February, pp. 94–6.

Teng, C. (1987) 'Film Critics in the Limelight', *Sinorama*, November, pp. 102–5.

Teng, W. (1987) 'Teng Wenji, Middle-Aged New Director' in G.S. Semsel (ed.), *Chinese Film: The State of the Art in the People's Republic*, Praeger, New York, pp. 115–24.

Thomas, S. (ed.) (1982) *Film/Culture: Exploration of Cinema in Its Social Context*, The Scarecrow Press, Metuchen, N.J. and London.

Tilden, N.A. (1975) 'Hong Kong Film', Masters thesis, San Francisco State University, San Francisco.

Time (1976) 'Asia's Bouncing World of Movies', 28 June, pp. 40–3.

Tiongson, N.G. (1980) 'Stage to Screen', *International Popular Culture*, 1: 1, pp. 60–7.

Tiongson, N.G. (ed.) (1984) *The Politics of Culture: The Philippine Experience*, Philippine Educational Theatre Association, Manila.

Tiongson, N.G. (1986) 'The Filipino Film Industry: History, Profile, Problems and Prospects' in National Conference on the Role of Communication in the Philippines after the Revolution, *Complete Set of Papers and Recommendations*, Philippine Association of Communication Educators and Asia Foundation, Laguna, pp. 1–26.

Tobias, M. (1981) 'Hong Kong Newcomers' Aim Beyond Chop Socky', *Variety*, 14 October, pp. 194, 222.

Tobias, M. (1982) 'Pass or Fail Time for Manila Fest in '83; Big Far East Push', *Variety*, 24 November, pp. 7, 30.

Tobias, M (1985) 'There's No Biz Like Shaw Biz', *Cinema India-International*, January–March, pp. 119–120.

Tobias, M. (1987a) 'The Cinema in Taiwan', *Cinema India-International*, 1, p. 115.

Tobias, M. (1987b) 'The Hong Kong Film Industry Grew To Be a Flourishing Biz From Ancient Roots in 1898', *Variety*, 6 May, p. 520.

Tobias, M. (1987c) 'Video Biz in Hong Kong Goes from Hole-in-Wall Venture to Big Industry', *Variety*, 6 May, p. 548.

Tripathi, S. (1989) 'Ganga Jamuna Saraswathi. Formula Failure', *India Today*, 31 January.

United Asia (1961) 'The Asian Film', 13: 5, pp. 257–311.

Urban Council (n.d.) *A Study of the Hong Kong Martial Arts Film*, Urban Council, Hong Kong.

Urban Council (1978) *Cantonese Cinema Retrospective (1950–1959)*, The Sixth Hong Kong International Film Festival, Urban Council, Hong Kong.

Urban Council (1982) *Cantonese Cinema Retrospective (1960–69)*, The Sixth Hong Kong International Film Festival, Urban Council, Hong Kong.

Urban Council (1984) *The 8th Hong Kong International Film Festival*, Urban Council, Hong Kong.

Urban Council (1985) *The Tradition of Hong Kong Comedy*, The Ninth Hong Kong International Film Festival, Urban Council, Hong Kong.

Urban Council (1986) *Ten Years of Hong Kong Cinema (1976–85)*, The Tenth Hong Kong International Film Festival, Urban Council, Hong Kong.

Variety (1976) 'South Korea Might Up U.S. Features', 11 August, p. 4.

Variety (1977) 'Crown Colony Censorship', 4 May, p. 58.

Variety (1978) 'Filipino Censorship a Model for Control over Pic Content', 17 May, p. 427.

Variety (1982) 'Sri Lanka Cuts Down on Imported Features', 6 October, p. 35.

Variety (1985a) 'Archives Shift to Snippers Hit', 16 October, pp. 339, 413.

Variety (1985b) 'Pres. Marcos' Anti-Piracy Edict Hits Plight of Philippine Film Biz', 16 October, pp. 339, 392.

Variety (1986a) 'Anti-Marcos Auteur Lino Brocka Returns with Pic, TV Projects', 22 October, p. 442.

Variety (1986b) 'Golden Harvest, Cinema City, Others Fill Vacuum Left in H.K. by Shaw Bros. Production Exit', 22 October, p. 443.

Variety (1986c) 'Indonesia's Unique in Way It Exhibits and Distribs Films', 22 October, p. 443.

Variety (1986d) 'Jakarta's Ali Hassan Bats 99% at Natl. B.O. with Lower-Class Pitch', 22 October, p. 442.

Variety (1987a) 'Hong Kong To Clarify Its Censorship Policies', 13 May, p. 56.

Variety (1987b) 'Taiwan Pic Industry Breaks Out of Nuts-and-Bolts Mold with a New Breed of Young Filmmakers', 6 May, p. 521.

Variety (1988) 'UIP Runs Korean Gantlet', 28 September, p. 8.

Vatikiotis, M. (1989) 'Indonesian Film Fare', *Far Eastern Economic Review*, 9 March, pp. 66–7.

Vertido, C. (1988) 'The Filipino Film Industry', *Media Asia*, 15: 3, pp. 128–33.

Warnasiri, D.B. (1977) 'Point of View', *Cinema Asia/Cinema Africa*, No. 2, pp. 4–8.

Warren, W. (1983) 'Thailand's Anonymous Andy Warhols', *Asia*, January–February, pp. 32–37, 48.

Weber, M.J. (1986) 'What Makes Run Run Run?' *American Film*, June, pp. 36–9.

Wong, K-C. (1979) 'A Song in Every Film' in The Third Hong Kong International Film Festival, *Hong Kong Cinema Survey 1946–1968*, Urban Council, Hong Kong, pp. 29–32.

Wong, S. (1986) 'Fighting for Their Lives' *On Video*, November, pp. 22–3.

Wong, S.Y. (1984) 'Death of the Swashbuckler', *Singapore Monitor*, 24 September, p. 16.

Woollacott, M. (1976) 'Carry on Copying', *Communicator*, October, pp. 35–6.

Xie, F. (1984) 'My View of the Concept of Film', *Film Art*, December.

Yajima, M. (1986) 'Tokushu: *Yari no Gonza*: Intabyu: Shinoda Masahiro' (*Gonza the Spearman*: Special Issue: Interview with Masahiro Shinoda), *Kinema Jumpo*, No. 927 (January), pp. 50–5.

Yoon, B-C. (n.d. ca 1966) 'A Veteran Recalls the Early Years', *Free World*, 16: 8, p. 39.

INTERVIEWS

Conducted by John A. Lent

Alcala, larry, cartoonist, Manila, Philippines, September 1988.

Arif Nizami, executive editor, *Nawa-i-Waqt*, Lahore, Pakistan, 9 July 1984.

Avellana, Lamberto, director and proprietor of Documentaries Co., Manila, Philippines, 15 June 1965 and 16 August 1986.

Bernal, Ishmael, director, Quezon City, Philippines, 16 August 1986.

Brocka, Lino, director, Quezon City, Philippines, 20 August 1986.

Chan, David, vice-president of production, Golden Communications Company (Golden Harvest), Hong Kong, 13 August 1986.

Chang, C.M., manager, Motion Picture Promotion Corporation, Seoul, Korea, 12 October 1982.

Chang King-Yuh, director-general, Government Information Office, Taipei, Taiwan, 6 August 1986.

Chao, Benny C.P., producer, head of productions, Central Motion Picture Company, Taipei, Taiwan, 5 August 1986.

Chen Kun-Hou, director, Taipei, Taiwan, 9 August 1986.

Chen, Yao-Chi (a.k.a. Richard Chen), movie director, Taipei, Taiwan, 7 August 1986.

Chiang Tsou-Ming, director, Motion Picture Department, Government Information Office, Taipei, Taiwan, 5 August 1986.

Chou, H.S., president, Motion Picture Association of Taiwan, Taipei, Taiwan, 4 August 1986.

Chou Ling-Kong, Fee Tang Motion Picture Co., Taipei, Taiwan, 6 August 1986.

Cinco, Manuel 'Fyke,' director, Quezon City, Philippines, 22 August 1986.

del Mundo, Clodualdo jr, scriptwriter, in Athens, Ohio, 8 October 1988.

Fabregas, Jimmy, actor, music scorer, Regal Productions, Quezon City, Philippines, 21 August 1986.

Fan, Frank, general manager, United Artists of China, MGM of China, Paramount of China, Universal of China, Taipei, Taiwan, 5 August 1986.

Fong, Allen (Fong Yuk-Ping), director, Hong Kong, 11 August 1986.

Gallaga, Peque, director, Regal Productions, Quezon City, Philippines, 20 August 1986.

Goonsekera, Anura, director-general, Rupavahini (TV) Corporation of Sri Lanka, in Singapore, 20 November 1986.

Han Chae Soo, film critic, Seoul, Korea, 7 October 1982.

Hsu, Li-Kong, director, Film Library; publisher, *Film Review*, Taipei, Taiwan, 8 August 1986.

Hu, Joe-Yang, president, Empire Audio Visual Company, Taipei, Taiwan, 6 August 1986.

Hu Ying Mon, actress, Taipei, Taiwan, 9 August 1986.

Huang, Paul, video section chief, Department of Radio and Television, Government Information Office, Taipei, Taiwan, 7 August 1986.

Krishnan, Dato L., managing director, Gaya Filem, Kuala Lumpur, Malaysia, 17 November 1986.

Kuang, Sunshine, director, Department of Radio and Television, Government Information Office, Taipei, Taiwan, 8 August 1986.

Lacaba, Jose "Pete," scriptwriter, Quezon City, Philippines, 22 August 1986.

Lam, Peter, distribution manager, Cinema City, Hong Kong, 12 August 1986.

Lan Tsu-Wei, reporter, Editing Department, *United Daily News*, Taipei, Taiwan, 7 August 1986.

Law Wai-Ming, director, Hong Kong, 12 August 1986.

Lee, Alan, Golden Harvest Motion Picture Co., Taipei, Taiwan, 4 August 1986.

Lee Daw-Ming, filmmaker, Taipei, Taiwan, 3 August 1986; Philadelphia, Pa., 10 August 1988.

Lee Jin Keun, president, Motion Picture Promotion Corporation of Korea, Seoul, Korea, 12 October 1982.

Lee Pai-Kwi, managing director, Golden Harvest Motion Picture Co., Taipei, Taiwan, 4 August 1986.

Lee, Ricky, scriptwriter, Quezon City, Philippines, 22 August 1986.

Li Cheuk-To, programme co-ordinator, Hong Kong International Film Festival, and editor-in-chief, *Film Bi-Weekly*, Hong Kong, 11 August 1986.

Li Yuan (Hsiao Yeh), creative director and scriptwriter, Central Motion Picture Corporation, Taipei, Taiwan, 9 August 1986.

Liao Hsiang-Hsiong, director, Department of Audio Visual Services, Government Information Office, Taipei, Taiwan, 7 August 1986.

Liu Shou-Chi, deputy director, Motion Picture Department, Government Information Office, Taipei, Taiwan, 5 August 1986.

Muzaffar Abbas, director, Pakistan Information Service Academy, Lahore, Pakistan, 12 July 1984.

Navarro, Mr, studio manager, Premiere Productions, Manila, Philippines, 9 June 1965.

Nettleton, John, director, Filem Negara, Kuala Lumpur, Malaysia, 25 January 1973.

Raman Kutty, K.V., film lecturer, University of Kerala, in New Delhi, India, 28 August 1986.

Rani, Devika, former actress, New Delhi, 21, 22, 23 July, 14, 15 August 1980.

Shi Nansun, director and executive manager, Cinema City, Hong Kong, 12 August 1986.

Suzara, Romy, director, Viva, Quezon City, Philippines, 22 August 1986.

Tchii, Danny, owner, ESC Incorporated, Taipei, Taiwan, 5 August 1986.

Tecson, Jeremias, studio manager, LVN Studios, 25 May 1965.

Tobias, Mel, film reviewer and *Variety* correspondent, Hong Kong, 13 August 1986.

Tu, Richard C., managing director, China Yu-Lo Motion Picture Co., Taipei, Taiwan, 4 August 1986.

Wan Jen, movie director, Taipei, Taiwan, 7 August 1986.

Wang Ming-Tsann, production manager, Hsiu-Cher Motion Picture Co., Taipei, Taiwan, 4 August 1986.

Yao, Wade, foreign sales director, Tom Son Motion Picture Co., Taipei, Taiwan, 4 August 1986.

Yu Hyun-Mok, director, Seoul, Korea, 7 October 1982.

Conducted by Keiko McDonald:
Ogawa, Shinsuka, documentary filmmaker, in Honolulu, Hawaii, December 1988.

Conducted by Manjunath Pendakur:
Anandan, Filmnews, journalist, 9 December 1985.

Broca, N.S., chief executive, Parakash Mehra Productions, Bombay, India, 13 July 1985.

Gandhiraman, Mohan, president, Film Employees Federation of South India, Madras, India, 11 December 1985.

Palekar, Amol, producer-director, Bombay, India, 17 July 1985.

Shetty, Manmohan, partner, Adlabs, Bombay, India, 5 July 1985.

Conducted by George S. Semsel:
Chen Mei, editor, *World Cinema*, Beijing, China, 2 February 1985; and Iowa City, Iowa, 14 April 1989.

Chen Xiaolin, branch head, China Film Distribution and Exhibition Corporation, Beijing, China, Winter 1985.

Cheng Jihua, film historian, Iowa City, Iowa, 14 April 1989.

Teng Wenji, director, Beijing, China, 1987.

Xie, Fei, deputy head, Beijing Film Academy, Beijing, China, Spring 1985; Athens, Ohio, Winter 1987.

CORRESPONDENCE

Ni Zhen, head of theoretical studies, Beijing Film Institute, to George S. Semsel, 16 March 1989.

Rani, Devika, former Indian actress, to John A. Lent, 20 and 22 October 1980; 27 February and 25 August 1981; 15 January 1982; 27 July 1983; 8 February and 24 July 1984 and 1 November 1985.

ABOUT THE
AUTHORS

Dr John A. Lent was a pioneer in the study of international communications, and especially Third World mass media. His works include at least 35 books and monographs he has written or edited and more than 300 articles published in journals in 30 countries. Many of Lent's works have been described as definitive. Listed in numerous biographical books, including Marquis' *Who's Who in the World* and *Who's Who in America*, Lent has studied in Norway, Mexico, Japan and India. He was a Fulbright Scholar to the Philippines; first co-ordinator of the pioneering mass communications programme in Malaysia, and visiting Benedum distinguished professor at Bethany (W.Va.) College. He has taught in many universities in the United States, Malaysia and the Philippines; he has been professor at Temple University since 1976. Professor Lent founded the Malaysia/Singapore/Brunei Studies Group, which he chaired for seven years; has been founding editor of *Berita* since 1975, and is managing editor of *WittyWorld*, an international cartoon magazine.

Dr Keiko I. McDonald is associate professor of Japanese literature and cinema in the Department of East Asian Languages and Literatures, University of Pittsburgh. She has written many articles on Japanese film and is a frequent presenter of papers at conferences.

Dr Manjunath Pendakur is associate professor and director, Program on Communication and Development Studies, Northwestern University, USA. He worked as associate director in the Indian film industry before going to the United States. Currently writing a book on Indian cinema, Pendakur has written numerous articles on mass communications.

Dr George S. Semsel, filmmaker and associate professor of film

297

at Ohio University, spent 1984 and 1985 working as a 'foreign expert' in the China Film Export and Import Corporation, Beijing. The experience brought him into frequent contact with many of China's filmmakers and led to his book, *Chinese Film: The State of the Art in the People's Republic*. Recently named a Fulbright Scholar at Xiamen University, Semsel is completing an English translation of contemporary film theory. His latest film, *China Lessons*, had its premiere at the 1989 Athens (Ohio) International Film Festival.

INDEX

Subject Index

acting
  Japan 43–5
  Korea 132–4
  Pakistan 260–1
  Philippines 165–73
  Taiwan 69–71, 77
  Thailand 219–20
  Sri Lanka 273–4
action films 173, 175, 260–1,
  275
adivasis
admission prices
  Bangladesh 265
  Burma 223
  Indonesia 209
  Japan 47–8
  Korea 134
  Philippines 165
  Singapore 198
  Thailand 215
advertising 215, 245
ancient costume musical 64
animal films 40, 56
animation
  Burma 221
  Japan 57
  Korea 132
  Philippines 156, 182
  Thailand 220
arnande 221
'art' films and theatres
  China 20, 28–9
  Hong Kong 119
  Japan 36
  Taiwan 87

bakya 157–89, 167
bangsawan 188
'black money' 236, 264–5
blockbuster films 38–9, 41, 131
bomba 157–8, 170, 174–5
bookers 209, 265
box office (*includes* audiences,
  marketplace) 29–30
  Bangladesh 265
  China 13–16, 23, 25, 30–2
  Hong Kong 100–1, 103, 107
  India 2, 234–5
  Indonesia 209
  Japan 34, 37, 41, 43, 46
  Korea 135–6, 141
  Malaysia 195
  Philippines 161, 164
  Singapore 198
  Taiwan 73, 81, 86
  Thailand 218, 220
budgets
  Hong Kong 104–5
  India 231–2, 235–6
  Indonesia 210
  Japan 41–2
  Malaysia 194
  Pakistan 258–9
  Philippines 160

Taiwan 66–7
Thailand 214–5
bumiputra 191, 193
casting 14, 45, 70
censorship 6, 24–5
  Bangladesh 266–7
  Burma 223
  Hong Kong 94, 117–18
  India 236, 242–5
  Indonesia 204, 206, 210
  Japan 48–51
  Korea 125, 137–8
  Malaysia 186–8, 196–7
  Pakistan 257–8, 261–2
  Philippines 149–50, 166, 174,
    176–8
  Singapore 198–9
  Sri Lanka 275
  Taiwan 65, 77–9

chambara 36
comedy 4–5, 37, 83–4
  Hong Kong 116
  Korea 139
  Philippines 174–5
comic-book movies
  Japan 39, 43, 58
  Philippines 155, 168, 173
commercialisation of film
  China 29–30
  India 2, 245–6, 248
  Japan 40, 54
  Philippines 157, 159–60,
    169–70
  Thailand 219
contract system 32–3, 68, 153,
  157, 159
co-productions 7, 31, 41, 63
  Hong Kong 100, 104
  India 237–8
  Indonesia 211
  Korea 131
  Malaysia 194
  Pakistan 259
  Philippines 162
  Thailand 217
copyright
  Japan 52–3
  Taiwan 80, 82, 90
  Thailand 214
critics 24
cultural films 132, 135, 188
dialect films
  Hong Kong 93, 95–6, 100,
    116
  India 230–1
  Indonesia 203
  Pakistan 256, 263
  Taiwan 63
directing
  Hong Kong 100, 110–3
  Japan 43–5
  Korea 132–4
  Pakistan 260–1

Philippines 165–73
Sri Lanka 273–4
Taiwan 69–71
Thailand 219–20
directors 5–6
  China 19–27
  Hong Kong 110–2
  India 251
  Indonesia 210–2
  Japan 38, 43–5, 54–5
  Korea 132–4
  Malaysia 260
  Philippines 158, 165–73
  Sri Lanka 268, 273–4
  Taiwan 61–2, 69–71, 79, 84,
    86, 89
  Thailand 219–20
documentary film 34, 57, 198,
  243–4, 255, 269
dubbers 213, 219
distribution
  Bangladesh 264–5
  China 15–6, 27, 31
  Hong Kong 95, 97, 105–9
  India 2, 233–5, 238–9, 241
  Indonesia 208–10, 224
  Japan 39, 42, 45–8, 51–3
  Korea 122–3, 134–7
  Malaysia 194–5
  Pakistan 255, 259–60
  Philippines 163–5, 179
  Singapore 198
  Sri Lanka 267, 269–73
  Taiwan 71–7, 79–80
  Thailand 217–19

equipment
  China 14, 18–19
  Korea 126, 130–1
  Malaysia 191
  Philippines 152, 161
  Sri Lanka 270, 274
  Taiwan 61, 87
  Thailand 215
escapist films 4, 114–15, 174
exhibition 31
  Bangladesh 264–5
  Hong Kong 105–9
  India 230, 233–5, 238
  Indonesia 208–10
  Japan 45–48, 53
  Korea 122–3, 134–5
  Malaysia 194–5
  Pakistan 259–60
  Philippines 154, 163–5
  Singapore 198
  Sri Lanka 270–3
  Taiwan 71–7
  Thailand 218–19
  see also theatres
experimental films 27–9, 88,
  117, 165

family films 55

fantasy films 174
film as literature 16–7
film festivals 7, 58–9, 88–9, 119, 143, 181–2, 198, 212, 239
foreign films (*includes* imports) 6, 46–7
  Bangladesh 264
  Burma 223
  Hong Kong 104–5
  India 240–2
  Indonesia 205–7
  Korea 122–3, 135–6, 143–4
  Pakistan 255
  Philippines 161, 176–7
  Sri Lanka 267, 269–72, 274
  Taiwan 74–6, 78, 81
  Thailand 216
foreign markets (*includes* exports)
  Hong Kong 103, 105–6, 109
  India 239–40
  Indonesia 208
  Korea 128, 136
  Malaysia 189, 194
  Pakistan 259–60
  Philippines 162–3
  Taiwan 71–2, 88–9
frottage 6
funding (*includes* investment)
  Bangladesh 263–5
  China 31–3
  Hong Kong 95, 101–3
  India 229–38
  Japan 37–9, 41–2
  Korea 127, 131
  Pakistan 258–9
  Philippines 156, 161
  Sri Lanka 269–71
  Taiwan 67–8, 77
genres *see* themes
government
  ownership 63
  protectionist moves 6, 190, 206
  regulation 48–52, 64, 66, 75–9, 81–2, 90, 117–18, 127–9, 137–9, 149–50, 175–81, 186–8, 192–3, 195–9, 209, 211–12, 214, 216, 222–3, 236–45, 257–8, 261–2, 266–7
  subsidies 17–8, 48, 67, 127, 149–50, 222, 236

han 139–40
history
  Bangladesh 262–3
  Burma 221–2
  China 20–22
  Hong Kong 92–101
  Indonesia 202–7
  Japan 35–9
  Korea 123–9
  Malaysia 186–93
  North Korea 143
  Pakistan 254–7
  Philippines 150–8
  Sri Lanka 267–70
  Taiwan 62–5
  Thailand 212–14
Hollywood 23, 25, 30, 35, 41, 98, 104, 136, 140, 150, 153, 159, 186, 211, 217, 242
horror films 84

independent filmmaking 34
  China 11–2, 16, 27–33
  Japan 40, 45
  Philippines 156–7, 182
  Taiwan 66
  Thailand 213
'interpolation' 243

jidaigeki 36–7, 58
jotra 266

kedgeree 3
kino-drama 124
komiks 155, 168, 173
kung fu films 4–5, 65, 71–2, 83–4, 100, 105–6, 115–16
kung fu comedy 5, 113, 116

lagare 165
'literary film' 23
love story films 83–4, 213

martial arts films
  China 30, 113
  Hong Kong 115–16
  Korea 136, 139
  Sri Lanka 274
  see kung fu films, kung fu comedy
masala films 3, 236
melodrama 5, 37, 65, 70, 96
  Hong Kong 113
  India 249
  Korea 139–40
  Malaysia 195
  Philippines 167, 172–5
  Thailand 224
monopolisation 159, 163–4, 169–71, 176, 192, 194, 218, 236, 245, 267, 269
movie posters 220
movies on television clubs (MTV) 81, 80–90
multilingualism/multiculturalism 3, 14, 192–3, 197, 245, 275
music 96, 133, 213–14, 229, 250
music video 30

naadagam 267
'new cinema'
  India 229, 231, 248–51
  Sri Lanka 269
  Taiwan 61, 66, 68–70, 83–7
  see 'new wave'
'new wave' (*includes* 'socially relevant')
  China 20, 28
  Hong Kong 100, 110–13, 117
  Malaysia 194–5
  Philippines 158, 166, 175
  Sri Lanka 273–4
non-resident Indians 241

ownership 6, 35, 40–1, 63, 68, 73, 99, 101–2, 194

pakikisama 158
'pene' films 6, 174
photography 133
plagiarism 253, 256, 263, 266, 268
politics and film 3, 30, 96–7, 105, 116–17, 180, 186–8, 202–3, 229, 243–5, 256–7, 263, 266, 270–1, 275
preservation of film (*includes* archives) 7, 87–8, 119, 142, 181, 212, 267
press 196
production
  Bangladesh 264–5
  Burma 222
  China 12, 30, 32–3
  Hong Kong 93–4, 99, 101–5
  India 230, 233
  Indonesia 207–8
  Japan 35–8, 40–2
  Korea 127, 130–2
  Malaysia 188–92
  Pakistan 256, 258–9
  Philippines 159–63
  Singapore 198
  Sri Lanka 270–3
  Taiwan 65–9, 77, 83
  Thailand 214–18
professionalism 7
  Bangladesh 267
  Hong Kong 119–20
  Indonesia 212
  Japan 58–60
  Korea 141–2
  Philippines 170, 181–3
  Taiwan 87–9
  Thailand 215–16
promotion of film
  Hong Kong 119
  India 239
  Indonesia 212
  Japan 58–9
  Korea 128–9
  Philippines 156
  Taiwan 72, 74, 87
propaganda films
  China 14, 23
  Hong Kong 93, 118
  Indonesia 202–5
  Korea 124, 132, 138–9
  Malaysia 186–8, 192
  Philippines 158, 180
  Taiwan 62–3, 83
pwe 221

quotas 6, 46–7, 74–6, 123, 135–6, 141, 161, 206–7, 272

ratings (classification) system
  Hong Kong 118
  Japan 49
  Korea 137
  Philippines 164, 178
  Taiwan 77–9
religious taboos 3, 118, 197
roman poruno 38

sarsuwela 150–1
science fiction films 39
scriptwriting

China 16–7
Hong Kong 110–13
India 237
Japan 43–5
Korea 131–4
Malaysia 185–6, 190–1
Pakistan 261
Philippines 165–73
Taiwan 69–71
seiten 36
sex themes (*includes* erotics,
    pornography, soft porn)
Hong Kong 100, 118
India 2, 242–3
Japan 36, 38–9, 42, 49–50
Korea 138–9
Malaysia 196
Pakistan 275
Philippines 157–8, 170,
    174–5, 181
Singapore 274–5
Taiwan 83
shomingeki 36, 38, 42
silent film 124–5, 151, 213,
    222, 262
'silver jubilee' 255
spectacular mega-comedy 116
star system
Burma 222
Hong Kong 104–5
India 233
Japan 45, 51
Philippines 157, 160–1, 169,
    171
Sri Lanka 268
Taiwan 65–7, 71
Thailand 213–15, 219–20
studios
China 12–6, 31
Hong Kong 105
Japan 36–9, 42
Korea 130
Pakistan 256
Philippines 152–5
Sri Lanka 268–9
Taiwan 62–3, 65
studio system 14, 89, 99, 103,
    153–5, 157, 170–1
swordplay films 64–5, 95, 113,
    115–16

taisaku shugi 38
taiyozuko 36
taxes 6
Bangladesh 264
India 234
Korea 134
Malaysia 194
Pakistan 257–60
Philippines 155, 161, 178
Singapore 198
Taiwan 62, 76, 79
Thailand 215–17
teenager (youth) films 39, 41,
    43, 195
televison 30
Burma 223
China 14–5
Hong Kong 100–1
India 238, 245–8
Indonesia 208
Japan 34, 37
Malaysia 189–90
Pakistan 258–9
Philippines 163
Sri Lanka 270–2
Taiwan 63, 80–1, 83, 87
theatres
Bangladesh 265
China 15
Hong Kong 97, 107–8
India 230, 23–4, 238
Indonesia 209–10
Japan 36, 42, 45–8, 53
Korea 134–5
Malaysia 195
Pakistan 260
Philippines 164–5
Singapore 198
Sri Lanka 271
Taiwan 72–4, 76, 80
Thailand 218–19
themes (*includes* genres)
Bangladesh 253, 266
China 23–5
Hong Kong 94
India 248–51
Indonesia 210–12
Japan 36–9, 54–8
Korea 139–41
Malaysia 195

Pakistan 275
Philippines 157–8, 173–5
Sri Lanka 269, 274–5
Taiwan 64, 83–7
Thailand 213–14
touring cinemas 230
training and education 7
Bangladesh 267
Burma 222
China 17–9
Hong Kong 111, 119–20
Indonesia 212
Japan 59
Korea 141–2
Malaysia 185, 194
Philippines 156, 170, 182
Singapore 198
Taiwan 87–9
Thailand 215

unions 88, 183, 267

videocassettes 4, 6
Burma 223
China 14–5
Hong Kong 105, 108–9, 118
India 235, 239–42, 248
Indonesia 208
Japan 34, 46, 51–3
Malaysia 195, 197
Pakistan 258–9
Philippines 161–63
Singapore 199
Sri Lanka 270–2
Taiwan 67–8, 71, 79–83,
    89–90
violence (crime) films 49, 114,
    157–8, 175, 197, 242

wages 232–3
war films 56, 139, 175, 266
wayang 206
wenyi 65
Western influences 2, 5, 18,
    22–3, 28–30, 140, 245,
    255, 261

yakusa 37
yoke thay 221

zat 221

Film Index

Aama (Nepal) 254
A Better Tomorrow (Hong Kong)
    110–1, 113
A Boat without a Boatman
    (Korea) 124–5
Aces Go Places (Hong Kong)
    103–4, 116
A Corner of the City (China) 20
Adara Kathawa (Sri Lanka) 275
Again to the Front (North
    Korea) 143
Age 18 (Indonesia) 210
A Girl Who Came to the City
    (Korea) 139–40
Ahas Gawwa (Sri Lanka) 274
Ah Fei (Taiwan) 86
Ah Fu (Hong Kong) 117
Ah Ying (Hong Kong) 113

Ai no Korida (Japan) 48
Akash-ar-Mati (East Pakistan)
    263
Akrosh (India) 246, 249
Ali Setan (Malaysia) 195
All the Youthful Days (Taiwan)
    85
*A Man Who Came to the World
    and He Made Good* (China)
    98
Ang Bayan Ko (Philippines) 166
Angela Markado (Philippines)
    166
An Jung Gun Shoots Ho Hirobumi
    (North Korea) 143
Ankahee (India) 238
Announcing to the World (North
    Korea) 143

Antha (india) 243
Apa Yang Kau Palupi?
    (Indonesia) 206
Apocalypse Now (US) 162
Apu Trilogy (India) 248
Arc Light, The (China) 26
Ardh Satya (India) 238, 246
Arirang (Korea) 124–5
Army Nurse (China) 26
A Time To Live. A Time to Die
    (Taiwan) 85
Awakening (China) 14, 24

Baja Membara (Indonesia) 203
*Bakayaro: Watakushi Okotte
    Imasu* (Japan) 43–4
Bambaru Avith (Sri Lanka) 274
Batch '81 (Philippines) 158

Battle Creek Brawl (Hong Kong) 100
Battle of Artillery – August 23 (Taiwan) 67
Beddegama (Sri Lanka) 273
Below the Lion Rock (Hong Kong) 101, 112
Bernapas dalam Lumpur (Indonesia) 206
Best Action series (Japan) 51
Best Selection Film (Japan) 51
Bhavni Bhavai (India) 249
Bhoomika (India) 249
Big Parade (China) 26
Bii Bappu Haisukuru (Japan) 58
Bima Kroda (Indonesia) 206
Bird in the Cage, The (Korea) 24
Black Cannon Incident (China) 19–20, 26, 33
Bokura no Shichinichi-kan Senso (Japan) 44
Bombay Our City (India) 243
Bona (Philippines) 166
Borderline between Male and Female (China) 26
Boy Kondenado (Philippines) 178
Boy Partisans (North Korea) 143
Bukan Sandiwara (Indonesia) 211
Buluh Perindu (Malaysia) 189
Butterfly Murders (Hong Kong) 112

Camera Sunbo (Korea) 132
Cannonball Run (Hong Kong) 100, 105
Cannonball 2 (Hong Kong) 47
Chanda (East Pakistan) 263
Chinese Boxer, The (Hong Kong) 115
Choke Song Chan (Thailand) 213
Chor Police (India) 242
Chuang Tsu Tests His Wife (Hong Kong) 93
Cinema Land series (Japan) 51
Cinta Pertama (Indonesia) 210
Citizen, The (Thailand) 220
Clerk, Shaheed and Farangi (Pakistan) 255
Cobra (US) 78
Coldest Winter in Peking, The (Taiwan) 117
Come On, Chinese Team (China) 26
Cops and Robbers (Hong Kong) 112
Cream Soda and Milk (Hong Kong) 111
Cute Girl (Taiwan) 84

Dalagang Bukid (Philippines) 151
Damul (India) 246
Dangerous Encounters of the First Kind (Hong Kong) 112
Darah dan Do'a (Indonesia) 205
Daughter of Fire, The (Korea) 141
Daughter of the Nile (Taiwan) 85
Dauntaun Hirozu (Japan) 42
Debshishu (India) 237
Deep Blue Night (Korea) 132, 141
Defense News (Korea) 126

Der Himmel Uber Berlin (West Germany) 47
Desa di Kaki Bukit (Indonesia) 211
Diary of a Woman, The (Korea) 126
Dilereng Gunung Kawi (Indonesia) 203
Doro no Kawa (Japan) 55
Dove Tree (China) 20, 26
Dragon Gate Inn (Hong Kong) 115
Dragon Inn (Taiwan) 64
Dream Nights (India) 243
Dreams (Japan) 6
Dukhey Jader Jibon Gora (East Bengal) 262
Dulla Bhatti (Pakistan) 255
Dun-Huang (Japan) 47
Dust in the Wind (Taiwan) 85
'Dynasty' 245

Emanuelle (US) 5
Emperor Chin Shih (Taiwan) 64
Enter the Dragon (Hong Kong) 100, 116
Equal Love (Burma) 223
Evening Bell (China) 31
Evening Rain (China) 20

Far Away from Headquarters (North Korea) 143
Fatal Attraction (US) 122
Father and Son (Hong Kong) 112, 117
Fengkuangenu (China) 32
Fist of Fury (Hong Kong) 115
Flames Spreading over the Land (North Korea) 143
Free Woman, The (Korea) 140
From the Highway (Hong Kong) 115

Gahanu Lamai (Sri Lanka) 273
Gamperaliya (Sri Lanka) 273
Ganashatru (India) 237
Gandahar (North Korea) 143
Gandhi (US) 237
Ganga, Jamuna, Saraswati (India) 234–5
Gangs (Hong Kong) 117
Ganito Kami Noon, Paano Kayo Ngayon (Philippines) 158
Garm Hava (India) 243
Genbaku no Ko (Japan) 57
Ghare Bhaire (India) 237
Gila-Gila (Malaysia) 195
Godzilla (Japan) 39
Golden Swallow (Hong Kong) 115
Gongchoga (Korea) 133
The Good, The Bad and the Loser (Hong Kong) 116
Great King Seijong, The (Korea) 140
Green, Green Grass of Home (Taiwan) 84
Growing Up (Taiwan) 61, 85
Gumnam (Pakistan) 255

Hachiko Monogatari (Japan) 40, 56
Hadaka no Shima (Japan) 48
Hamburger Hill (US) 162

Hana Ichi,onme (Japan) 55
Harimau Tjampa (Indonesia) 206
Harta Karun (Indonesia) 205
Hatsukoi Jigokuhen (Japan) 38
Hei no Naka (Japan) 58
Hei no Naka no Pureiboru (Japan) 58
Her Nights (India) 242
Hero Hiralal (India) 250–1
Hijo Aaj Bholi (Nepal) 254
Himala (Philippines) 168
Himatsuri (Japan) 45, 55
Hissatsui (Japan) 58
History of Unyong (Korea) 124
Hi Taruru no Haka 57
Home in Hong Kong (Hong Kong) 117
Horse Thief (China) 25–6
House of Death (Korea) 141
Hwang Chin-i (Korea) 141

Ichimannen Kizami no Hidokei: Magino-mura Monogatari (Japan) 34
If I Were Real (Taiwan) 117
Ikiru (Japan) 54
Iko ka Modoro ka (Japan) 47
In Our Time (Taiwan) 85–6
Insiang (Philippines) 158, 166
In the First Armed Unit (North Korea) 143
In the Realm of the Senses (Japan) 49–50
In the Wild Mountains (China) 14
Inugami-ke no Ichizoku (Japan) 39
Invited People (Korea) 137, 140
Ishq wa dosti (Afghanistan)

Jago Hua Savera (East Pakistan) 263
Jaguar (Philippines) 166
Japan Film Worldwide series (Japan) 59
Jejaka Perasan (Malaysia) 195
Jeung-un (Korea) 133
Jibon Thekey Neya (East Pakistan) 263
Jogakusei Geisha (Japan) 50
Jokbo (Korea) 133
Just Like Weather (Hong Kong) 104, 113

Kabut Sutera Ungu (Indonesia) 211
Kadawunu Poronduwa (Sri Lanka) 268
Kagemusha (Japan) 48
Kaliyugaya (Sri Lanka) 273
Kapit sa -atalim (Philippines) 158
Karumakkarayo (Sri Lanka) 275
Kawin Lari (Indonesia) 210
Kaze no Nakano Naushika (Japan) 57
Kazoku (Japan) 43, 55
Kemakmocran (Indonesia) 204
Kembara Seniman Jalanan (Malaysia) 195
Kerikil-Kerikil Tajam (Himala) (Indonesia) 211
Key of the Heart (Taiwan) 83

'Khandan' 245
Kimi wa Hadaka no Kami o Mitaka (Japan) 59
Kimura-ke no Hitobito (Japan) 55
King of the Children (China) 26
King of the White Elephants, The (Thailand) 213
Kisapmata (Philippines) 158
Kissa Kursi Ka (India) 243
Koi no Kariudo (Japan) 50
Kokotsu no Hito (Japan) 55
Komniku Zasshi Nanka Iranai (Japan) 55
Koneko Monogatari (Japan) 40, 56
Kongbuyie (China) 32
Konna Yuma Mita (Japan) 44
Kontroversyal (Philippines) 166
Koshikei (Japan) 38
Kozure Okami (Japan) 39
Krisis (Indonesia) 205
Kung Fu Kids (Taiwan) 83–84
Kuraimu Hantaa (Japan) 53
Kuroi Yuki (Japan) 50

Laila Majnum (Malaysia) 188
La Mujer Filipina (Philippines) 151
Landscape of Kyongsong City, The (Korea) 124
La Sombre de la Armada (Philippines) 151
Last Day of Winter, The (China) 26
Last Emperor, The (US) 47, 50, 52
Last Sun, The (China) 26
La Venganza de Don Silvestre (Philippines) 151
La Vida Rizal (Philippines) 151
Lewat Jam Malam (Indonesia) 210
Liang Shan-po and Chu Ying-tai (Taiwan) 64
Liberty News (Korea) 126
Living Daylights, The (US) 122
Lonely Murderer, The (China) 26
Love the Future (North Korea) 143
Lutang Karasarung (Indonesia) 203

Maihime (Japan) 44
Mandala (Korea) 133, 141
Manila by Night (Philippines) 158, 168–69
Manila in the Claws of Neon (Philippines) 166
Man on the Brink (Hong Kong) 112
Man on the Road, The (Korea) 125
Man without a Promised Land (Hong Kong) 118
March of Justice (Korea) 126
Maririn ni Aitai (Japan) 41, 56
Marusa no Onna Ni (A Taxing Woman) (Japan) 47, 54
Max, Mon Amour (Japan) 44
Mekanik (Malaysia) 195
Mementos (Indonesia) 210
Mesuneko no Nioi (Japan) 50
Minsa 'y Isang Gamu-Gamo (Philippines) 158

Miracles of Love (Philippines) 152
Mirch Masala (India) 237, 249–50
Miss Colombo (Pakistan) 260
Miss Hong Kong (Pakistan) 260
Miss Singapore (Pakistan) 260
Missing in Action III (US) 162
Money, Money, Money (Taiwan) 65
Mon Rak Luk Tung (Thailand) 213–14
Moonlight (Indonesia) 203
Moral (Philippines) 178
Mukh-o-Mukhosh (East Pakistan) 262
Myiitta Hnit Thura (Burma) 221
My Memories of Old Beijing (China) 20
My Lucky Stars (Hong Kong) 100, 116
My Mother and the Boarder (Korea) 126
My Native Place (North Korea) 143

Nankyoku Monogatari (Japan) 40, 56
Narrow Lane (China) 20
Native Call (China) 20
Naxalites (India) 243
Neighbours (China) 20
Never Can Live Like That (North Korea) 143
Nihon Chinbotsu (Japan) 39
Nikudan (Japan) 38
Ningen Johatsu (Japan) 37
Ningen no Yakusoku (Japan) 55
Nippon-koku Furuyashiki-mura (Japan) 34
November 1828 (Indonesia) 210
No Yo na Mono (Japan) 43
Nunal sa Tubig (Philippines) 168

Objective Burma! (Hong Kong) 98
One and Eight (China) 19–20, 22–4, 26, 28
One Armed Swordsman (Hong Kong) 99, 115
On the Elevator (China) 13
On the Hunting Ground (China) 12, 19–20, 23, 25–6, 28, 33
Opera Jakarta (Indonesia) 211
Orang Village (North Korea) 143
Oro, Plata, Mata (Philippines) 169
Ososhiki (Japan) 44, 54
Otako wa Tsurai yo, Tora-san (Japan) 37–9, 42, 44, 55
Oyster Girl (Taiwan) 64

Pae Kao (Thailand) 220
Pagdating sa Dulo (Philippines) 168
Palangetiyo (Sri Lanka) 275
Parasathumal (Sri Lanka) 274
Pareh (Indonesia) 203
Parivartan (Nepal) 254
Patria Amore (Philippines) 152
Peluru dan Wanita (Indonesia) 211

Penarik Beca (Malaysia) 190
Pengemis dan Tukang Becak (Indonesia) 210
People in Darkness (Korea) 140–1
Petualang-Petualang (Indonesia) 210
Pisau Surit (Indonesia) 203
Platform (Japan) 51
Platoon (US) 162
Pleasant Heroes (China) 26
Plighted Love under the Moon, The (Korea) 124
Podiputha (Sri Lanka) 268
Ponirah Terpidana (Indonesia) 211
Potato (Korea) 137
Project A (Hong Kong) 47
Puen -aeng (thailand) 220
Punyal na Ginto (Philippines) 152
Puteri (Malaysia) 195
Puitri Giok (Indonesia) 211

Qatil (Pakistan) 255

Rainbow over the Kinmen Bay (Taiwan) 64
Raja Harishchandra (Nepal) 254
Ramayan (India) 247
Rambo (US) 114–15
Ran (Japan) 42, 45, 48
Ranjang Pengatin (Indonesia) 210
Rashomon (Japan) 36
Redressment of Justice by a Porcelain Pot (Hong Kong) 92
Red Sorghum (China) 19, 26, 31, 33
Rekawa (Sri Lanka) 269, 273
Rembulan dan Matahari (Indonesia) 211
Re Men Chu China) 62
Return of the Taxing Woman, The (Japan) 54
Reverberations of Life (China) 20
Righteous Revenge, The (Korea) 124
Righteous War (North Korea) 143
Road (China) 20
Road to Happiness, The (North Korea) 143
Rock 'n' Roll Youth (China) 26
Rokku yo, Shizuka ni Nagareyo (Japan) 44
Roopha (East Pakistan) 263
Rouge (Hong Kong) 93
Royal Adventure (Sri Lanka) 267

Sadgati (India) 246
Sagarayake Jalaya (Sri Lanka) 273
Sagarayak Meda (Sri Lanka) 275
Sakada (Philippines) 158
Sakay (Philippines) 154
Sakuratai Chiru (Japan) 57
Salaam Bombay! 237
Sampaguita (Philippines) 151
Sandesaya (Sri Lanka) 273
Sandwich Man, The (Taiwan) 84, 86
Sannrizuka (Japan) 34

Saraba Itoshiki Daichi (Japan) 45, 55
Sarungale (Sri Lanka) 174–5
Sayonara Jupita (Japan) 39
Scorpio Nights (Philippines) 169
Scout (North Korea) 143
Sealed with a Kiss (Hong Kong) 111
Secret, The (Hong Kong) 112
Secret Decree (China) 19–20, 23–6
Sembilan (Indonesia) 206
September (China) 26
Seputih Hatinya Semerah Bibiruya (Indonesia) 211
Sesshui to Barentnino (Japan) 44
Setouchi Shonen Yakyudan (Japan) 57
Seven Fairies (Taiwan) 64
Shadow over Angkor (Cambodia) 201
Sha'ou (China) 20, 24
Shogun Iemitsu no Ranshin: Gekitotsu (Japan) 58
Si Doel Anak Modern (Indonesia) 210–1
Si Mamad (Indonesia) 210
Sing Song Girl, Red Peony (China) 96
Si Pincang (Indonesia) 206
Six Talents in West Chamber (Taiwan) 63
Small Ball Tossed by a Dwarf, The (Korea) 138
Somewhere (Philippines) 160
Somewhere in the Midst of Clouds (Taiwan) 70
Song of Yesterday (Hong Kong) 97
Sorekara (Japan) 43
Spinning Gold and Silver Threads in a Lom (Burma) 223
Spinning Wheel, The (Korea) 141
Spooky Bunch, The (Hong Kong) 112
Story of Chunhyang, The (Korea) 125
Star of Korea (North Korea) 143
Story of the Imperial Capital (Japan) 41

Story of Wu Viet, The (Hong Kong) 112
Story-Teller (China) 26
Stray Bullet, The (Korea) 126
Suci Sang Primadona (Indonesia) 210
Sudsakorn (Thailand) 220
Suito Homu (Japan) 44
Summer at Grandpa's (Taiwan) 85
Super Citizen (Taiwan) 86
Suvarna of Siam (Thailand) 213

Taehan News (Korea) 126, 132
Taipei Story (Taiwan) 85
Taketori Mongatari (Japan) 44
Tale of Simchong (Korea) 124
Tale of Sisters of Janghwa and Hongnyon (Korea) 124–5
Tamas (India) 246
Tampopo (Japan) 54
Tamu Agung (Indonesia) 205
Tatlong Hambog (Philippines) 151
Taw Myaing Soon (Burma) 221
Tenka no Shiro Ruputa (Japan) 57
Teri Yaad (Pakistan) 254
Terrorists, The (Taiwan) 85
That Day on the Beach (Taiwan) 85
Thon (Thailand) 220
Tjitra (Indonesia) 205
Tjoet Nia Dhien (Indonesia) 211, 223–4
Tokyo Monogatari (Japan) 54
Tomorrow: Asu (Japan) 57
Tonari no Totoro (Japan) 57
Tonko (Japan) 41
To Steal a Roasted Duck (Hong Kong) 92
Tropical Flowers (Korea) 141
Troubled Laughter (China) 19
Tsu-Feh Sofiah (Malaysia) 195
Two Monks (Korea) 138

Uchu Senkan Yamato (Japan) 57
Ugetsu (Japan) 36
Ugly American, The (US) 201
Uma (Japan) 56
Umi to Dokuyaku (Japan) 56–7

Un Capullo Marchito (Philippines) 151
Unknown Heroes (North Korea) 143
Uod at Rosas (Philippines) 169
Uthumaneni (Sri Lanka) 274

Valmathwuvo (Sri Lanka) 274
Video Library series (Japan) 53
Village in the Mist, The (Korea) 141

Wai Olawon (Thailand) 220
Wajah Seorang Lelaki (Indonesia) 210
Wandering Swordsman, The (Hong Kong) 115
Wanted: A Perfect Mother (Philippines) 167
Warm It Was That Winter (Korea) 132–3
Way of the Dragon (Hong Kong) 115–16
Whale Hunting (Korea) 132–3, 141
When Love Breaks Through (Indonesia) 210
Wind and Cloud on Ali Mountain (Taiwan) 63
Woman of Wrath (Taiwan) 83

Yadanabo (Burma) 221
Yagyu Ichizoku no Inbo (Japan) 38–9
Yahalu Yeheli (Sri Lanka) 273
Yamaha Fish Stall (China) 13–4
Yari no Gonza (Japan) 44
Yasei no Shomei (Japan) 39
Yeh Kahani Nahin (India) 244
Yellow Earth (China) 12, 14, 19–20, 22–6, 28, 31, 33
Yuganthaya (Sri Lanka) 273
Yukiyukite Shinngun (Japan) 57
Yume Miru Yo ni Nemuritai (Japan) 41
Yushun (Japan) 56
Yuyn, Patient in a Mental Hospital (Indonesia) 210

Zamboanga (Philippines) 153
Zatoichi series (Japan) 58

Name Index

Abbas, K.A. 243
Abe, Joji 58
Abeyasekera, Tissa 275
Abdul Jabbar Khan 262
Abdus Sadeq 262
Academy of Cinematography, Indonesia 212
ACTION (Action Against Movie Monopoly) 159
Actors Workshop Foundation 182
Acuña, Isabel 152
Advertisement Short Film Department, Taiwan 68
Afghan Films 254
Afghanistan 254
Agcaoili, T.D. 151

Agricultural Educational Film Corporation 62–3
Ahmad, Nordin 189
Alcala, Larry 156, 182
Algameen Nederlands Indische Film Syndicaat (ANIF) 203–4
Ali Hussan 208
Alliance of Artists 180
Always Good Film Company 102–3
American Film Marketing Association 123
Anderson, Joseph 35, 37, 58
Andjar Asmara 205
Anglo-American Tobacco Company 123

Antonioni, Michelangelo 2
Annusorn, Prince 213, 220
Anwardi Jamil 195
Anwar Kamal 255
A-1 Film Company 221
Apex 217-218
Apricot Entertainment Inc. 35
Aquino, Corazon 149, 174, 179–80, 183
Araneta University 156
Arranya Namwong 219
Arifin C. Noer 210
Army Film and photography Unit, Malaysia 188
Art Theatre Guild 37–8, 59
Asawin Films 213
ASEAN Film Festival 7

ASEAN Motion Picture
Producers Association 7
Asia Film Company 92
Asian-Pacific Film Festival 7, 64,
119, 126, 190, 198, 205–6,
210–2, 223
Asian Wall Street Journal 118
Assessment Committee,
Malaysia 196
Association of Film Producers
and Distributors,
Philippines 150
Association of Indonesian Film
Companies 208
Association of Motion Picture
Arts, Korea 124
Ateneo de Manila University
182
ATV 83
August Eight Film Studio 14
August First Film Studio 13
Avellana, Lamberto 149, 154,
156–7, 174–5, 179, 182
AVM 233
Ayub Khan 263

Babra Sharif 260–1
Bachan, Amitabh 234
Bachtiar Siagian 203
Bae Chang-ho 132, 141
Balink, Albert 203–4
Bandaranaike, Felix 275
Bandaranayake, Dharmasiri 274
Bang Bang Motion Pictures
101–2
Bangladesh Better Cinema Front
267
Bangladesh Censorship of Film
Rules, 1972 266
Bangladesh Filmmakers
Association Film Awards
267
Bangladesh National Film
Awards 267
Bazin, Andre 22
Beijing Agricultural Film Studio
21
Beijing Film Academy 17–9
Beijing Film Institute 13, 20–1
Beijing Film Processing Lab 21
Beijing Film Studio 13, 16–7,
21, 32
Bell, Hesketh 186
Bengal, Shyam 244, 246, 249
Bergman, Ingmar 22
Berlin Film Festival 26
Bernal, Ishmael 5, 149–50,
158, 162, 166–9, 171, 174,
179, 183
Berry, Chris 14–15
Bhanu, Prince 23
Bhutto, Benazir 276
Bhutto (Ali) government 257
Big Four 155–7
Board of Censorship for
Cinematographic Films,
Philippines 150
Board of Film Censors,
Bangladesh 266
Board of Film Censors,
Singapore 198
Board of Review for Motion
Pictures and Television,
Philippines 178

Board of Standards, Philippines
177
Bo Ho Films 102
Bombay Talkies 1
Booty, Kasma 189, 191
Borneo Film Company 197
Brando, Marlon 201
British Burma Film Company
221
Brocka, Lino 4–5, 149, 158,
166–71, 173–4, 177,
179–80
Brown, Harry 150–1
Bungei-za 45
Bunka Eiga Gekijo 188
Burma Film Company 221
Burma Socialist Programme
Party 222

Cai Cushing 20
Cambodia 201
Cannes Film Festival 166–9,
238
Cathay (*includes* Cathay
Organisation, Cathay
Productions) 65, 97,
99–100, 106, 188–9, 195
Cathay-Keris productions
189–90, 192–4, 197–8
Catholic Mass Media Awards
183
CBS/Fox 51–2
Censorship of Films Act, 1963
255, 261
Central Board of Film Censors,
Pakistan 257
Central Board of Film
Certification, India 242
Central Motion Picture
Corporation 63–70, 73, 83
Century Films 83, 102
Cervantes, Behn 158, 166
Ceylon Entertainments 268
Ceylon Theatres Ltd. 267–9
Chakravorty, Utpalendu 237
Chan, David 105
Chang Cheh 115
Chang King-Yuh 78, 81
Chang Shin-Kuan 96–7
Chan, Jackie 47, 100, 104, 106,
114
Chao, Benny 72, 83
Charoenkrung Company 213
Chatri Chalerm Yukol, Prince
220
Cheng Jihua 19
Chen Kaige 5, 13, 19, 21–6,
28, 30
Chen Kun-Hou 61–2, 69, 72,
84–5, 87
Chen Lizhou 20
Chen Mei 11–2, 16–7, 21
Chen Xiaolin 15
Chen Yao-Chi (Richard Y.
Chen) 65, 72, 74, 79, 84,
87, 89
Chen Yuewe 32
Cherd Songsri 5, 220
Cheung Kwok-Min, Alex 112
Chiang Kai-shek 25
Chiang Pai Yin 94
Children's Film Studio 13
China Arts Motion Picture
Company 64

China Educational Film Studio
63
China Educational Recreational
75–6
China Film Association 28, 30
China Film Board 25
China Film Corporation 14,
30–1
China Film Distribution and
Exhibition Corporation 15
China Film Export and Import
Corporation 11–12,
15–16
China Movie Studio 62–4
China Screen 4
Chinese Cultural Movietown 68
Chisty 188
Chittampalam A. Gardiner and
Associates 267
Chiu, Deacon 101
Choi, Clifford 112
Chong Chang-hwa 126
Chong Gay 198
Chongqing Hardware Store 32
Choongang University 142
Choson Kinema 124
Chou, H.S. 66, 82
Chou Ling-Kong 74, 78
Chow, Raymond 97, 99–100,
102, 111, 115
Chung Jin-won 133
Chung-joo University 142
Cinco, Manuel 'Fyke' 163–4,
168–9, 174, 183
Cine Journalists Association
Awards 267
Cinema Centre Productions
198
Cinema City 6, 73, 102–7,
109–12, 116, 120
Cinema India-International 4
Cine Manila 166
Cinemas Ltd. 269
Cinemathèque Française 251
Cinematograph Act of 1918,
South Asia 253, 261
Cinematograph Films
(Censorship) Act 1952,
Malaysia 195–6
Cine Saison 41
Cine Vivant 41
Cino Motion Picture
Corporation 203
Citizens Council for Better
Motion Pictures,
Philippines 182
C. Itoh and Co. 44, 53
Citra Awards 212, 223
Code of Motion Picture
Censorship, Philippines 176
Columbia 76, 216
Columbia Classics 119
Commission of Inquiry into the
Film Industry, Sri Lanka
269
Concerned Artists of the
Philippines 167, 177
Concio, Lupita 158
Conde, Manuel 156
Crown Film Unit, Malaya 189
CTS 83
Cultural Convenience Club 53
Cultural Revolution 11–12, 17,
19–22, 24, 27, 30–1

Dacca Studio 263
Daiei 36–8, 42, 64
Daini-Toei 36–7
D and B films 6, 101, 103, 107, 120
Dangal 183
Deegar Cinema 156
de la Rama, Atang 151
De La Salle College 182
de Leon, Doña Narcisa Buencamino vda. (Doña Sisang) 153
de Leon, Gerardo 155–6
de Leon, Mike 158, 171
del Mundo, Clodualdo, jr. 165, 171, 182
Desai, Manmohan 234–5
Devi, Rukmani 268
Diaz Abaya, Marilou 166
Disney 216
Djamaluddin Malik 202–3, 205–6
Djayakusuma, D. 206
Dokdin Kanyaman 220
Dolphy 5
Donggook University 142
Doordarshan Television 238, 245–8

Eastern Film Management Corporation 162
East-West Film Journal 4
Eddie Romero Productions 155
Edison Carnival Tent 221
Efren Reyes Productions 155
Ehtesham 263
Eihai (Motion Picture Distributing Company) 204
Eirin 48–51
Emei Film Studio 13, 16, 32
Empire Audio Visual Company 83
Enquiry Committee on Film Censorship 244
Entertainment Licensing authority 95, 118
Entertainment Philippines Inc. 162, 180
Equipe de Cinema 59–60
Eros Djarot 211, 223–4
ESC Incorporated 76
Estela, Ramon 156
Estrada, Joseph 164, 175, 182–3
Excelsior 153
Experimental Cinema of the Philippines 149–50, 158, 168, 178, 181

Fabregas, Jimmy 160, 163–4, 166
Fan, Frank 75
Far East Film Company 97
Far East Motion Picture Development Ltd. Far East 101
'Feature Film' 42
Federal 254
Federation of Indonesian Film Importers, Producers and Distributors 207
Federation of Theatre Owners of Korea 128, 142
Fee Tang Motion Picture company 66, 74

Fellini, Federico 22
Feng Huang (Phoenix) Motion Picture Company 97, 100, 103, 112–3
Fernandez, Gregorio 156
Fernandez, Rudy 175
Fernando Poe Productions 155, 159
Film Finance Corporation, India 237
'Fifth Generation' 14, 19–27, 28–33
Fiftieth Year Film Company 97
Fifties Film Company 95
Filem Negara 192
Filipino Academy of Movie Arts and Sciences (FAMAS) 156, 169, 181–3
Filippine Films 153
Film Academy of the Philippines 177, 180, 183
Film Archives, Philippines 177–8, 180–1
Film Art 142
Film Artists' Foundation, Indonesia 212
Film Bi-Weekly 119
Film Board, Philippines 177
Film Censorship Board, Malaysia 196
Film Centre, Philippines 149, 178, 180–1
Film Council, Burma 222
Film Critic's Award 267
Film Cultural Centre 119–20
Film Development Corporation, East Pakistan 262–4
Film Development Foundation of the Philippines 178, 180
Film Director's Guild 95
Film Employees Federation of South India 232
Film Exporters and Importers Association of Korea Inc. 128
Film Export Corporation, India 237
Film Fact Finding Commission, Pakistan 256
Film Finance Corporation, East Pakistan 255
Film Institute of the Philippines 182
Film Library, Taiwan 88
Film Ratings Board, Philippines 178, 180
Film Review 88
Films Act, Singapore 199
Film School Board of the Philippines 182
Film Workshop 114
First Manila Short Film Festival 182
Fong, Allen 5, 101, 104, 112–13, 117
Fonseka, Gamini 274–5
Fotocine Film Production Ltd. 102, 108
Fox 76, 216
'FPJ sa GMA' 163
Franken, Mannus 203
Free-the Artist Movement 167, 177
French Film Company 47

Fuji Television 40, 46
Fukasaku, Kinji 38
Furansu Eigasha 46

Gabungan Pengusaha Bioskop Seluruh Indonesia 209
Gala Film Distribution 102, 107
Gala Theatres 102
Gallaga, Peque 150, 160, 162, 168–70, 174–5, 179
Gandhiraman, Mohan 232
Gandhi, Sanjay 243
Garbo Films 102
Gandhi, Sanjay 243
Geawon Art School 142
Ghose, Goutam, 251
Go Brothers Films 217–18
Godrej 245
Golden Bear Award 26
Golden Cluster Awards 88
Golden Communications 102, 194
Golden Harvest 6, 67, 71, 73, 81, 83, 99, 101–3, 105, 107–9, 111–12, 116, 216
Golden Horse Award 62, 64, 67, 77, 89
Golden Horse Awards International Film Festival 62, 88
Golden Princess Amusements 102–3, 108
Golden Princess Gala Film Company 102–3, 107
Golden Rooster Award 26
Golden Wave Productions 102
Goonsekera, Anura 271–2
Gopalkrishnan, Adoor 251
Government Film Unit, Indonesia 207
Government Film Unit, Sri Lanka 269
Government Information Office, Taiwan 64, 66, 73, 75, 77, 79, 81–3, 85, 88–9
Government Task Force on Film, Philippines 179
Grand Bell Awards 127, 135, 141–2
Grandview 94, 97
Grand Movie Company 64
Great China Motion Picture Company (Dazhonghua) 94
Greater Metro Manila Theatres Association 163–4
Great Wall Films 96–7, 100, 103
Gross, Edward M. 150–1
Grumman, Elizabeth (Lee) 14
Guang Li 100
Guangxi Film Studio 13, 21
Gul, G.A. 255
Gunasinghe, Siri 274
Guo Lien 68

Hafsham (Othman Samsuddin) 194–5
Haiyu-za 45
Hani, Susumu 38
Hanumarn Films 213
Hanyang University 142
Hara, Kazuo 57
Harris, George F. 152–3
Hata Entertainment Enterprise 46

Hata, Masanori 40
Hayashi, Kaizo 41
Herald Enterprise Inc. 43, 46
Heuveldorp, L. 203
Himawari 45
HKTVB 83, 99, 101, 109, 112
Ho Ah Loke 189
Hong Kong Baptist College 119
Hong Kong International Film
    Festival 92, 119
Hong Kong Movie News 99
Ho, Leonard 102
Hou Hsiao-Hsien 84–5
Hou Jianping 24
Hou Ping 89
Hsiao Yeh 85–6
Hua Da 100
Hua Guo Movie Productions 68
Huang Fei Hung 115
Huanl Jianxin 19–20, 26
Huangpu Keren 32–3
Hu Bing Liu 20
Hu Chin-Chuan 64
Hui, Ann 112
Hui, Michael and Samuel 5
Hu King 115
Hu Mei 26
Hundred Flowers Award 26
Hu Ying Mon 69–71, 87

Ichikawa, Kon 39, 44
Ikatan Karyawan Film dan
    Televisi 212
Imamura, Shohei 37
Im Kwon t'aek 133, 141
Imperial Company 221
Independent Film and Video
    Festival 182
India 1–3
Indian Films 1
Indonesian Film Festival 207,
    212
Inem films 208
Inner Mongolia Film Studio 12,
    32
Interim Board of Censors for
    Motion Pictures,
    Philippines 177
International Film Company 64
International Film Distribution
    Company 97
International Motion Picture
    Studios 64
Iqbal Films 262
Itami, Juzo 44–5, 54
Ito, Shunya 55
Izumi, Seiji 44

Jade Video 108
Jakarta Seisakujo 204
Japan Academy of Visual Arts
    59
Japan Film Library Council
    (Kawakita Memorial Film
    Institute) 59
Japan Herald Film 46, 51
Japan Video Association Rental
    System 52
Jarunee Sukswadee 219
Jawa Eiga Kosha 204
Jayamanne, B.A.W. 268
Jayamanne, Eddie 268
Jayatilaka, Amarnath 270
Jayewardene, Junius 270–3

Jha, Prakash 246
Jiang Haiyang 26
Jissoji, Akio 41
Joy Pack Film Inc. 51

Kabir, Alamgir 253
Kadokawa Publishing Company
    39–40
Kam Ping-Hing 110
Kam Productions 108
Kaneko, Shunsuke 44
Kapoor, Raj 242
Karachi Studio 254
Kasaravalli, Girish 251
Katigbak, Maria Kalaw 178
Katsu, Shintaro 58
Kawakita, Kashiko 59–60
Keris 97
Keris Film Productions 189
Khalil Qaiser 255
Khan, Amjad 242
Khosla, G.D. 244
Khurshid Anwar 255
Kim Do-san 124
Kim Hee-gap 133
Kim Song-min 126
Klm Soo-yong 133
Kinema Jumpo 38, 43–4, 51,
    54–7
King George V 186
King Hoi Lam (David King)
    117
King Mahendra Bir Bikram
    Shah Dev 254
Kinkuan Picture Corporation 94
Kinoshita 45
Komatsu, Sakyo 39
Korea Cinema 142
Korea Motion Picture Institute
    142
Korean Automobile and
    Transport Workers Union
    139
Korean Cultural and Advertising
    Film Producers Association
    142
Korean February 8 Film Studio
    143
Korean Film Archive
    Incorporated Foundation
    129, 142
Korean Film Unit 130, 132
Korean Motion Picture
    Distributors Association
    129, 134, 142
Korean Performance Ethics
    Committee 123
Korean Public Performance
    Ethics Committee 137
Koritan Entertainment 123
Kowloon Developments 103
KPS Video Retail Shops 108
Kraucauer, Sigfried 22
Kriangsak Chomanan 217
Krishnan, Lakshmana 185, 189
Kruger, G. 203
Krung Srivilai 219
Kuang, Sunshine 81–2
Kukrit Pramaj, M.R. 201
Kumai, Kei 56
Kumarasinghe, Geetha 275
Kurahara, Koretsugu 40
Kuroki, Kazuo 57

Kurosawa, Akira 4–6, 36, 42,
    44–5, 48, 54
Kurosawa, Kiyoshi 45
Kwan Tak-Hing 115
Kwon Ming 94

Lacaba, Jose 'Pete' 165, 171–3,
    179
Lam, Peter 110
Lan Tsu-Wei 71, 86
Lap Yan Films 102
Latif, Reshid 254
Lal, Diwan Sardari 254
Lawo Films 213
League of Japanese Filmmakers
    58
Lebran 155–7
Lee, Bruce 92, 99–100, 104,
    115–16
Lee Chang-ho 132, 140–1
Lee Daw-Ming 68, 86–7, 89
Lee Doo Yong 133
Lee Gang-chon 126
Lee Gyu hwan 124–5
Lee Han-Hsiang
Lee Hyun-mok 126
Lee Kyong-son 124
Lee Man-hui 126
Lee Myong-u 125
Lee Pil-u 124
Lee, Ricky 163–4, 166, 169,
    171–4, 182
Lee Tsu Yung 97
LEKRA 202–3
Leopoldo Salcedo Productions
    155
LESBUMI 202
Leung Po-Chi 112
Liang Shaobo 92
Lian-Hau Film Company 93
Liao Hsiang-Hsiong 65 Li
    Cheuk-to 119
Lien Pun 68
Li Li 31–3
Li Min Wei 92–3
Literary Song 153
Liu Guoquan 32
Liu Shou-Chi 78
Liu Yi 89
Liwayway 153
Li Yuan (Hsian Yeh) 68
Li Xiahong 14
Lo Chi-Keung 101
Loke Wan Tho 97, 99, 188
London Art Films 221
Louey, Lawrence 103
Luo Yijun 30
LVN Studios 153, 155

Maarof, Mustapha 189
McRay, Henry 213
Madan Theatres 267
Maha Sway Film Company 221
Maha Vizzadhor Films 221
Mahmud, Ahmad 189
Mak, Carl 102–3
Makinilya 183
Malayan Movies 151
Malayan Pictures Corporation
    151
Malay Film Production Ltd. 189
Malaysian Chamber of Film
    Companies 192
Malaysian Film Academy 194

Malaysian Film Distributors 198
Manansala, Julian 152
Manifesto Politik' 202
Manila Chronicle 167
Manila International Film
  Festival 119, 181
Manila Times 156
Manuel Conde Productions 155
Manunuri ng Pelikulang
  Pilipino 183
Mao Zedong 24
Marcos, Ferdinand and Imelda
  149–50, 158, 168, 170,
  176–7, 179–82
Marcos, Imee 178
'Maria Clara Awards' 156
Marubeni Trading Corporation
  41–2, 53
Marx, Fred 27
Maya 205
Mehta, Ketan 237, 246,
  249–51
Metro Manila Film Festival 158,
  176, 182
Metro Manila Theatres
  Association 163–4
MGM 75, 122, 159, 216
Mid-Week Magazine 171
Mifune, Toshiro 44
Mi Jiashen 32
Min Kyong-Sik 126
Min-Xin (New People) Film
  Company 93
Mishima, Yukio 50
Mitchum, Robert 104
Mitsubishi Trading Company
  40–1
Mitsui Trading Company 40
Miura, Tomokazu 39
Miyazaki, Shun 57
Mizoguchi 36
Mmamura, Shohei 59
Mohammad Ali 257
Mohd. Auzam 221
Molina, Titay 150
Monteverde, 'Mother Lily' 150,
  159, 163, 166, 170, 172–4
Mori, Ogai 44
Moritani, Shiro 39
Morita, Yoshimitsu 43–5
Moscow Film Festival 48
Motion Picture and General
  Investment Company Ltd.
  99
Motion Picture Anti-Film Piracy
  Committee, Philippines 162
Motion Picture Association of
  Taiwan 66, 79, 82, 87–8
Motion Picture Censorship
  Committee, Korea 137
Motion Picture Council
  Organisation Committee,
  Burma 222
Motion Picture Critics
  Association, Korea 142
Motion Picture Development
  Board, Philippines 177
Motion Picture Export
  Association of America
  74–5, 122–3, 130,
  143–4, 201, 217, 219,
  240–2
Motion Picture Industry Act
  (Lumauig Bill) 176–7

Motion Picture Marketing,
  Singapore 198
Motion Picture Ordinance
  1979, Pakistan 261
Motion Picture Producers
  Association of Korea Inc.
  128, 142
Motion Picture Production
  Association of the Republic
  of China 87
Motion Picture Promotion
  Corporation of Korea
  128–30, 135–6, 139,
  141–2
Motion Picture Promotion
  Union, Korea 128–9
Motion Picture Association of
  Korea 128, 142
Movement 182
Movie and Drama Association,
  Taiwan 87
Movie and Drama Weekly 68
Movie and Television Review
  and Classification Board,
  Philippines 178, 180
Movie Pictorial Monthly 68
Movie Town 92, 98–9
MOWELFUND 180, 182–3
MOWELFUND Film Institute
  182
Mumei-juku 45
Muzaffar Ali 246

Nagasaki, Shunichi 44
Nagayama, Toshihiro 35
Nair, Mira 237–8
Nakadai, Tatsuya 45
Nan Kuen 96
Nan Kwok (Southern) 96
Nan Luen 94
Nasir Jani 194
National Academy of Theatre
  Indonesia 210–1
National Commission for
  Culture and the Arts
  (Philippine Commission on
  Culture and the Arts) 180
National Film Center, Japan 59
National Film Commission,
  Philippines 179–80
National Film Committee,
  Philippines 180
National Film Corporation,
  Malaysia 192–3
National Film Corporation, Sri
  Lanka 269–71
National Film Council,
  Indonesia 194, 207
National Film Development
  Corporation, India
  237–42, 248
National Film Development
  Corporation, Malaysia 185,
  193–4, 197
National Film Development
  Corporation, Pakistan
  256–7, 259–60
National Film Institute, Sri
  Lanka 270
National Film Production
  Council, Indonesia 206
National Film Studio of North
  Korea 143

National Film Theatres
  Association 134
National Media Production
  Centre 156
Na Un-gyu 124
Navketan 233
Nawak 262
Nayagam S.M. 268
Nepal 254
Nepomuceno, Jose 151–3
Nepomuceno-Harris-Tait
  Partnership 151
Nepomuceno Productions 151
'New Chinese Cinema' 20
New Delhi International Film
  Festival 239
New Five Stars 218
New Hsin Hwa Company 97
Ne Win 222
Newport Entertainment Ltd.
  107
Nichi' ei (Japan Motion Picture
  Company) 204
Nihalani, Govind 238, 246, 249
Nikkatsu 5–6, 36–42, 46, 50,
  64
Nikkatsu Rapponica 42
Nippon AVC 52
Noorbhai, A.G. 267
Nordin, Mazlan 194
Number Three Studio 93
Nusantara 189
N.V. Multi 205
Nyuu Serekuto 46

Obaidal Huq 262
Obeyasekera, Vasantha 275
Ofuna Studio 42
Ogawa, Shinsuka 34
Oguri, Kohei 55
Okamoto, Kihachi 38
Om Gil-son 143
Onn, Hussein 192
Opera Stambul 203
Ordinance No. 200
  (Cinematograph Film),
  Malaysia 187
Oshima, Nagisa 5, 38, 44, 48,
  50
Ozu, Yasujiro 5, 54

Pabst, G.W. 1
Padilla Brothers Productions
  155
Paimpol Cheyaroon 220
Pakistan Film Exhibitors
  Association 260
Pakistan Film Festival 255
Palekar, Amol 238
Pamantasan ng Lungsod ng
  Maynila 182
Pan Asia Films 102
Pancasila 202
PAPFIAS 202
Paragon Films 102
Paramount 75, 122, 216
Paranjpe, Sai 246
Park Chung-hee 130–1, 138
Parlatone Hispano-Filipino Inc.
  151–3
Parliamentary Select Committee
  on Controversial Films,
  Malaysia 196
Patanakorn Company 213

Pathe 124, 150
Pathiraja, Dharmasena 274
Patwardhan, Anand 243
Payuth Ngaokrachang 220
Pearl River Studio 13–14, 16
People's Daily 31
People's Liberation Army (PLA) 12–13
People's Pictures 156
Perfima (Malaysian Film Industries) 191–2
PERFINI 205
Peries, Lester J. 5, 269, 273–5
Peries, Sumitra 273
Perlis Plantations 197
Pernas 192
PERSARI 203, 295
Persatuan Artis Film Indonesia 212
Petchara Chaowaray 220
Petchrama-Metro-MacKenna 217
Petroni, Gulio 269
Philippine Educational Theatre Association 167
Philippine Motion Pictures Producers Association 159, 162
Philippine Herald 153
Phoenix Cine Club 119
Piak Poster 220
Pinga, Ben 182
Poe, Fernando, Jr. 171, 175
Polaski, Benjamin 92
Polychrome Motion Picture Corporation 152
Pony Canyon 52
Poon, Dickson 101
PPFI 202, 205
Prasad 233
Premiere 155–6
Presidential Awards, Pakistan 255
Presidential Commission on Good Government, Philippines 180
Pridi Panomyong 213
PT Perfin 209
Pura Mas 191
Pusat Produksi Filem Negara 207
Pyongyang University of Cinematics 143
Pyramid Entertainment Group 217

Quaisar 254
Quality Film Examination System 135

Raden Mochtar 203
Radio Television Singapore 198
Rahim Razali 194–5
Rai, Himansu 1
Rainbow 94
Rajhaus, B.S. 188
Rama VI, VII 213
Ramlee, P. (Teuku Zakariah bin Teuku Nyak Putih) 189–91
Ramos, Antonio 150
Rani, Devika 1–3
Ray Chaudhuri, Biplab 244
Ray, Satyajit 2, 4–6, 231, 237, 239, 246, 248, 251

Reddy, B.N. 249
Red, Raymond 165
Regal 6, 150, 159–63, 166, 170–3
'Regal Presents' 163
Republic Act 3060 176
Revilla, Ramon 175
Reynolds, Burt 100, 104
Richie, Donald 35, 37, 58
Rimau Productions 189
Rizalina Film Manufacturing Company 150
Rizvi, Shaukat Hussain 254
R.J. Studios 195
Roekiah 203
Roerich, Svetoslav 1
Romero, Eddie 158
Rothchild, Amy 27
Royal Nepal Film Corporation 254
RTHK 101, 112
RTV 101
Rumpun Melaya 191
Rupavahini Television 271
Ryu Ho-son 143
Ryu, Taisuke 45

Sabah Film 191
Saeed Mirza 246
Sagar, Ramanand 247
Saha Mongkon 216, 218
Salahuddin 263
Saloma 189
Salumbides Film Company 153
Salumbides, Vicente 152
Sampaguita 152–3, 155–6
Santiago, Ciriacio 155
Sasaki Entertainment Enterprise 46
Satay, Wahid 189
Sato, Junya 41
Satyu, M.S 243
Scholars Motion Picture Company 67, 73, 83
Seasonal 103
Seibu Saison Group 41, 46
Seiko 6, 159, 163, 173
Sekera, Mahagama 274
Sek Studios 143
Sen, Mrinal 251
Seoul Specialised Arts College 142
Serra, Federico 269
Shahnoor 254
Shamsuddin, Jins 189, 191
Shantaram 249 Shao Mujun 28–9
Shashi, I.V. 242
Shaw Brothers 6, 64–5, 94, 97–101, 103, 108–9, 111–12, 188–90, 192–3, 197–8, 216
Shaw, Naseeruddin 250
Shaw, Run Run 94, 97–9
Shek, Dean 102
Shimizu, Hiroshi 59
Shi, Nansun 111
Shindo, Kaneto 38, 48, 57
Shinoda, Masahiro 38, 44, 57
Shin Sang-ok 126
Shin-Toho 36–7
Shochiku 6, 36–40, 42, 46, 51–2, 58
Shochiku-Fuji 46–7, 50–1

Shui On Group 108
Siam Rath 201
Sihanouk, Monique 201
Sihanouk, Norodom 201
Silberman, Serge 44
Sil-Metropole 102–4, 107
Singapore Feature Productions 198
Singapore International Film Festival 198
Singh, Heera 254
Sinhala Cinema 269
Sino-American Film Company 93
Slamet Rahardjo 211
Smedley, Agnes 14
Sogang University 142
Sombat Metanee 215, 219
Soong, James 62
Sorapon Chatri 219
South China Co-operative Society 93–4
Southern Film Corporation 102
South Pacific Film Corporation 205
Sovexport Film 240–1
Spielberg, Steven 44, 132
Sri Krung Film Company 213
Star Awards 183
State Film Authority, Pakistan 260–1
State Film Corporation, Sri Lanka 270, 272–3
State Film Production Centre, Indonesia 207–8
State Film Promotion Board, Burma 222
Studio Merdeka 189–90
Studio One 119
Sugawara, Hiroshi 44
Sukarno 202
Sundara Sound Studio 268
Sunn, Joseph 96–7
Suntory Ltd. 41
Suphannahong Committee Awards 215–16
Supravat Jongsiri (Supaksorn) 220
Suraswadee Awards 216
Survey Research Malaysia 195
Suzara, Romy 160, 168–9, 173, 179, 183
Syumandjaja 210–1
Sze Tak Kwok Ka 94

Tahimik, Kidlat 165
Tai Kuang 96
Tai Kwong Ming Film Company 95–6
Taipei Actors Association 88
Taipei News Picture Association 62
Taiwan Film Studio 62–4
Taiwan Motion Picture Association 62–3
Taiwan Provincial Motion Picture Association 87
Taiwan Provisional Motion Picture Company 68
Taiwan Television Enterprises 63
Takabata, Isao 57
Takano, Etusko 60
Takita, Yojiro 55

Talmadge, Richard 221
Tam Ka Ming 112
Tan and Wong Brothers Co. 205
Tanin government 216–17
Tan Khoen Hian 203, 205
Tan's Film 203
Tata 245
Tayama, Rikiya 40
Tchii, Danny 76
Teguh, Karya 5, 210–1
Tekechi, Tetsuya 50
Tekemura, Hajime 50
Television Malaysia 193
Teng Wenji 14, 20, 22, 24, 27
Teshigawara, Hiroshi 38
Tetra Finance 102
Thai Film Industry Promotion Committee 216
Thai Motion Picture Producers Association 216
Thai Tukatatong Awards 215
The Cinematograph Films (Control) Enactment, 1927 186–7
The Economist 133
The Five Major Studios' Treaty 51
The Japanese Film: Art and Industry 35
The Motion Picture Code of Ethics 48–9
The Motion Picture Law, Korea 127, 130, 134, 137
The Teng Chun 203, 205
The Theatres Enactment of 1910 187
Thirty-One Audio Visual Company 67
Thomas, Jeremy 44
Tian Zhuangzhuang 19, 21, 26, 28
Tien Yat (Tan Yee) Studio 94, 98
Toei 6, 36–7, 39–40, 42, 46–7, 52–3, 55, 58
Toei Classics 46, 51
Toei Yoga 46
Toho 6, 36, 39–42, 46–7, 52
Toho-Towa 46–7
Tokuma, Yasuyoshi 42
Tokyo Broadcasting System 41
Tokyo International Film Festival 58–9
Tokyu Group 40
Tom, David 68
Tom Shu-Fen 68
Tom Son Motion Picture Company 65, 67–9, 83–4
Toyoda, Shiro 55
Tsai Sung-Lin 67, 73
Tsui Hark 112
Tu, Richard C. 75–6

TV-3, Malaysia 208

Union Film Company 64
Union-Odeon 216–17
Union of Videogram Distributors 82
United Artists 75, 108, 216
United Daily News 71
United Estates Projects 197
United International Pictures 46–7, 122
United States Information Service 126, 142
United States Majors' Philippine Federation Against Copyright Theft 162
Universal 75, 122, 216
University of the Philippines Institute of Mass Communication 182
U Nyi Pu 221
U Nyunt 221
U Ohn Maung 221
Urban Council 119
Urian Awards 183
Usmar Ismail 202–3, 205
U Tin Maung 221
U Tin Nwe 221
Uttaran Film Award 267
U Tu Kha 223
Uzumasa Studio 36, 42

Valentino, Rudolph 221
Vera, Jose O. 152–3
Vera, Pedro 152–3
Verdull Ltd. 101
Vichit Kounavudhi 220
Vico-Viva 180
Videogram Regulatory Board, Philippines 162, 178
Viva 6, 159, 163, 170, 173
'Vodka Zobel' 170

Wang Ming-Tsann 73
Wang, Peter 89
Wang Rui 11
Wan Jen 66, 69, 80, 84–5
Warner 52, 76, 100, 216
Warriors Film Company 102
Wasuvati 213
Wendt, Lionel 273
Wen San 96
Wimalaweera, Sirisena 268
Wim Unboh 206, 210
Wolmi Island Creation Company 143
Wong brothers 203, 205
Wong Chi 101
Wong, Raymond 102
Wong Wah Kei 112
Woo, John 110–1
World Cinema 28
World Festival of Film 201

Wu Tianming 13, 22, 27
Wu Yigong 20, 21
Wu Ziniu 19–21, 26

Xia Hong 24
Xi'an Film Studio 16, 27–8
Xie Fei 13, 17–19, 27, 29–30
Xie Fengsong 13
Xie Jin 20, 30
Xin Lian 100, 103
X'Otic Films 152–3

Yamada, Yuji 37–8, 44, 55
Yamaguchi, Momoe 39
Yamakawa, Naota 44
Yamamoto, Kajiro 56
Yanagimachi, Mitsuo 45, 55
Yang De-Chang (Edward Yang) 84–6, 89
Yang Shichuan 20
Yang Yianjin 19–20
Yao Wade 65, 68–9
Yearsly, Albert 150–1
Yi Dynasty 125
Yien Yue Hsiang 94
Yin Ho 112
Yin Tingru 14
Yi Tu-yong 141
Yiu Kui 94
Yokomizo, Seishi 39
Yoon Bong-choon 125
Yoshida, Yoshishige 38, 55
Yoshimitsu, Morita 55
Youngwha 142
Youth Film Studio 13
Yu Hyun-mok 131–2, 138
Yun Baek-nam 124
Yung Hwa Company 97
Yung, Peter 112
Yu, Ronnie 112
Yusari Film Sdn. Bhd. 191
Yushin (Revitalising Reform) Constitution 129

Zahir Raihan 263–4
Zaiton 189
Zem, Rachel 112
Zhang Dan 35
Zhang Junzhao 19, 23, 26
Zhang Liang 13–4
Zhang Nuanxin 20, 24, 30
Zhang Yimou 5, 14, 19, 21, 26, 28, 30
Zheng Dongtian 20–2
Zheng Junli 20
Zheng Zhenqui 20
Zhen Ni 33
Zhong Lian 100
Zia Ul Huq 257–8, 261
Zulkiflee, Sarimah 189
Zulueta, Jose 152